THE WORLD OF MELODRAMA

THE WORLD
OF
MELODRAMA

FRANK RAHILL

THE PENNSYLVANIA STATE UNIVERSITY PRESS

University Park and London

1967

Preface

I have included France, England, and the United States in this survey of melodrama because these three nations constitute an intelligible field of study. It is impossible to tell the whole story of English melodrama without constant reference to the drama and theatre of France, and American melodrama likewise cannot be understood in isolation. As for France, melodrama in its very origins there owed as much to English as to native sources. The situation with respect to Germany is somewhat different. The influence of that nation was strong in the beginning, particularly in the area of subject matter, but it faded gradually and is not conspicuous after the eclipse of Kotzebue (circa 1815) except occasionally as with *Der Freischütz*.

There was constant traffic among the theatres of England, France, and America throughout the period in which melodrama flourished, a period coinciding roughly with the nineteenth century. It was a traffic in production methods and devices as well as in general ideas, themes, plays, character types—and playwrights. Probably the most popular police and crime melodrama of the nineteenth century in England and America was *The Ticket-of-Leave Man* with its immortal detective, Hawkshaw; Tom Taylor, an English playwright, signed his name to it, but it was really a French play. Also French was *The Bells*, a play closely associated with the fame of Henry Irving as an actor. The most affectionately cherished of all hero types in British melodrama, the semicomic sailor man, later caricatured in *Pinafore*, enjoyed his first major triumph in the character of Long Tom Coffin, created in the American novel, *The Pilot*, written by James Fenimore Cooper in 1823 and transferred to the stage in an adaptation by a hack English playwright in 1825. The presentation of English and American melodrama was revolutionized at the middle of the century by three men: a French actor, Charles Fechter; an English actor-manager, Charles Kean (son of the great Edmund) who got much of his inspiration in Paris; and a cosmopolitan Irishman, Dion Boucicault, actor, playwright, and manager, who, on the threshold of his career as a melodramatist, spent three years studying the theatre in Paris.

The extent to which American melodrama was dependent on foreign theatres appears from various standard collections of American plays of the last century. Of the four plays presented before 1875 which are included in *The Most Successful Plays of the American Stage*, edited by Bennett Cerf and Van H. Cartmell, two are foreign melodramas (the French *Two Orphans* and the English *East Lynne*). In the "America's Lost Plays" series, published by Princeton University Press, there are no fewer than twelve foreign melodramas; one volume of the twenty comprising the set contains three French works and another four. The only playwright represented by more than one item in Arthur H. Quinn's *Representative American Plays* was Boucicault, who came to the United States in middle life. Boucicault is perhaps the most important single figure in American melodrama; it was thanks largely to him, and to the essentially French playwriting technique which he may be said to have introduced, that melodrama on American themes reached something like maturity in the later decades of the century.

Free trade in the theatre of melodrama during the nineteenth century was encouraged and promoted by a number of circumstances including the absence until 1891 of any effective international copyright, the gypsy proclivities of the acting profession, and the unimportance of a playwright's name on a playbill. More considerable than any of these factors in contributing to the internationalization of melodrama was the peculiar nature of the beast. Melodrama is predominantly situation, action, and spectacle; and the appeal of this sort of thing knows no national or linguistic boundaries. A passage at arms, a wild ride, a shot in the dark, the appearance of an avenging ghost—these would go over equally well with audiences in Paris, London, and New York. Like the novels of Cooper and Jack London—and like *Gone with the Wind* in our own times—melodramas need suffer little, and might even gain, in translation. *The Ticket-of-Leave Man* and *The Bells* were more effective plays in English than they were in their original French.

The treatment no less than the scope of my book has been determined by the international nature of the material. The basic divisions are chronological within nations, but this scheme is not followed out rigidly, and my approach is thematic in the main. The few murder mysteries written in France and England are noted in the chapter devoted to this type of composition in the American section of the book, and there are similar transpositions elsewhere. Considerations of reader interest likewise influenced me here; melodrama, for me, is something exciting which happened in the theatre, and telling its story thematically seems to be the best way to communicate that excitement.

A history of melodrama is inevitably a history of its theatre also; the chronicler cannot afford to neglect circumstances of creation and presentation in this most theatrical of all dramatic forms, a closet example of which is almost unthinkable. The business organization of theatrical enterprise, the physical playhouse, the personalities of certain performers and managers, producing and acting techniques, the composition of particular audiences, and even theatrical legislation are all bound up with the construction, point of view, choice of themes, and literary merit—or lack of it—in melodrama. Consequently many of my pages are given over to discussion of such matters as the royalty payment for plays; admission prices; acting styles; the size, location, and finances of individual theatres; the repertory organization; and the patent grants and the Theatrical Licensing Act in England.

In the Bibliographical Notes at the end of the book I attempt to lay down guide lines on the subject of play texts and provide some information on where they may be found. In quoting passages from plays I have not pinpointed sources as a rule because definitive texts are rare owing to the chaos prevailing in playwriting, theatrical production, and play publication (and non-publication!) in melodrama, which approached the conditions of folk art. In instances where something like standard texts are extant, I have given publication data, e.g., for *Le Cause célèbre, Cœlina, Shore Acres, The Mysterious Husband*, etc. Translations of extracts from French plays are my own unless otherwise indicated.

For facts of production and publication of plays produced in England, the reader is referred to Allardyce Nicoll's six volume *A History of English Drama, 1660–1900*. The alphabetical catalogue of plays in Volume VI may be used in conjunction with the Hand-Lists incorporated in each volume. No such reference source exists for French or American plays.

Contents

Contents

Setting the Stage

When I use a word it means just what I choose it to mean. —
Humpty Dumpty in *Through the Looking Glass*

"No one that I ever met or heard of has appeared to know what
melodrama really is," said William Gillette, author and actor of
melodrama, in an address delivered in Chicago in 1913; and he went
on to suggest that only a fool would attempt a definition.

This helplessness is understandable. In 1913 melodrama had long
since lost its once clear-cut individuality, its primitive integrity—
certainly in the carriage-trade theatre for which Gillette worked;
and the word had degenerated into a loose and usually emotive tag
for sentimentality and other emotional extravagance, inflated declamation, dramatic conflict on a physical level, intrigue for its own
sake, and theatrical crime—severally or in combination. "A term
generally used with some contempt," is the way Fowler leads off his
definition in *A Dictionary of Modern English Usage* (1st ed.).

In the generation following World War I, through a change in
aesthetic fashions, the word tended to shed its pejorative overtones
without acquiring any greater accuracy. During the thirties, in the
course of a single Broadway season three world classics of the tragic
stage, *Oedipus Rex, Electra,* and *Hamlet,* each produced by a
different management, were all advertised as melodramas. Critics of
the present century have been of no help in the matter, adding to
the confusion if anything. They have used the term for plays as
different from one another—and from true melodrama—as *The Jest*
(*La Cena delle beffe*), *The Second Mrs. Tanqueray, Mourning
becomes Electra,* and *No Exit* (*Huit clos*).

The clue to a definition of melodrama lies in its history, and this
has been investigated only fragmentarily or superficially. No serious
and comprehensive study of melodrama has appeared in any language. This neglect is astonishing. Certainly the form is important
enough to justify more attention than it has received. On the basis
of sheer bulk it cannot be ignored; examples may be counted in
thousands in France, England, and the United States during the
nineteenth century. It dominated our Western theatre for prolonged periods and throughout the century virtually monopolized
the spoken stage of the popular theatre except for farce (and
Shakespeare!); and more recently it has enjoyed a posthumous
popularity in the films and on television and radio. Moreover the

importance of melodrama was more than merely a matter of bulk. Many excellent plays were written under its banner, plays which stand up today quite as well as anything done in more pretentious genres during the same era. (Jean Louis Barrault has used the word "masterpiece" in reference to *Le Bossu*). And melodrama's influence is to be seen everywhere in the theatre of its own day and later, notably in such areas as mise-en-scène and direction. How much the basic techniques of the motion pictures owe to melodrama has been spelled out in A. Nicolas Vardac's *Stage to Screen*.

Melodrama emerged simultaneously in France and England as the eighteenth century drew to a close. Its base was blood and thunder, which, of course, had always existed in the theatre; but this was no more than the base—the marrowbone of the soup. Stirred into the pot by the Frenchman Guilbert de Pixerécourt (1773–1844), who is generally accepted as the father of the form, and by other pioneers was a variety of ingredients assembled from a variety of sources in and out of the theatre: the heroic pantomime of the minor theatres of the people; the homiletic *drame sérieux* of Diderot and his school; the popular music drama; and contemporary pastoral and romantic fiction, especially German and English bandit and horror novels, including the gothic.

Hodgepodge though it is, melodrama nevertheless simmers down to a consistency, its recipe being no less precise than that for neoclassic tragedy, for example, or comedy of manners. Certainly it is reducible to a definition, and a fairly hard and fast one, with due respect to Gillette. I shall attempt one: Melodrama is a form of dramatic composition in prose partaking of the nature of tragedy, comedy, pantomime, and spectacle, and intended for a popular audience. Primarily concerned with situation and plot, it calls upon mimed action extensively and employs a more or less fixed comple-ment of stock characters, the most important of which are a suffering heroine or hero, a persecuting villain, and a benevolent comic. It is conventionally moral and humanitarian in point of view and sentimental and optimistic in temper, concluding its fable happily with virtue rewarded after many trials and vice punished. Characteristically it offers elaborate scenic accessories and miscel-laneous divertissements and introduces music freely, typically to underscore dramatic effect.

Insofar as it remained a popular diversion—I mean a diversion of the *populus*—melodrama continued to be cut on this pattern until the liquidation of the popular theatre itself in our own times; and if nothing remained but this theatre to be considered, there would be no problem of finding a definition that would stick. The drama of the cheap gallery-house melodrama ("ten, twent', thirt' ") in the United States and that of Drury Lane in England for a generation or so at the turn of the nineteenth and twentieth centuries differ only superficially from that offered a century earlier in the Boulevard du Temple theatres of Paris and in both the patent houses and the minor theatres of London.

However, melodrama did not confine itself to the popular theatre, and from this circumstance arises much of the confusion, voiced by Gillette, as to what melodrama is and what it isn't. It spilled over into the theatre at large, especially the theatre of the middle classes. Here, reacting to audiences of greater sophistication, it underwent a gradual change as the nineteenth century moved into its second half. The "heart" became the target of playwrights rather than the simple nervous system, and firearms and the representation of convulsions of nature yielded the center of the stage to high-voltage emotionalism, examination of soul-states, and the observation of manners. The employment of music was curtailed and the more extravagant embellishments in the field of scenic display were discarded. Something like subtlety was attempted here and there in characterization, with the result that stock types lost some of their primitive rigidity. Increasingly as the century wore on heroines were to be discovered who were less than blameless, especially in love, villains who were more to be pitied than censured when all the evidence was in, and even heroes who refused to fight! The unhappy end became common. As Théophile Gautier noted on June 8, 1870 in his obituary for Joseph Bouchardy, a master of melodrama, these changes reflected a loss in naïveté and something approaching a revolution in morals.[1] They resulted in a species of transitional melodrama for which the definition as given is unsatisfactory.

Various aspects of this modified melodrama are illustrated in *La Dame aux camélias*, the historical dramas of Victorien Sardou, much of that French drawing-room melodrama introduced to the English stage at the middle of the century by Tom Taylor and others, many of the famous "Adelphi dramas" associated with the professional career of Celine Celeste, the Henry Irving repertory at the Lyceum, and *East Lynne*. In the United States relevant items were *Way Down East* and the plays of Bartley Campbell and James A. Herne.

Gillette's own plays afford an interesting exhibit of what had been

[1] *Histoire du Romantisme* (Paris, 1874), p. 186.

happening to melodrama. *Sherlock Holmes* is a sheer situation melodrama of an almost primitive type, its plot turning upon a purely external conflict between good and evil. *Secret Service*, on the other hand, though it has its share of old-fashioned melodrama, depends for its chief interest on a conflict wholly within the breast of the protagonist. Captain Thorne in that admirable play must make a choice between his duty to his country and his love for a lady—a moral decision. While it is not always easy to draw the line between the one type and the other—melodrama in its pure and in its diluted or etheralized form—a distinction must be made in the interest of precision. I suggest the qualifying adjective, classical, an adjective employed by René Charles Guilbert de Pixerécourt, "father of melodrama," to distinguish his orthodox brand of product from Romantic drama.[2]

Besides splitting horizontally into middle-class and proletarian, melodrama divided vertically also. There was the play written merely to entertain and the play with a message. Purpose was no new thing in drama at the beginning of the nineteenth century, even in the popular theatre. As a matter of fact, it pervaded the new free forms of the drama which preceded melodrama and out of which melodrama evolved, taking at first the form of a vague humanitarianism associated with the word "nature" as Rousseau and the *philosophes* used that term. It later tended to focus on specific causes, often class-conscious or political in character.

Melodrama, in its dramaturgic apparatus of a villain-heroine conflict, a persecution plot with a happy end, and a *raisonneur*, inherited from the theatre of Diderot an almost perfect instrument for propaganda—an apparatus contrived indeed with that very end in view. During the nineteenth century this instrument was pressed into the service of innumerable crusades: national patriotism, anticlericalism, abolition of slavery, prohibition, and even tax and prison reform, to name only a few. There was an avowedly Socialist school of melodrama in France during the period when the Communist Manifesto was proclaimed, and the American James A. Herne wrote single-tax sermons into *Shore Acres* (the original title of which was *Shore Acres Subdivision*) and other plays.

The effectiveness of the theatre, especially the theatre of melodrama, in rousing men to action has never been adequately assessed. It is possible to reconstruct the history of a century of agitation from the repertory of the popular theatres of the "Boulevard du

[2] "Le Mélodrame," *Paris ou le livre des Cent-et-un*, VI (1832), 342.

Crime," the Surrey Side of London, and New York's Bowery; there were moments when reverberations from their humble stages shook the world. *Uncle Tom's Cabin* and *Ten Nights in a Bar-room* are but two of a large company. Showboat performances up and down the Hudson of an English antilandlord play, *The Rent Day*, played a part in the "tin-horn rebellion" of the "Calico Indians" against Patroon feudalism in the 1840's. A production of a melodramatic opera, *Masaniello*, by Auber and Scribe, proved the spark which ignited the revolution that won national independence for Belgium in 1850. *Le Chiffonnier de Paris*, a spirited and inflammatory polemic in melodramatic form by Félix Pyat, given at the Porte Saint-Martin in 1847, had as much to do with rallying the people of Paris to the barricades in the Revolution of '48 as any other single immediate factor. The historic march upon the Bastille in 1789 may be said to have begun in the Boulevard du Temple, stronghold of the little theatres of the proletariat, where the heroic pantomime and *drame*, ancestors of melodrama, preached as boldly as they dared in the last decades of the old regime the doctrine of the rights of man.

Whether in the form of the propaganda play or the play intended solely to entertain, melodrama gives us a fresh perspective on nineteenth-century life and affords an insight into popular feeling which cannot be had from any of the familiar source materials of history. These forgotten plays are especially valuable for revealing the tastes and opinions of the inarticulate *faubourgs*, East Ends, and Boweries of the Western world in the period when our capitalist-industrial society was in the throes of adolescence.

These were people who, for the most part, could not read and were not permitted to vote and whom the laws of the time prevented even from associating together in organizations like trade unions for orderly and democratic action to improve their lot. Cut off thus from participation in the determination of their destinies and denied normal avenues for self-expression, they seem to have turned to the theatre and adopted it as a sort of substitute franchise and a vehicle for the criticism of life. Through their attendance at one play or another and their patronage of this cheap theatre or that, the uprooted and disinherited poor of the typical nineteenth-century city have left us a kind of composite self-portrait. In the plots of melodrama, its choice of heroes and villains, and its resounding tirades can be read resentment at the insolence of authority and the heartlessness of greedy wealth, a mistrust of lawyers, a sneaking admiration for a bold and hearty rogue, and a persistent taste for blood—and along with this a staunch fidelity to orthodox morality and an optimism which can only be described as incorrigible. With the changing repertory of melodrama as a clue, it is possible to put a finger on specific emotions which swept the people of this nation or that during the century: the enthusiasm of the great masses of Frenchmen for the Napoleonic legend, the special affection of Britons for the sea, rural America's mistrust of the growing cities. Melodrama, springing as it did from the people, speaks with their voice and is impressed with their image.

Even if it were intrinsically sterile and worthless, melodrama would yet have claims on our consideration for having provided the masses of the people with diversion they could get in no other way. The bills of the despised theatres of melodrama were frequently all that made life tolerable for uncounted thousands, especially in the great cities, during the era which two of its historians in England, the Hammonds, have called "the bleak age." To the whipped apprentice, the dockside drudge, the factory serf, the domestic slavey, the work-worn wife, these shows brought precious moments of release and fulfillment.[3] At the playhouse of his choice, in the quickening fellowship of his kind, the poor man, warmed with his pint of porter and his dish of fish and chips, could taste life at its carnival peak, forgetting for a while the heavy burden of his wretched existence in rapt contemplation of a magic world of pinchbeck splendor unfolded spectacularly on the stage before him.

These plays diverted him, and they did something more. Justice triumphs in the essentially identical plots; men of good will come into their own. The little people, harried and hunted, despised and cast out, rise in their might and crush their oppressors to the earth. The villain of melodrama was frequently designated generically as the *tyran* in the French theatre early in the century. Imbedded in that convention are the social implications of the genre, forged in the fires of revolution: Jacques and Pierre, Tom, Dick, and Harry, as they poured into the streets at the final curtain of the melodrama of the evening, could say to themselves that a man, after all, might throw off his tormentors and be free.

[3] "It was the worst epoch of the industrial age; there has never been such poverty or drabness of life. . . . It is no wonder that the joys of the people took on a somewhat ferocious tinge, that they loved melodrama, crudities of blood and terror, and the cheap beauties of tinsel."—Sacheverell Sitwell, writing of early nineteenth-century London in *The Dance of the Quick and the Dead* (Boston, 1922), p. 325 ff.

I
FRANCE

I

A Melodramatic Apprenticeship

It was the best of times and the worst of times. —DICKENS, *A Tale of Two Cities*

Toward the close of the eighteenth century the petty nobility of Lorraine counted upon its rolls a Major Charles Nicolas Georges Guilbert, head of an inconspicuous Nancy family of some antiquity. Aspiring to a marquisate, he sold his modest seignory of Pixerécourt and bought up a more pretentious estate, investing all his fortune in the speculation. It proved ill-timed. Before he was able to settle down in his newly acquired demesne of Saint-Vallier, the National Assembly, in session at Versailles, decreed on August 5, 1789 the abolition of all feudal privileges in the realm, and the Major was ruined—cheated of his hopes and despoiled of his property. This personal disaster, not unnaturally, confirmed him in all his inherited political prejudices; and as the drift to the left proceeded in the Assembly and in the nation at large, he became the bitterest and most irreconcilable of Royalists.

Though a military man of sorts, the Major was at no time outraged to the point of taking up arms in defense of his principles and his property, but he had a seventeen-year-old son, René Charles, and in him he found a ready, if not a particularly willing, instrument of vengeance against the Revolutionary cause. René, a serious-minded young man completely absorbed in the study of law, was snatched from his books in '91 and packed off to take his place in the Army of the Allies—"to make war," as he was to put it later, "he knew not why nor against whom."[1] He went without protest, knowing that protest would be useless, the Major being a gentleman of harsh temper and brutal instincts accustomed to ruling his family with an iron hand.[2] The "heavy father" of melodrama, a theatrical form of which René was to be in large measure the inventor, owes something to this formidable parent.

René's soldiering with the Emigrés in the Legion of Condé was uneventful enough, but somewhere in the cantonment of Erntz he

[1] Pixerécourt, "Souvenirs de la Révolution," *Théâtre choisi* (Paris & Nancy, 1841–1843), Vol. II, p. viii.

[2] Pixerécourt, "Souvenirs du jeune âge," *Théâtre choisi*, Vol. I, pp. xviii–xxi.

learned German, which was to prove useful to him in after years, and fell in love with his teacher, one Clotilde. The romance, as he recounted it to his intimates later, bears a suspicious resemblance to one of his own theatrical pieces. "His budding passion, doubtless by presentiment, assumed the hue of melodrama," wrote Jules Janin in his memoir of Pixerécourt; "even in his loves, the young man carefully arranged and disposed his effects, his settings, and his surprises."[3]

An ancient abbey and a picturesque ruin—that favorite romantic property of the age—decorate the background of this autobiographical idyl; trysts are kept "in the shade of a somber forest," and a brook—a babbling brook in fact—carries love messages downstream from Clotilde to her René, waiting by an ancient willow on its banks. Clotilde was strictly in the melodramatic style, an orphan and a great heiress, beautiful and of an approved romantic pallor. She and her soldier-lover sang duets at the clavichord in the convent of which her aunt, "the Baroness X——, of an ancient Teutonic house," was abbess, and planned their future together over a German grammar.

There was a parting with vows exchanged, and when René returned some time later to claim his beloved, she was dead at the age of sixteen. While he lived, he cherished the memory of this ideal lost love (which may help to explain his failure as a husband); her image, shining through his fifty-odd dramas, helped establish a stereotype in stage heroines which endured for more than a century.

The parting of the lovers occurred when Pixerécourt was transferred to the Army of the Ardennes. He was restless and unhappy in his new billet, and he obtained a month's leave of absence to visit his home. On his way there he met with the first of those exciting adventures which, throughout his youth, seem to have been attracted to him by a kind of melodramatic destiny. As he passed through Pont-à-Mousson disguised as a beggar (a characteristic touch), he aroused the suspicions of the local gendarmerie. He took to his heels and there was a chase. He eluded his pursuers by lying in the mud of a ditch for hours, flat on his belly, while they hunted him, passing and repassing, at times so close to where he lay that he could hear their oaths. Only when night fell was he able to make his escape.

---

[3] Jules Janin, *Histoire de la littérature dramatique* (Paris, 1855), Vol. IV, pp. 311–313.

He may have had desertion in the back of his head when he applied for his leave, since he had no relish for the profession of arms and little enthusiasm for the Royalist cause; in any event, he made no attempt to rejoin his regiment when the leave expired. Instead, he lurked about Nancy for a while, dodging the Jacobins who had by this time won control there, and finally set out for Paris after obtaining a passport from a relative in a neighboring town. He made the journey on foot and reached the capital early in March of 1793. He was without funds and a complete stranger in the city, but he had the good fortune to meet an old schoolmate, one Michel, who was living in the mean attic of an old house in the Rue de Bouloi. There René found shelter.

Paris of 1793 was a melodramatist's nightmare—a city shaken by hysteria and a prey to mobs. One thing the mobs clamored for unceasingly: vengeance on aristocrats and counterrevolutionaries. That cry was everywhere—on the floor of the Convention, in the clubs, at the Palais Royal, along the boulevards and in the starving, desperate *faubourgs*. Pamphlets, posters, and the journals took up the chorus, and the very songs in the streets echoed it:

> Ah! ça ira, ça ira, ça ira!
> Les aristocrat' à la lanterne;
> Ah! ça ira, ça ira, ça ira!
> Les aristocrat' on les pendra!

and:

> Epouvantail des scélérats, vengez-nous
> Effroi des artistocrats, vengez-nous.

The Rue de Bouloi abutted upon the Rue de Saint-Honoré in the very heart of Paris; under his window the young aristocrat often heard those songs, as he heard the tocsin and saw the fierce rabble of pikemen swarm out of the sections time and again at its summons. And when the horrible procession of tumbrils began across the Pont au Change from the Conciergerie and along the Rue Saint-Honoré to the Place de Réunion where the guillotine awaited, he saw that too.

Recalling this trying time, Pixerécourt was to write: "I lived in an attic, exposed to pay at any moment the death penalty for having obeyed my father in leaving France at the age of seventeen. Alone, three hundred leagues from my people, I awaited death daily, hourly, in the blood-stained capital. Each night after watching the death-carts go by loaded with victims for slaughter, noble souls whose courage I admired and whose example I resolved to imitate when my time came, I would throw myself upon my wretched bed. It can easily be imagined that my thoughts were of the deepest black."[4] For once the tremolos of that highly theatrical style have a certain justification.

Disaster threatened Pixerécourt often but never struck. Summer wore on and he was left unmolested in his attic. Meanwhile he sought distraction from his dark thoughts. Sober, scholarly lad that he was, he turned to books. In the reminiscences quoted above he mentions the volumes that engaged him during this trying vigil; they make a precious exhibit in the genealogy of melodrama. At the head of the list are the *Meditations* of the Rev. James Hervey, and *The Complaint, or Night Thoughts* of the Rev. Edward Young, characteristic works of that school of English mortuary moralists so widely read and extravagantly esteemed on the eve of the Revolution especially in France.

Hervey, a country parson, was a bachelor and a hypochondriac who, according to an anonymous biographer, found "a melancholy but pleasing satisfaction in contemplating the latter end of the righteous,"[5] an occupation to which he devoted several volumes. *Meditations among the Tombs*, to give the exact title, are pulpit exhortations with epitaphs for texts; they are saturated with evangelical piety (John Wesley had been his tutor at Oxford), overcast with puritanical gloom, and distended with biblical quotations. Their quality may be savored in chapter headings like "Promiscuous lodgment and amicable agreement of corpses, suggesting humility and concord" and "The wonderful changes which take place in the tomb, displayed in several particulars." The moral is thumped home vigorously in these discourses, as it will be in melodrama, and the style is that involved, magniloquent one which later will distinguish the tirades of generations of actors in the theatres of melodrama.

monly called, a sort of compendium of English melancholy, which the French called *le spleen anglais*.

Young had inspired Hervey; his poetry deals with the same subjects as his imitator's prose. With personal bereavements for a point of departure, he produced in *Night Thoughts*, as it is com-

[4] Pixerécourt, "Souvenirs de la Révolution," *Théâtre choisi*, Vol. II, pp. xvi–xvii.

[5] James Hervey, *Meditations and Contemplations, containing his Meditations among the Tombs and Reflections on a Flower Garden . . . together with the life of the author* (Philadelphia, 1849), p. 14.

A trifle apologetically, Pixerécourt refers to certain other volumes of a more worldly complexion which he read at this time: *Le Comte de Comminge, ou les amants malheureux* (1790),[6] a *drame sérieux* by François Marie Baculard d'Arnaud; Louis Sébastien Mercier's works in the same genre; and the short tales of Jean Pierre Claris de Florian. It is an interesting sidelight on the taste of the period that these light works should for the most part show the same characteristics as the compositions of Young and Hervey: a resolute moral didacticism, a morbid preoccupation with grief and misfortune, a noxious and all-pervading sentimentality, and an almost total absence of a sense of humor. All these were to be in the inheritance of melodrama.

Gloom predominates in D'Arnaud's play; this writer, another admirer of Young, proclaimed himself the inventor of the *genre sombre*. His play is based on a semiautobiographical romance, *Les Mémoirs du Comte Comminges* (1735), by Claudine-Alexandrine Guérin, Marquise de Tencin, renegade nun, mother of D'Alembert (out of wedlock), mistress for a while of Louis XV and of the Regent, and conductress of a famous salon. Like its source, the dramatic work is a passionate depiction of frustrated love punctuated with disaster. D'Arnaud (or the Marquise) drew upon local color to intensify his lugubrious effects, notably in the final scene wherein the ill-starred lovers, separated for many years, are brought together at the woman's death. The scene is the burial place of the austerely penitential monastery of La Trappe. Mute monks in somber cowls move on and off, a passing bell tolls, and death's heads lie about on opened graves. Pixerécourt's *Valentine ou la séduction* and *Alice ou les fossoyeurs écossais* were to be in the same *genre sombre*.

The theme of suffering innocence recurs in the little tales of Florian, softened, however, by a certain elegiac, pastoral touch deriving from this author's gentle and winning nature, to which all his contemporaries testify. Florian was related by marriage to Voltaire, but spiritually his kinship was with a very different sort of soul, Rousseau, though the ingrown vanity of that difficult genius was happily absent in the disciple. He sang the praises of simple domestic life and the natural virtues of unspoiled, primitive man. The tales deal with various misfortunes which befall sensitive, generous souls, who bear up under them with edifying fortitude and

[6] Date of first theatrical production.

never hesitate to sacrifice their personal happiness and risk their lives in the interest of others. Unlike *Comte de Comminge*, these little stories end happily; that was to be the rule in melodrama.

The Rousseauistic religion of nature and the cult of sensibility are animated with a jauntier spirit in the works of Mercier, a bustling, controversial person, Paris-born and -bred, and *au courant* with the effervescing intellectual life of the capital, which is echoed in his plays. He put the theories of the *philosophes* more fully into his plays than any of the major prophets themselves, not excepting Diderot, exemplifying if fleetingly, their program as stated by the modern historian of the genre: "a spectacle intended for a bourgeois or popular audience and presenting a moral and affecting picture of its surroundings."[7] Kings, when they appear in his pieces, usually yield the center of the stage to peasants and merchants; the leading character of *La Brouette du vinaigrier* is the humble tradesman indicated in the title, and the plot turns on a commercial failure. Like Sedaine, Mercier occasionally mixed comedy with his serious fable, contrary to classical precedent, which he scorned; and like Diderot, he was given to a similarly unconventional preoccupation with the minutiae of mise-en-scène, as in *L'Indigent*, in the printed version of which are specified all manner of realistic properties for scenes in a notary's office and a poverty-stricken hovel. Prose was his only medium. Finally, he summarized most succinctly the common purpose of melodrama and *drame:* "to immortalize the innocent, persecuted by a stronger power."[8] The theatrical experiments of the *philosophes* and their allies came to be designated *drame* (or *drame sérieux*) generically during a period from 1765 to 1800. The term was first proposed by P. F. Guyot, the Abbé Desfontaines, an eighteenth-century critic and journalist.[9] Beaumarchais used it for the first time in connection with a specific play, his *Eugénie* (1767).

The influence of *drame* came from many sides to affect the content, form, and moral mood of melodrama during its formative years—from the German August von Kotzebue, and the *drame lyrique* for example; but it is reasonable to adjudge the early exposure of Pixerécourt to the plays of Mercier as decisive. After a prolonged study of this writer and Sedaine, he himself tells us that

[7] Félix Gaiffe, *Le Drame en France au XVIIIe siècle* (Paris, 1908), p. 93.

[8] Jules Marsan, "Le Mélodrame et Guilbert de Pixerécourt, *Revue d'histoire de littéraire de la France,* July 1911, p. 203.

[9] Desfontaines, *Observations sur les critiques modernes* (Paris, 1737), XXV, 25.

he came to understand that, in order to succeed in the theatre, it was necessary to choose a moral and dramatic subject, natural dialogue, and a simple and true style; to mix gaiety and serious interest in the plot; to recompense injured virtue and punish crime in the denouement; and to call upon the resources of mise-en-scène to assist illusion at all times.[10]

What homely simplicity and verisimilitude melodramas like *Cœlina* and *Valentine* possess, they owe chiefly to the example of *drame*. Yet the debt is for vices as well as virtues. If melodrama's characters are wooden abstractions yanked about in accordance with the exigencies of a highly artificial intrigue; if its concealed identities, repeated coincidences, and *coups de théâtre* approach the fantastic at times; if resounding moral platitudes are dragged in by the heels on every occasion, blame must be laid ultimately at the door of those didactic eighteenth-century reformers who, in turning to commonplace people for their subjects, felt it necessary to invest their lives on the stage with a meretricious glamor and an edifying moral tone.

The effects upon the ardent young Pixerécourt of this bouillabaisse of exhortation and idyl, dirge and romance, as represented in Hervey and Young, D'Arnaud, Florian, and Mercier, was to bring to a head an ambition which had accompanied him to Paris—if it had not really inspired that slightly mad excursion: Suddenly one day he is furiously busy at the writing of a play, his private woes forgotten. With the knowing theatricality of Mercier for a model, he turns a tale of Florian's, "Sélico" into a four-act drama, *Sélico, ou les nègres genéréux*,[11] accomplishing the task in a week's time.

The tale has for its hero the exemplary young negro of the title. He lives with his six brothers and an aged mother on a little plot of land in Africa, which yields enough to maintain them in frugal Rousseauistic simplicity. At a village fete Sélico sees and straightway loves the chief's maiden daughter, a virtuous, amiable, and devoted creature. She returns his love, and they are formally betrothed. (It is an idyllic country of the mind here, where class distinctions do not exist.) Plans for the marriage are dashed when the barbarous king of Dahomey invades the land; Sélico and his kin are driven into the jungle and he is separated from his beloved, of whose fate he is left in ignorance. In the wilds the little family contrive to keep alive through heroic effort and self-denial, the sons

---

[10] "Dernières Reflexions sur le mélodrame," quoted by Willie G. Hartog in *Guilbert de Pixerécourt* (Paris, 1913), p. 171.

[11] It was never printed.

competing with one another in making sacrifices in order that the mother may want nothing.

Sélico is disconsolate at the loss of his sweetheart; he exhibits all the familiar romantic symptoms of unhappy love (which Prévost and Rousseau had standardized), wasting away and wandering about half mad. Meanwhile the problem of subsistence grows more and more desperate. Supplies are exhausted; game is scarce. Finally, faced with starvation, the brothers decide to draw lots to determine which one of them shall be sold into slavery to procure the means of keeping the others alive. Sélico, anxious for death now that reunion with his beloved appears impossible, will not hear of lots; he insists on being the one who shall be sold. Reluctantly the others consent, and the hero and one of his brothers set out for the slave market at the Dutch colony on the coast. Arriving in the town they learn that the king of Dahomey is stopping there and come upon placards offering a large reward for the capture of an audacious native who had contrived to penetrate to the king's seraglio and gain access to one of his wives. The reward far exceeds the sum that would be paid for a slave, and Sélico is inspired to impersonate the trespasser and have himself turned over to the king. After tearful protestations the brother agrees to the plan and carries it out, thereby obtaining sufficient money to insure the comfort of their mother as long as she lives.

For his supposed crime the hero is condemned to die at the stake. The fire which is to consume him is lighted, and tribesmen gather in full panoply—a magnificent opportunity for one of those grand spectacles of which melodrama will make so much. Then the guilty woman is led out to share the fate of her supposed partner in sin. To his horror, Sélico recognizes in her his lost beloved—a perfect melodramatic situation. At this agonizing moment, who should appear but the old chief, the girl's father, with a confession that *he* is the guilty one; a parent's love led him to violate the privacy of the royal harem. Sélico's noble sacrifice is revealed, and the king pardons him, releases the girl announcing that she has always resisted him, and bestows a general blessing.

Fiction at the end of the eighteenth century had gone that far along the way to melodrama. It is not the whole journey. This tyrant-king is a humane man at bottom, capable of generosity and mercy. The blood and thunder drama was to tolerate no such flabbiness in its scoundrels. It was to create—or resuscitate—the villain.

II

The Villain Enters

I write in the genre of Sedaine.—GUILBERT DE PIXERÉCOURT

With the manuscript of his first play, *Sélico*, under his arm, Pixeré-court sallied from his attic in search of a manager. He had not far to go in order to find one willing, not to say eager, to give him a hearing; in the Paris of 1793 playwrights were in demand, even tyros at the profession. A veritable passion for the spectacle had taken possession of the city at the outset of the Revolution, and new theatres were springing up on every side to cater to it. Only the supply of new plays remained inadequate.

At two of the new houses, the Marais (built by Beaumarchais) and the Molière, he received attractive offers for his maiden effort, and finally sold it to Villeneuve at the Molière for six hundred francs. This was an auspicious beginning surely, and the young man's hopes rose. *Sélico*, however, was not destined for production just yet. With the approach of the Terror and the increasing official scrutiny of the theatre by the Revolutionaries, the manager found it expedient to confine himself to pieces of more positive Republican sentiments, the more so after one of his actors lost his head for a lack of zeal in this direction. The play was shelved.[1]

Meanwhile word came to Pixerécourt, as he scribbled away at other pieces, that he had been drafted for service in the Republican army at Nancy, through the *levée en masse* of August 13. He decided to obey the summons, and late in 1793 turned his back on the capital without having had his dearest wish gratified. Arriving at his home, he was enrolled in a regiment of cavalry—his old offense of having borne arms against the Republic apparently having been overlooked or forgotten.

This second period of military service, though briefer than the first, was more important for Pixerécourt's development as a play-wright and consequently for melodrama. At Nancy he encountered a prototype of an essential ingredient of the theatrical form with

---

[1] Pixerécourt, "Souvenirs de la Révolution," *Théâtre choisi*, Vol. II, p. xvii.

which his fame is so intimately bound. This was that picturesque and terrifying puppet which distinguishes melodrama from earlier French theatrical forms: the deep-dyed villain (*traître* or *tyran* in French stage nomenclature), fomentor of conspiracies, deviser of snares, abductor of maidens, and persecutor of innocence. Pixeré-court was given the opportunity to observe a living villain of the first luster at close range and sketch his portrait. It was to prove an experience he would not soon forget.

Extremes of perfidy, cruelty and sensuality, and violent effects generally were repugnant to the nice taste of eighteenth-century France, besides running counter to that favorite dogma of the age, the essential goodness of humanity; and novelists and playwrights respected these prejudices. Prévost discarded the shocking death and funeral scenes in *Clarissa Harlowe* when he translated the novel, and Voltaire permitted little of Iago's infamy to filter through into his *Zaïre*, imitated from *Othello*. The forthright scoundrels of English prose drama were invariably subjected to a similar French dry cleaning in the course of adaptation for the Paris stage.

Even in that group of playwrights in revolt against the stiffness and artificiality of tragedy, the group which accepted Diderot as a leader, these precautions were taken.[2] Diderot himself emasculated Stukely, in a manner of speaking, when he reworked *The Gamester* (as *Beverli*); Desforges took similar liberties with the Fellamar of Fielding in his *Tom Jones à Londres;* and Sedaine and Collé, in their versions of *The King and the Miller of Mansfield*, expunged Lord Lurewell's seduction of the maiden. Mercier, most intransigent of nonconformists, meekly bowed to convention in sparing French playgoers the spectacle of the murder of the merchant by his nephew in *Jenneval*, the *drame* he wrote on the basis of Lillo's *The London Merchant*, and in modifying the wickedness of the prostitute Millwood. Félix Gaiffe, in *Le Drame en France au XVIIIe siècle* (p. 300), remarks that it was decidedly not easy to place a villain on the stage of any of the principal theatres of France in the late eighteenth century.

Along the Boulevard du Temple, home of the popular theatre in Paris during this period and later, tastes were less nice and theatrical

---

[2] The villains of *drame*, such as Juiller of Mercier's *Le Faux Ami*, the Comte de Clarendon of Beaumarchais' *Eugénie*, and the Commandeur of *La Père de famille* of Diderot, are comparatively mild examples of the type and usually reform before the final curtain.

practice much freer. In the unpretentious heroic pantomime played at the little theatres there (which will be considered in subsequent pages), Arnould-Mussot and his imitators were sketching in the tentative outlines of a figure that was to develop into the villain of melodrama. The Revolution was providing excellent models. The spectacle offered by that upheaval made heinous wickedness credible and familiar; cherished illusions of native human goodness could not well survive the 10th of August, the 2nd of September, and the carnival of the guillotine repeated throughout France. Monsters were everywhere in those terrible times. Barras, Collot d'Herbois, Tallien, Carrier, Le Bon, Fouché, Stanislas Fréron—any one of these might have sat as model for those stage scoundrels whom sophisticated audiences late in the century came to laugh at as examples of melodramatic extravagance.

Pixerécourt's private villain was named Mauger but he had added the prefix Marat to his name and proved himself entirely worthy of it. Among other crimes committed while he served as self-appointed agent of the Convention at Nancy was the violation and murder of a young girl of the city who had gone to plead with him for the life of her father, a political prisoner. Indignation flared among the townspeople over this outrage, but no one could do much about it. Pixerécourt, an acquaintance of the murdered girl, heard of the affair and set out to avenge her in the only way that lay in his power: writing up the despoiler in a play. With his customary facility he finished the piece in a few days and with incredible imprudence took it to the local theatre where *Sélico* had finally had its premiere a few weeks earlier.

It is hardly necessary to report that the good people of Nancy were denied the grim satisfaction of seeing their oppressor trepanned on the stage. *Marat-Mauger ou le Jacobin en mission, pièce en un acte, melée de vaudevilles* (1794) was turned over to the Comité de Surveillance of the local Revolutionary committee for its approval. The critics comprising this jury, after examining the composition, decided that it would be a good thing for the French stage if the author were taken into custody and promptly guillotined—a judgment in which many subsequent students of the drama have heartily concurred. The committee, it is necessary to mention, had been hoaxed by Mauger, an impostor, who had by this time taken himself off after being exposed; what its members took particular umbrage at was the rôle of clown to which they were collectively assigned by implication in the *dramatis personae*. The inevitable order of arrest was issued.

Pixerécourt must have had more than an inkling of the consequences to be expected of his rash act, since he had provided himself in advance with a leave of absence; and when the guard sent to apprehend him entered his lodgings by the front door, he left by the rear—a perfect melodramatic exit. Free of the city, he found himself once again a deserter and a fugitive. A second time he turned toward Paris. He had drawn his first villain, and he had defied the wicked powers that be. Though doubtless he did not regret it, the episode taught him a lesson; in the future he was to let the civil authorities severely alone in their iniquities. Thereafter he confined himself to noncontroversial themes, save for a single Napoleonic piece at the Revolution of July and an anti-Jesuit play, which, however, owed more to the collaborator Ducange than to him. He was to be remorseless in his condemnation of abduction, rape, theft, brigandage, and assassination and tireless in his eulogies of honesty, constancy, and benevolence; further than that he would not go. Other hands were to develop the propaganda melodrama.

If Nancy was difficult for Pixerécourt in 1794, the capital was hardly an improvement. Merlin de Douai's terrible Law of Suspects was still in effect, with its penalties for "those who have not constantly given evidence of their attachment to the Revolution"; and on top of that the Convention, aroused by Royalist plots and threats of invasion, had passed the Law of 27 Germinal An II, directing the imprisonment or exile of everyone of noble blood remaining in France—an act which drove Florian into banishment. Only artists were exempt, and the fledgling playwright, desperate, seized upon that. He went straight to Barrère, chief of the Committee of Public Safety, and gave a full and frank account of himself. "I am too young to die," he pleaded passionately. "Something within me tells me that I was made for better things. I want to work and devote myself to writing for the stage. Give me my liberty; you will be doing a good deed and I shall be grateful to you." Surprisingly Barrère granted him exemption, amused no doubt by the comical ardor of this serious, intense youth. He went further, securing him a post under Carnot, who in turn became Pixerécourt's protector.[3]

[3] Pixerécourt, "Souvenirs de la Révolution," *Théâtre choisi*, Vol. II, p. xxi ff.

From the haven of a clerkship in the War Office, René watched the Terror rise to its climax. The experience constitutes an indispensable clue to the peculiarities of the genre which he was to help create; melodrama incubated in the shambles of that shocking purge.

The circumstances of the Revolution explain the drama that followed it, and they help also to explain the response of the audiences which found their pleasure in this drama. In the early decades of the nineteenth century there was no complaint from playgoers on the score of the improbability of the characters and situations presented before them nightly on the boards of the Gaîté, the Ambigu, and the Porte Saint-Martin—a complaint that was to be heard increasingly as the end of the nineteenth century approached. Nothing was improbable to people who had lived through Thermidor.

No less important than the Revolution and the printed word as influences upon Pixerécourt in the formative years he spent in Paris during the closing decades of the century were theatrical conditions of the place and time. A new kind of theatre was coming to maturity during these years and a new audience with it, and an understanding of melodrama is impossible without some knowledge of both. Accordingly, in the two chapters which follow we shall take our leave temporarily of Pixerécourt and explore the exciting environs of the Boulevard du Temple and the entertainments on view there.

III

The "Boulevard du Crime"

The only mall that counts at all—
It thrills me like a lover's call—
The promenade that's gay and free:
The Temple Boulevard, Paree!
—Eighteenth-century Paris street song

In the course of the same decade in which the Comédie Française and the Opéra obtained recognition as subvened monopolies, a beginning was made on a municipal improvement in Paris which, within a century, was to develop into the stronghold of a feared and detested rival of those two august foundations. Two years before Lully was granted letters patent for the exclusive presentation of the musical drama imported from Italy and ten years before the company of players at the Hôtel Bourgogne was consolidated with those at the Palais Royal and the Marais and made the sole repository of the classical drama, a royal command (1670) placed upon the map of the city the Boulevard du Temple, that promenade fated to attain picturesque immortality in theatrical annals as the "Boulevard du Crime"—so called on account of the atrocities perpetrated and the blood made to flow nightly along its lively length under the auspices of melodrama.

A crumbling bastion of the old fortifications in the Temple quarter was demolished, its moat filled in, and an avenue opened up as far as the Porte Saint-Martin from the point where the Rue des Filles du Calvaire came to a dead end. After it had been decked out with lawns and planted with pleasant shade trees, Parisians found the spot to their liking and, afoot and in equipages, flocked here on bright afternoons to gossip, flirt, sun themselves, and keep rendezvous. Coffee shops and billiard parlors opened, *grandes dames* held court under the spreading horse chestnuts, beggars whined for alms, *filles de joie* circulated in the crowd.

In the wake of the idlers came the forerunners of the modern hokeypokey and hot-dog merchants, hawking fruit, cocoa, lemonade, Nantes cakes, sweet barley sticks and hot Lyons chestnuts; and after them the nondescript tribe of popular entertainers from the fairs and their satellites—the buskers, grifters, fixers, shills, and pitchmen of immemorial carnival tradition. Freaks and automatons were exhibited, trained animals went through their paces, clowns, dancers, ropewalkers, ventriloquists, tumblers, and prestidigitators displayed their dexterity, and puppeteers set up their stands.

Here came "Sieur" Nicolas Vienne (professionally, "le Grimacier," or "Beauvisage") to regale the crowds with his mugging from atop a cart and pass the hat; "Sieur" Comus, half charlatan and half scientist, to attract the notice of Diderot and amass a fortune with his phantasmagoria (grandfather of the cinema), his physical and electrical experiments, his artificial hand that wrote out one's secret thoughts, and his sibyl who answered questions; and "Sieur" Gaudon with his ropedancers and actors from the fair at Saint-Germain, to set up the first booth, bringing in his train Guillaume Nicolet, father of the more famous Jean-Baptiste, a young man who was to elevate Boulevard entertainment from the status of a vagabond's racket to that of a big business.

At first it was all outdoors, the performers offering their specialties on carts and rude trestles or in the temporary shelter of booths, which were flimsy affairs of wood and canvas that could be knocked down and transported readily from one to another of the fairs held seasonally at different places in the city. In 1765 Nicolet *fils*, as a novice entrepreneur built the first proper auditorium, a modest frame structure, half booth and half hall, in which he augmented his earlier show of performing animals with tumblers, tightrope walkers, and strong men. A redoubtable competitor soon appeared on the Boulevard, Nicolas Médard Audinot, who offered a new type of marionette, caricatures of his sometime associates at the Italiennes, in plays which parodied the repertoire of that company.

The seventies saw further progress on the Boulevard and precipitated a crisis in its fortunes. Visitors were being attracted in greater numbers by the increased elegance and variety of the spectacles. The population of this lately rural district was growing by leaps and bounds, and the erection of permanent, substantial playhouses continued. "Beauvisage" had passed the hat to such good purpose that, in partnership with one Louis Gabriel Sallé, he was able to build the Théâtre des Associés in 1774; the Délassements Comiques joined the ranks in 1785; and Nicolet, after a fire in 1769, rebuilt his Grands Danseurs du Roi in imposing style as a real theatre. After generations of buffetings and vagabondage, the performers of the fairs were at last finding a safe refuge. It was an important stage in their evolution, foreshadowing a prosperous, autonomous, popular theatre, safe from the petty persecutions of its enemies, professional and political.

Emboldened by success and the prestige of command performances before the King and Pompadour at Choisy, the two outstanding entrepreneurs of the Boulevard made further additions to their bills. In Nicolet's new house the plebeian ropewalkers, strong men, and acrobats were relegated to the intermission in order to make room for "works of spectacle," ballets, pantomimes, and even little spoken pieces—*grivoiseries*—comic and for the most part obscene, devised by Toussaint-Gaspard Taconnet. Audinot, not to be outdone, supplemented his marionettes in 1771 with juvenile actors (succeeded not long after by adults) appearing in miniature comedies and ballet-pantomimes, some of them the work of Arnould-Mussot, of whom more later. Gradually Audinot, like Nicolet, began to adopt dialogue, chiefly in the so-called *ambigus*—melanges of parody, *drame*, comedy, song, and dance. At about this time (1770) he changed the name of his playhouse to Ambigu Comique.

These innovations brought the Boulevard theatres into sharp conflict with the official theatres, which, for all their lofty pretensions, were not above recourse to the civil arm of the law for the purpose of suppressing competition. The Français took exception to speech, the Opéra to dancing, orchestra, and song, and the Italiennes to ariettas and vaudevilles; and all three had certain rights of censorship. Police were kept busy up and down the Boulevard, harrying this resort for introducing kings upon the stage, closing that one for the use of verse, and requiring a third to stretch a net between stage and audience for miscellaneous trespass—the net, associated with acrobats, being a shameful reminder of lowly status.

A final crisis in the affairs of the little theatres before their liberation was precipitated in 1784 when the Opéra was assigned all the privileges of the Boulevard spectacles. This august institution proceeded to shake down Nicolet to the tune of 24,000 livres a year. Audinot, already paying heavy tribute, resisted a further imposition and was dispossessed. However, two year later he was back in a new theatre on the Boulevard where he did pretty much as he pleased.

As the Revolution approached, the little theatres generally were subjected to less and less of this sort of persecution. The Boulevard entrenched itself deeper in popular favor and acquired that importance which comes with affluence. With the overthrow of the monarchy—celebrated jubilantly on the Boulevard, which was Jacobin to the core—the oppressive regulations went into discard, their cancellation being officially confirmed in the act of the National Assembly of January 13, 1791, which abolished the monopoly and removed all restrictions save political ones on the opening and operation of theatres in Paris and threw open the repertory of the classics to all and sundry. Then did the Boulevard houses taste sweet revenge for their long subjection, playing Racine, Voltaire, Corneille, Molière, LeSage, and Marivaux to their hearts' content—with *citoyen* substituted for *monsieur* in the dialogue, and the valets transformed into captains. Molière became a special favorite; Tartuffe was roundly hissed at the Gaîté (as the Grands Danseurs du Roi was tactfully renamed) and the author loudly called for at the curtain. New houses sprang up as if by magic: the Elévès de Thalia, the Petits Comédiens Français, the Théâtre Minerve, and resorts like the Café Yon and the Café Godet—ancestors of the modern night club. Side shows multiplied. The triumph of the Boulevard was complete when Audinot erected his handsome new Ambigu in 1791, the largest theatre in the country.

From Nicolas Brazier and other contemporary sources it is possible to reconstruct the scene at this period of the Boulevard's history: the pandemonium of peddlers ringing their hand bells and crying everything from prints to pomade; the blaring of clarinets and the booming of bass drums; the noisy *parades*, or balcony farces, beginning one after another at about noon; Madame Malaga, tightrope dancer, exposing her voluptuous curves in gold-spangled red tights on the trestles outside her booth in her celebrated come-on; "Sieur" Sallé, one-eyed actor-manager of the Associés, doubling as barker at the door of his theatre to extol the richness and variety of his company's wardrobe; the uproarious holiday throng milling about, guzzling in The Turk or The Green, fighting for places on the carrousels, pressing into Curtius' Wax Works—where kings and celebrated criminals were on view in effigy, a narrator in sepulchral tones reciting their histories to the accompaniment of clinking chains—and pushing over into the Faubourg du Temple, where Astley, the Londoner, had his Cirque Anglais, offering feats of horsemanship, tightrope performers, and wild animals.[1]

It was a swarming, Hogarthian mob, turbulent, illiterate, and

[1] Nicolas Brazier, *Chroniques des petits théâtres de Paris* (Paris, 1883), Vol. I, p. 6 *ff.*

unwashed, recruited from the city's rowdies and reinforced by
bands of cutthroats from the provinces. In rags and tatters or ill-
gotten finery—a cassock or chasuble, as like as not—sucking
oranges, munching sausages or apple puffs, and smelling of sweat
and garlic, these emancipated citizens took their pleasure by day and
by night, clowning, brawling, lovemaking, carousing, and bellowing
the "Marseillaise," the "Bourbouillaise" and

> Dansons la carmagnole
> Vive le son du canon.

The young clerk of the War Department, René Pixerécourt,
haunted the Boulevard through these years, peddling the plays he
was eternally busy writing and observing meanwhile with a sharp
eye the vagaries of the ebullient thoroughfare—studying the psychology of its habitués and noting the methods of its successful
managers. To appreciate the influence of it all upon him one has
only to look at this works; the clatter of the midway, the shrill
treble of the barker resound through every play he ever wrote. For
all that he owed to literary men such as Young, Hervey, Florian,
and D'Arnaud, Pixerécourt was first, last, and always the playwright
of the "Boulevard du Crime." He was never to deny it, content with
his modest niche as "Shakespeare of the Boulevard" and "Corneille
of melodrama." Though a scholar of sorts and a bibliophile, pos-
sessing the friendship of men of the type of Nodier and Jules Janin,
he avowed like Bouchardy after him that he wrote "for those who
cannot read."

The popular audience and the commercial theatre came into their
own simultaneously at the Revolution, to complement each other.
With no subventions and no hereditary, organized audience to
depend upon for support, the Boulevard theatres had to adjust their
programs to the tastes of their patrons—had to give the public what
it wanted; hence the shows there came to be weighed by the single,
inexorable standard of box office. The managers' philosophy was
stated frankly by Prévost, one of the most successful of them, who
took over the Associés in 1797, naming it, with a fine sense of the
appropriate, the Théâtre sans Prétentions. Dramatic authors, he said,
must be guided in their choice of subjects by the taste of the public.
As taste changes, one must change with it—to the marvellous,
fairytale spectacles, *diablerie*, crime plays, the supernatural. One
troubles oneself no longer about theatrical rules. Any improvement
in the situation is up to the more enlightened part of the populace

exercising its franchise at the box office. A manager who attempted to play anything of a high order would be ruined. One must, of necessity, follow the mode. A decade later a commentator on Boulevard affairs, Armand Charlemagne, writing under the pen name of Placide le Vieux, went a step further in a pamphlet entitled *Le Mélo-drame aux boulevards* (1809) stating that the people have the right to demand amusement to their taste.

One by one the appurtenances of this democratic theatre made their appearance. The scalper began to take his stand in the environs of the Ambigu early in the nineteenth century; and Corsse, manager of this house from 1798 onward, invented the giant poster to provide space for advertisement of all those "spectacles demanded by the ambassadors" and the like. For *Latude,* given in 1834, Pixeré-court had the inspiration for the last word in exploitation, the lobby display. On exhibit at the Gaîté were authentic relics of the escape of the celebrated prisoner, Henri Massers de Latude, whose career was set forth in the play—a rope woven from sheets, a candlestick hack-saw, and a hammer made from a large spike. It is the atmosphere of twentieth-century Broadway.

IV

Pantomime Into Melodrama

In melodrama, the logical evolution of the entire theatre of the eighteenth century is achieved. —JULES MARSAN

Shows on the Boulevard during the eighteenth century ran the gamut from acrobatics and performing dogs to tragedy and *opéra seria.* Wrestling, pugilism, vaudevilles, *drame,* comedy, *opéra comique*—all were to be seen here. Most assiduously cultivated were comedy in the broad vein of Toussaint-Gaspard Taconnet and pantomime. The history of the dramatic advances made by the popular theatre in this period is essentially the history of the latter; out of pantomime, as it absorbed new elements and improved its technique, melodrama issued at the end of the century.[1]

Pantomime, in the loose sense of the word, is an ancient diversion, probably Italian in origin, which came early to France with its farcical imbroglio, its stock characters—each with a distinguishing costume—its acrobatic acting and its elaborate conventionalized gesture which was made necessary in the beginning by the wearing of masks. Typically it was in dumb show, though not always; official regulation tended to keep it thus in Paris, where it made its way from the seasonal fairs to the Boulevard du Temple during the late decades of the eighteenth century when the performers at the fairs were converging on that thoroughfare and finding a permanent home there. It became acclimated to the Boulevard in various forms such as the *Arlequinade,* featuring the antics and stratagems of the rowdy guzzler and playboy from whom it got this name, and the fairytale spectacles, which derived from the Countess d'Aulnoy's and Charles Perrault's[2] collections of nursery tales both published

---

[1] This theory of the evolution of pantomime is developed most fully by Alexis Pitou in "Les Origins du mélodrame français à la fin du XVIII siècle," *Revue d'histoire littéraire de la France,* June 1911, pp. 256–296.

[2] No fewer than five of Perrault's plots survived into the twentieth century in English pantomime. His tales, like the melodramas of Pixerécourt and his imitators, conclude with a moral and draw a sharp distinction between good and bad fairies.

late in the seventeenth century. This latter type of fiction, with its sympathetic heroine caught in the toils of an evil ogre's enchantment from which she is eventually extricated through the more potent charms of a good fairy or the valor of her princely lover, faintly foreshadowed the persecution theme of melodrama. Harlequin, discarding his mask and changing his costume, was to survive as the comic in the formula of Pixerécourt.

The prohibition of speech at the little theatres in Paris prevented the pantomime from making any progress along literary lines, but few restrictions were imposed upon purely visual displays, and it was to development in this field that Boulevard directors applied themselves, attaining an increasing degree of magnificence as time went on. Swelling receipts made possible increased expenditures for this purpose, and the enlarged facilities of the permanent, commodious playhouses, which were erected in the seventies and later, provided scope for the most ambitious effects. At the end of that decade costumes were varied and elaborate; dank dungeons, towering castle keeps, and wild, mountainous landscapes were being reproduced with some measure of realism; storms and tempests were counterfeited after a fashion; the assault of fortresses went forward with brilliance; machines were called into play for the manipulation of various magical effects in fairytale spectacles; "Sieur" Torré introduced fireworks in pantomime; and military evolutions climaxed by pitched battles alternated with ecclesiastical processions and tournaments in full chivalric panoply. It was thanks largely to these eye-filling stage settings, this bustle and variety, that pantomime—and melodrama after it—won and held the patronage of Boulevard audiences.

Certainly the fables themselves could have generated only the slightest interest; they were in most instances thin, trivial, stereotyped, dull. It was this deficiency and a tendency to ribaldry in the pantomime that impelled Jean-François Mussot, who called himself Arnould-Mussot, to undertake a reform of the genre in 1779 in association with Audinot at the Ambigu. Arnould-Mussot's renovations took the form of a more serious plot, usually strong in sentimental interest, a stricter—even a puritanical—morality, and new themes drawn from recent and medieval history and current events, with character types in conformity. This was heroic pantomime, immediate ancestor of Boulevard melodrama.[3]

[3] Pitou, p. 259.

Like its predecessor, Arnould-Mussot's pantomime was performed in dumb show, placards with explanatory legends in the
tradition of the fairs (*pièces à écriteaux*) being displayed at intervals
to assist in an understanding of the story. Accompanying the
performance was music, often written and performed with great
care, intended to clarify the action and enhance the dramatic effect
further.[4]

One of the earliest of these reformed pantomimes, *Les Quatre Fils
Aymon* (1779), which Bachaumont's *Mémoirs secrets* mentions
for its pathos and its popularity, retold the medieval geste in a
series of tableaux charged with suspense and replete with thrilling
action. It was popular until the end of the century in London and
New York as well as in Paris. The plots of the reformed pantomimes were prevailingly simple, but occasionally they presented
complications which Audinot's illustrative action and descriptive
music could not resolve. The remedy adopted in these cases was the
inevitable one: here and there mimes became actors for the nonce,
dropping into speech. Introduced sparingly at first, dialogue showed
a tendency to increase; and pantomime eventually became *pantomime dialoguée* on the program, a mongrel term for a mongrel
genre, precursor of melodrama, which, at least in its heroic form,
Ribié claimed to have invented in his *La Prise de Mitylène ou les
princes infortunés* (1783). Dialogue, of course, had been used much
earlier in more primitive forms of the pantomime and in comedies at
Nicolet's and the Ambigu and at the *foires*, a specific example being
L'Élève de la Nature (1781) cited by Gaiffe.

Meanwhile on the Boulevard there appeared the *fait historique*, or
dramatization of some sensational episode from recent European
history, a type of piece which grew in popularity with the increasing political tension of the times. *Baron de Trenck* (1788), in verse
and with a musical accompaniment, was one of the most successful
of these. *Drame* also was heard from but not often; examples, sometimes in three acts but usually shorter, occasionally met with a
favorable reception. They tended to raise the moral tone of the free
and easy popular theatre and to accustom its audiences to realistic
atmosphere on the stage and a certain naturalness of dialogue.
Mercier's *La Brouette du Vinagrier* and *Jenneval* were given at the

[4] Maurice Albert, *Les Théâtres des Boulevards* (Paris, 1902),
p. 20.

Associés in 1776, and Mayeur de Saint-Paul's *L'Élève de la Nature* (with music) had its premiere at Nicolet's five years later.

More interesting than either of these as a specimen of *drame*, and more popular, was *L'Artiste infortuné*. In this play by Destival de Braban, habitués of the Ambigu in 1781 were permitted to exercise their sensibility on the poignant misfortunes of the Orval family, impoverished by a miscarriage of justice, driven from pillar to post in their distress, and reduced to the verge of starvation. Back of all this is a lascivious villain (a financier) with evil designs on the lovely daughter. When all seems lost, a virtuous young merchant whom Orval in his prosperity had befriended steps into the picture with assistance and an offer of honorable marriage to the girl. It is virtually a domestic melodrama.[5]

Pieces of this type, however, were the exception; it was the heroic pantomime in the Arnould-Mussot manner that gained and held the favor of Boulevard audiences, the preferred theme continuing to be the persecution of an innocent maiden by a brutal, libidinous tyrant—burgomaster, prince, or oriental despot—who sets wild beasts upon her track, throws her into a dungeon, lashes her to the stake, and the like when she spurns his advances. They are *pièces d'action* and justify the label by the rapidity of their mimed business and the multiplicity of their episodes.

The Revolution diverted the pantomime into political channels, of course. After 1791, feudal abuses are attacked, convents and monasteries "exposed," and Republicans flattered and their ideas propagated. *Grands seigneurs* and priors step into what were to be called the *troisième*, or villain, rôles; and the Vendéean insurrectionists became ferocious, inhuman brigands. The robber joined the ranks of major characters in pantomime appearing first in the production of *Robert, chef de brigands*, which stirred revolutionary fervor along the Boulevard in 1792 with its figure of a high-minded outlaw avenging the wrongs of the poor on their noble oppressors, to the accompaniment of much resounding rhetoric. The author of this piece, Lamartellière, took extensive liberties with his source, *Die Räuber* (whose creator, the young Friedrich Schiller, was commended by the *Moniteur* as a true Girondist), among them being the substitution of a happy end. The life of Amelia is spared by her brigand sweetheart, whose offenses in turn are pardoned by the

[5] Gaiffe, p. 480.

Emperor in a speech freighted with appropriate Girondist sentiments.

Bandits noble and ignoble, many of them, like Robert, of Teutonic origin, were to kidnap, waylay, and pistol their way through piece after piece on the Boulevard for fifty years and more. At times they would redeem and justify themselves in pompous words and heroic deeds, after the manner of Schiller's Karl Moor; as a rule, however, they were to be outright villains, providing those thrills so necessary to an audience which demanded suspense, action, and violence above all else.

Bandits were particularly ferocious in *La Forêt périlleuse ou les brigands de la Calabre* (1797), often called the first melodrama. In this piece by Loaisel-Tréogate a sinister outlaw captain carries off Camille, the heroine, to his cave, puts her behind bars there when she declines to become his mistress, and seizes Colisan, her lover, when that noble youth blunders into a secret passage to the cave while searching for the maiden. In *Les Miquelots ou le repaire des Pyrénées* (1797), by J. G. A. Cuvelier de Trye, another candidate for the honor of having invented melodrama, the abducting robber chief, Barbanamo, captures his victim's lover, as in *La Forêt périlleuse*, and forces him to fight against a rescuing party.

Boulevard audiences by no means lost their taste for comedy, and, though Arnould-Mussot did not cater to it particularly, other playwrights did. Along with the brigand, there is a clown in *La Forêt périlleuse*, Fresco by name, squire to the dauntless hero Colisan; he is an extravagantly chickenhearted creature, eloquent in counsels of prudence, like the *gracioso* of Spanish drama. The comic became a popular accessory in heroic pantomime after his successful debut in another of Loaisel-Tréogate's *comédies héroïques* (as this author called his exercises in the genre), *Le Château du diable*, a four-act piece entirely in dialogue, given at the Marais in the same year as *Robert*. Half fairytale and half melodrama, this effort presents a courageous young knight who penetrates the haunted castle of a cruel ogre and encounters there all manner of ghostly perils and voluptuous temptations, only to discover in the end that these apparitions have been contrived by the father of his prospective bride as a test of his spirit and fidelity. It is the trick ending of the modern mystery play—of *Seven Keys to Baldpate* and *Under Cover*. The humorous personage in Cuvelier's *C'est le diable ou la Bohémienne* (1798) is an ageing coquette. There are comics in

Marsolier's *Camille ou le souterrain* (1791), *Les Mystères d'Udolphe,* and other pantomimes of this period, and in *L'Artiste infortuné* and other *drames.*

Alien novels supplemented alien plays in shaping the destiny of the evolving pantomime in the middle nineties, and it was with the rise of this influence that melodrama definitely emerged. Romances, like human interest items in the newspapers, had supplied the authors of *drame* with subjects—Mercier wrote that a play ought to be merely "a romance in action"—but melodrama was to borrow from fiction to an extent never approached before or since. In the beginning it was fiction in its more horrific aspects which attracted the playwrights, chiefly the German ghost and brigand literature and the English gothic school of Matthew G. Lewis and Mrs. Anne Radcliffe. Ribié's version of Lewis' *The Monk* launched the gothic vogue in 1795 on the Boulevard. The play did full justice to that nightmare of violence and bestiality. The playwright contrived among other tidbits to include the scene in which the devil himself appears to drag off the sex-mad monk to his doom. The devil is the heavy villain in *C'est le diable ou la Bohémienne,* a carnival of horrors.

After the establishment of the Directory, when the bourgeois resumed theatregoing along the "Boulevard du Crime," a reaction against these atrocities set in; milder pieces in increasing numbers occupied the stage. It was at this point in the evolution of the pantomime—now being called *mélo-drame* in some instances—that Pixerécourt finally achieved Paris production of one of his plays after having had sixteen of them accepted in two years without actually being put on the stage. It was with an adapted novel that he did it, *Les Petits Auvergnats,* by Ducray Duminil. After an unexplained absence of two years, a wife returns to her husband, who believes that she deserted him and their children. Actually she was carried off by a villain and imprisoned. Letters are produced which confirm her story, and there is a touching reconciliation. In one act, *Les Petits Auvergnats* was given at the Ambigu in 1797.

Pixerécourt's next work, and his first full-length play to reach the boards in the capital, was *Victor ou l'enfant de la forêt* (Ambigu, 1797) a bandit piece owing something to *Die Räuber.* Its history illustrates the curious state of solution to which the various dramatic forms—once so fixed, so homogeneous, and so distinct—had been reduced in the crucible of the Revolutionary theatre and throws light upon the complicated and diverse ancestry of melodrama.[6] *Victor* was planned and written as a musical drama or *drame lyrique* with a score composed by another Nancy citizen, one Solié. As such it was accepted at the Favart and had got as far along as rehearsal at this musical house when the manager suddenly decided to lay it aside in favor of another version of the Ducray-Duminil romance of the same name from which it had been taken. Thereupon the indignant Pixerécourt took his script to the Ambigu where it was mounted as a *drame en prose et à grand spectacle* without any change save the suppression of the songs.[7] *Victor* made an acceptable melodrama as it would have made an acceptable musical drama. The difference between the two forms was of the slightest as they developed side by side in these years. The musical drama, originally entirely comic since it evolved from vaudeville, had gradually, under a variety of labels, acquired a serious main plot wherein virtuous, "sensible" leading characters are exposed to a succession of perilous adventures and subjected to various touching misfortunes before being rewarded by happiness in the end. The comedy, meanwhile, was confined to special comic personages introduced at intervals to relieve the pathetic situations. This evolution was due chiefly to Michel Jean Sedaine, a genuinely gifted man of the theatre who, discouraged at the Française where his *Philosophe sans le savoir* (1765) had contributed to *drame* its solitary work of enduring merit, turned to the lighter form, furnishing the less exacting and more popular stage of the Italiennes with a succession of light *opéras comiques larmoyantes,* of which *Le Déserteur* (1769) set a standard and established a school.

The most cursory inspection of the musical drama reveals its affinities with melodrama. Pixerécourt himself wrote that "a melodrama is nothing but a musical drama in which the music is played by the orchestra instead of being sung"—and elsewhere that his plays were "in the genre of Sedaine."[8] The musical drama relied

[6] Writing in August, 1802 to Frederick Reynolds, Henry Harris, who was son of Drury Lane manager Thomas Harris, derived the word from mêler (mix), a natural error. Actually, of course, it is from *melos* (Gr.), song. See Chap. XVI.

[7] Pixerécourt, "Souvenirs du jeune âge," *Théâtre choisi,* Vol. I, p. xxxviii.

[8] Marsan, p. 203.

upon external incident for the advancement of its intrigue, cultivated rapid action, utilized the monologue, and betrayed an increasing weakness for spectacular stage effects. *Richard Coeur-de-Lion*
(1784), one of the most successful of Sedaine's musical dramas—
thanks somewhat to Grétry's charming score—was rewritten to
include a rousing assault upon the prison-fortress, in which the king
is rescued amid the clash of arms and the collapse of pasteboard
masonry.

Pixerécourt called his *Victor* "firstborn of modern melodrama"[9]
but the play is not exactly that since it lacks a comic and an unregenerate villain. (It was produced as a *drame lyrique*.) A later
work of his was to embody the complete formula. This was *Cœlina
ou l'enfant du mystère*, melodrama's first great international success,
performed in 1800.

[9] "Le Mélodrame," *Paris ou le livre des Cent-et-un*, VI, p. 325.

V

Cœlina, Child of Mystery

We are awaiting a genius who will combine pantomime with dialogue, mingling dumb-show with spoken scenes. —DIDEROT

The first scene of *Cœlina ou l'enfant du mystère* opens in the household of a Savoyard squire, M. Dufour, where an important visitor is expected, Trugelin, a powerful neighbor, coming on behalf of his son to bespeak the hand of the maiden of the title, Dufour's orphaned niece and ward. Cœlina, introduced in the opening scene, is young and beautiful, and the perfection of her person is matched by the kindness of her heart and the nobility of her soul. Her conduct and sentiments in any given situation—and even her language—can always be predicted with certainty, not only for the period of the three acts of Pixerécourt's play but also throughout the thousands of weepy dramas of wronged orphans in which she will be reproduced throughout the Western world for upward of a century with scarcely any change save in name, costume, and nationality.

The character of this heroine owes little or nothing to Pixerécourt. He found this fine flower of femininity, along with the rest of the material for the first two acts of his piece, in a romance (also called *Cœlina*) from the pen of Ducray-Duminil, whom Saintsbury has called "a writer of kitchen French." He might have found her in virtually any contemporary *drame, opéra comique,* romance or heroic pantomime, so common was the sensible, dutiful, and impregnably virtuous ingenue in the literature and drama of the day. She had made her French stage debut in the "tearful comedies" of La Chaussée, who seems to have discovered her in the pages of the English novelist Samuel Richardson.

Dufour is disposed to look favorably upon the suit of Trugelin though a sincere reciprocal affection exists between his own dutiful son Stéphany and the heroine. He prefers a stranger as spouse for his ward, because the girl is an heiress, and he would not have it thought that he is after her money! Dufour is a formidable prig, the synthetic "good man" of encyclopaedist theorists; he is given to spouting the fashionable humanitarian cant and striking moral attitudes like his predecessors in *drame*. The "good man" was to prove useful in melodrama, his booby guilelessness making him fair game for the scheming and unprincipled villain.

Stéphany is a younger Dufour, a masculine Cœlina; each is cut from the same white cloth, all wool and a yard wide. He is courageous, high-minded, devoted, incorruptible; such faults as he has are venial and generous ones, for example, impetuosity. Somewhat stupid, he will often be outwitted by the clever villain in his long stage career, but not in a hundred years will he be worsted in fair fight. Like his sweetheart and parent, this model youth was a stock literary property of the times.

Trugelin, unlike Dufour, has no delicate scruples about Cœlina's dowry; indeed, the girl's substantial estate is the single motive for his matrimonial overtures. Trugelin is the *tyran*, or *traître*—scheming, venal, cruel, cowardly, and treacherous, a Marat-Mauger of private life. At intervals in the course of the play he will let the audience in on the kind of life he had led, the state of his conscience at the moment, what he has been doing before he came on the stage, what he proposes doing in the next scene, and how he will go about it. The soliloquy is an ancient theatrical device, but the informative aside as it will flourish in melodrama is largely a relic of those times when the *forain* theatres were restricted by law to a single actor on the stage at a time.

Hints of the true nature of this reptile are thrown out at the very beginning of the play through the fear and distrust which his expected visit arouses in the breasts of the gentle Cœlina and her robust, plainspoken confidante, Tiennette, Dufour's aged housekeeper, one of the play's two comic rôles. If the melodramatist allows his good men to be taken in by plausible villains, he plays no such tricks on his audience.

Shortly after his entrance, Trugelin is much taken aback upon encountering a mysterious stranger in the Dufour household, a wanderer newly come to the neighborhood. Their meeting, like all significant and exciting moments in the play, is signalled by appropriate music from the busy orchestra. This stranger, who goes under the name of Françisque Humbert, is a kind, gentle old man, quite poor but bearing himself with a certain placid dignity which is plainly meant to indicate gentle birth. This was the premier rôle.

Cœlina has befriended Françisque from the first, not only from her natural goodness of heart, but also in response to a strong feeling of sympathy for which she cannot account; this is the famous "voice of the blood" indicating otherwise unsuspected relationship. Used frequently in *drame* and in novels of the period, this device became a peculiarly melodramatic one. Humbert, on his part, has been hovering tenderly about Cœlina, so much so that his attentions to the girl are noted by another character. The ground is being prepared for the big recognition scene, the *reconnaissance* or discovery scene in English theatrical terminology, which will provide the climax in the second act.

Nothing is known of Françisque save that years before the opening of the play, through the treachery of an enemy, he was sold into the hands of pirates, who cut out his tongue; and that more recently he has been viciously assaulted in a wild mountain pass nearby and left for dead. His mutilation makes it necessary for him to express himself entirely in pantomime.

Françisque is that pawn which melodrama will find so useful in its romantic intrigue: a figure out of the past, returning to his familiar haunts after a long absence in disguise or changed beyond recognition, his reappearance serving to bring to a head a situation growing out of his disappearance. He may be a villain, as in *La Femme à deux maris;* the "good man," as in *Le Monastère abandonné;* or the hero, as in *L'Homme à trois visages.* The return commended itself particularly to playwrights working within the restrictions imposed by the classical unities, since it made possible a point of attack close to the denouement and thus helped solve the frequently troublesome problem of holding the action within the classically required span of twenty-four hours. Insofar as his subjects and the tastes of his audiences permitted, Pixerécourt respected the unities, particularly the unity of time; he departed from classical precedent on this score only three times in his plays, apologizing on each occasion. No radical iconoclast, "the Shakespeare of melodrama" was humbly respectful of tragedy, which he admitted to be a form far superior to the humble one in which he worked; until the 1830's he kept almost all his pieces within three acts[1] because he felt that only the statelier drama of tradition was worthy of five.

The late point of attack usually necessitated considerable exposition, and the customary method of melodrama was to accomplish it in the opening scene by means of a frank monologue or explanatory

---

[1] Three exceptions were *La Citerne* (1809), *Le Moulin des etangs* (1826), and *La Tête de mort* (1827), all of which were in four acts. *Latude* (1834) had five acts, as did *La Ferme et le chateau* (1834).

dialogue, got through with as rapidly as possible. Pixerécourt managed it more skillfully in *Cœlina*—he was not always to do so well—filling in adroitly with the necessary background as the action proceeded.

In a passage with the second heavy, his henchman Germain, Trugelin reveals himself as the perpetrator of the assault on Françisque eight years before. He now fears that the old man's presence may interfere with his plans, and he plots to murder him that night. Now Cœlina happens to be concealed in a convenient spot nearby during this conversation, thanks to one of those coincidences upon which melodrama leans so heavily. She overhears everything and proceeds to warn Françisque, so that when the conspirators descend upon the old man that night—for the first thrilling episode of the play—he is ready for them with pistols. It was ingenuity in contriving situations of this stirring kind that was to establish Pixerécourt as master of his genre.

The household is aroused by the clash and all gather on the scene, whereupon Trugelin charges Françisque with attacking him. Dufour, indignant at this seeming abuse of his hospitality, orders the old man from the house. However, Cœlina interposes with the true version of the affair, and it is Trugelin who is turned out. Revealed in his true colors and cheated of his hopes of the profitable marriage, the villain shows his teeth; he makes his exit on one of those resounding threats which will become classic, provoking many a chorus of furious hisses and imprecations from generations of aroused gallery gods: "If I do not receive your consent [to the marriage] by ten o'clock tomorrow, tremble! A single word will break off the nuptials you plan [with Stéphany] and that word I shall utter. Adieu!"

For the second act the scene changes to the garden of Dufour's house; melodrama will always provide at least one new stage picture with each act, a practice for which there was precedent in tragedy itself. As the scene opens, preparations are afoot for the immediate marriage of Stéphany and Cœlina, Dufour having dropped his objections to the match after the unmasking of Trugelin. There is a brief comic dispute between two yokels; villagers gather in picturesque costume for the festivities (ballet); and the notary arrives for the ceremony. Before the business can proceed, however, Germain bursts rudely upon the scene with a note to Dufour from Trugelin; that scoundrel is playing his trump card. With a great show of plausibility and reference to enclosed documents, the note conveys the startling information that Cœlina is not what Dufour has always supposed her, namely, the daughter of his deceased brother, but the illegitimate offspring of none other than old Françisque, with whom the girl's mother—who was Trugelin's sister—betrayed her husband.

At this disclosure Cœlina throws herself into the old man's arms, her vague feeling of kinship confirmed. This is the *reconnaissance*. The obvious dramatic value of this piece of hokum had been discovered long before Pixerécourt; Aristotle approved it, and such eminent playwrights as Euripides (in *Ion*), Molière (in *L'Avare*) and Shakespeare (in *King Lear*) all used it. Cuvelier, in his *C'est le diable ou la Bohémienne* (1795) introduced the device into Boulevard heroic pantomime, inspired no doubt by its prevalence in fiction of the day. It was a favorite device with Mercier. Melodrama was to cling to the *reconnaissance* as tenaciously as to the theme of persecuted innocence itself.

Dufour does not share the ecstatic emotion of father and daughter. He feels that he has been the victim of an imposture and, angered, drives the old man out and repudiates Cœlina, calling her "the child of adultery and sin." This is a most unreasonable, not to say brutal, thing to do, since, as Stéphany points out, the girl is an entirely innocent party. Certainly the outburst is not in keeping with Dufour's character, which has been represented as all that is generous, kind, and noble. Imperious necessity demands it, however; where would melodrama be without its wronged heroine, its long-drawn-out pathos? The unfeeling father or guardian is as necessary as the unscrupulous villain. Françisque and Cœlina go off.

Before the second act is over, an old and trusted friend of the family, Dr. Andrevon, brings the intelligence that it was Trugelin who waylaid and assaulted Humbert eight years before. For no good reason this effects a complete change of heart in Dufour toward the girl and her father. He now feels remorse and would have his beloved Cœlina near him again. But it is too late. Father and daughter are already far off—they travel fast in melodrama. Meanwhile the villain, learning that he has been denounced by Andrevon to the authorities, takes to the woods. Slowly and somewhat creakingly the wheels of retribution begin to turn.

Driving the heroine out into the cruel world serves another purpose: it provides Pixerécourt with an opportunity for that big spectacular scenic effect which, appearing in all his plays in one form or another, explains the phrase, *à grand spectacle,* tacked on to the titles of his works. The wild and desolate mountain pass in Savoy whither the audience is transported for the third act is no mere stage picture to be enjoyed for its own sake but a carpenter's set, carefully designed to reflect the mood of the turbulent scene to be enacted there and realized in numerous "practicables," which will play an important part in the animated denouement. Everything is carefully set down in the minute stage directions: Alpine peaks and towering pines represented on the drop; a mountain torrent upstage spanned by a useable bridge, up to which a narrow path leads; a mill (its wheel turning) with a door opening toward the wings, a window facing the audience, and a stone seat under the window.

During the entr'acte the noise of thunder is heard.

TRUGELIN (*disguised as a peasant*). (*His gaze traverses half of the theatre.*) Where can I flee? Where can I hide my shame? Having wandered all morning through these mountains, I seek in vain a refuge which would appease the torment in my mind. I have not found a den dark enough, a cave deep enough to conceal my crime. Under these coarse garments, which conceal my identity from the most penetrating eye, I betray my guilt; and casting my glance to the earth, I can do nothing but tremble when questions are put to me. It seems to me that all nature unites to accuse me. These terrible words re-echo without cease in my ear: No repose for the assassin! vengeance! vengeance! . . . (*The echo of his words is heard.*)

TRUGELIN (*turns around sharply in fright*). Where am I? What is this menacing voice? Heavens, what do I see? This bridge, these rocks, this torrent. 'Tis here that my criminal hand shed the blood of an unfortunate man. O my God, thou whom I have so long ignored, behold my remorse, my sincere repentance. Stop, wretch, do not blaspheme against heaven! Consolation for such as you! That favor is reserved for the innocent and you will never enjoy it. Tears, the scaffold—that is the lot that awaits you, and you will never escape. (*He falls exhausted on a bench.*) Ah! if one only knew the price one has to pay for leaving the path of virtue, there would be few wicked men on the earth. (*During this scene the storm has continued.*)

Michaud (first comic), the miller who eight years before came upon the wounded Françisque on this very spot, appears now from

his house, greets the wanderer, and offers him shelter. Not recognizing the villain in his disguise, he proceeds to regale him with an
account of the assault on Françisque, much to his listerner's secret
dismay. Archers enter and read a description of the fugitive, which
mentions a scar on the hand by which he can be identified. They go
off. A few moments later Michaud, upon shaking hands with his
guest, notices the telltale scar. Still he does not associate him with
Trugelin.

Trugelin enters the mill as Cœlina and Françisque wander on
stage; they are exhausted after the long day's tramp in the wilds.
Michaud is delighted to see father and daughter and embraces the
old man, telling him that the villain is being pursued and that he
cannot escape capture. Françisque goes to enter the mill at his host's
invitation but, on looking within, recoils, "horror in his face."
Michaud and Cœlina go to him.

> (*Françisque indicates in gesture that he has locked up his enemy
> in the mill.*)
>
> CŒLINA. What do you wish to say?
>
> MICHAUD. That man, has he frightened you?
> (*Françisque indicates that he has recognized him; he shows his
> hand to Michaud, recalling to him that it was by that sign that
> he was able to recognize his assailant.*)
>
> MICHAUD. Is it possible? Can that be Trugelin?
>
> CŒLINA. Trugelin, O heaven! (*Françisque indicates that it is he.*)
>
> TRUGELIN (*apart, without being seen*). The appearance of that
> man disturbs me. What do I hear? My name has been spoken.
>
> MICHAUD. Oh, curses! The archers were here and I wasn't able
> to recognize him! And yet it was so easy. And that scar . . .
> Ah! Michaud! Michaud! Where were your brains?
>
> CŒLINA. Let us flee, my father, far away from this wicked man.
>
> TRUGELIN. I too must make off. I know enough. (*He re-enters
> and closes the window.*)
>
> MICHAUD. Be well on your guard and get away. There is still
> time to repair my stupidity. The archers can't be far off. I am
> going to run after them and bring them back; It is well that the
> monster should receive his punishment where the crime was
> committed.

(*Françisque stops* MICHAUD *and indicates the mill and makes him understand that* TRUGELIN *is able to make his escape.*)

MICHAUD. You are right. Scatter-brain that I am. I forgot that the essential thing is to secure the exits. (*He closes the door. Moves toward the window.*) Let us inspect the house. Good, it is secure. Be on the lookout. Have you arms? (FRANÇISQUE *shows pistols.*) Keep this one, it will be of assistance in keeping our man under control, if he attempts to escape; give me the other one. If I can't make my cries heard by the archers, my last resource will be to fire a shot to draw them to this side of the hill.

CŒLINA. Go quickly, think of my father!

MICHAUD. Heaven watch over both of you. (*He ascends the bridge and disappears.*)

CŒLINA. Stay here, father: I am going up on the bridge so that I will be able to catch sight of Michaud sooner or summon anyone who comes in sight.
(*She ascends the bridge;* FRANÇISQUE, *seated at the edge of the torrent close to the door of the mill, his head turned from the window and regarding his daughter.*)

TRUGELIN (*reopens the window*). I hear no more. They have no doubt gone off; the moment is favorable. Let me flee while they are busy searching.
(*He climbs through the window, leaps down onto the stone seat which is under it, and from there to the earth; then he moves softly to the corner of the mill. Arriving there, he perceives* FRANÇISQUE *at two paces from him; then he recoils and draws his pistols, covering* FRANÇISQUE.)

TRUGELIN. One move and you are a dead man!

(FRANÇISQUE *leaps up quickly to seize his arm.* TRUGELIN *discharges his piece but it misses fire.* CŒLINA *gives out a piercing cry.*)

CŒLINA. Michaud! Michaud!

(*In the distance is heard the report of a pistol.* FRANÇISQUE *hurls himself at* TRUGELIN *and blocks the path skirting the torrent, and* TRUGELIN *is forced to return along the side of the house.* CŒLINA *has come down; she throws herself in front of her father and draws him after her into the mill.*)

(TRUGELIN *flees along the road which skirts the torrent and goes to cross the bridge but an archer suddenly appears and confronts him with an upraised sabre.* TRUGELIN *hurls himself upon the archer, disarms him, and flings him into the torrent. More archers appear and* TRUGELIN *is forced back across the bridge toward the mill, where a lively combat ensues between him and the archers. He upsets one and swerves to elude the other, when the armed peasants arrive and throw themselves on him and prepare to cut him down.*)

Defour restrains their fury. "Leave him to the law," he says (the law took on a new majesty at the Revolution) and directs the archers to take the villain off for punishment.[2]

I have reproduced this scene in detail because I think it is one of the most important in the whole range of the modern theatre. With *Cœlina*, action—action integrated with an elaborate, built set—came on the French stage from the pantomime to galvanize a spoken play.

Realistic settings and properties had been used before this at the Boulevard theatres, and romantic effects in scenic investiture and machines were developed to a high degree of perfection in the court pageants and opera of the Baroque era in Italy, France, and England. What *Cœlina* did was recapitulate this progress in a theatrical piece which combined the everyday and the romantic. Such amalgamation was no doubt inevitable in view of the direction which the theatre was taking in these years, but it was *Cœlina* more than any other single play which brought all the strands together.

It is not easy for modern playgoers to realize what a static affair a performance at the Française was in those days. *Drame*, under the influence of Diderot and Voltaire, had done something to enliven stage management, but prevailingly the presentation of a play at the end of the eighteenth century in France consisted of a wordy debate among characters arranged in a hard semicircle beneath the chandelier. The verse and its proper declamation was the important thing; pantomime, properties, and settings were frowned upon as meretricious. The conservative foundation of Louis XIV and Napoleon, the first theatre of Europe, was to wage a stubborn fight

[2] Translated from the text found in *Nineteenth Century French Plays*, ed. Joseph L. Borgerhoff (New York & London, 1931), pp. 23–43.

against the embellishments which *Cœlina* established, but it was to be a losing fight.

Vice is punished in *Cœlina*, and virtue rewarded. After Trugelin has been taken away for the law to deal with, Françisque vindicates himself and clears his child's name. He was secretly married to Isoline, the girl's mother, he reveals; Isoline's marriage to Dufour's brother was a later and a bigamous one, forced upon the woman through terrible threats and over her impassioned protests by her evil brother Trugelin, who saw in the union a way to increase his wealth. Cœlina is reunited to Stéphany, Michaud sings a jolly ballad, and "all dance."

VI

The Art of Pixerécourt

Melodrama has never been "placed"; its birth dates from Cœlina.—
JULES MARSAN

Cœlina, first produced at the Ambigu during September, 1800, marked the ripening of Pixerécourt's talents and the beginning of his reign as "king of melodrama." A career of success scarcely paralleled in all previous theatrical history lay ahead of him. Fifty-nine melodramas, twenty-one of them in collaboration with other writers, were to come from his pen in the thirty-seven years of his activity as a playwright, in addition to sixty-one plays of other types.[1] They were to set such a high standard of popularity that when, as in the case of *Christophe Colomb* (1815), a play did not survive one hundred and fifty performances, it was adjudged a failure. Five hundred was average. The staggering total of thirty thousand performances is recorded of his works between 1797 and 1834 in Paris and the provinces; *L'Homme à trois visages* was given 1,022 times, *Le Chien de Montargis,* 1,158, *Tékéli,* 1,334, *Le Pèlerin blanc,* 1,533, and *La Femme à deux maris,* 1,346. At times, Pixerécourt's name could have been seen on the billboards of as many as three Parisian theatres simultaneously.

Foreign productions were frequent. At least seventeen of the plays were given in England. From there they made their way to the United States, where one, *Le Pèlerin blanc* (in the version of the Englishman Theodore Hook, *The Wandering Boys*) was given fifteen hundred times. *Valentine* was printed twice in the U.S.A. prior to 1820. There were numerous German, Italian, Dutch, and Portuguese adaptations, and even a few in Russian and Polish. It was thanks largely to Pixerécourt that melodrama swept the Western world in the early decades of the nineteenth century; he fixed the form that remained an international standard for generations and furnished the models which two continents copied.

[1] *Opéras comiques, drames,* vaudevilles, comedies, fairytale spectacles, farces, and even a one-act *comédie-anecdotique* in verse for the Français, *Une Visite ou Madame de la Vallière* (1818).

With success came fame; "I know nothing comparable to the popularity of the illustrious author of *Babylon*," wrote Jules Janin, famous *Débats* critic; "men, women, children, young girls, the aged, followed him at a distance . . . when he deigned to promenade on the Boulevard du Temple, enveloped in his velvet cloak, decorated with the Cross of the Legion of Honor. He was followed in silence, he was pointed out with an impassioned gesture. 'It is he—there he is, the great punisher of all crimes, the exalted judge who reads in perverted hearts . . .' "[2]

Pixerécourt's success may be attributed partly to conditions prevailing in the France of his day. The passion for the theatre which manifested itself at the outbreak of the Revolution continued unabated through the Directory, the Consulate, the Empire, and the Restoration. There were twenty-three theatres in the city in 1789 (Holcroft noticed the posters of as many as eighteen open at one time), and this number had increased to thirty-two when the Napoleonic decree of 1807—in effect for a comparatively short period—reduced it to seven. A quarter of a century later when Pixerécourt was still writing, he commented that Parisians were able to choose from among no fewer than forty-four in their quest for entertainment.[3] Between 1815 and 1830, hundreds of melodramas had their premieres in the city.[4]

Audiences were for the most part naïve, ignorant, and uncritical, being of that unschooled generation which passed its minority in the chaotic years of the Revolution. They entered the theatres of the Boulevard desiring simply to be amused; their response to a spectacle was not complicated by aesthetic prejudices or intellectual preconceptions. Nevertheless, diverting these people called for special knowledge, a special gift; and these Pixerécourt possessed to a degree unique in his time and profession. No contemporary equalled him in number or magnitude of hits, because none approached him in insight into popular psychology or in knowledge of his trade.

[2] *Histoire de la littérature dramatique*, Vol. IV, p. 309.
[3] "Le Mélodrame," p. 347.
[4] C. B. Wicks (*The Parisian Stage*, Part I) lists 236 productions designated melodrama in advertisements in Paris newspapers during these years, which does not take into account pieces listed under various other classifications (including *drames*, *faits historiques*, and *mélodrame-féeries*) but actually indistinguishable from melodrama as a rule, so that this figure may reasonably be doubled. M. Albert's figure is 280 (*Les Théâtres des Boulevards*, p. 285).

He knew the value of surprise, but surprise that is led up to and prepared for; of rapidly changing and executed incident that never permits the vagrant interest of the untrained mind to wander or lag; of the regular alternation of comic and pathetic, and of the sharp contrast of black villainy and spotless innocence personified in the appealing form of women, children, the poor, and the afflicted; of the glamor of resounding names from history and legend; of the heroic attitude, the flamboyant word, the striking gesture; of regal majesty on the one hand, and simple, familiar things on the other. Giving his Boulevard public all this in strong doses, he knew that they would not strain at the improbable or even the preposterous. He realized that they looked for that sort of thing, demanded it— that they saw in those chance meetings, those last-minute rescues and reprieves, those providential acts of God and retributory accidents—collapsing bridges, thunderbolts, volcanic eruptions, floods, earthquakes—the obscure workings of a higher order, a more perfect economy, a more rigid justice than prevailed in the unsatisfactory world where they suffered, struggled, and failed.

A factor in his success was his sincerity; Pixerécourt never wrote with his tongue in his cheek. He believed in his work and took it quite seriously, defending the dignity and usefulness of melodrama with all the force at his command in more than one pamphlet on the subject. It may be noted here that with the possible exception of Boucicault no major practitioner of the melodramatist's art was consciously the charlatan. Owen Davis, last of the line, noticed that when he allowed himself to yield to a cynical mood in composition the piece invariably failed. "When I wrote *Nellie the Beautiful Cloak Model*," he confessed in his reminiscences, *I'd Like to Do It Again*, "I was honestly moved by the lady's misfortunes."[5]

Pixerécourt had the acuteness to perceive that fully half the success of a play is made on the stage, and he became a close student of the theatre and an active participant in production. Two, or at the most, three weeks sufficed him for the mere writing of a piece; the more important business of translating a script into a show, however, was a labor of months. Every detail of the mounting of a play was arranged, rehearsed, and perfected under his sharp, exacting eye—casting, music, scenery, properties, acting, direction. Like Boucicault and Sardou after him he became a martinet behind the scenes, the terror of actors, scene painters, machinists, carpenters,

[5] Owen Davis, *I'd Like to Do It Again* (New York, 1931), p. 107.

and musicians. The results were revolutionary; this now forgotten melodramatist added a new dimension to the theatre. He made plays live on the stage as plays had never lived before his time.

Each of his plays offered at least one spectacular scenic effect: *Tékéli*, a *fête militaire; Charles le Téméraire*, a flood and an assault; *Marguerite d'Anjou*, a forest fire; *La Citerne*, an explosion; *Robinson Crusoë* and *Christophe Colomb*, full-rigged ships; *La Fille de l'exilé*, an inundation with the heroine borne across the stage clinging to a floating log, a mechanical effect which the playwright invented; *Les Chefs écossais*, the storming of Stirling castle and "a ballet of citizens of Edinburgh" at an audience with King Edward. All were woven into the dramatic action and managed with great skill. The success of the various plays owed a great deal to these embellishments, and Pixerécourt felt that many of his works did not prosper as they might have in the provinces because the staging was neglected.

Pixerécourt got his material from a wide variety of sources: Goethe, Schiller, Kotzebue, Werner, Prévost, Florian, Ducray-Duminil, La Harpe, the poet Bernard, Nodier, Chateaubriand, De Kock, Mme Cottin, Mrs. Radcliffe, George Sand, Defoe, Jane Porter, Godwin, Walter Scott, and Shakespeare were drawn upon for subjects, plots, situations, characters, devices; and in addition to these he used *The Thousand and One Nights*, chronicles of exploration, and the newspapers. Like Shakespeare, he seldom borrowed without rehandling and transforming and always with the special requirements of the stage in mind. He took little or much as suited his purpose, often drawing upon several sources for one play. In his adaptations of novels and dramas characters disappear or are combined with others, episodes are suppressed or added with a free hand, the order of events is changed, denouements are rewritten.

The use he made of his various English sources illustrates his methods, and at the same time reveals his constructive talents. In *L'Évasion de Marie Stuart ou le Château de Loch-Leven* (1822) only the second half of Walter Scott's novel, *The Abbot*, is used. Mary's escape, which it narrates, forms a single dramatic action. There is further simplification in the compression of time and the combination of characters—Lindsay with Ruthven, Dryfesdale with Randal, and Lady Fleming with Catherine Seton. Details are changed; incidents invented. The Queen refuses to sign the papers for her abdication, and Douglas gives his life to assure her escape—

improvements on the novel from the melodramatic point of view. As in so many of his adaptations, Pixerécourt here availed himself freely of the novelist's dialogue. Niceties of language do not count for much in melodrama; dramatic situations, mimed action, striking stage effects—these are what made a play successful on the "Boulevard du Crime."

Several such effects are introduced in *L'Évasion de Marie Stuart.* The faithful Catherine Seton thrusts her arm through the staples of a door in place of a missing bolt in order to hold off the pursuers of her royal mistress;[6] Lord Lindsay pinches the Queen's arm with his mailed gauntlet (as the Duke of Guise will pinch the arm of Catherine of Cleves in Dumas' *Henri III et sa cour*); Lady Loch Leven herself places the lamp in the loophole of the tower, not suspecting that she is thereby signalling Mary's friends that the hour of the planned escape has arrived. This last was partially at least the adaptor's invention. An even better example of theatrical imagination at work is entirely's Pixerécourt's own. It occurs in the second act. Two of Mary's friends meet at the Kinloss Fair. Not daring to speak openly lest they betray themselves, they convey to each other by means of the various figures of a quadrille the names of the men who can be trusted and the hour of the Queen's escape attempt.

Whether he borrowed or originated them,[7] Pixerécourt in his fifty-nine melodramas[8] managed to make use of virtually every one of the effects of this kind which became classic in the genre: the transfer of poison cups, striking clocks which set conspiracies in motion, casks in which troops are smuggled into besieged cities, telltale scars and identifying birthmarks, rings and lockets, papers that clear up mysteries, pretended invalids exposed by a discreet application of fire or the like, disguised heroes or heroines participating in councils which plot their doom, fellow criminals killing each other in mistake for their intended victims.

Charles Nodier called Pixerécourt the inventor of a new genre, dismissing melodrama as it had been written previously on the

---

[6] Many a melodramatist was to copy this scene which was Scott's invention: Dumas in *Henri III et sa cour*, Ben Webster in *The Golden Farmer*, the anonymous English author of *The Merchant's Daughter*, and Frank Hitchcock Murdock in *Davy Crockett*.

[7] Jules Marsan (p. 207) writes: "Of all the classical effects of melodrama, there are few which he did not discover."

[8] Hartog's figure.

Boulevard as a "misshapen, abortive, monstrous concoction."[9] Marsan maintained that it was thanks to Pixerécourt alone that melodrama established itself in its full character.[10] This is magnifying the shortcomings of the pioneers perhaps, but the judgment is essentially just. Certainly it is indisputable that Pixerécourt was the first master melodramatist of the Boulevard.

[9] "Du Mouvement intellectuel et littérair sous le Directoire et le Consulat," *Revue de Paris*, XIX (1835). Also included in Nodier's introduction to Pixerécourt's *Théâtre choisi*.

[10] Marsan, p. 201.

VII

The Plays of Pixerécourt

Domestic and Historical Melodrama

*If I could give an account of all that I owe to great predecessors
and contemporaries, there would be but a small balance in my
favor.*—GOETHE to Eckermann

Cœlina was a domestic melodrama, to employ a term invented by
early nineteenth-century reporters of the drama to distinguish
pieces in which fireside interest prevailed over larger matters like
the travail of Mary Stuart and the iniquities of Charles the Bold;
these latter were lumped under the general head of historical. Gaiffe
justly observes that domestic and historical are no more than "classifications of convenience." The adventures which take place in
domestic melodrama can be quite as harrowing and fantastic as those
of the historical pieces, and the characters are the same wooden
puppets whether they appear in the Bagdad of Haroun al Raschid's
reign; the Venice of the Renaissance; the Spain of the Moors;
primitive Africa; or nineteenth-century France, Scotland, or Italy.
The language scarcely ever varies from one classification to another.
Pixerécourt invented an astonishing gibberish for his aborigines in
Christophe Colomb, employed provincial dialects for many of his
comics as Molière and the Italian comedy had done before him, and
sprinkled archaic expressions through some of his period plays;
otherwise his dialogue relied upon the pedestrian and the pretentious.

The affinities of domestic melodrama are with *drame*. This mixed
form, a sentimental, moral, middle-class tragi-comedy in prose
deriving from the theories of Diderot, Beaumarchais and Mercier,
had lost caste as a distinct dramatic genre at the Français before the
Revolution. It survived in a modified form at the Opéra Comique,
but it never had been received with any enduring enthusiasm on the
Boulevard. When repudiated in the country of its origin it had
taken refuge across the Rhine, where it won wide prestige. Lessing
extolled Diderot's program and put it into practice with far greater
dramaturgic skill than Diderot himself, notably in *Minna von Barn-*

helm. His example was followed with less success by other German playwrights including Kotzebue whose *Menschenhass und Reue* was given two productions in 1799 in Paris: at the Français as *Misanthropie et repentir*, adapted by Mme Molé, and at the Jeunes Artistes on the Boulevard, meeting with enormous success as did other adaptations in London, Madrid, Philadelphia, New York, and elsewhere.

Meinau, the misanthrope referred to in the title, is a deceived and deserted husband, soured by his misfortunes though his native goodness of heart remains untouched. The repentant is Eulalia, the wife who left him years before to run off with a young admirer—a brief escapade which she has never ceased to regret and do penance for in deeds of charity (though such benefactions as she indulges in during the play are all at the expense of her employer as Thackeray pointed out). With considerable theatrical skill, Kotzebue brings these two together on the country estate where Eulalia is employed as a housekeeper, and he builds up gradually to a meeting and a reconciliation. In this climax the propulsion upon the scene of the couple's two young children to complete a heart-rending group plays a determining part. Language as well as situation fairly drool with that pathetic sentimentality so highly regarded at the time.

Pixerécourt must have seen one or both of the Paris productions of the Kotzebue play. Certainly he knew of it and in the original, since he translated Kotzebue's entire works and borrowed from the German's store for at least three of his plays. To *Menschenhass and Reue* may be attributed some of the qualities which appear in *La Femme à deux maris* (1802), though the outline of the plot is taken from a novel by Ducray-Duminil. The heroine, Eliza, wife to Édouard, Count de Fersen, is a woman with a past like Eulalia. In her youth, rebelling against parental authority, "that authority which has its origin on high," she ran off with and married Isidor Fritz, a villain, who, after treating her badly, deserted her and apparently died in jail, leaving her with an infant son. This child, Jules, is fifteen when the play opens; he is a model of dutiful obedience and precocity, expressing himself in elaborately balanced periods. The Countess has never acknowledged her child, though she has him always by her and lavishes love upon him. One of the reasons for her silence is that she would spare her kind, generous husband the pain which the knowledge of having a felon's offspring in his household might cause him. Her old father, blinded for melodramatic purposes, is now a pensioner on her husband's estate but is kept in ignorance of the identity of his benefactress.

In the first act Eliza is visited by one of those presentiments which never play a character false in melodrama. It is confirmed when Fritz puts in an appearance to start the plot boiling. The document certifying to his death was a forgery, it is revealed, and the scoundrel has come to execute a grandiose blackmailing scheme. The woman's frantic offers of money and jewels are scorned; nothing less than the entire estate of the Count will buy Fritz's silence. He seeks out Jules and tells him of his parentage, in the hope that the revelation will turn the boy against his mother. Disappointed in that quarter, the villain approaches Ferzen with his story. That upright gentleman treats him with contempt. Then Fritz demands his child.

A Major de Goltz, uncle to the Count and his guest at the moment, recognizes the villain as a deserter from his regiment under sentence for a capital crime. He arrests him and turns him over to be shot. Ferzen, however, is concerned about the disgrace that may thereby fall upon Jules, and he arranges a compromise, procuring Fritz's release and giving him money on condition that he take himself off. For morality's sake, the innocently bigamous husband sadly prepares to separate from his beloved Eliza. Fritz agrees to the proposal in order to save his neck, but he is far from being reconciled to the collapse of his scheme, and he plans to murder the Count. A confederate is posted in a tree, from which he is to drop upon the Count and stab him as he passes below, decoyed by Fritz. The plot goes awry thanks to the good comic Bataille—perhaps the first of the many faithful old sergeants of melodrama—and instead of Édouard it is Fritz who is fatally knifed by the assassin.

La Femme à deux maris is the usual shrewdly compounded mélange. There is a ballet introduced as part of a fête to welcome the "good man" upon his return from a journey. Comedy is introduced, and domestic tenderness and sentimentality generally are played up throughout. One scene, was particularly appealing: the innocently bigamous wife Eliza pleading with her blind father for forgiveness using the third person.

The play ran 451 times in Paris and was a hit in various foreign capitals including London and St. Petersburg. The skeleton of the plot was to be used over and over again in melodrama—in Hunted Down, The Parson's Bride, My Pal and My Partner Joe, Nuits de la Seine, and Fairfax.

Another play of Pixerécourt's with a similar appeal, *Le Chien de Montargis,* was one of the most popular dramas of the century throughout Europe and America. The plot is based on a medieval legend which was treated in a twelfth-century *chanson de geste.* The action occurs at and near a country inn where a company of archers is billeted for the night as the play begins. It deals with a blind boy, Eloi, falsely accused of a murder and saved from execution at the last moment by an extraordinary dog detective who had been at the scene of the crime, but was tied to a tree by the villains while they committed it. As Eloi is being conducted to the scaffold in the last act, the dog, joining the crowd, sees the murderer, flies at his throat, and justice is done.

Count de Fersen, the "good man," had uttered the customary moralizing tag at the conclusion of *La Femme à deux maris*—"an offended father who pardons is the most perfect image of the divinity"; in *Le Chien de Montargis* it is the crushed villain who performs this office. "Heaven is just," he cries; "it saves the innocent and strikes down the guilty at one and the same time." This is the essence of melodrama.

"*Sensible,* lovable characters like Eloi, Eliza, and Cœlina suffer in all the plays Pixerécourt wrote; he never neglected that pathetic interest which had proved so potent with Mercier and Florian. This element, however, usually takes second place to the breathless hurry of the plot from one exciting situation to another. Dynamic conduct of the fable is the supreme virtue of this playwright and was the most important factor in his success. Suffering heroines not infrequently accommodate themselves to it, stepping out of their characteristically passive roles to fight back at their persecutors and thus in some measure usurping the role of the hero. There is a distressed maiden, Seraphine, in *La Citerne* (1809), but her energetic sister Clara steals the show with various ingenious and audacious moves to check the villain. In *La Forteresse du Danube* (1805), Celestine supplies the excitement and suspense by gaining entrance, in the disguise of a male Savoyard entertainer, to a stronghold where her father is held prisoner and distracting the guards with her singing and dancing while the old man makes his escape. The heroic, resourceful female is a mother in *Charles le Téméraire* (1814), Léontine, daughter of the Governor of Nancy. She penetrates the camp of the Burgundians who are besieging the city, learns their plans, retrieves her child who has been taken as a hostage, fends off the sack of the city by a stratagem, and finally opens the dikes to inundate the area where the troops of the enemy are encamped; then, vizor down—borrowing from Schiller's *Die Jungfrau von Orleans*—slays the evil Duke himself in single combat.

It is in *L'Ange tutélaire ou le démon femelle* (1808), however, that the intrepid woman reaches the heights. The Flora of this Renaissance drama is a veritable female demon in her fierce energy, her bold courage, and her subtle craft exercised on behalf of her lover, the Duke of Ferrara, whose guardian angel she becomes, crushing a conspiracy hatched by his faithless brother. Among the disguises assumed by this busy amazon are those of a gypsy, a page boy, an old man, a court dame, and a magician.

Such plays are definitely in the zone of historical melodrama. Here as in domestic melodrama Kotzebue must be considered an influence. *Rollas Tod*, written by the German on the basis of an adventure tale by Marmontel, was given at the Porte Saint-Martin when that theatre was reopened in 1802, and Pixerécourt himself did an adaptation produced in the same year, *Pizarre ou la conquête du Pérou*. Kotzebue's play contains no comic and ends unhappily, but its battles and pursuits, its pathos and its preaching are all in the melodramatic style. There were, of course, other influences which led Pixerécourt and his French contemporaries to seek stirring themes in history: *Richard Coeur-de-Lion* and other *opéras comiques*, tragedies such as Chenier's *Charles IX*, Goethe's *Goetz von Berlichingen*, Schiller's dramas, Shakespeare's chronicle plays, and the heroic pantomime. And, of course, his early exemplar, Mercier.

Pixerécourt's historical melodramas stand apart from these works, German, English and French, most obviously in that quality of headlong speed which has been noted above, that frenetic press of episode upon episode which was to be his most valuable legacy to the genre and to which Hugo and Dumas were indebted. *L'Homme à trois visages* (1801), the earliest of them, has this quality in a superlative degree. The setting is Venice, and the hero Vivaldi, a noble youth proscribed through the machinations of a powerful enemy, Orsino, and banished from the Republic. Since his ostracism he has been a soldier of fortune and, under the name of Edgar, has risen to the command of a powerful body of mercenaries, as ironic chance will have it now in the employ of his native city. In his military capacity, he intercepts a letter from the city to a certain ferocious Florentine bandit, Aballino, in which that cutthroat is apprised of a conspiracy on foot to overthrow the Republic, and his professional service is solicited for the assassination of the Doge. The writer is Orsino.

Vivaldi captures and executes the outlaw and proceeds to Venice, where he appears in the opening scene as he meets his old friend Alfieri and acquaints him with a heroic program he has resolved upon: to clear his name, regain his position, claim Rosamonde, daughter of the Doge, his secret bride of eight years, and save the Republic from the peril which threatens it. Only to Alfieri and Rosamonde does he reveal himself in his proper person. As Edgar he warns the Doge of the danger hanging over him and the state and obtains permission to substitute his own troops as a palace guard. In the disguise of Aballino he proceeds to a rendezvous with Orsino and his fellow conspirators to learn the particulars of the coup which they plan.

It is in the energetic hero's lightning-like changes from one to another of his *trois visages*, or three faces, and in the dangers he thereby exposes himself to, that the breathless interest of the piece resides. The climax comes in a grand session of the Council of State at which the traitors have agreed to act. After skillfully decoying them into showing their hand, the hero tosses off his disguise (which includes a bandit's stock red beard) and reveals himself as Vivaldi, come to save Venice from a disaster he himself has been unjustly convicted of plotting. At his signal his troops swarm into the chamber and overpower the conspirators. The Republic is preserved, the Doge is saved, and husband and wife are reunited.

Tékéli ou le siège de Mongatz (1803), which Pixerécourt thought of most highly among all his plays, gets into more definitely historical matters: the Prince from whom the title derives was a seventeenth-century Hungarian patriot who led his people in revolt against their Austrian oppressors. The play was something of a tour de force in that it made a romantic hero of a character who for the greater part of an act remained hidden in a barrel while his foes searched for him. Melodramatic heroes as a rule disdain such undignified shifts preferring to fight it out in the open be the odds what they may.

Contemporary history was another field wherein Pixerécourt opened up new paths for melodrama. His *Le Suicide ou le vieux sergeant* (1816) was the first of that vast library of shockers based upon recent crimes. It dealt with the attempt of a provincial family of some eminence to place blame upon an old servant for a murder committed by one of its own members. Another of Pixerécourt's dramas of this kind was *La Chapelle des bois ou le témoin invisible* (1818), an arrangement of the notorious Fualdès case, one of the strangest crimes in police annals. H. B. Irving has retold the story of this fantastic murder in his *Occasional Papers*. Gericault used it as the subject of a famous painting shown in the exhibition of 1824.

Meanwhile melodrama was flourishing on the Boulevard, and other playwrights were making important contributions to its evolution.

VIII

Pixerécourt's Contemporaries
Propaganda, Horse, and Courtroom Drama

Make us weep, gentlemen, and you'll always be certain to succeed.
—GOETHE to Eckermann

Had Pixerécourt never been born, there would still have been melodrama. It might not have been compounded after the precise formula which became standard, but it would have been substantially the same in mood, matter, and manner. The elaborately mounted play of broad effects and sharp contrasts, optimistic in tone and moral in purpose, employing stock characters and introducing comic relief in its serious, action-filled fable was the end toward which theatricals had been tending for upward of a century and was a logical evolution.[1] The neoclassic genres were not immune.

The Revolution accelerated a process to which Corneille, Crébillon, and Voltaire had contributed in various ways. (Geoffroy called Crébillon "one of the fathers of Boulevard melodrama.") The apparatus of melodrama was already assembled in nearly complete form in Boutet de Monvel's *Victimes cloîtrées*, given at the Français in 1791 and labelled a tragedy. This is an antimonachal polemic with much action and mimed stage business and spectacular scenic embellishment. A divided set showed two adjoining cells in a forbidding dungeon. The heroine is a prisoner in one and the hero in the other. For a climax, the latter smashes through the intervening stone wall to rescue the girl. She is an escaped nun and victim of the persecution of a sulphurous clerical villain, Père Laurent, of gothic derivation. This romantic thriller ran for eighty performances.

The domestic note, deriving from *drame*, is struck in another melodrama-oriented composition, *L'Abbé de l'Épée*, by J. N. Bouilly (out of Kotzebue), which enjoyed similar success also at the Français in 1800. The ideological wind had veered since *Victimes cloîtrées*, and the "good man" here is the abbé of the title, modelled

---

[1] Marsan, p. 196.

after a clergyman of the day, the Abbé Sicard, a benefactor of the afflicted in the tradition of St. Vincent de Paul. He devoted his life to the care and education of deaf mutes, whom he taught a sign language of his own invention. The hero (or *jeune premier*), a deaf mute, is Julio, a defrauded heir of tender years, who had been brought to Paris from Toulon and abandoned there by a faithless guardian, Darlemont. The priest rescues him from the streets and becomes his protector and tutor. By means of his newly acquired sign language the lad, though handicapped by loss of memory, is able to communicate some hint of the identity of the villain to the priest and some of the circumstances of his antecedents. Together they travel to Toulon, track down Darlemont, confront him, and obtain justice and the restoration of Julio's considerable estate. They are assisted by an accomplice of Darlemont, whose testimony assures the conviction of that villain. This accomplice declaims the concluding speech: "Let us hope that the example of this unprotected orphan may terrify the unjust man from the abuse of trust, and confirm the benevolent in the discharge of all the gentle duties of humanity."

Julio was the first of those physically afflicted unfortunates whom melodrama treated with a reverential awe that has something medieval, something almost superstitious, about it. Françisque, in *Cœlina*, and Eloi, in *Le Chien de Montargis*, are the type, and there were to be hundreds more including the lame Pierre and the blind Louise of *Les Deux Orphelines*. Often the mutes are aphasia cases, losing the power of speech as a result of shocks such as come from witnessing, for example, the murder of their parents and regaining it under similarly melodramatic circumstances. Blindness provided innumerable touching and exciting situations, as witness those in *La Femme à deux maris* and *Valentine* and a famous scene in an English play by Captain Hewetson, *The Broken Sword* (1807)—a classic of the toy theatre—in which the orphan boy-hero recognizes the slayer of his father by the feel of his hand. Virtuosity in portraying such rôles was highly esteemed.

Curtail the rather lengthy speeches of *L'Abbé de l'Epée*, increase the laughs, insert a combat, provide a ballet and stage spectacle, add music, and you have approximately the model Pixerécourt standardized in its milder, domestic form. Except for the comedy and the combat all these melodramatic ingredients are present in *Le Jugement de Salomon*, a Boulevard piece by L. C. Caigniez, given in January, 1802 at the Ambigu, the same theatre where *Cœlina* had its premiere. This play deserves consideration for various reasons; it was the first courtroom melodrama and the first melodrama to use a biblical theme. Certain liberties were taken with the simple Old Testament narrative in working it up into an affecting piece a la Kotzebue, liberties which anticipated the work of Cecil B. De Mille in the films. The child in dispute is here the illegitimate offspring of an Israelite girl of a noble but impoverished family, Leila, and the philandering father is no less a personage than the King's brother, Eliphal, whom the author of the Book of Kings overlooked. As the play opens, the child is in the possession of the villainess, Tamira, who, having procured it by stealth three years previously leaving her own dead child in its stead, has in the meantime passed it off as her own while her husband lived and now, since his death, finds it useful in furthering her designs to marry Eliphal. He, as a prince of the blood, is naturally concerned about the fertility of his prospective bride.

Leila encounters the child by chance and, convinced that it is hers not only through the "voice of the blood" but also by tangible evidence in the form of a birthmark, goes straight to Solomon with her plea to have it restored to her. The climax comes when Leila, her mother's-heart speaking, gives up her child to save its life—only to win it to her breast and Eliphal into the bargain, that gentleman never having suspected his fatherhood and being still in love with the mother. *Le Jugement de Salomon* ran three hundred times, and its smash scene was copied interminably.

The plays of Pixérécourt had no influence on this piece, but, as his successes multiplied along the Boulevard, other melodramatists began to pay him the compliment of imitation. They caught his trick of whipping up the action and giving fuller play to the comic and helped themselves to his plots, character types, and devices. *Thérèse ou l'orpheline de Genève*, by Victor Ducange, recalls *Cœlina*. The heroine, unknowingly a daughter of the nobility, is the victim of brutal persecution at the hands of Walter, who covets her person and her inheritance. Jailed as a result of his false accusations, she escapes but only to find herself at her persecutor's mercy some time later at a country place where she has found employment under another name. The villain reveals her past and procures her dismissal, then attempts to murder her one night in the darkened pavilion of a farm house where her recent employer, Mme de Senages, happens also to be lodged. It is this elder woman whom he fatally wounds instead of Thérèse, but he does not discover his mistake. Lightning strikes the pavilion at the moment of the crime for a magnificent stage effect; it awakens Thérèse, who runs to save her former mistress. Thérèse is discovered bent over the dead body by members of the household and is formally charged with the crime. Her guilt appears certain. However, heaven provides a powerful defender in the person of the "good man," Pastor Egherton.

Thérèse anticipates some of the psychological third-degree methods of subsequent literary and theatrical sleuths. At a somewhat irregular judicial inquiry, the heroine, pale and dishevelled and habited in graveclothes, is led in by the pastor to confront the villain, who, believing her to be dead from his knife thrust, takes this awesome apparition for an avenging ghost and blurts out a confession. The play was a prolonged success everywhere; in New York the future Mrs. John Drew, then in her teens, played Thérèse to Forrest's Walter Carwin for a famous triumph.

The Pixerécourt influence appears in various other pieces; Paul Ginisty notes similarities to *Les Mines de Pologne*, an early and inferior work of Pixerécourt, in Caigniez's *Le Fôret de Hermenstadt*, and to *Le Pèlerin blanc* in Caigniez's *Les Enfants du bûcheron*.[2]

The plays of the contemporaries of Pixerécourt—Boirie, Cammaille de Saint-Aubin, Hapdé, Frederic, Melesville, Cuvelier de Trye, and others—are seldom as cleverly contrived as his, and a detailed survey of them would serve no purpose here. In a few instances, however, these minor writers made important contributions to melodrama. What may be called the reformed-convict, the zoological, the propaganda, and the circus types of the genre owe their beginnings to one or another of these men.

Caigniez produced the first of the zoological pieces when he collaborated with Daubigny in 1815 on *La Pie voleuse ou la servante de Paliseau*. A cover of silver is missing from the household of Dame Gervaise, and a poor servant girl, the dutiful and virtuous Annette, is suspected of stealing it. Damaging evidence is produced against her in an inquiry pushed by a villainous bailiff, whose improper advances she has spurned. A Jew tells of buying a cover from her, and the precise amount of money he gave for it is found on Annette's person. Really the girl is the victim of cruel circumstances. The plate she sold was not her mistress' but the property of Annette's old father, a soldier, who, pursued by a patrol from a regiment he has deserted after a brutal beating, made his way to his

[2] *Le Mélodrame* (Paris, 1910), p. 127.

daughter and entrusted to her this, his sole earthly possession, in order that she might dispose of it for him. She dare not reveal this, however, lest it betray the old man. Furthermore, she has sworn silence, and an oath—even an oath on a most trifling matter—is invested with the most portentous solemnity in melodrama. Justice, meanwhile, is swift and drastic; Annette is condemned to die. She is being led out to her doom (dead march, and a scaffold shown upstage) when providence interposes through the agency of the comic. To this character, Blaisot, Annette has committed a silver cross, her last possession, with instructions to sell it and place the money he receives in the hollow of a certain old tree where she arranged with her father to leave what she was paid for the cover. The stage is cleared to allow Blaisot to enter and count out the money on a bench. When he turns away for a moment, a magpie swoops down and, seizing one of the coins in its bill, flies off with it. Blaisot follows the bird to its nest in a nearby belfry and finds the missing cover. Annette is cleared and released, and a way is found to secure a pardon for the old soldier.

The Magpie or the Maid? a play which Hazlitt called delightful in Pocock's adaptation at Covent Garden in 1815, contains many ingenious theatrical situations. In one, widely imitated in melodrama, Annette is shown with her fugitive father, who is disguised as a farmer. The villain enters with a proclamation describing the deserter and directing his apprehension. He is without his spectacles and gives the notice to the girl to read, which she proceeds to do as she sees fit, changing, suppressing, and improvising as necessary to shield her father. *La Pie voleuse* was used as the basis of the libretto of Rossini's *La Gazza Ladra*, a work which launched the school of domestic *opéra comique* to which *La Sonnambula* belongs. In various adaptations, Caigniez's play was one of the most popular items on the English and American stage throughout the first half of the century.

After Pixerécourt, Victor Ducange (née Brahain) was the melodramatist who opened up most new trails for the genre. His *Trent Ans ou la vie d'un joueur!* (1827) written in collaboration with Prosper Gobaux, was the first of many melodramas which carried on the Calvinistic tradition of plays such as *The London Merchant* and *The Gamester* by exposing the wages of gaming, wenching, and boozing. The protagonist, Georges, caught in the toils of his fatal passion for play, is driven to more and more desperate expedients to recoup his fortunes. Losing the money given him by an upright father to purchase diamonds for his bride, he accepts stolen gems from the villain, Warner, who, pretending friendship, really plots Georges' ruin in the hope that he may succeed him in the affections of the fair and virtuous lady to whom he is affianced. Georges is arrested on his wedding day for the theft of the diamonds, and sees his parent die of the disgrace, cursing his undutiful son with his last breath. He is jailed but escapes and flees the country with his bride after Warner attempts unsuccessfully to compromise the lady in a scene lifted from *The Gamester*. He cannot shake off his vice, which drags him lower and lower as years pass. He squanders his wife's inheritance and beggars his children. In the horrible denouement, imitated from the German "fate tragedy," *The Twenty-fourth of February*, by Zacharias Werner (or perhaps from Lillo's *Fatal Curiosity*), Georges treacherously murders a traveller for his purse and then kills his own son with the same motive without recognizing the boy, who, sent away as a child to school, has returned to seek out his parent having funds on his person with which he hopes to restore him to respectability and obtain for him a pardon for the early offense which forced him to flee France. The "good man" in the piece is an uncle of the unhappy wife—she is an orphan—who drives home the moral with cudgel blows at every opportunity in the dialogue.

French melodramatists were not far behind their English colleagues in dramatizing Scott's romances, which were enormously popular in translation. Here again Ducange was in the van with his *La Sorcière ou l'orpheline écossaise* (1821) from *Guy Mannering*. He followed this up five years later with *La Fiancée de Lammermoor*. In the interval *Kenilworth*, *Woodstock*, *Heart of Midlothian*, *Ivanhoe*, *Rob Roy*, and *The Abbot* were adapted by other hands. Three Scott adaptations were running simultaneously in Paris in 1827.

The blackmailed ex-convict was too promising a theme to escape for long the sharp, roving eyes of the early melodramatists, particularly since the subject of prison abuses generally was a mooted one in France in the early years of the nineteenth century. Here Boirie was a pioneer with *Les Deux Forçats ou la meunière du Puy-de-Dôme*. Produced in 1822, it was still running a year later at the Porte Saint-Martin when that most famous of all fictional fugitives from the galleys, Jean Valjean, noticed it on the poster outside that house. In the first act of this drama François, a respectable miller of unknown antecedents, is about to marry the lady of his choice when an evil-looking stranger puts in an appearance. He is an escaped convict who recognizes the bridegroom as an old cell-mate, a situation which he proceeds to turn to his profit. Bought off by the distraught miller, he agrees to leave him in peace, but before doing so he robs his victim's fiancée in such a way as to throw suspicion on François. That unlucky youth is arrested and, being unable to explain his past, faces tragic consequences. However, as Thérèse had her Egherton, so François has his M. Derville, a god dropped from the machine in the last act to exculpate the hero and clear up the mystery of his early years. The miller has, indeed, served a jail term but only because of his noble generosity in assuming the penalty for a brother's crime; M. Derville has papers which attest his pardon.

Pixerècourt wrote in the tradition of Gallic rationalism, eschewing the supernatural in his dramas; only in an early adaptation of *Udolpho* did he approach this theme, and here the apparition is an imposture, as is almost invariably the case in Mrs. Radcliffe's stories. Ghosts and demons, however, were eagerly seized upon by the rank and file of melodramatists, the gothic school and the Germans providing material and inspiration. Redactions of various spine-chilling tales and legends followed one another on stages along the "Boulevard du Crime"—the werewolf, the bleeding nun of Lindenburg, the doppelgänger, the diabolic Duke of Normandy (whence came Scribe's libretto for *Robert le diable*), and others. The vampire became a theatrical property in 1820 through Charles Nodier's drama of that name, adapted in collaboration with Jouffroy from the tale begun by Byron and completed by Dr. John William Polidori who was his secretary for a time.

One further development of melodrama falling within this period deserves a glance, namely, the hippodrama. As in England this form grew out of exhibits of horsemanship, specifically a famous show set up in 1782 by an Englishman, Philip Astley, in the Faubourg du Temple, a byway of the Boulevard. In 1793 Astley found it prudent to dispose of his Cirque Anglais, as he called it, selling it to Antonio Franconi. The new proprietor removed it to another location, and it was to occupy two other sites before being returned to its original spot by Franconi's sons, who continued the business after his retirement in 1805, after 1807 under the name of the Cirque Olympique. Here for nine glorious years beginning in 1817, triumph succeeded triumph as elephants were added to the performers, and a long series of famous animal dramas was staged. Shakespearean adaptations were given on horseback including

Hapdé's *Les Visions de Macbeth* and Cuvelier's *La More de Venise,* but the backbone of the repertory consisted of "national military mimodramas," among them *L'Entrée d'Henri IV à Paris, La Jeunesse du Grand Condé, Condé et la victoire de Rocroy, La Mort de Kléber,* and *La Mort de Turenne.*

A fire destroyed the Cirque in 1826, but it was destined to rise grandly from its ashes in the following year in a new structure, located this time on the Boulevard proper alongside the Ambigu where it occupied the most extensive premises and presented the most imposing facade of any theatre on the thoroughfare. The third generation of Franconis took over in 1828, and five years later Cirque Olympique became the Théâtre National du Cirque. There were further changes in name, location, fortune, and management. However when it became the Théâtre Imperial du Cirque in 1853, the track was removed ending horse melodrama in Paris.

IX

Harbingers of Romantic Drama
The Morals of Melodrama

Justice is done only in the melodramas of the Boulevard. —GEORGE
SAND

The shadow of advancing Romanticism lies across the early melodrama of France faintly discernible in the second decade of the
nineteenth century and deepening in the twenties. It assumes a
variety of shapes in the plays of Pixerécourt and his fellow playwrights of the Boulevard: an increasing disregard of classical precedent particularly with respect to the unities, a posturing mood of
melancholy and despair a la Byron, and a gradual relaxation of the
strict morality of early days illustrated notably in the treatment of
love.

Like *drame* and, to a lesser degree, *opéra comique* before it, early
melodrama in France voluntarily assumed the yoke of the unities,
permitting itself scarcely greater liberty with time and place than
Voltaire had assumed in tragedy at the Français itself; in 1814 Pixerécourt apologized for changing his scene within the act. Five
years later, however, in his dramatization of Mme Sophie Cottin's
romance of *Elizabeth ou les exilés de Sybérie*, which he called *La
Fille de l'exilé* (the first of innumerable Siberian melodramas), the
unities of both time and place went by the board. The events of
eight months were represented in two hours, as the subtitle of the
play put it (*Huit mois en deux heures*), and the action wandered
from Siberia in the first act to Moscow in the third, with a stopover
midway between in the intermediate act.[1] Ducange, in arranging
for the stage another favorite romance of the day, D'Arlincourt's *Le
Solitaire*, as *Élodie* (1822), got around the difficulty of the twenty-
four hour limitation by the device of the prologue—the Romantics

---

[1] "*La Fille de l'exilé*, by Pixerécourt, was for the destruction of
the unities what Mairet's *Sophonisbe* had been for their establishment."—Maurice Albert, *Les Théâtres des Boulevards* (Paris, 1902),
p. 298.

were to be partial to prologues—portraying events which occurred six months before those with which the play proper deals; and he changed his scene frequently within the act. When this author came to write his masterpiece, *Trent Ans* (1827), he went off the deep end in both respects as Pixerécourt had done in *La Fille de l'exilé*. In the debacle of the thirties Pixerécourt followed the drift of the times. His last melodrama, *Latude ou trente-cinq ans de captivité* (1834), embraces thirty-five years and includes scenes at Versailles, in the Bastille, and in Holland. It is in five acts and also has fewer monologues.

The morbidity of the Romantics, that *mal du siècle* which *emigrés* brought back with them to France from exile in the lands of *Hamlet, Manfred,* and *Werther,* began to infect melodrama a decade and more before *Hernani* and *Chatterton* appeared on the stage. In 1816 Pixerécourt brought forward the familiar Romantic property of the doomed man, or *héros fatal,* on the Boulevard; and in 1821 he offered an unhappy end. Gérard, in *Le Monastère abandonné ou la malédiction paternelle* (based on a tragedy by Zacharias Werner, a German writer of the Sturm und Drang), is a mild example of the hero under a curse. He believes himself the slayer—through an accident—of his brother. For this supposed crime he has been banished from his native city of Geneva with a father's curse on his head. When the play begins, he has gone to an abandoned monastery where, by way of expiation, he offers succor to strayed and benighted travellers. Misfortunes befall him here. A guest is murdered, and circumstances point to the guilt of Gérard. He is arrested and charged with the crime. When the parental malediction appears to be taking its toll, a stranger, Captain Bellerose, appears on the scene to champion the cause of Gérard.

A paralytic, Sebastian by name, was in the hospice when the murder was committed, but his infirmity has diverted suspicion from him. Bellerose is not so easily taken in. He sets fire to the room in which Sebastian is quartered, whereupon the supposed paralytic displays a most unnatural agility in getting out. The crime is ultimately fixed on this impostor, and Gérard's mysterious advocate reveals himself as the very brother he was accused of having slain!

The Byronic mania had gained great momentum in France by 1818 when Pixerécourt wrote *Le Belvéder ou la vallée de l'Etna,* taking his subject from Charles Nodier's romance, *Jean Sbogar*—which also inspired one of Scribe's few melodramas, *Les Frères invisibles.* Here the atmosphere of fatality is deeper. *Die Räuber* is drawn upon for the portrayal of the gloomy Loredan, who turns corsair when he is unjustly proscribed and banished from his native Sicily. The Charles the Bold of Ducange's *Élodie* and Pixerécourt's *Le Mont sauvage ou le Duc de Bourgogne* (both from D'Arlincourt's romance of the same name) is another representative of the dismal tribe. In Ducange's play, the Duke, after a sentimental love affair with the girl of the title, is carried offstage to hell by a frightening entourage of specters and demons in a pantomimic epilogue rich in stupefying supernatural effects. Falkland in Pixerécourt's *La Tête de mort* (1827) looks forward to hell, tortured, like Charles, with remorse for his past.

The unhappy end is alien to the spirit of the popular theatre. The people require from their drama something grosser than that catharsis which, in the rationalization of Aristotle, is the end of tragedy. What they look for and need is poetic justice in a denouement, with virtue emerging victorious from its trials, its heel on the neck of villainy overthrown; nothing less than a physical demonstration of accomplished retribution can satisfy their pedestrian moral sense.

Until the twenties Pixerécourt's plays end happily without exception. Sources are departed from when they do not lend themselves to this pattern, and historical fact is sacrificed on occasion. *L'Évasion de Marie Stuart* (1822) marks a change; Douglas, who loves the Queen and assists her to escape prison, gives his life for her in the end, whereas in Scott's *The Abbot* he is alive when the story concludes. In *Alice ou les fossoyeurs écossais* (1829) and *Valentine ou la séduction* (1829), two tragedies of unhappy love, the heroines themselves die. The denouement of *Alice* is not only sad, but horrible; Dumas at his worst has scarcely surpassed it. The girl of the title is in love with a young medical student, Édouard, whom she nursed back to health when, wounded in a duel, he was carried into the café where she was a servant. Her devotion takes a heroic form; when money is required for Édouard's care, she offers herself as a kind of human vivisectionist subject to provide it. Nevertheless, her lover abandons her. Unable to believe him false, she follows him to his native town where he has already taken steps to wed another. While searching for him Alice is waylaid and slain by ghouls, and her body is brought to Édouard's office and offered to him for sale. He lifts the veil which covers her face, and the play ends upon his cry of self-accusation and despair as he recognizes her.

Love is an emotion which, above all others, distinguishes Romantic drama. Hugo, writing as a youth in 1819, called "its treat-

ment as an overwhelming passion [one of the] two foundations
upon which, and upon which alone, the action of the new drama
must be built"—a program which he and Dumas were to follow
faithfully. From Pixerécourt's ideal world of paternal, filial, and
conjugal affection, this irrational, destructive force as it is seen in
Angelo and *Marion Delorme* is strictly excluded prior to 1818.
There is no love interest in *La Fille de l'exilé* (a departure from its
source, Mme Cottin's novel), *Marguerite d'Anjou*, *Christophe Colomb*, *Robinson Crusoë* or *Le Pèlerin blanc*. Where a love affair
does figure in the plot in any of Pixerécourt's early plays, courtship
is an extremely brusque and formal affair, as in *Cœlina*. Ardent
wooers, of whom Zamoski of *Les Mines de Pologne* is an example,
are all villains.

Pixerécourt, like Molière and Shakespeare, was married unhappily, and the bitterness of his feelings toward his wife from whom
he was separated continued to the end of his life. However, the
distress which the binding character of the marriage vow evidently
caused him never affected his reverence for it. A surprisingly large
proportion of his heroines are already married—and they are nearly
all happily married—when the curtain rises as in *Tékéli*, *La Femme
à deux maris*, *Pizarre*, *Charles le Téméraire*, and other plays. In
L'Homme à trois visages, Rosamonde is the wife of Vivaldi and not
merely promised to him as she is in H. H. D. Zschokke's German
romance from which it was taken. One of the most successful of the
plays, *Les Ruines de Babylone ou le massacre des Barmécides*
(1810), deals with a marriage triumphing over the most formidable
objection and interference.

Suddenly and rather startlingly in *Le Belvéder* (1818) the passionately enamored hero appears, using the very language of the
Romantics. Loredan in this play loves even to madness; possession of
his Emilia seems to him preferable to all the treasures of the earth,
and he contemplates suicide should she reject his suit. Three years
later a heroine, Valentine, does more than talk of self-destruction;
she accomplishes it. *Valentine ou la séduction* is the finest thing
Pixerécourt ever did, the only one of his plays which rises above the
limitations of the genre in which he worked. Absent for once are
the orphan heiresses, the missing fathers, the kidnapped children, the
brigands, the papers, the birthmarks, the *reconnaissance*, the providential accidents—leaving only a touching, human story of a girl
coming gradually to a realization that she has been cruelly betrayed
in love and that there is no hope for her. The play is actually not a

melodrama at all; its affinities are all with the earlier *drame* or the later plays of Dumas *fils*.

Valentine is a simple country girl tricked into a sham marriage with a nobleman who, representing himself as a struggling artist, has won her confidence and her love. The play opens on the morning after the mock ceremony, with the girl learning of the heartless ruse and making her way home with her blind father. This proud old man does not learn the whole truth, but he knows of his daughter's love for Édouard, of whom he disapproves; and he demands a promise from her to part with him, which she sadly gives. Later the guilty lover calls on Valentine at her home; he is stricken with remorse and confesses his treachery. The old father overhears him without understanding the situation completely; he enters from an adjoining room and drives Édouard from the house. A heavier blow is in store for the unhappy Valentine. A stately lady from the court arrives to inform her that she is the Countess, wife of Édouard. Haughty and contemptuous at first, the visitor ends by being touched at the plight of the girl and offers her protection. This time the father has heard all. He denounces his daughter and calls upon her to curse her lover if she wants his pardon. Valentine cannot bring herself to do that. Cheated, abandoned, she still loves Édouard.

The last act occurs at the palace of the Duke, a "good man." Here the father comes to pour out the story of his grief and plead for justice. It is not the Duke whom he sees, however, but the villain of the piece, impersonating his sovereign for the occasion. This is Count Ernest, the heartless, wanton instigator of the whole affair, who played the part of the clergyman at the mock marriage. After the old man has been dismissed by the impostor, Valentine appears. Without revealing herself as the victim of Édouard's baseness, she appeals to the Duke to take care of her aged father, saying that he is alone in the world now, his child being dead. A note of gayety is cleverly introduced at this point by means of a ballet. When it is over a figure is seen leaping from a bridge in the background into the lake. It is Valentine. She is rescued only to die in her father's arms.

Valentine represents a weakening in the moral front of melodrama; its merit as a play arises from its very violation of that draconic code of conduct which Pixerécourt himself had been instrumental in imposing upon the genre. The heroine is no longer a paragon of her sex, no longer entirely the persecuted innocent. Not only has she loved passionately, an impropriety itself in this austere world, but she has also persisted in a love stained by betrayal in the face of paternal authority, which was vested with a truly scriptural dignity in melodrama. Nevertheless, her creator has only tenderness and pity for her. In his preface to the printed version of the play, Pixerécourt went so far as to suggest extenuating circumstances for the seducer himself; love has blinded him and driven him beyond his strength; he is a weak, unhappy mortal rather than a scoundrel—the plaything of Eros, more to be pitied than censured. It is the fatal passion of Tristan and Iseult, a curious exotic in the neat kitchen garden of melodrama.

There is no such compromise with sin elsewhere in Pixerécourt's plays. Villains are wholly black in this admirably simplified universe, and the virtue of the virtuous has that ironclad invincibility which in life is nature's bounty to the stupid. The durable, impregnable heroine and the dauntless, dependable hero are moral automata geared for nothing but benevolence, duty, obedience, self-sacrifice, and pure love. Drama, accordingly, is reduced to a purely external conflict between the sharply differentiated forces of good and evil. There is no recognition of those hesitations, temptations, and weaknesses, those fatal flaws which make genuine tragedy possible.

Valentine is a step along the road to the moral anarchy of Romantic drama, and its heroine is a prototype of those courtesans whom a great love makes virginal again, those monsters who are tender and solicitous parents. Later, however, when the godless generation of 1830 supplanted him on his own Boulevard, Pixerécourt was indignantly to disclaim responsibility for them. Writing in 1843, he called the Romantic works "dangerous, evil, immoral plays, devoid of interest and truth." These monstrous concoctions, he asserted, had neither his ideas, his language, his plan of constructing a play, his "heart," nor his "conscience."

The king of melodrama was also its pope; he took great pride in that conscience of his. Moral instruction, he wrote, was his first object; and the inculcation of virtue through the word and example of his characters his constant concern. In all his plays the popular virtues are extolled and the obvious vices reprobated. Wickedness is shown not to pay, and virtue has seldom to be content with itself as its only reward, receiving its due in dollars and cents before the evening is out. Preaching is scattered thick in the plays; and, as in *drame*, maxims occur on virtually every page.

More than one of Pixerécourt's eminent contemporaries set a high value on his work as an evangelist among the people. Nodier called him an agent of providence—and something like an accessory to the police. "In the absence of religious worship," he wrote, "I have seen him take the place of the silenced pulpit, and, under an attractive form which seldom failed to make an impression, bring home serious and profitable lessons to the souls of his audience." Melodrama, as Nodier saw it, was "the morality of the Revolution."[2] The worldly Jules Janin echoed this sentiment, if half mockingly. "You write dramas and we believe in God," he quotes someone as saying; and he mentions the outburst of a mother upon surprising her young son in a theft: "Of what use was it to take you to the plays of Pixerécourt?"[3]

Moral purpose in drama in this narrow—this constabulary—sense is traceable back through Sedaine and Mercier to Diderot and his school. One of the most cherished superstitions of these professedly implacable enemies of superstition was that the theatre could be used effectively in reforming human nature. D'Alembert and Grimm, who wrote no plays, and Destouches, Sedaine, Beaumarchais, Marmontel, and Diderot, who wrote many, all expressed themselves strongly on this point, the single dissenter being that maverick, Rousseau, who, in an incomparable polemic, his *Letter to M. D'Alembert on the Theatre*, remorselessly dissected the proposition and laid bare its fallacy.[4]

This moral purpose was set forth in the prefaces of the printed versions of the plays and in theoretical and critical works such as those of Mercier, who asserted that it was not for the quality of their talent that he judged and esteemed dramatic authors, but for the morality that resulted from their plays.[5] Though not formally of the school of the *philosophes*, Destouches shared their point of view in this matter, writing in the preface to *Le Glorieux* that the theatre ought to aim at correcting morals and picturing virtue in such a fair light as to attract public esteem and veneration.[6]

Virtue was closely linked with sensibility in the philosophy of

[2] Pixerécourt, *Théâtre choisi*, Vol. I, p. iii.

[3] Janin, Vol. IV, p. 309.

[4] Jean Jacques Rousseau, *Politics and the Arts, Letter to M. D'Alembert on the Theatre*, trans. Allan Bloom (Glencoe, Ill., 1960).

[5] Louis Sébastien Mercier, *Du Theatre ou nouvel essai sur l'art dramatique* (Amsterdam, 1773).

[6] 2nd ed. (Paris, 1789), p ii; the play was originally produced in 1732.

this school. "It is sensibility that makes us realize the value of existence," in the words of D'Arnaud; "and the emotions which it procures to the soul necessarily beget virtue and good actions." Diderot wrote to the same purpose in his famous *Discourse on Dramatic Poetry* and Beaumarchais in his preface to *Eugénie*. Here Rousseau saw eye to eye with the others. "A feeling fool is better than a cold wise man," he wrote in his *Confessions*. Accessibility to the softer emotions became a touchstone of virtue; and the innate goodness of man, which tended to atrophy in the poisonous air of modern society (so the doctrine ran), might be stimulated to action by an appeal to the heart. Potential villains are won over to righteousness by such treatment in the typical *drame*, Mercier's *Le Déserteur* and *L'Indigent* and Beaumarchais's *Eugénie* for example.

The authors of *drame* used the same methods to reform their public en masse, writing their plays designedly to move an audience to sympathetic tears. Hence the disasters which befall good folks, the persecutions they are forced to endure, the atmosphere of woe in which they are presented. Pixerécourt was the continuator of *drame* in this as in other respects; his plays fairly drip sentimentality. It is apparent not only in his plots, his situations, and his character types, but also in the very texture of his language, as witness those recurring epithets which are such a distinguishing mark of his style—*père tendre, ami généreux, amant fidèle, époux sensible*, and the like. He fixed sentimentality with a moral purpose so securely upon melodrama that it has never entirely shaken it loose.

X

The Impact of Romantic Drama

Romantic drama is nothing but melodrama dressed up in the artificial pomp of lyricism. —CHARLES NODIER

Pixerécourt's angry disclaimer of any responsibility for Romantic drama has been mentioned in the preceding chapter. The Romantics, for their part, were equally emphatic for reasons of their own in denying that they owed anything to melodrama. (Hugo pointedly avoids mentioning it in the preface to *Cromwell.*) Disinterested observers, however, including critics from Nodier at the beginning of the century to Brunetière at its end, have thought otherwise, pointing to the plays themselves, particularly the plays of Hugo and Dumas, where the debt is plain to see: the picturesque, violent puppets, the frame of external action, the strong theatrical effects, the comedy, the stage settings, and the music.[1]

Rejected at the Français—no less on account of its melodramatic extravagance than its disdain of the rules—Romantic drama betook itself to the Boulevard, setting up shop at the Porte Saint-Martin, the very citadel of melodrama, and taking over the chief actors of that genre as its interpreters—Lemaître, Dorval and Bocage. It had a tremendous success there; and the playwrights of melodrama, impressed, proceeded to imitate its vices. Theatrical infanticides, adulteries, and parricides, and horrors generally became the fashion of the hour in melodrama, not only at the Porte Saint-Martin but at the Ambigu and Gaîté as well.

Nicolas Brazier, when he wrote about the "Boulevard du Crime" in 1838, thought that melodrama proper was being driven from the boards. Gone, he mourned, are the knights, the tyrants, the mute and courageous children of five years, the brigands, the venerable old men. And the language—what a change there! Instead of those

---

[1] See Petit de Julleville, *Le Théâtre en France* (Paris, 1927), pp. 358–359. For a detailed analysis of the debt of Romantic drama to melodrama, see Hippolyte Parigot, *Le Drame de Alexandre Dumas* (Paris, 1899), Part I, Chap. IV, pp. 114–159. Alexander Lacy, *Pixerécourt and the French Romantic Drama* (Toronto, 1928) deals with many particulars.

ringing tirades—instead of "Monster, receive the just chastisement of your horrible offenses" . . . "Villain, learn that sooner or later crime is punished and virtue rewarded" . . . and "See that they be loaded with chains and thrown into a dungeon, with all the honors of their rank"—one now hears "Darlings!" "Companions!" "My dagger!" "Vagabonds!" "Stand back!" "To the rescue!" "Curses!" "Hell!" and "Damnation." "It is quite a new speech, and I doubt that the apple-munching lounger in the *parterre* and the nut-cracking urchin in the gallery will ever be able to get it into their heads."[2] A few years later Théophile Gautier shed mock tears over the passing of "the Aeschuyluses of the Gaité and the Euripideses of the Ambigu." The impression that the old drama had run its course was encouraged by the disappearance of the first generation of melodramatists from the scene at this time. Caigniez had ceased to produce, Ducange's last play, *Il y à seize ans* was given in 1831, and Pixerécourt wrote finis to his prolific career with *Latude* in 1834.

Melodrama of the traditional pattern did not die, however. In the heyday of Romantic drama it held its own along the Boulevard as Brazier might have seen for himself; not even at the Porte Saint-Martin itself was it entirely eclipsed. While the new drama was agitating the controversies in the salons and the journals, the old was drawing the crowds with such plays as *Le Sonneur de Saint-Paul* (three hundred performances), *Gaspardo le pêcheur* (two hundred performances), *Lazare le pâtre*, *La Grâce de Dieu*, *Paris le Bohémien*, *Jean le cocher*, *L'Abbaye de Castro*, and *Geneviève de Brabant*—all famous successes of the thirties. And when the ranks of the Romantics began to break—when Dumas deserted in 1839 and Hugo withdrew to his tent after the disastrous failure of *Les Burgraves* four years later—melodrama won back its old place as undisputed mistress of the Boulevard. By this time a new generation of playwrights had appeared on the scene to carry on—one more vigorous and more prolific, on the whole, than its predecessor: Joseph Bouchardy, Victor Anicet-Bourgeois, Félicien Mallefille, Adolphe Dennery, Paul Meurice, Eugène Grangé, Francis Cornu, Paul Foucher, Marc Fournier, and Anthony Béraud. Many of these men had learned their trade collaborating with Pixerécourt and his contemporaries, and in the main they continued faithful to the ideals of their old masters. If their language has not quite the same quality of epic flatulence as that of the great legislator and founder of the

[2] *Chroniques des petits théâtres de Paris,* Vol. I, pp. 312, 314.

genre, if their subjects do not at all times have the heroic exaltation of his, this second generation, nevertheless, possesses those essentials so conspicuously lacking in the Romantics—what Pixerécourt meant when he referred to his heart and his conscience: Heroines are *sensible* and pure and heroes conventionally dutiful and un-adulterous, unnatural crimes are absent, and virtue is rewarded after many trials, and vice punished.

On the technical side, the unities are disregarded, sometimes by means of the prologue, which the Romantics fancied; the mono-logue is used with greater restraint than in the early days; the plays (called simply *drames*) are commonly in the five-act form used by Hugo and Dumas; and there is a marked tendency to increase the number of characters and complicate the intrigue.

The ghosts, the underground passageways, and the bandits mod-erate somewhat. Later (1863) Bouchardy went so far as to travesty the highwaymen pieces—biting the hand that fed him. The charac-ter of the title role in his *Philidor* is an actor condemned by his physique to play *troisième* roles though by nature he is the kindest and gentlest of men, like the famous London transpontine villain, O. Smith. Bouchardy, like Dennery, could be highly amusing in his comedy. The comic in this piece is an incredibly lazy dresser with acting ambitions who attributes his failure to obtain roles to the jealousy of the claque.

The stock low-comedy character, incidentally, would appear to have been threatened with extinction after 1830 along with other standard ingredients of melodrama if we are to judge by Brazier (p. 309) and by the plays themselves. He is absent in Bouchardy's *Le Sonneur de Saint-Paul* (1838) and in his *Gaspardo le pêcheur*, a revolutionary drama laid in Venice. But, as Brazier himself wrote, the comic could not die. He has been restored in *L'Abbaye de Castro* (1840), a medieval convent piece by P. Dinaux and Gustave Lemoine, based on a quasi-historical tragedy of passionate love in seventeenth-century Italy, and in *Geneviève de Brabant*, by Anicet-Bourgeois and Valory, a redaction of the enduring Merovingian legend of a falsely accused wife. In the former he is a slashing, fearless soldier of fortune, very much in the Dumas style, seasoning his audacity with practical jokes; and in the latter a stunted bump-kin shivering with terror inside an oversize suit of mail as he is thrust into all manner of perilous situations.

If bandits and ghosts were checked in French melodrama in the wake of Romantic drama, other extravagances had free reign. The world of the genre remains the small one of yore; old friends and old foes have a way of meeting in the most unlikely places, and all hands contrive to be in at the death for the concluding tableau—an invention of melodrama. Documents continue to be stolen and miraculously recovered (there is one in *Philidor*); orphans turn out to be missing heirs; and the *reconnaissance* remains a fixture. Never for long out of sight is the hand that pulls the strings.

A typical example of post-Romantic melodrama is *Le Sonneur de Saint-Paul*. The setting is the England of the Commonwealth and Restoration. In the prologue John, the hero, a former London tavern-keeper, is living happily in a remote part of the Scottish Highlands with his secret bride, Clara, whom he saved from death in London a short while previously at the time of the Cromwellian rebellion and subsequently married. Clara is many years his junior and far above him in station, being the daughter of Lord Richmond. Richmond himself, supposedly dead, puts in a dramatic appearance; he is tracked by spies, who also discover Clara's identity. The only hope for father and daughter lies in their escaping the country, and they start off together for the coast to take ship for America. John is shot while covering their flight as the curtain descends.

The action of the play proper begins in London twenty years later. Charles II has by now ascended the throne of his ancestors, and Richmond has been restored to his old position as minister. Clara has had a son—John's son—and believing the father dead, has, at the command of her father, made a political marriage ("a marriage in name only") with a villain, Lord Bedford. Clara's son, Henri, is in love with a beautiful young girl, Marie, a commoner evidently, since her foster-father is the bell ringer of St. Paul's. This character is a blind old man who, the audience learns, lost his sight as the result of a wound received in Scotland twenty years earlier; this identifies him as John. Marie is the daughter of one of John's Scottish neighbors by a certain mysterious William Smith, who deserted his wife and betrayed his king in the prologue. In the denouement, which occurs at a masked ball where the king is in attendance, Bedford is revealed to be Smith, John's sight is restored, he is reunited with his wife—who has never ceased to love him—and the barriers are removed for the wedding of Marie and Henri.

It is the political rather than the literary or moral reverberations of the Revolution of July that are heard most persistently in the melodramas of this period: antimonarchical and anticlerical senti-ment and the resuscitated Napoleonic legend. In *La Curé et l'archevêché* (1833), an archbishop is pictured as an immensely rich debauchee, a forger, a political intriguer, a corrupter of young girls, and an incendiary. Capuchins and Dominicans become sottish clowns on the stage; and the Jesuits, unregenerate villains. Ducange's *Le Jésuite* really belongs in this era also having been written in 1830. Many other dramas follow the same lines. Hatred of the Society of Jesus and of the Confraternity, a quasi-political organization popularly supposed to be headed by a Jesuit, reached its climax on the stage some years later (1843) in *Le Juif errant* from Eugène Sue's novel of that name, the most elaborate and the most successful romance of the century. Its action begins in a menagerie at Leipzig (an opportunity for a display of real wild beasts in the stage version mounted at the Porte Saint-Martin in 1844), touches at the North Pole, and reaches its climax in Paris. The story tells of a gigantic conspiracy by the two Jesuit villains, one worse than the other, to obtain for their order the reversion of an immense estate accumulated over generations. The villains contrive the murder of all the legal heirs, one by one. The play offered a profusion of highly charged scenes in low-life and high-life backgrounds anticipating *Les Mystères de Paris*. Like *Monte Cristo*, it was in two parts given on consecutive evenings.

The Jesuits were the favorite villains and Bonaparte was the favorite hero of the thirties. Napoleonic pieces were everywhere—at the Gaîté, the Ambigu, the Opéra Comique, the Odéon, the Porte Saint-Martin, and most of all at the Cirque Olympique. Private gratitude as much as public enthusiasm impelled this establishment to outdo its rivals in honoring the memory of the Emperor; after it had been suppressed by the decree of 1807 regulating the number of theatres and their respective repertoires, Napoleon had exempted it from the provisions of that edict permitting it to operate as usual. The facilities of the Cirque were ideally suited to the staging of the type of military show in which he was most fittingly commemorated. In these dramas artillery roared, infantry maneuvered, cavalry charged, trenches were taken at bayonet point, flags were captured and recaptured, traitors shot. Supers were pressed into service on a colossal scale—five and six hundred in a production. Recruiting Cossacks was a problem for the management; only an exceptional honorarium would overcome the repugnance of a good Frenchman to appearing in one of the hated uniforms, whereas members of the Old Guard could be hired for little or nothing.

The Cirque was basically a circus ring. About this a track ran, communicating at either side with the huge stage. When the moment of battle arrived, the stage curtain opened, giving access to a parade of the French army moving up a ramp from the track at one side, across the stage, and off at the other side. Then the enemy was seen surging from the back of the theatre, and the action broke out in all quarters of the house as the two armies came to grips. "Cavalry galloped, bugles sounded, drums beat the charge, rifles were fired, the cannon thundered, smoke filled up the hall and the curtain fell on the tableau in the midst of the uproar as the spectators applauded in a frenzy."[3]

The greater number of these spectacles were written by Ferdinand Laloue, Villain de Saint-Hilaire, and Fabrice Labrousse, though Dennery and Anicet-Bourgeois provided many. A few titles will indicate the subjects: *L'Empire et les Cent Jours, Les Pages de l'Empereur, Le Prince Eugène et l'Imperatrice Joséphine, Austerlitz, Le General Foy, Le Soldat de la République, Murat, Bonaparte en Egypte, Schoenbrunn et Sainte-Hélène.*

There was a revival of interest in these Napoleonic spectacles after Louis Napoleon's coup d'etat. One of this later crop, Dennery's *L'Histoire d'un drapeau* given at the Théâtre Imperial du Cirque in 1860, introduced a novelty in play construction that would be important to future melodrama: the short comic scene on the forestage, designed to permit the change of an elaborate built set further up on the stage.[4]

[3] M. J. Moynet, *L'Envers du théâtre* (Paris, 1874), pp. 244–247.
[4] Georges Cain, *Anciens théâtres de Paris* (Paris, 1920), pp. 64, 65.

XI

The Cape-and-Sword Hero

History is a pawn shop where theatrical tableaux are dressed.
—ALEXANDRE DUMAS, *père*

Romantic drama survived in the living theatre only by becoming frankly melodrama. Dennery collaborating with Dumanoir made a melodrama out of the character of Don César de Bazan (from Hugo's *Ruy Blas*) in 1844, and other playwrights used matter from Romantic dramas as points of departure for melodramas.

What happened specifically to Romantic drama on the Boulevard was that it degenerated into cape-and-sword melodrama. This transformation was owing somewhat to Dumas, who gave it momentum in 1845 with his dramatization of his own novel, *Les Trois Mousquetaires*. Two years later under the patronage of the Duke of Montpensier, Dumas built his own house, the Théâtre Historique. It was here that the cape-and-sword drama enjoyed its most brilliant success in that series of rousing historical plays adapted from the romances: *La Reine Margot, Le Chevalier du Maison-Rouge, Une Fille du régent, Intrigue et amour, Le Comte Hermann, Pauline, La Jeunesse des mousquetaires, Le Chevalier d'Hermenthal, Monte Cristo, La Dame de Monsoreau, Les Frères corses,* and others. The actor Mélingue made his reputation in them.

The most noteworthy contribution made by Dumas to melodrama was the cape-and-sword hero. Superficially he was not new; Vivaldi, of *L'Homme à trois visages*, is of the breed. But Vivaldi, for all his heroic enterprise, is but a pale shadow alongside the passionate supermen put upon the stage by "the ventripotent mulatto," as Stevenson called him, "the great eater, worker, earner and waster, the man of much and witty laughter, the man of great heart," whose tremendous appetite for life is reflected in these creatures of his. Buridan, of *La Tour de Nesle*, was the first—Buridan the proud swaggerer, Buridan the iron-willed and fearless soldier of fortune for whom adventure is daily bread, Buridan the ruthless and cunning intriguer who rises from nothing to become master of a queen and master of France.

Buridan is no lover, but most of his successors are—gallant, passionate lovers. The typical cape-and-sword hero dares every-thing, sacrifices everything, for love. A romantic passion for the queen he has never seen inspires Savoisy to plan an audacious rescue of Marie Antoinette in Le Chevalier de Maison-Rouge; and when it fails he risks his life to gain access to her in the Temple and give her a knife with which she may forestall the guillotine. Linday, the ardent young Republican in the same play, must choose between his lady's service and the cause he has given his life to; he bows to the lady and betrays the cause.

Dumas was not afraid to bring the old bandits, the old horrors, and the old underground passageways, even the old ghosts back upon the stage. In one of the most powerful of the dramas from his stories, Les Frères corses, adapted by Montepin and Grangé, the elder De Franchi learns of the killing of his brother through a vision shown on the stage; and the vision recurs in the last act after he has hunted the slayer down and run him through in a thrilling duel fought with broken swords. In Le Vampire, reworked from Nodier's play in the fifties, a veritable supernatural carnival is introduced. Dumas managed to bring it all off; he was, in that hackneyed but indispensable phrase, a born dramatist. Nearly every-thing he wrote for the stage is alive with dynamic action and nervous with expertly contrived suspense.

After the great Alexandre, various other writers practiced the genre of the cape and sword, none of them to such good purpose, however. Weiss thought that the best of the crop were Dugué and Anicet-Bourgeois' La Bouquetière des innocents, written about the St. Bartholomew's Day massacre, and La Famille des Gueux (1869). Other cape-and-sword pieces which received wide acclaim were La Sorcière ou les États de Blois, by Anicet-Bourgeois and J. Barbier; Fanfan la tulipe, by Paul Meurice; La Jeunesse de Roi Henri, by Ponson du Terrail; La Belle Gabrielle, by Maquet, Dumas's col-laborator; and Le Fils de Porthos, by M. E. Blavet. The most popular of the lot, however, were Don César de Bazan (1844) and Le Bossu (1862), the latter by Anicet-Bourgeois and Paul Féval.

Don César derives as much from Hugo as from Dumas. Its central figure, the Spanish nobleman of the title, Don César, had appeared previously on the stage in Hugo's Ruy Blas as a minor character, brought on briefly in the first act and again in the last to serve as an instrument—he proves a not very manageable one—of the designing villain, his uncle, who appropriates his title to bestow it upon a lackey as part of a tortuous intrigue to disgrace the queen. César is no willing accessory to this contemptible plot; on the contrary, when his participation is solicited, he refuses indignantly, spurning the gold offered him, with the result that his scoundrel uncle finds it necessary to have him abducted. Spurning gold is no easy thing for Don César to do since he needs it badly; a scapegrace nobleman, he has brought himself to the condition of a penniless vagabond through his extravagances and convivial habits. Adverse fortune, however, has not tarnished the luster of his Castilian honor in the code of which there is nothing about paying merchants' bills; nor has it weakened his chivalrous instincts, soured his Falstaffian humor, or dulled the point of his wit. It is in the character of an engaging, picaresque rogue that he appears in *Don César de Bazan,* by Dennery and Dumanoir.

He is presented in the opening act returning clandestinely to Madrid, whence he has been banished in disgrace for divers rakehelly adventures—and by the concerted action of an army of creditors. In the first scene in which he appears his impulsive generosity gets him immediately into trouble. A brutal captain is preparing to flog a boy in his company, Lazarillo, and Don César interposes, quite respectfully, with a plea for mercy. He is answered with contempt. It happens to be Holy Week when duelling is prohibited under penalty of death; and the shabby adventurer submits humbly as the captain insults his rags. But his sword is itching in its scabbard. The boy has mentioned that his lieutenant pleaded for him also. "I think," the Don tells him finally, "that I shall make that lieutenant of yours a captain. . . . Stand behind me; you have for defender César and his sword." The mean cape is tossed back with a certain gesture and a wisp of gleaming steel hisses from its folds; the happy-go-lucky roustabout has become a lion. Casting prudence to the winds, César will fight it out for a poor boy. Only the thinning ranks of old-timers who remember Coquelin or Edwin Booth in that magnificent moment—and many another like it in the play—can know how much there was in it to rouse the blood.

César goes off with the captain and returns presently, wiping his sword; the lieutenant is in line for a captaincy. As luck will have it, however, an alcalde passing with a patrol has seen all; and the duellist is arrested in the name of the King and taken off to pay the penalty for his offense. Death has no terrors for him, however; he has drained the cup of earthly pleasures, he says; he has loved, he has drunk, he has gamed.

As he awaits execution in jail, the King's minister, De Santarem, who is César's kinsman, comes to him with the proposition that he marry a beautiful young street singer, Maritana, for undisclosed reasons. Taken with the piquancy of the idea, César consents. He goes gaily through with the ceremony, and takes leave of his heavily veiled bride with a quip on his lips—on his way to face a firing squad.

Like Don Sallust in *Ruy Blas*, De Santarem has a tortuous project in mind. The King, Charles II, is secretly enamoured of Maritana, but her low estate makes a regular liaison out of the question. The Minister, on his part, loves the Queen—unsuccessfully; he hopes by introducing Maritana to the court as the widowed Countess de Bazan to promote the consummation of the King's romance and thereby arouse the jealousy of his consort to his, De Santarem's, advantage. The affair is complicated by the circumstance that Maritana is a good girl and will hear of nothing but marriage. To get around her scruples, De Santarem represents the man she married in jail as the monarch, and, after much maneuvering, leases a secluded house in the suburbs, installs her there, and tells her to await the connubial visit.

In due course the monarch arrives, but Maritana is not entirely convinced. Her melodramatic instinct tells her that this is not the man she wed, a man whose image and legend she has come to love from reports picked up about the court of his bold courage and great heart. The King makes out a plausible case for himself, however, and she sadly acquiesces to his will. She moves into the adjoining bedchamber. The King starts to follow when he is dramatically interrupted. A shot rings out, and the figure of a man enters precipitately by a window at a balcony upstage—an entrance Bernard Shaw borrowed for his travesty of romantic heroics, *Arms and the Man*.

The newcomer is Don César; there were blanks in the arquebuses of the firing squad in the gaol yard, thanks to the surreptitious intervention of the boy Lazarillo whom César had saved from the flogging (Gillette borrowed this bit for *Secret Service*, and Sardou —with a bitter twist—for *La Tosca*). At the execution the bridegroom feigned death and subsequently found a way to escape. Since then he has been out of the country. It is curiosity concerning his bride that brings him back now to Madrid—and into this scene. Passing by, he has been told that this is Don César's house; and, he has reasoned, where else but in Don César's house may Don César's wife be found?

To the indignant King, thus surprised, he says merely—as cool as can be—that he has glimpsed a lovely lady at a window and, the door being barred, has found another way in despite the most inhospitable conduct of the lookout with the arquebus, who took a shot at him.

KING. Impertinent! I desire you to quit this room.

DON C. After the trouble I've had to get here? Are you—

K. The master of this house.

DON C. The master of the house—hum! the house where I have seen the Countess of Bazan.

K. (*haughtily*). I am (*pauses, looks at the door of Maritana's chamber*), I am Don César de Bazan. (*Sits.*)

DON C. Eh! Don César de Bazan! (*Aside.*) Egad, I excel the phoenix, for two Don Césars have arisen from my ashes.

K. Now that I have satisfied you, I demand to know your name.

By this time César, recognizing the King, has sized up the situation. He is equal to it—thanks, it must be, to his recollection of a famous scene of *La Estrella de Seville*, long mistakenly attributed to Lope de Vega.

DON C. If you are Don César de Bazan, I am the King of Spain! . . . and that astonishes you, to see His Majesty, Charles II, without suite, in the dead of night, close to a wife that is not his? . . . As you see, César, Our Majesty is bored, Our Majesty comes to distract himself.

In the course of this byplay, César learns for the first time that a pardon in his behalf was signed by the King while he was in prison—a pardon obviously withheld by De Santarem; he makes a mental note of the fact against the time when he will close his account with that traitor. His ignorance of the pardon, of course, convicts him of imposture and ends the comedy.

KING (*presses him*). Who are you really?

DON C. A man who can walk with his face uncovered, and who has no need to hide his title and his name. I am—

The man on guard at the door enters before he can finish and interrupts. He brings an urgent message for the King, who, glancing through it, learns that he has been betrayed by De Santarem and exclaims: "What do I read? Treason! I have been forestalled. She is at the palace. My horse!"—and he hurries out, flinging an order to the guard to see to it that no one leaves the house until he returns.

César turns to his wife, who has no notion who this nonchalant madman may be. He is struck with the girl's beauty, but he is in no dallying mood. Answering her question, he identifies himself: "I am a man who can demand an account of your actions and your thoughts. . . . What have you done, madame, with my honor and my name?"

The tangled coils of the whole affair are unravelled in the dramatic interview that follows. When it is over, the two see that they can at least trust and respect each other. They consult about what to do. Maritana, who, as a singing girl, has won the favor of the Queen, suggests to her newfound spouse, as a way out of their plight, that he hurry to that great lady and make an appeal for her intercession.

> MARITANA. I demand of you a great sacrifice, that you go else-where to beg from a woman when there are men here to be fought. But if you will do that, yours is my heart, my soul and my life.
>
> DON C. Madame, you perform a miracle! . . . Don César the adventurer exists no longer; Don César the gentleman is reborn. (*He goes.*)

When he returns in the next scene, the King is with Maritana on the point of forcing her. César enters and locks the door, putting the key in his pocket. Then he confronts his sovereign and rival. All masks are off now; each knows everything about the other.

> DON C. If you were merely a gentleman, I should know what to do. In cases like this, one does not merely fight; one kills.

But this is his king; and he throws his sword from him being afraid to trust himself with it. The fury that is in his heart he vents in a subtler and crueller way. He begins by explaining where he has been: at the Escorial, to see the Queen—running the gauntlet of the guard, scaling the wall of the royal park as shot whistled past him, and climbing up to the window of the royal bedchamber, whence, as he clung to the ivy beneath the sill, the sound of voices came to him—one the voice of a man!

The enraged King blurts an interruption, but his tormentor goes imperturbably on with his narrative.

It was the voice of the King's trusted minister that he overheard, speaking words of love, soliciting the Queen's—and his, the King's —dishonor; attempting to inveigle his unwilling and distracted listener with a story of how at that very moment in a secluded villa her royal consort was with the wife of another man.

> DON C. Sad equality! While dishonor enters the house of a gentleman, outrage penetrates the palace of the king . . . That which you would do to me, another has done to you . . . And you shall not leave!

The King, in a frenzy now, springs for the door.

> KING. Don César! Take up that sword and defend yourself. I am not the King of Spain. You do not know me. Let it be iron against iron, blood against blood!—since it is necessary to trample your dead body in order that I can leave this house.

> DON C. It is too late.

> KING. Too late?

> DON C. Since when, if you please, in this old Spain of ours does a gentleman not know enough to defend his Queen from insult? Can you believe that I could hear all that without chastising the infamy? . . . Look! here is the collar with which your royal hand decorated that man; I have taken the liberty of removing it from the carcass . . . I have saved your honor (*kneeling*); now, dispose of mine.

A great clatter of hurrying troops breaks in upon this tableau; it is the guard that De Santarem arranged to be sent in the hope of surprising the King *in flagrante delicto*. Charles, a chastened man now, addresses the guardsmen as they enter the house—to commend as the most loyal and most faithful of his gentlemen, his host, Don César, and to announce the appointment of that rehabilitated noble-man to the Governorship of Valence, fifty miles from Madrid.

"It is too close," the Don whispers, in great agitation; "make it Grenada"—which the monarch quickly does. Grenada is several days' march from the capital, and out of the range of those insatiable creditors.[1]

The second of the two most popular cape-and-sword dramas after those of Dumas was *Le Bossu*. Its hero Lagardère is the familiar type: chivalrous and generous, hungry for adventure, cool in danger, fertile in stratagems, uncanny at disguises, and as ready with his tongue as with his sword. Jean-Louis Barrault revived the play triumphantly in Paris in 1949 and it was also made into a film. It was Victorien Sardou who originally wrote *Le Bossu*. His drama, never produced, was novelized by Paul Féval (Justin H. McCarthy did one of the five contemporary English translations), and the story was adapted for the stage by Anicet-Bourgeois. Sardou, a master of melodramatic effects, manipulated the imposing pageantry and flamboyant action of historical drama with superlative dexterity in various other plays, notably *Patrie* (1869) and *La Haine* (1874). These pieces are cape-and-sword dramas crossed with tragedy; like the Romantic dramas, they end unhappily. *Patrie*, the first of them, is based on an episode of the siege of Leyden by the Duke of Alba in 1568 as recounted by the American historian Motley, to whom the play was dedicated; it deals with the betrayal of a patriotic conspiracy by an unfaithful wife. The intrigue unfolds in a succession of melodramatic devices commonplace enough but superbly managed—belfry tocsins, hoot-owl signals, ambuscades, betrayals by scars and piled up mass effects full of color and magnificent archaeological detail.

As good as any of the business in either of these plays is that magnificent melodramatic episode in the fourth act of Sardou's *La Tosca* (1887), Act II of the opera. The singer-heroine has just thrust a table knife into Scarpia—"Tosca's kiss"—and he lies stretched out dead on the floor. Repulsive to her in life, he is doubly so to her now; but she conquers her feelings long enough to drop to her knees at his side and wrest Mario's safe-conduct from his stiffening grasp. She goes to leave with her precious paper but something checks her at the door. Monster though Scarpia has been, death has its proprieties; and she retraces her steps. Two splendid candelabra light the supper table; Tosca takes them up and sets them down upon the floor like ritual tapers at the head of the gaping and convulsed corpse; and, wrenching a crucifix from the wall, places it

[1] Translated from Dennery and Dumanoir, *Don César de Bazan*, Acts IV and V.

gently upon the dead man's breast. Again she kneels, this time for a brief prayer. Then, rising and drawing her cloak about her, she hurries out into the Roman dawn while drums in the court below beat a grim reveille.

Sardou's other reconstructions of past ages on the stage included *Théodora, Cléopâtre, La Sorcière, Gismonda, Fédora, Madame Sans-Gêne, L'Affaire des poisons* and *Thermidor* (commissioned by Henry Irving), and *Robespierre*. Sarah Bernhardt graced many of them. All were mounted with the same conscientious accuracy and the same lavish display of what was then known as the upholsterer's art.

At the end of the century the cape-and-sword drama lighted its torches and brandished its swords once again in France, and in England and America also. In New York three versions of *The Three Musketeers* were given during 1897 and 1898, one starring James O'Neill, who had been identified with *Monte Cristo* (a version by John Brougham) for seventeen years; and in London Sir Beerbohm Tree's D'Artagnan raced Lewis Waller's to the stage. New plays appeared in England and America as well as in France, the greater number of them adapted from current fiction. Edward Rose's dramatization of Stanley Weymann's *Under the Red Robe* was successful at the Haymarket in London, and Frohman brought it out on this side with William Faversham starred. A *Gentleman of France* (with Kyrle Bellew) and *The House of the Wolf* (with Richard Mansfield) were also adapted. When Anthony Hope discovered a new region of romance in his imaginary Baltic principality of Ruritania, managers were quick to recognize its suitability for the theatre; *The Prisoner of Zenda* had long runs on both sides of the Atlantic, and its sequel, *Rupert of Hentzau*, succeeded it at the St. James and the Empire, with George Alexander and E. H. Sothern starred, respectively. There were original cape-and-sword dramas also, but only a few; Justin H. McCarthy's *If I Were King* (the best of them); Louis N. Parker's *The Cardinal* (Richelieu) and *The Vagabond King;* R. S. Stephenson's *An Enemy of the King;* and Victor Mapes *Don Caesar's Return.*

It was in the congenial air of this cape-and-sword drama—and with the aid of careful cultivation by the canny Frohman—that the matinee idol flourished; between luncheon and tea a million virgin hearts of the Gibson Girl era were wont to flutter against frilled shirtwaists as these godlike creatures fought and made love on the stage in costumes out of the picturesque past. An unsympathetic commentator—some envious and inadequate male, no doubt—coined a punning phrase, "the sword and caper drama," twitting certain of these performers, Waller in particular, on the excessive virility they affected in such roles and their athletic, not to say acrobatic, style. It was a good style for its purpose, nicely keyed to the spirit of Dumas romance. Lemaître and Bocage doubtless created it, and Mélingue and Fechter refined its effects. The latter introduced it to the English-speaking stage, impressing the ladies particularly by his perfervid wooing. Charles Kean, Charles Dillon, Lester Wallack, and Henry Irving borrowed many of its tricks, but its essence is outside the range of the Anglo-Saxon temperament.[2] With the passing of Lou Tellegen it disappeared entirely from our theatre, though a caricature of it survives in some of the screen performances of the late Douglas Fairbanks, Sr. Recently the cape-and-sword repertory of the middle of the last century has been enjoying a vigorous revival in French films.

[2] Henry James observed: "Unhappily for us as actors, we are not a gesticulating people."—*The Scenic Art* (New York, 1957), p. 6.

XII

Low Life and High

The Melodrama of the City

Long live the melodrame at which Margot has wept! —ALFRED
DE MUSSET

A more important fact for melodrama, as for the theatre in general, a more pervasive and compelling influence than either Romantic drama or the Napoleonic legend in shaping its course and determining its substance, was the daily life of the times, particularly the kaleidoscopic spectacle of modern city life. From about 1824 onward the genre grew more urban and contemporary.[1] The early plays of such men as Dennery and Bouchardy show this tendency. The first act of *La Grâce de Dieu* (1837), a melodramatic comedy by the former, is laid in the mountains of Savoy, which is the locale of *Cœlina;* but the heroine is promptly transported to Paris, where she is discovered successively in a humble garret, an elegant salon, and the anteroom of a great mansion. In the forties the drift of melodrama's population from the country to the town became more pronounced.

Dumas *père* may have directed the attention of Boulevard dramatists to the rich possibilities of this milieu; he dealt with modern Paris and London in several of his Romantic dramas, notably *Kean ou désordre et génie* (*Kean* in English) and *Antony.* The latter, which was the first of the modern triangle plays, confines itself to a *haute bourgeois* background; but *Kean* roams widely in its action, taking its characters into the dressing room of a theatre and a low dive along the Thames, The Coal Hole, where the actor-hero is shown engaging a bruiser at fisticuffs and besting him. This was to be the plan of the new melodrama—to paint the animated, colorful panorama of a metropolis in its entirety, showing pestholes and palaces and revealing each social stratum at work and at play. The mansions of high society alternate with the counting houses of the bourgeoisie, workmen's hovels, courtrooms, jails, billiard parlors,

---

[1] Maurice Albert, *Les Théâtres des Boulevards,* pp. 300–301.

and dives as settings for scenes within the same play. A restaurant and a hospital are shown in *Marie-Jeanne* (1842), by Mallain and Dennery.

If the early realistic plays of Dumas gave the initial impulse to city-life melodrama, the chief source of inspiration was the work of other writers, particularly Scribe and the novelists Paul de Kock and Eugène Sue, who provided reading matter for a huge middle-class and popular public. In 1844 appeared Sue's "bizarre epic," as Gautier called it, *Les Mystères de Paris*, eight volumes of nightmarish metropolitan adventures with an overpowering climax in every chapter. There are abductions, robberies, torture scenes, murders, pursuits, duels, nick-of-time rescues, hairbreadth escapes, drownings, gigantic swindles, evictions, and love intrigues, involving persons of every social level and all shades of virtue and depravity—ill-treated waifs, defrauded orphans, starving workmen, chaste grisettes, diplomatic spies, avaricious and libidinous lawyers, juvenile criminals, evil hunchbacks, savage thieftakers and fences, desperate smugglers and river pirates, vicious old hags, epileptics, profligates of high rank, droll concierges and an English comic butler, Murphy by name!

Sue was an inexhaustible mine of material for later writers; novels as diverse as *Dossier 113*, *Les Misérables*, *The Prisoner of Zenda*, *Crime and Punishment* and *L'Assomoir* owe something, directly or indirectly, to his stupefying compendiums of melodramatic effects. He was no doubt influenced to some extent by the English chroniclers of the poor, but the writings of a compatriot supplied the element in *Les Mystères de Paris* that meant most to its success, namely, the naturalistic transcript of that society of human derelicts which huddled in warrens in the old *Cité* and at the barriers—its code of conduct, its language, its economics, its habits and diversions. This compatriot was François Eugène Vidocq, successively juvenile felon, army deserter, self-confessed swindler, convicted forger and counterfeiter, jailbreaker, stool pigeon, alleged fence, *agent provocateur*, officer of the Brigade du Sûreté (established in 1812), and private criminal investigator. He was probably the first official detective. His *Mémoirs*, published in 1829, created a sensation with their revelations of the underworld and inspired many literary men besides Sue—Poe and Victor Hugo among them. Vidocq had an enormous melodramatic progeny, chiefly through the medium of Sue.

Les Mystères de Paris was promptly dramatized (1844) in an episodic but effective version by Prosper Gobaux (one of eight contemporary adaptations), which scored a decided hit with Lemaître as Jacques Ferrand, the rascally lawyer-villain; and in the same decade came the first batch of those imitations and derivations which were to continue indefinitely: *Paris la nuit* and *Le Canal Saint-Martin*, by Depeuty and Cormon; *Les Bohémiens de Paris*, by Grangé and Dennery; *Les Marches de Londres*, by Brisebarre and Nus; *Les Mystères de Londres*, by Féval; *Les Puritains de Paris*, by Dumas; *Les Nuits de la Seine*, by Marc Fournier; and Felix Pyat's *Les Deux Serruriers* and *Le Chiffonnier de Paris*.

Les Bohémiens de Paris (source of Boucicault's *After Dark*) was one of the earliest and one of the best of these imitations. As the play opens, two bohemians (at that time a term for petty racketeers) Montorgueil and Digonard, are planning a Napoleonic coup. The daughter of a certain Desrosier family, heiress to a half-million francs, is betrothed to Charles Didier, who has been absent for years in India; and the villains, familiar with the situation, propose to advance the date of the marriage by one means or another, substitute Charles' brother Paul, who resembles him closely, as the bridegroom, and collect a percentage of the dowry. Paul, the family black sheep, is down and out—a bohemian like the others—and he consents though reluctantly to go through with the imposture, signing a bond for two hundred thousand francs payable to the villains. The cat's paw already has a wife, the devoted Louisa; but he deserts her at the order of the masterminds of the conspiracy. The plot is progressing when Charles, unexpectedly back from the Orient, puts in an appearance.

At this point the various lines of the complex plot begin to converge. Louisa's father, Crévecour, a decayed gentleman, has descended to the bohemian class also; he is living under the Pont Neuf in a loose community of vagrants there. Here one evening he sees a woman fling herself from the bridge into the Seine in an attempt at suicide. It is Louisa, but, having been long separated from his child, he does not recognize her. Charles, happening to be in that particular part of Paris at that particular moment, leaps into the river and brings the girl ashore. Father and daughter are reunited in a highly emotional scene.

Crévecour has an old score to settle with one of the villains. Years before his wife was ruined by Digonard, a tragedy which has made the old man what he is. The finding of Louisa gives him a new grip on life and leads to his regeneration. It is he who eventually wrecks the swindling scheme and unscrambles the affairs of the Didier and Desrosier families. (The man-who-came-back theme was exploited in hundreds of melodramas in the latter half of the century; *The Silver King, The Ticket-of-Leave Man,* and *Chinatown Charley* were three of them.)

In the concluding act of *Les Bohémiens* Charles goes to a low resort to treat with the racketeers for the return of the contract. He is drugged and dropped through a trap door, and the place is set afire. Crévecour, who has followed him to the rendezvous, makes his way to the cellar by a stratagem, drags the insensible body from the burning house, and recovers the papers.

Les Bohémiens opens with a lively scene in the courtyard of the Messageries Royal, terminal of the stage lines. Billstickers are to be seen posting up notices; travellers are arriving and departing; peddlers mill about crying matches, canes, and guidebooks; and drunks, bootblacks, urchins, panhandlers, and guards mingle in the crowd. This was one of many such scenes in the play reproducing familiar localities in Paris—a billiard parlor, a thieves' den, on the Pont Neuf by moonlight with the city glimpsed through its arches on the backdrop. At Hoboken in 1929, Christopher Morley and Cleon Throckmorton turned Boucicault's English version into a hilarious romp.

The trail of metropolitan crime leads down to the waterfront in Marc Fournier's *Les Nuits de la Seine,* in which a mob of river rats are seen plotting miscellaneous deviltry on orders from an aristocratic smuggler-villain. A gang of counterfeiters do the plotting in Édouard Louis Alexandre Brisebarre and Eugene Nus's *Léonard ou la retour de Brest.* This piece was a success in Paris but was a far greater and more lasting one in England and America, thanks to Tom Taylor's creative adaptation, *The Ticket-of-Leave Man,* which will be described in a later chapter.

Brisebarre and Nus were the authors of *Les Pauvres de Paris* also; given first at the Ambigu in 1856, this piece became probably the most resounding international success of all city-life melodramas. The villain, Villebrun, is a banker, a profession prolific among theatrical evildoers in the French popular drama, particularly from the forties onward when socialism and communism became lively issues in Paris and industrial cities such as Lyons.

In the prologue of *Les Pauvres de Paris,* Villebrun, now in Bordeaux, is tottering on the brink of a ruin he richly deserves. He is preparing to abscond with what liquid assets he can lay his hands on, when a ship's captain, Pierre Bernier, calls at the banking office. This worthy old man has with him the entire savings of a frugal and industrious life, which he desires to place in trust for his wife and children. The unscrupulous financier takes the money and the captain leaves. He returns shortly afterward in great agitation; he has learned of the precarious state of the Villebrun establishment, and he demands his money back. His excitement induces a heart attack, and he dies. The banker makes off after buying the silence of his confidential clerk, Fabien de Roquefeuil, the comic, who is privy to his peculations generally.

In the first act it is fifteen years later and the scene is Paris whither Mme Bernier and her two children, André and Antoinette, have removed from Bordeaux. The little family is quite poor, depending for bare necessaries upon a workingman's charitable family. (The virtuous, benevolent workingman is the urbanized version of Rousseau's natural good man.) Their landlord is a certain hardhearted and purse-proud banker, who turns out to be Villebrun reestablished in the world by means of old Bernier's money.

All roads lead to Paris; Fabien is the next to turn up, having come directly from the galleys. He has in his possession a highly valuable paper, the receipt which Villebrun made out for the money Bernier turned over to him in Bordeaux; and he approaches his old employer (who, he feels, has treated him badly) with the object of blackmail.

Meanwhile Antoinette has obtained work as a seamstress, and, of all the ladies of Paris, it is to Villebrun's daughter, the spoiled and arrogant Alida, that she is sent on assignment by her employer. In the banker's mansion, by yet another chance, Antoinette encounters one to whom in more prosperous days she was espoused, the patrician Planterose, an old school chum of André's. This young man, like the Berniers, has met with reverses, and it is his wounded pride at his altered circumstances rather than caprice or any unworthier motive which has led to his estrangement from Antoinette. A hard necessity brings him to the Villebruns now; needing money badly, he has come to accept the terms which the parvenu banker, ambitious for his daughter to shine socially, has set for a loan: marriage to Alida. When Planterose sees Antoinette again, he realizes that he cannot go through with his mercenary bargain; and he renews his offer of marriage to the impoverished heroine on the spot. That unselfish young lady, however, has learned of his situation from Alida, and she pretends that she does not love him telling him so with a brave face. Alida later attempts to press a purse upon the heroic seamstress as reward for her noble renunciation. It is rejected with a scalding rebuke: "No, madame; its touch would degrade my poverty. I did not sell my happiness, I gave it freely for his sake, whom, in riches or in poverty, living or dead, I shall never cease to love—to love" (*Exit wildly*).

Things go from bad to worse for the Berniers. They are assembled by the author in the fourth act for a grand contrapuntal effect of woe in a scene representing the Boulevard close to the Chemin de Fer de l'Ouest (trains to be seen through the grill work at the back). André, weakened by hunger, is unable to lift a trunk and so fails to get work as a porter; Mme Bernier attempts to pawn her wedding ring—"dear bond of early love and wedded faith"; Antoinette comes on, the picture of destitution, begging; and all three solicit alms of one another before recognition.

Later, in the fourth act, the scene shifts to 2, Rue de la Hachette, in a wretched quarter of Paris. Two adjoining attic apartments are shown in the divided scene. In one Fabien is discovered; he reveals in a monologue that he awaits Villebrun coming to dicker for the papers. In the other Mme Bernier, in despair, is burning charcoal in the grate, hoping to die by its fumes. Antoinette enters and, after a pathetic passage with her mother, agrees to die with her as the fumes gradually fill the room. Meanwhile the banker has arrived in Fabien's apartment. He proceeds to business with his difficult antagonist and contrives to drop a powder into the liquor Fabien is drinking. Taking his leave, he promises to return with the sum demanded.

At this point someone is heard bursting in the door of the other apartment, and a moment later André is visible through the smoke, smashing the window glass and ministering to the now unconscious mother and sister. Fabien dozes off from the effects of the powder, but the noise awakens him. Suspecting what Villebrun has done, he rouses himself with an effort and thrusts the papers under a loose board in the floor for concealment. He has sunk into a coma when the banker reappears. The villain commences rummaging in the prostrate comic's pockets. He is surprised by André entering to ask for assistance. Once more Fabien revives and, recognizing André, points out Villebrun to the lad as "the robber of your parent." The powder gets in its work before he can say where he has hidden the incriminating receipt, however. He appears to be dead as he lies on the floor. The villain turns to André with "a smile of scornful triumph," and the curtain falls on the fourth act.

It takes more than an overdose of a narcotic to kill a good comic, especially one with a secret such as Fabien's locked in his breast; he reappears at a dramatic moment in the last act. The scene is the exterior of the church where Planterose is to be married to Alida, and the wedding party is seen moving across the stage. The Bernier family in full strength is watching from the side lines, and, as Villebrun passes, André bursts out in an elaborate rhetorical denunciation of his villainies. The two are exchanging abuse when Fabien enters, flourishing the papers and accompanied by two policemen who take Villebrun off with them to explain, if he can, a certain shady bankruptcy of fifteen years before. This is a cue for the somewhat unsatisfactory Planterose to decide that it is Antoinette after all and not Alida whom he wishes to marry.

It may have been from *Le Chiffonnier de Paris* that the authors of *Les Pauvres de Paris* got the idea of Antoinette's fine gesture of renunciation as well as other details of their plot. This city-life drama by Félix Pyat, first put on in 1847 at the Porte Saint-Martin, was a major factor in agitating the insurrection of 1848. Both plays make a point of contrasting "the wretched condition of honest poverty with the callous extravagances of rapacious wealth"; *Les Pauvres de Paris* concludes with a speech addressed to the audience in the manner of *L'Abbé de l'Épée* on society's responsibility to the poor and friendless. Pyat was a militant socialist and fought on the barricades in '48. *Le Chiffonnier* and another militantly proletarian melodrama of his, *Les Deux Serruriers*, were forbidden the boards in Paris after 1852.

Critics and other close observers of the French stage began to notice a falling off in the popularity of melodrama (or *drame*, as it was then designated in France) in the middle years of the Second Empire and later, concurrent with the rise of a new and bastard form of drawing room drama, the *drame à thèse*, which owed much to melodrama. The critic of *L'Année littéraire et dramatique* in 1866 expressed the opinion that melodrama of "Boulevard du Crime" ancestry was losing ground daily to the "social studies" presented by such writers as Augier and Sardou; and he cited the fact that the entire season of 1865 had passed at that onetime stronghold of melodrama, the Porte Saint-Martin, without a single new piece of the type having been given.

Five years later in 1870 on the occasion of the death of Joseph Bouchardy, Théophile Gautier in the *Moniteur universal* mourned the genre along with the man and undertook to give reasons why melodrama was losing its appeal. He blamed it on a loss of naïveté in audiences and a deterioration in moral standards. Of Bouchardy, his old companion in arms in the days of the Little Cénacle and the stirring battles for Romantic drama, he wrote: "He loved to develop those grand commonplaces which are the very foundation of the human spirit, but which provoke only an evil smile on the lips of the skeptic: paternal love, fidelity, devotion, loyalty, chivalry, the point of honour, and all the noble motives which can determine action. These things have become ridiculous, and the *naïf* Bouchardy was astonished at the failure of his last works, into which he had put the same talent as his early ones."[2]

Gautier's eulogy proved premature, as had a similar pronouncement by Brazier a generation earlier. Henry James, reviewing the first American production of *The Two Orphans* in the *Nation* early in 1875, noted that the success of the original production in Paris during the previous year had "fairly rejuvenated the rather defunct type to which it belonged."[3] The author of this masterpiece, Adolphe Dennery, was to give further demonstration that he was worthy of his illustrious fathers.

[2] *Histoire du romantisme*, p. 186.
[3] *The Scenic Art*, p. 24.

XIII

Adolphe Dennery and the Last Days of French Classical Melodrama

Dennery is not to be despised; we have reasons for admiring him.
—THEOPHILE GAUTIER

Children were useful in the families of melodramatic actors; they could be lifted from the cradle and put to work even before they were weaned. Mrs. John Drew went on in her mother's arms as an infant and was kept professionally busy from that time forward, progressing in due course to such juvenile "breeches" rôles as Prince Ahib, the rightful heir in *Timour the Tartar*. There was need for an "infant phenomenon" in every company to play that ubiquitous orphan who is lost or stolen in the prologue and who turns up full-grown at a dramatic moment in the third act to claim his usurped patrimony, avenge his foully murdered kin, retrieve his aged mother from the poorhouse, or expose and crush the nefarious conspiracy threatening the kind old duke, who, it transpires, is really his father.

Children on the stage were chiefly desirable as an infallible tear-jerking device in a theatre in which no appeal was more potent than a sentimental one. They were usually presented by playwrights as neglected, abused, deprived of parental love and care, or menaced in their very lives by bloodthirsty villains. Infant appeal in one form or another played an important part in the success of hundreds of melodramas, if not thousands. Among them were *Le Jugement de Salomon, Le Pèlerin blanc, Charles le Téméraire, L'Illustré Aveugle, Il y a seize ans, Les Deux Gosses, La Voleuse d'enfants* in France; *The Adopted Child, The Foundling of the Forest, The Broken Sword, The Green Bushes, East Lynne, The Sea,* and *The Silver King* in England; and *Horizon, Uncle Tom's Cabin, Ten Nights in a Barroom,* and *No Mother to Guide Her* in the United States.

The melodramatic permutations of the lost child and the bereaved parent were worked out most exhaustively perhaps by Adolphe Dennery, one of the most prodigious playwrights in theatrical history, in what amounts to a whole library of excruciating dramas given from the early forties to the end of the century. Among them

93

were *L'Escamoteur* (collaborator, Brésil), *Casper Hauser* (based on a famous pretender case since novelized by Jacob Wassermann), *Paillasse* (collaborator, Marc Fournier), *Les Deux Orphelines* (collaborator, Cormon), *Marie-Jeanne*, *Une Cause célèbre* (collaborator, Cormon), *Les Médecin des enfants*, and *La Prière des naufragés* (collaborator, Dugué). Dennery used spectacular mechanical devices in *La Prière des naufragés* which made it one of the major box office attractions of the late nineteenth century. In *Une Cause célèbre* (1875) he uses subtler emotional effects.

On the eve of the battle of Fontenoy, Corporal Jean Renaud of the French army rescues a dying man from a plundering scoundrel between the lines. The victim is Count de Mornas, scion of a proscribed noble house, who has been attempting to flee the country with the ancestral jewels. Before expiring in the arms of his Good Samaritan, he turns his treasure over to him with an appeal that he convey it to his relatives when the occasion offers. This constitutes the action of the prologue, a section of the play for which even Zola had the highest praise.

The opening scenes of Part One show the Renaud home near the battlefield some hours later. Jean enters hurriedly, having stolen away from his company. He greets his wife Madeleine affectionately, relates his adventures, and places the jewels in an old cabinet for safekeeping. While husband and wife are together, their child, Adrienne, is put to bed in an adjoining room. Madeleine then sees Jean off. When she reenters the house, she discovers a stranger there. He is Lazare, De Mornas' thieving assailant, who has followed Jean to his home. He forces the woman to reveal the hiding place of the jewels and stuffs them in his pockets; and when Adrienne, alarmed by the upraised voices, calls from the next room, he compels the mother to say, "Be quiet, I am with your father." Then he stabs Madeleine and she dies.

In Part Two at the inquiry and court-martial next morning after the battle in which Jean has distinguished himself by capturing an enemy flag, the child innocently reveals her father's visit home, mentions the quarrel she overheard, and repeats her mother's command. Jean has a reputation as a quarrelsomely jealous husband; this and the damaging testimony of the child condemn him. Stricken, he takes farewell of his daughter, saying, "You have ruined me, my child, but remember that I love you, remember that I forgive you."

Twelve years later (in Part Three) the scene is the palatial Château d'Aubeterre. Jean's colonel, who condemned him to the galleys, is now a general and lord here, a duke. He has an eighteen-year-old daughter—or to all appearances his daughter—the gentle and beautiful Adrienne, another Cœlina. The girl loves her supposed parents, is loved by them, and possesses everthing she can desire, yet she is vaguely unhappy. She is troubled by strange dreams in which the tragic face of an old man appears and a grief-stricken voice utters these words: "You have ruined me, my child, but remember that I love you, remember that I forgive you." Adrienne, it must be mentioned, is another victim of an affliction endemic in melodrama, amnesia; all of her life which preceded a grave illness of her childhood is a blank.

A gang of prisoners from the galleys is passing through the country, and Adrienne, wandering down to where they are temporarily quartered, is strongly attracted to one among them, an aged man. His face proves to be the one of her dreams, and when she engages him in conversation, "That voice!" she exclaims—as hundreds of her sisters have done on like occasions. For it, too, recalls her dreams. Why was he condemned, she asks. "For the murder of my wife." But he is innocent, he says; and she believes him. The labor, the humiliation of his life are nothing, he tells her—nothing compared to the torture of his soul.

> JEAN RENAUD. What has become of my child, my daughter? Abandoned, without support, without succor, she is perhaps dead from suffering and hunger. And perhaps instead of one grave there are two, with no one to utter a prayer over them or shed a tear.

He tells her his story. The name Madeleine occurs in it, and Adrienne interrupts.

> ADRIENNE. It is strange! that name resounds at the bottom of my heart . . . (*with emotion*) Madeleine! In pronouncing it, tears come to my eyes. . . . Go on, say it again—if you wish.
>
> JEAN. Do I wish! . . . Oh I do not fear to pronounce it, the name of my good and dear Madeleine.
>
> ADRIENNE. It is like an echo from afar that I hear. . . . That name, a great many of our friends bear it, and I have heard it repeated so often. How does it happen then that I am moved as I am by it now . . . when it is you who pronounce it? Madeleine! . . . I feel dawning in me I know not what confused memories . . . yes . . . I see myself very tiny, my hands joined and . . . Madeleine praying! . . . (*with warmth*) St. Mary

Madeleine, patron of my mother, pray for her . . . (*suddenly stunned.*) What have I done. Have I gone insane.

JEAN. Who taught you that prayer, mademoiselle?

Adrienne cannot say. But step by step, the interview builds up to the big *reconnaissance*—one of the most moving in all melodrama. Jean speaks of his last words to his child.

ADRIENNE(*breathless*). And when you separated from her . . . what were your last words?

JEAN. I said: My daughter, may my last words remain graven in your memory.

ADRIENNE. In your memory, yes . . .

JEAN. You have ruined me, poor child.

ADRIENNE. That's it! You have ruined me!

JEAN. But remember that I love you—

ADRIENNE (*with animation*). Remember that I pardon you.

JEAN (*with force*). Ah, you know that, my child! My daughter alone heard these words; my daughter alone could repeat them.

At this point the good comic of the piece comes on, Chamboran, now the old and trusted servant of the Duke and devoted guardian of Adrienne. In him Jean recognizes his old companion in arms at Fontenoy, to whom he entrused Adrienne years before.

JEAN. Before God who watches over us and hears us, tell me what has become of my child . . .

CHAMBORAN. Your . . . your daughter . . .

JEAN. Before God! Before God!

CHAMBORAN. I made her the adopted daughter of the Dutchess of Aubeterre.

ADRIENNE. My father . . . (*falling on her knees and bathing her father's hands with her tears*). It is my father! my father who is innocent and whom I have, unhappily, made miserable.[1]

The two children in Dennery's *Paillasse* (1850) are neither lost, stolen, orphaned, nor abused, but they are exposed to no less dis-

[1] Translated from *Une Cause célèbre, drame en six parties* (Paris: Libraire Stock, 1922).

tressing vicissitudes for all that and are made the agency of no less heartrending pathos. The fat part in this play was that of the father, Belphegor, a clown; and the big moment—or, rather, the biggest of the many big moments—is the scene in the second act when, accompanied by his son and professional associate, the boy Henri, he returns joyfully to his humble attic with a gay shawl for his wife, bought as a surprise with a little hoard he has secretly scraped together. He discovers that she has deserted him, and he takes his child in his arms and breaks into a prolonged scene of hysterical grief. (Dickens touched up this passage in one of the several versions given in London during the fifties and sixties and frequently afterward.) No contemporary audience was able to resist that celebrated piece of business as put over by the giants of the Romantic school of melodramatic acting—Lemaître, Fechter, and Charles Dillon particularly. The intellectuals no less than the gallery gods succumbed to it—among them Gautier and Janin—and even hardened professionals themselves. Joseph Jefferson found tears in his eyes when Fechter ran through the scene one night for him and a few companions back stage. But alas for the extravagance of our forefathers' taste—or the blindness of our own! "An absurd farrago of bombast and pathos," Walkeley called *Paillasse* when Wilson Barrett revived it in 1891 at the Princess in London in a production that proved a dismal failure.

Best-remembered of all Dennery's *succèses des larmes* is *Les Deux Orphelines* (1874). Possibly no play ever written equals it in emotional voltage if the quantity of tears made to flow in the theatres of Christendom during the final quarter of the nineteenth century is a criterion. Louise, a sweet, gentle blind girl of mysterious parentage, falling into the hands of an abandoned old hag who exploits her in a begging racket on the streets of Paris; the crippled child of this fiend, Pierre, bullied and abused by her and his vicious brothers because he pities and shields and even fights for the unfortunate girl; Louise's foster-sister, the beautiful Henriette, abducted by one nobleman with wicked intentions and rescued by another with honorable ones; the titled mother of Louise, seeking everywhere for traces of the child she allowed to be taken from her at birth—and missing her by inches time and again as they pass without recognition on the stage; here, surely, are elements that would be hard to improve upon for beguiling audiences which enjoyed nothing so much as a good cry. And they are compounded with a wizard's skill though the formula has long since lost its magic; nothing is lacking from the standpoint of acting opportunities and nineteenth-century theatrical effectiveness. Quite under-standable is the enthusiasm of a man such as Daniel Frohman; he once called *The Two Orphans* the perfect play.

Again and again in his plays Dennery returned to the lost–child plot, and it seldom failed him with audiences; only the journalists were supercilious and facetious. One of these light-minded fellows, a writer for the *Trombinoscope*, a journal of the day in Paris, pictured the playwright in his cradle, a precocious and melo-dramatic infant, demanding a knife with which to scratch an identifying cross on his buttocks, so that everything would be in order for a fifth-act *reconnaissance*. The same irreverent commen-tator undertook to provide an explanation for the sudden change in the author's signature from Dennery to D'Ennery. "It is believed that he added that aristocratic apostrophe one day when he dis-covered noble ancestry for himself upon ripping up an old pair of trousers belonging to the great-uncle of his grandfather, who had hidden his papers in the lining because a son of one of his sisters, kidnapped in infancy by mountebanks passing through the region, had carried off an obscure young woman whose family, pursued in '93, had, in fleeing, hidden in the handle of a broom, scooped out by a devoted old domestic, the documents which proved that poor Raoul, accused wrongly of having stolen the diamonds of the Marquise . . ."

Late in his career Dennery turned his hand to a type of melo-dramatic entertainment which he made virtually his own province, the so-called scientific spectacle, usually an adaptation of a Jules Verne yarn. The earliest was *Around the World in Eighty Days*, which lasted for 417 performances at the Porte Saint-Martin when it was first given in 1874. Following this success came *Voyage dans la lune*, with its astronomical wonders and its magic phial; and later *Le Voyage à travers l'impossible*, offering a castaway hero, a thrilling rock-slide from a mountain side into the sea, and whale-fishing episodes and *Les Enfants du Capitaine Grant* with comparable marvels. *Twenty Thousand Leagues under the Sea* was not adapted for the stage apparently; but in 1877 Ferdinand Dugué dramatized a story by another novelist, H. Cortambert, which appears to owe something to this most famous romance of Verne written in 1869. *Un Drame au fond de la mer* was the name of the piece, and its sensation scene represented a desperate submarine duel in which the villain severs the air tube of the hero's diving suit.

Personal data on Dennery is disappointing. In his proper person this supreme melodramatist was no veteran of adventures like Pixerécourt, no hirsute, brawny Bouchardy in physique, no gargantuan Dumas in temperament and in appetites. The contriver of all those thundering climaxes, the inventor of that legion of virile heroes and maleficent villains, the activator of all that mighty chorus of heaving sighs, deep sobs, convulsive shudders, and abdominal guffaws which rocked the playhouses of two hemispheres for the greater part of a century, was a shy, mild-mannered bourgeois with a watery eye, a drooping moustache and a receding chin. He was regular and methodical in his habits and circumspect in his behaviour, and he never ventured out of doors without his umbrella, which was of white silk.

Dennery, who began his career in the thirties, is the link which connects the first generation of melodrama with the last. He was one of the prepotent trinity which maintained the genre at its best during the Second Empire—Anicet-Bourgeois who died in 1870 and Bouchardy were the others—and dying in 1898 he was the only one of the three who survived into the final years of the century when melodrama went into its decline. During these years his plays shared the boards with those of Brisebarre, Nus, Xavier Montépin, and younger writers—Adolphe Belot, Jules Mary, and Pierre Decourcelle. None of these was of his stature.

At the Ambigu and the Porte Saint-Martin (the Gaîté had surrendered to the musical drama in the early seventies) and at such newer houses as the Théâtre de la République (formerly the Cirque) and the Chatelet were to be seen elaborately staged pieces of an exotic and romantic cast, typical of which were *Michel Strogoff* (1880), by Dennery from a Jules Verne story, and *La Venus noire*, laid in French Équatorial Africa; miscellaneous *causes célèbres* and adapted novels, from *Les Misérables* (1878) and *Quo Vadis* (1908) to *L'Homme a l'oreille cassée* (1893) and Belot's *L'Érangleur de Paris* (1880); seduction dramas like *Le Maître d'armes* (1892) by Montépin and Grisier; detective dramas, a few from Gaboriau; patriotic exhibits inspired by French colonial expansion under the Ministry of Ferry, among them Mary's *La Chanson du pays* (1901) and Hugues le Roux and Decourcelle's *L'Autre France* (Morocco) (1900); convict dramas like *À perpète!* (1899), by Decourcelle, Lapelletier, and Xarnof; and the eternal courtroom affairs, from Mary and Grisier's *Roger la Honte* (1886)—given successfully in English by first-rate companies at the Haymarket in London and Daly's in New York—to Belot's *Madame X*, which brings the story down to the eve of World War I.

Aside from the spectacular scenic and mechanical effects of the scientific drama and the contributions of Dennery, two props sustained melodrama in its declining years as a major theatrical form in Paris: a few great actors, many of them of the school of Lemaître, the last of the noble line bred on the "Boulevard du Crime," and the great masterpieces of the past. In the eighties and nineties it was still possible to see Jenneval in *Les Pauvres de Paris*, Paulin Ménier and Lacressonnière in *Le Courrier de Lyon* and *Le Juif errant*, Taillade in *Les Crochets du Père Martin*. The great players passed finally, and without them even the best of the old melodramas came to sound a trifle loud and even silly. Audiences here and there began to laugh at the time-honored formulae if not at the old plays themselves; at the Ambigu itself in 1895 *Les Ruffians de Paris* suffered this ignominy. Melodrama, nevertheless, was far from being vanquished, even at the end of the century. It was not the failure of acting, the rise of new dramatic forms, the halting inspiration of melodramatists or increased sophistication on the part of audiences that finally routed it utterly. The blow came from a monstrously potent offspring of those *ombres chinoises* and phantasmagorias which had first amused habitués of the "Boulevard du Crime" in the knockdown shanties of the eighteenth century: the cinema. It was to this enemy that Decourcelle, best of the younger writers, finally deserted but not before writing a melodrama which demonstrated that the traditional pattern had not lost its power to enchant. *Deux Gosses* (1897) was an old-fashioned play and it scored an old-fashioned triumph, running for 751 performances to break a Paris record set by *Around the World in Eighty Days*. With its two little unprotected wanderers, exposed to the perils of an unfriendly world, this wholly delightful piece was strikingly like *Le Pèlerin blanc* and *The Children in the Wood* of a century earlier. The wheel of melodrama had come full circle.

The "Boulevard du Crime" itself did not survive to witness the end of the drama which had been its lifeblood. A dread municipal ukase utterly wiped out its remaining theatres in 1862 as a precaution against disastrous fires. Six theatres were demolished, including the Ambigu (the Gaîté had removed to the Square des Arts-et-Metiers after a fire in 1822); and into oblivion with them went the picturesque old cafés and wine shops where the great Frédéric Lemaître had drunk—too much, alas!—and in one of which Franz Liszt, between the acts of a shocker at the Ambigu, had first met the Lady of the Camellias.

II
ENGLAND

XIV

The English Background

. . . tis a drama of our own invention, and the fashion of it is enough to proclaim it so; here a course of mirth, there another of sorrow and passion, and a third of honor and a duel: thus in two hours and a half, we run through all the fits of Bedlam. —JOHN DRYDEN, *Dramatic Poesy*

Thomas Holcroft, an English actor and playwright of note in his day (1745–1809) spent two years in Paris during the peace at the beginning of the century, attending the theatre conscientiously while there. He saw *Cœlina* at the Ambigu, and, recognizing its possibilities for London, prepared an English version in two acts, which he offered to Kemble at Covent Garden. It was accepted and mounted as an afterpiece under the title of *A Tale of Mystery* on November 12, 1802—a date which thus marks the formal introduction to England of French *mélodrame* under that name.

Melodrama in fact was no novelty for London audiences. If we put aside for consideration in Chapter XVI their innovations in the use of music—and these were in degree rather than in kind—the works of Pixerécourt can be distinguished only by the greater dexterity of their workmanship from many plays that preceded them on the English stage. The outstanding successes of the season of 1798–1799 at Drury Lane had been *The Stranger, Pizarro,* and *The Castle Spectre;* and in 1801 *Adelmorn, the Outlaw* had run briefly at the same house. In these plays—the first two adaptations from Kotzebue's *Menschenhass und Reue* and *Rollas Tod* and the others original pieces by Matthew Gregory ("Monk") Lewis—the mood and machinery are those of melodrama. *The Stranger* and *Pizarro* foreshadowed respectively the domestic and historical types of the new form. *The Castle Spectre,* like *L'Homme à trois visages,* is a historical melodrama without the history (to paraphrase Saintsbury's phrase for *The Castle of Otranto*) and *Adelmorn* has affinities with both the bandit and supernatural melodrama then flourishing on the "Boulevard du Crime."

The kinship of Kotzebue and Pixerécourt has already been pointed out in these pages. Lewis came even closer than the German to the Frenchman's formula. In *The Castle Spectre* are to be encountered the lovely orphan maiden, Lady Angela, in the clutches of the lascivious villain, Lord Osmond, a usurper like all his breed, having done away with his fair captive's father and seized his demesne; the peasant hero, who turns out to be Earl Percy in disguise; and a comic, bibulous monk, who helps checkmate the villain. The setting is a mysterious gothic castle; there is a ghost, the spirit of the girl's dead mother, come to aid her child in a moment of peril wielding a very material dagger; and a brace of sinister blackamoors, servants to Osmond. Surprise, coincidence, and suspense are introduced frequently in the action, and there is a happy end. Adelmorn in the play by that name is a noble youth falsely accused of the murder of his father and driven into exile by a usurping wicked uncle. After joining an outlaw gang he returns and establishes his innocence, assisted by an impressive apparition which terrifies the villain into a confession.

The Castle Spectre and *Adelmorn*, though written by an Englishman, owed as little to English sources as the Kotzebue plays themselves—less, indeed, when it is considered how much Kotzebue was indebted to Lillo and Moore. Lewis travelled extensively on the Continent in 1791 and 1792, and while there was exposed to the Teutonic bandit and spook literature and the French monacal drama. He was at Weimar when the works of Iffland, Kotzebue, and Babo were prominent in the repertory of Goethe's theatre there; he met that great man, read *Werther, Die Räuber* and Zschokke's novels—sources of much English and French melodrama —and translated Bürger's ballads and *The Tales of Wonder*, works packed with sensational incidents and supernatural horrors. A direct fruit of his Parisian sojourn is his adaptation of the pre-Pixérécourt *Les Victimes cloîtrées* as *Venoni; or, the Novice of St. Mark's*, 1808. Borrowings from both French and German sources are apparent in *The Castle Spectre* and *Adelmorn* and other of his plays produced during the first decade of the century.

Elsewhere in the repertory of the English theatre of the time may be found ample evidence that melodramatic elements were coming to the fore independently of alien influence. It is not too much to say that from 1770 onward precedent had been set in English plays by Cumberland, Boaden, Morton, Colman, MacNally, Hoare, Cobb, Dibdin, Kelly, O'Keefe, Morris, and Arnold as well as Holcroft for virtually everything Pixérécourt and his French colleagues offered in the way of theatrical sentimentality and sensationalism. Sheridan burlesqued many of these extravagances as early as 1779 in *The Critic.* The virtuous young female orphan turned out into the cruel world by a villainous guardian who has wronged her father drew tears from the susceptible in *The Fashionable Lover* (1772), a sentimental comedy by Cumberland, the resemblance of which to *Cœlina* is heightened by the reappearance of the supposedly dead parent and the eventual punishment of the persecutor. Two children are the objects of a fiendish plot of another usurper in Morton's *Children in the Wood* (as adapted in 1793 from Percy's *Reliques*) as in *Le Pelèrin blanc.* Cumberland's *The Mysterious Husband* (1783) used bigamy for purposes of melodramatic intrigue, which Pixerécourt was to do in *La Femme à deux maris.* As in *L'Homme à trois visages* the proscribed hero returning in disguise after a long absence to recover his patrimony from a villainous usurper figures in Morton's *Zorinsky* (1795), which also has a comic character in the manner of Pixerécourt, a belligerent Irish soldier. A kidnapped and imprisoned wife is the center of an exciting plot in Samuel Birch's *Albert and Adelaide* (1789), as in *Les Petits Auvergnats;* and the man who mistakenly believes himself a murderer of one of his kin, finally discovering his innocence through a succession of exciting adventures and an act of God, was presented to Drury Lane audiences in Morton's *Speed the Plough* (1800) a full decade before a like figure appeared at the Ambigu in *Le Monastère abandonné.*

The identical devices to be encountered in Pixerécourt, as well as his plots, had been employed by English playwrights before him: the eternal papers which establish innocence, guilt, legitimacy, and the like are in Colman's *The Iron Chest* (1796) and Boaden's *Fontainville Forest* (1794); the "voice of the blood," in Cross's *The Purse; or, the Benevolent Tar* (1793) and Birch's *The Adopted Child* (1795); the convenient shipwreck which throws villain and hero together on the same shores where they had crossed swords years before, in Cumberland's tragedy, *The Carmelite* (1794); the curfew bell which gives the signal for an attack on a castle, in Cobb's melodramatic farce, *The Haunted Tower* (1789); the last-minute reprieve in Colman's *The Surrender of Calais* (1791); false accusation, in *The Purse; or, the Benevolent Tar* (1793); along with the other useful contrivances such as eavesdropping, black conspiracies, secret marriages, clandestine births, *reconnaissances* (discovery scenes, in English stage parlance), infants transposed in their cradles.

The sticky language melodrama employed with its heavy moral seasoning is out of the same pot used by Cumberland in his comedies; what more could one ask from the pen of Pixerécourt at his most inspired than this monologue of Lord Davenant, the villain of Cumberland's *The Mysterious Husband* when his sins find him out: "Cursed be the hour in which I wronged this man! What a clear spirit! what a lofty soul! There is stateliness and grace in virtue which guilty pride can never imitate—'sdeath! how I loathe myself—Damnation! what a wretch am I! If I had worlds, I'd give them to be free—Vain lamentation! vain remorse!—this precipice has no degrees;—down, down he falls at once, plunges into the fathomless abyss, and sinks forever!"[1]

The themes no less than the plots, devices, and language are identical: history, banditry, and the supernatural. With Shakespeare for precedent, famous figures out of the past were resuscitated to tread English stages before Tékéli, Charles the Bold, and Mary Stuart arrived by way of French and German adaptations. Robin Hood and his merry men were frequent revenants on the stage; Queen Margaret, the Prince of Wales, and the Earl of Warwick appear in Colman's *The Battle of Hexham* (1799) dealing with the Wars of the Roses; Polish annals supply the characters for *Zorinski*.

Britain bred her own spooks and bandits and put them into stories and plays before the German and French influence had begun to operate to any great extent. The former are to be encountered in the precise gothic backgrounds in which melodrama was to exploit them as early as *The Castle of Otranto*, published in 1765. This romance by Horace Walpole anticipated all the spine-chilling apparatus of such later romancers as Mrs. Anne Radcliffe and Matthew G. Lewis and a whole battalion of gothic playwrights. The period of the tale is medieval and the setting a sinister Italian castle. There is a persecuted female, Isabel, importuned by the usurper villain, Prince Manfred; a mysterious peasant coming to her aid in that stock property of melodrama, the underground passageway through which she is fleeing from her persecutor; and a comic maid, confidante of the heroine. The supernatural *dramatis personae* include a ghostly hermit appearing in the chapel and various members of a gigantic armed figure, portents of the impending doom of

---

[1] (London, 1753) Act II, sc. i.

Manfred; and thunder and lightning are introduced at dramatic moments. Devices such as the return and concealed identities are employed, and the climax turns upon a recognition scene in which the peasant hero is revealed to be the son of the old chaplain (really a distinguished nobleman) and hence the rightful heir. No German legend could do more.

In 1781 Jephson dramatized *Otranto* as a tragedy under the title of *The Count of Narbonne*, and about a decade later Mrs. Radcliffe's "tales of terror" underwent adaptation for the stage in Boaden's version of *The Italian Monk* (*Fontainville Forest*, 1793) and two versions of *Udolpho* (Henry Siddons's *Sicilian Romance; or, the Apparition of the Cliff*, 1794, and Miles Peter Andrews' *The Mysteries of the Castle*, 1794). Boaden reworked Lewis' *Monk* for Kemble in 1799 under the title of *Aurelio and Miranda*.

As for chivalrous, romantic banditry, as early as 1778, or three years before *Die Räuber* was written, Holcroft was writing *The Noble Peasant*, though it was not produced until 1784. Freebooters invade the scene also in the younger George Colman's *The Iron Chest* (1796), O'Keefe's farce, *The Castle of Andalusia* (1782), in the aforementioned *The Battle of Hexham* (1799), and in MacNally's *Robin Hood* (1781).

Many of these works are "comic operas" along the same lines as Sedaine's musical pieces, at least two of which were adapted for the English stage during this period—*Le Déserteur*, by George Colman, in 1790, and *Richard Coeur-de-Lion* twice, by General John Burgoyne and by MacNally, both in 1786. As in France, this genre was gradually adopting a sentimental, romantic type of main plot, the comedy confining itself more and more to distinct and exclusively humorous characters. With its strong admixture of music in the form of solos, duets, glees, and choruses, it was to be something like a godfather to English, as to French, melodrama.

Sentimentality, so integral a part of the melodrama formula, was an international phenomenon in western Europe during the eighteenth century, but its infiltration into stage works probably began earlier and became more pervasive in England than on the Continent. Addison and Steele played important rôles; the latter's *The Conscious Lovers* (1722) united in one stage piece for the first time the two elements of an exciting romantic intrigue and that morally orientated softness of emotion commonly designated sentimental. This amalgamation was not achieved in France until La Chaussée's *Fausse Antipathie* (1733), the first example of *comédie larmoyante*.

The premiere of *The Conscious Lovers* at Drury Lane in November of 1722 fell within the period of Destouche's residence in London, where he was an aide to the French ambassador from 1716 to 1725, attending the theatre regularly. This playwright's *Tambour Nocturne* (1736) is a version of Addison's *The Drummer; or, the Haunted House*, a classic of the English school of sentimental comedy, and his work is generally recognized as a formative influence on *comédie larmoyante* and *drame*.

Pre-melodrama stage works in England did more than tend in the same direction as French melodrama, anticipate its effects, and prepare English audiences for the finished article when it appeared in the works of Pixerécourt; the rise of melodrama in France may be attributed in some measure to the example of the British plays. When we penetrate to the fundamentals of the form, its juxtaposition of tragedy and comedy, its taste for crime and *diablerie*, its scenic splendors, and its protestant moral earnestness, we are on what is almost wholly English ground. Violence and supernatural horrors, like that other weakness of melodrama, bombastic declamation, are thick in English drama from the time of the Elizabethans, who perhaps came by them through the medium of Seneca. Among the French critics of things of this sort in English drama Voltaire was perhaps the chief; he was quite severe in his strictures on the drama of England, unembarrassed, it would seem, by the circumstance that his own plays were the channel through which much of what he called "English savagery" passed into the practice of French tragedy along with other ingredients alien to its genius. It was after his return from England in 1729 that he began to espouse innovations of Shakespearean inspiration in tragedy: the historical themes, the ghosts, the combats, the changes of scene, the pageantry, the deaths upon the stage. Geoffroy was to blame the rise of melodrama on this *anglomanie*. In the propagation of English moral seriousness on the French stage, the apostolate of Voltaire is no less important. His *Nanine* (1749), one of three dramatizations of Richardson's *Pamela* done in Paris, is a comedy in the sentimental vein of *drame*, and *L'Écossaise* (1760) belongs in the same general class.

Borrowing from English sources was direct and extensive in *drame* proper. George Lillo's *The London Merchant; or, the History of George Barnwell* and Edward Moore's *The Gamester* (1753), dealing with middle-class characters and ringing with moral lessons, provided Diderot and his disciples with models when they launched their reform of dramatic ideals and practice. Steele, Addison, and other lesser known practitioners of sentimental comedy, including Dodsley, were represented in the contents of various multivolume collections of English plays published in Paris between 1745 and 1784. French playwrights also acquired knowledge of the English theatre at first hand; besides Destouches, La Chaussée and Beaumarchais spent periods of residence across the Channel.

A cult of all things English flourished in Paris during this era. English manners, clothes, coiffure, sport, vehicles, and even cuisine ("ros' bif," punch, and tea) became the fashion. It was in the field of ideas, however, that enthusiasm was keenest. A fortnightly periodical devoted exclusively to British matters made its appearance; writers as unlike one another as Sterne, Chesterfield, Gibbon, Walpole, and Hume were feted in Paris; and translations of English books came thick and fast, many of them running into several editions. Hervey and Young have been mentioned previously in these pages, and there were many other English writers who acquired a French following. Ossian was admired as intemperately there as in Germany; Richardson was accepted as a novelist of genius—by La Chaussée, Prévost, Rousseau, and Diderot, the latter bracketing him with Moses, Homer, and Sophocles in a glowing tribute. Thomson was imitated by Florian. Madame du Deffand put English novels above French; and Baculard d'Arnaud commended the taste of the English nation at the expense of that of his own country, his criterion being, however, accessibility to the charms of graveyards, ghosts, and demons.

There was no more pronounced or vociferous Anglophile than Mercier before patriotism effected a change in his views at the end of the century. He did two adaptations of Shakespeare—his "favorite author"; cited Shakespearean precedent in the course of the wordy warfare he waged against "the rules"; and preached and practiced that very English infraction of the neoclassic code, mixture of the genres. The genres had been mixed in *opéra comique* before this, Sedaine showing the way in *Le Déserteur* (1769). Sedaine began his career in the musical drama with an adaptation of Dodsley's *The Miller of Mansfield* (*Le Roi et le fermier*), another version of which, Collé's *Partie de chasse de Henri IV*, was the most frequently reprised piece in the repertory of the Française in the decade preceding the Revolution. Sedaine, who thus can be said to have cut his teeth upon English plays, was the writer who introduced the note of moral improvement in *opéra comique*.

Finally it was the English romance that determined the last phase in the evolution of the pantomime into melodrama as has been noticed above. The gothic tales of Mrs. Radcliffe and "Monk" Lewis took Paris by storm. Several editions of both *Udolpho* and *Ambrosio; or, the Monk* were issued in quick succession in translation, and dramatic versions of each were numerous on the Boulevard—four, in the case of *Udolpho*. Gothic romance leads to the villain himself; "what distinguishes *Le Moine* from all pantomimes which preceded it," writes Alexis Pitou, "is only the inconceivable blackness of its villains . . ."[2] After running through the record one feels justified in asserting that melodrama, when it made its way onto the British stage at the dawn of the nineteenth century, did so not as an interloping alien but rather as a returning native son, whose unfamiliar aspect was nothing more than a superficial polish acquired on the Grand Tour.

[2] "Les Origines du mélodrame français à la fin du XVIII siècle," *Revue d'histoire littéraire*, June 1911, p. 281.

XV

Patent House Melodrama

O superb theatres, too small for parks, too enormous for houses, which exclude comedy and comfort, and have a monopoly for performing nonsense gigantically! —BULWER-LYTTON, *Paul Clifford*

Mr. Vincent Crummles had bought a real pump and two washing-tubs, he told Nicholas Nickelby at their momentous first meeting on the road to Portsmouth; and of that promising young man he bespoke a drama for the Crummles' travelling theatrical company in which these imposing acquisitions might be given the opportunity they deserved—a composition that might serve them as *Pizarro* served his donkey. "That's the London plan," he assured his astonished companion, new to the ways of the profession. "They look up some dresses and properties and have a piece written to fit 'em. Most of the theatres keep an author on purpose."

It *was* the London plan; Dickens' fooling was not far off from sober fact. The theatres of the metropolis set great store by more or less spectacular visual effects; from pumps to cataracts and volcanoes, realistic exhibits were introduced on every possible occasion. A process was working itself out not unlike that which has been noticed on the Boulevard du Temple: the consolidation of the pantomimic spectacle with the spoken drama, and the frame upon which it went forward was the same as in Paris, namely, the melodramatic play. One important difference must be pointed out, however; in England the stages of the great theatres, corresponding to the Comédie Française, were the laboratory.

At the end of the eighteenth century there was no "Boulevard du Crime" in London, no area consecrated by tradition to the popular theatre; and a decade or more was to elapse before anything comparable to it in size and importance came into existence across the river on the Surrey Side. Meanwhile, with the growth of the city a new theatrical public was coming into being, and it was crowding into the great houses for its entertainment. There was plenty of room for this popular audience, and certainly it was welcome. The new Drury Lane of 1794 accommodated more than 3,500 people, compared to the 2,000 of its predecessor, and the new

Covent Garden was greatly enlarged to seat 3,000 in 1808. Built and furnished on a lavish scale, both structures involved tremendous outlays. The fixed charges arising from these investments were a heavy burden which fell upon the lessees. Under these conditions it became a matter of life and death to attract crowds.

As audiences grew larger they necessarily grew less discriminating; the small and select company which had quickened to the wit of Wycherley and Congreve became diluted in Garrick's time and later was engulfed in what was frequently little better than a miscellaneous mob. The galleries gained control; paying the piper, they insisted on calling the tune. And what a tune it was! These new patrons of the art of the drama, addicted hereditarily to cock-fighting, pugilism, and bull-baiting (not outlawed until 1820) in their diversions, demanded something more lively than refinement of character development, beauty of language, or subtlety of wit. A show was what they wanted—and the louder, gaudier, and longer it was, the better they liked it.

As to the recipe for these shows, experience was agreed. Time and again melodramatic spectacle with circus trimmings—introduced as early as Garrick's time—saved the day for both houses. In 1803 Frederick Reynolds' *The Caravan; or, the Driver and His Dog* replenished sadly depleted coffers at Drury Lane. This was a crude melodrama of Spanish setting, with dungeons, trap doors, processions, combats, and thrilling escapes, the chief attraction being the rescue of a drowning child by a dog. In 1823 another financial catastrophe was averted by Moncrieff's *The Cataract of the Ganges* with its twelve changes of scene, two "grand processions," singing, dancing and—the *pièce de résistance*—a cataract reproduced realistically on the stage (with running water), which the heroine scaled on horseback amid flames and musket fire at the thundering climax. During a return engagement in 1823 of "Mr. Ducrow and his magnificent stud of horses" in Lewis' *Timour the Tartar*, which had a similar scene and a cavalry combat, the management found it necessary to post notices announcing that, on account of "the extra overflow" from every part of the house, no "orders" would be admitted.

At Covent Garden, "the destruction of the Temple of the Sun by an earthquake in *The Virgin of the Sun* and of a large Moorish vessel by a waterspout in a revival of Dryden's *Don Sebastian, King of Portugal* were two of the principal features of these successful pieces," writes Frederick Reynolds discussing the season of 1811–12 in his autobiography; and the same chronicler, who was reader and adviser to the management, records additional facts bearing on the financial importance of spectacles: "The largest annual receipt ever taken at Covent Garden was in the season of 1810–11, 100,000 pounds . . . the whole of the additional sum, over the usual receipts, was entirely produced by the introduction of cavalry upon the stage. . . . The first forty-one nights of *Bluebeard*, revived with the horses, produced above 21,000 pounds."[1] Manager Harris, in a chancery suit, gave testimony that his theatre had not made a shilling on regular drama from 1808 to 1821, but had subsisted entirely on pantomime, spectacle, and melodrama.

In play after play, ghosts, vampires, and Frankensteinian monsters menaced mortal maids in lurid moonlit glens, thunderbolts struck down villains in the last act, men-o'-war exploded magnificently and sank in seas of real water, forests and castles burst into flames, walls tottered and fell before the onslaught of besiegers, bridges collapsed carrying scoundrels to their doom, avalanches and inundations transformed the stage into scenes of desolation, and jumbles of pantomime, opera, and farce rode to triumph on the backs of prize bulls and real elephants. It was the exception rather than the rule for the legitimate theatre, as serious literary drama was called, to make money.

Even great acting, in worthy or unworthy vehicles, lost much of its appeal. John Philip Kemble, save at the end of his career as Alfred Bunn pointed out, played to prevailingly lean rather than overflowing houses, even with his imperial sister, Mrs. Siddons, to support him; and Edmund Kean's popularity was fluctuating, attaining its peak in Maturin's pinchbeck tragedy, *Bertram* (1816), which provided him with his most successful part. The greatest audiences of this outstanding tragedian were dwarfed alongside the throngs which pressed into Covent Garden in 1804 to witness the thirteen-year-old "boy Roscius," Henry West Betty ("Master Betty"), "whose celebrity was so excessive that though *unseen* and *untried* on the London stage, it was with truth averred that not a place could be procured for the first six nights."[2] The freak always outdrew the artist, and this juvenile was in the nature of a freak, like the horse, wild beast, and dog dramas, which were in constant

[1] *The Life and Times of Frederick Reynolds* (London, 1827), Vol. II, pp. 390, 403–404.
[2] *Ibid.*, p. 359.

demand: *Jocko, the Brazilian Monkey* (in which the ape steals a pardon); *El Hyder Ali* (lions attacked soldiers, and boa constrictors entwined themselves about the hero in this one); the various versions of *Le Chien de Montargis* and *La Pie voleuse* (three of the latter in one season); *The Ravens of Orleans* (from one of the *Ingoldsby Legends*); Reynolds' *The Dog Gellert;* and *Thalaba the Destroyer,* wherein the ostrich made its first appearance on any dramatic stage.

Since it contributed little to the box office, the traditional classical drama was put more and more in the shade. Melodramatic spectacles in the form of afterpieces shared the boards with poetic tragedy—and the tail wagged the dog. To assure the success of Macready's Shakespearean debut at Covent Garden in 1816, the management had the happy thought of putting *Aladdin* on the same bill; the crowds came to see the elephants and tolerated *Othello.* At this house in the following season *Romeo and Juliet* and *Hamlet* had the benefit of sharing the stage with *Puss in Boots* and Pocock's *The Miller and His Men* respectively. This last was a famous thriller whose popularity persisted for upwards of three quarters of a century throughout the English-speaking world and even longer in the toy theatre. It is deserving of a moment's attention.

In the guise of an honest, respectable miller, the villain Grindorf presses his aged competitor, Kelmar, whom he has brought to the verge of ruin, for his lovely daughter, Claudine. She, however, loves Lothair, the poor hero. This young man is able to extract a pledge from Kelmar that the parental blessing will be forthcoming if he, Lothair, succeeds in ridding the region of a gang of nocturnal brigands led by a mysterious character known as "the Wolf." Now "the Wolf" is really Grindorf, as Lothair discovers when, in disguise, he joins the gang and penetrates to the cave which is their headquarters.

The villain leads a midnight raid on Kelmar's cottage in an attempt to abduct Count Friberg, a nobleman of the region who, with his garrulous comic servant Karl (the names suggest a German source), has taken shelter there for the night. The raid is repulsed, and Grindorf, barely escaping exposure, succeeds in turning suspicion away from himself and toward Kelmar. Meanwhile he has carried off Claudine to his retreat and placed her in the custody of Lothair, whose identity he never once suspects, melodramatic disguises being impenetrable.

Combats, raids, and pursuits pile up in the rattling climax; Grindorf is unmasked; Friberg's vassals arrive in force and move on the cave to attempt a rescue of Claudine; Lothair escapes, bearing the fainting heroine in his arms; and the brigands are blown up *en masse* when a mine, laid by the hero, explodes with a magnificent roar.

This was the very pattern of a stage success in the patent houses: a violent romantic intrigue, its exciting incident set off against overpowering stage effects and varied at intervals by broad comedy. Constructed along the same lines were William Dimond's *The Hunter of the Alps, The Ethiop; or, the Child of the Desert* and *The Foundling of the Forest; or, Twice the Dagger Struck*, Edward Fitzball's *The Devil's Elixir; or, the Shadowless Man*, William Thomas Moncrieff's *Zoroaster; or, the Spirit of the Star*, Fanny Kemble's *Illusion; or, the Trances of Nourjahad*, James Robinson Planché's *The Red Mask; or, the Council of Three* and *Ali Pacha; or, the Signet Ring*, John Howard Payne's *The Two Galley Slaves*, Frederick Reynolds' *The Black Prince; or, the Edict of Charlemagne*, Isaac Pocock's *For England Ho!* and *Alfred; or, the Enchanted Standard*, and Richard Brinsley Peake's *The Haunted Inn*. All these were given at one or the other of the patent houses during the first thirty years of the century.

The sources of this early melodrama were foreign plays, historical anecdotes and patriotic reminiscences, operatic libretti, romantic narrative poems by Southey, Byron and Scott, romances, and the Arabian Nights Entertainment. France, of course, was an important source of foreign plays. Bouilly's *L'Abbé de l'Épée* had been given at Drury Lane in Holcroft's version, *Deaf and Dumb*, nearly two years before the premiere of *A Tale of Mystery*, and Caigniez's *Le Jugement de Salomon* six months after at the Haymarket in a version by Boaden, *The Voice of Nature*. Other Parisian successes followed in large numbers. *Tékéli*, by Pixerécourt, was a huge success in London, and there were four versions each of this author's *La Peste de Marseille, L'Homme à trois visages* and *Charles le Téméraire*. The dog and bird dramas were received with acclaim. Virtually every English dramatist of the era did at least one adaptation from the French, and some of them, Planché for example, as many as thirty. Allardyce Nicoll estimates that fully half of the plays written in England during this period (1800–1850) must have been suggested by Parisian models and many were literally adapted by English authors. A heavy proportion of them were melodramas, as may be seen from his "Hand-List of Plays Produced between 1800 and 1850."[3]

Melodrama did not make its way onto the boards of the patent houses without a fight. A minority of intelligent and cultivated playgoers was fully alive to the meretricious character of the repertoire, as were the critics. Opposition even became militant and organized at times, but that melodrama was preferred to the contemporary serious drama was not entirely the fault of the public. The serious drama as written during this period showed a sad decline, and the writers to whom one might naturally have looked for something better failed to rise to the occasion. Bulwer-Lytton is an example of the literary man who did succeed in the theatre by looking to the contemporary drama of France for his models. His *The Lady of Lyons; or, Love and Pride*, given first in Macready's production of 1838 at Covent Garden, was the most popular five-act play of the century, virtually every romantic actor on both sides of the Atlantic appearing in it down to Irving and Booth.

Claude Melnotte, a gardener's son, but extraordinarily gifted with all the romantic virtues and accomplishments, writes verses to Pauline Deschappelles, the fair daughter of a wealthy bourgeois of Lyons. He is rewarded with scorn for his pains by the haughty beauty when she discovers his lowly station, and in revenge he lends himself to a cruel hoax devised by one Beauséant, a noble villain who has a similar grievance against the lady. Masquerading as the Prince of Como, the gardener's son woos the snobbish damsel, astonishing everyone by the brilliancy of his wit and the elegance of his manners—and wins. After the marriage ceremony has been performed, however, he finds that he cannot go on with the comedy. He loves Pauline too deeply to deceive her further and confesses everything. She spurns him, and he leaves for the wars in despair, pausing only long enough to cross swords in her behalf and sustain a wound—a service which softens somewhat the heart of the cheated bride toward him.

It is three years later when the last act begins. Pauline, who is procuring a divorce, has consented to marry Beauséant, in order to save her father from financial ruin, though by now she has come to love the absent Claude and to regret her hasty dismissal of him. The

[3] In *A History of English Drama, 1660–1900*, rev. ed. (Cambridge, 1952–1959), Vol. IV: *Early Nineteenth Century Drama, 1800–1850*.

families are assembled to sign the marriage contract. In the company
is a mysterious Colonel Morier, back from the wars rich and loaded
with honors—Melnotte in disguise, of course; he stands in a corner
holding a cloak before his face.

BEAUSÉANT (*from the table*)
The papers are prepared—we only need
Your hand and seal.

MELNOTTE
          Stay, lady—one word more.
Were but your duty with your faith united,
Would you still share the low-born peasant's lot?

PAULINE
Would I? Ah, better death with him I love
Than all the pomp—which is but as the flowers
That crown the victim!—(*turning away*). I am
     ready.

(MELNOTTE *rushes to* DAMAS)

DAMAS [*the Notary*]
This is the schedule—this the total.

BEAUSÉANT (*to* DESCHAPPELLES *showing notes*)
                              These
Are yours the instant she has signed; you are
Still the great house of Lyons!

(The NOTARY *is about to hand the contract to* PAULINE, *when*
MELNOTTE *seizes it and tears it.*)

BEAUSÉANT
                    Are you mad?

MONS. DESCHAPPELLES
How, Sir! What means this insult?

MELNOTTE
                    Peace, old man!
I have a prior claim. Before the face
Of man and Heaven I urge it; I outbid
Your sordid huckster for your priceless jewel.
(*Giving a pocket-book*)
There is the sum twice told! Blush not to take it:

There's not a coin that is not bought and hallowed
In the cause of nations with a soldier's blood!

BEAUSÉANT

Torments and death!

PAULINE

That voice! Thou art—

MELNOTTE

Thy husband!

(PAULINE *rushes into his arms*)   [Act V, sc. 2.]

Bulwer's *Richelieu; or, the Conspiracy* (1839) was only a little less popular than *The Lady of Lyons*, and it has endured longer in the theatre; Walter Hampden played it to crowded houses in the early 1930's, and George Arliss made a movie of it. The plot concerns itself with an elaborate conspiracy at the court of Louis XIII to assassinate the Cardinal-Duke and depose the king in favor of the Duke of Orleans; it is frustrated by the old churchman's cunning and courage, the fidelity of his page boy, and the gratitude of a young cavalier in love with the Cardinal's niece—not to speak of the incredible fumbling of the conspirators themselves. The intrigue turns upon the possession of an incriminating dispatch (the papers), which changes hands several times in the course of the action under highly dramatic, and usually preposterous, circumstances. But the thing acted. The rôle of the old cardinal, created by Macready, was one of which actors dream. What situations! What lines! Richelieu in disgrace, relinquishing state papers to his successor and firing keen questions at him which lay bare his utter incompetence, while the king looks on and shudders; Richelieu discovering that he can no longer wield his sword and consoling himself with the epigram: "Beneath the rule of men entirely great, the pen is mightier than the sword"; Richelieu rebuking his faltering page boy and spurring him on to redoubled exertions with the immortal line: "In the lexicon which fate reserves for a bright manhood, there is no such word as fail!"; Richelieu in that scene which Booth is reported to have done so magnificently, drawing an imaginary circle about a defenseless girl and saving her from the lust of a king with the thundering challenge: "Mark, sire, where she stands! About her form I draw the awful circle of our solemn church. Set but a foot within that holy ground, and on your head—

yea, though it wear a crown–I launch the curse of Rome!" (Act IV, sc. 1.)

Though they are written in blank verse and have no specifically comic characters, these plays are essentially melodramas, with their simplified character types, their flamboyant heroics, and their happy ends; and they were adopted enthusiastically into the melodramatic repertoire everywhere.

Bulwer as a playwright came upon the scene on the eve of the revocation of the privileges of the patent houses with the passage of the Theatrical Regulation Act (1843), which placed all London theatres on the same footing–officially on the same footing, it should be said, since this legal action, long overdue, did little more than recognize a condition which had existed in fact for upward of a generation. The real life of the English theatre had already departed from the patent houses, taking refuge in various minor theatres, many of them across the Thames on the Surrey Side. Preliminary to dealing with them, however, it is necessary to fill in some background on the relationship of music to melodrama, a relationship of special importance in the development of minor house melodrama in England.

XVI

The Opera and Music in Melodrama

PUFF: *Now then for soft music.*
SNEER: *Pray what's that for?*
PUFF: *It shows that Tilburnia is coming—*
nothing introduces your heroine like
soft music.
—SHERIDAN, *The Critic* (1779)

William Gillette, in a speech in 1913 before the Academy of Arts and Letters, complaining of the inadequacy of theatrical terminology, fixed upon melodrama as an example—"certainly not drama with music," he said. With due deference to so distinguished a writer and interpreter of the genre, it must be insisted that this is exactly what melodrama was for a long period of its history, though it was never merely that. To a certain extent it was still drama with music at the end of the nineteenth century and into the twentieth. Gillette must surely have seen Booth in *Richelieu* and Irving in *The Bells* and *The Corsican Brothers*, if not *Gambler of the West*, *Chinatown Charlie*, and other items of the "ten, twent', thirt'" repertoire. All these productions gave the musicians in the pit plenty to do. We have the testimony of Augustus Thomas on the subject, in a reference to the "Adiós, amor" air which accompanies the character of Tony throughout this writer's *Arizona* (1899): ". . . it being a melodrama and having the powerful old-fashioned advantage of the right to use identifying musical themes," writes this dramatist, a contemporary of Gillette, in his reminiscences, *The Print of My Remembrance*.[1]

There can be no question of the importance of music in the early days. Pixerécourt and his contemporaries used an orchestra throughout their plays; both in France and England a musical score was written especially for virtually every melodrama given at the principal houses, the composer's name being mentioned along with the playwright's in the printed version of the play. Nowhere save in opera did music play a more important part. There were a few

[1] (New York, 1922) p. 360.

identifying bars played at entrances and often at exits, a convention which became more or less standardized in an ominous rumble of the contrabass for the villain, a trumpet fanfare for the hero, flute trills for the heroine, and a ribald guffaw from the bassoon for the comic. Songs were introduced here and there; accompaniments were played to the ballets and divertissements introduced so frequently in the plays; and descriptive passages sustained the prolonged stretches of dumb show (as in the third act of *Cœlina*) and accompanied dialogue to heighten various dramatic effects, the crash of brass at catastrophes, and the soft music for tender and pathetic scenes being examples.

Buzby's music for *A Tale of Mystery*, Holcroft's adaptation of *Cœlina*, which probably followed Quaisin's score for the original production in Paris, may be taken as an example of the thoroughgoing way in which the orchestra followed each turn of the plot in early melodrama. At the beginning of the play, when the heroine and Tiennette discuss the arrival of the villain, "music to express discontent and alarm" is directed. It is played "alarmingly" at the entrance of Dr. Andrevon, "piano" when he begins to speak, and "loud and discordant" when his eye catches Trugelin's. Subsequent directions run the gamut of the emotions: "hurrying" and "confused" music, music "to express chattering contention" and "pain and disorder," "music of doubt and terror," "soft music" after the conspirators plan their murders followed by "music expressing pain and alarm," and then "the successive feelings of the scene." "Terror, confusion, menace and command" are the rather bewildering demands for the climactic scene in which the villain's letter is read; and when Cœlina shrieks, the music "likewise shrieks." Such a music plot was not original with Pixerécourt. He borrowed and adapted rather than invented as was his custom generally. A generation and more of Boulevard and *forain* experimenters had prepared the way for him.

In hunting down the immediate origins of music in melodrama, we find the trail leading to a strange source. Although Jean Jacques Rousseau wrote no melodramas as we understand the term, and he had no traffic with the theatres of the Boulevard where the form began to take shape toward the end of his life (he died in 1778), he did bequeath it a name though unwittingly. *Mélo-drame* is his term, invented in 1766 (or borrowed from the Italians, who applied an equivalent term to opera) to describe his *Pygmalion*. Considered by itself this work, written in a style known formally as *scène lyrique,* seems a long way from the dramas of action and spectacle which came to be designated as melodramas. It is a dramatic monologue introducing the classical figure of the title, who, as the curtain rises, is discovered chiselling and apostrophizing a nearly completed nude marble figure of a beautiful woman. After his considerable flow of ardent rhetoric, Galatea sighs marmoreally, stirs, and, breathing a few words, falls into the arms of her adoring creator. This is all; no spectacle, no murders, no conspiracies, no villain, no crowds on the stage, no bustle—no moral lesson even. Turning to the music which accompanies this fable, however, we discover some grounds for linking it with melodrama.

Pygmalion was a by-product of the controversy over the respective merits of Italian and French opera, the war of the Lullists and the Buffonists, which raged in Paris at the middle of the century and in which Rousseau was a participant. At first (1751) a partisan of the Lullists or "the Queen's party," which opposed the Italians, he changed sides in his *Letter on French Music* (1753), contending that the French language was unfitted by its harshness for recitative in the Italian manner. *Pygmalion* was in the nature of an attempt to find an alternative method of using music in a dramatic production. In this *mélo-drame*, music expressive of the emotions of a situation is played, the actor meanwhile filling in with appropriate pantomime; when the music ceases, the actor begins to speak, putting into words what has previously been conveyed by airs and gestures. This alternation continues.

The work was given at Lyons in 1771, at Weimar in 1772, and at the Français four years later, with music in part of Rousseau's own composition. It was well received by the public, if not by the critics, and remained in the repertory until 1816, but it failed to launch a school and effect a fundamental reform in French opera.

In the meantime, Georg Benda, a Bohemian, and kappelmeister to the Duke of Gotha, had brought out his *Ariadne auf Naxos* (*Ein Duodrama mit musikalischen Zwischensatzen*) at Gotha in 1774. This was an opera with libretto by Jean Christian Brandes using music in the *Pygmalion* manner, which the composer would seem to have hit upon independently. He carried his work to Paris in 1781 where it was given unsuccessfully at the Italiennes in a version by Dubois called a *mélodrama*. Returning to Germany, Benda pushed his experiment a step further in *Medea*, arranging for the dialogue to be "spoken through" the music—"a recitative with instruments, the actor speaking instead of singing," in the words of Mozart, who employed it in two long passages in *Zaïde* (1789). This is melo-drama as it is understood by musicians. It has had quite a career under respectable musical auspices, especially in Germany. A very beautiful example occurs in the grave-digging scene in *Fidelio*.

Not long after *Pygmalion* and *Ariadne* had their debuts in Paris, popular entertainments were to be met with at the fairs and along the Boulevard which used music in the manner which these works introduced. In Mayeur de Saint Paul's *La Pomme ou le prix de beauté* (1779) and Florian's *Galatheé* (1785) an orchestra sustained dialogue; and in *Baron de Trenck* (1788) pantomimic interludes are accompanied by tunes from current operas and passages indicated as *airs d'action*, *airs de combat*, and the like. Gaiffe attaches great importance to this line of descent for melodrama; in his study of *drame* during the eighteenth century he traces the steps by which the unpretentious little musical shows, originally monologues or short scenes with two characters, increased the number of per-formers and substituted a realistic contemporary milieu for a pastoral-mythological one. He cites *L'Élève de la Nature* (1781) as being virtually a domestic melodrama.[2]

Meanwhile *opéra comique*, whose influence upon Pixerécourt has been noted in Chapter IV, was adopting melodramatic libretti, and Audinot was using descriptive scores throughout his dumb show spectacles at the Ambigu. When these latter productions took on speech at the Revolution to become *pantomime dialoguée*, the music was retained. *Lente et terrible* is a contemporary description of the accompaniment played to the unearthly adventures of Raoul in *Le Château du diable*.

The word *mélo-drame* was applied generally throughout this transitional period in the literal sense of drama with music. During 1784 and 1785 at the Beaujolais, rustic comedies accompanied by potpourris of airs in the mode were called *mélo-drames*.[3] The term became definitely and exclusively attached by association to our genre in the first decade of the new century. A. W. Schlegel uses it in this sense, writing in 1818.[4] Pixerécourt is mainly responsible for this engrossment. His early plays were labelled either *drame à grand spectacle* or simply *comédie*, but from *La Femme à deux maris*

[2] Gaiffe, p. 238.
[3] Pitou, p. 258.
[4] *A Course of Lectures on Dramatic Art and Literature* (London, 1846), p. 334.

(1802) onward they are all *mélo-drames*. Lesser playwrights followed his example. After 1830 in France melodramatists in the main called their works *drames*, imitating the Romanticists. Ducange was the earliest to do so with his *Il y a seize ans* (1835). Pixerécourt was one of the few who held to the old term; his last play, *Latude* (1834), was advertised as a *mélodrame*—the hyphen by this time being generally discarded.

There was no abatement in the use of music in melodrama during the lifetime of Pixerécourt, and Romantic drama imitated its humble precursor in this as in other particulars. Music had early begun to insinuate itself into the drama in the London patent houses, where the aesthetic objection to it was less formidable than in the first theatre of France. Ballad operas of the type of *The Beggar's Opera* and Italian opera accustomed playgoers to the introduction of tunes in the regular theatre. Garrick had soft music played offstage through the recognition scene of Lear and Cordelia and slow music accompanied the descent of the final curtain on *Werther* (1786), *The Gamester*, and a few other dramas given at the patent houses in the last quarter of the century.

Eventually the demand for more and more melodies resulted in a species of entertainment which was a confusion of tragedy, comedy and opera. Colman's *The Mountaineers* (1793) was probably the first example of the mixed form. *The Battle of Hexham, Robin Hood*, and Colman's *The Iron Chest*, a "comic opera" derived from *Caleb Williams*, are other examples. Michael Kelly, the singer, tells in his memoirs of composing an accompaniment for the appearance of the ghost in *The Castle Spectre;* and in *Perouse; or, the Desert Island* (1801) from Kotzebue there is that specific melodramatic device, stretches of dumb show with music, precedent for which can be found in English as well as French pantomime. *Mélodrame* in the manner of *Pygmalion* was not unknown; "Monk" Lewis' *The Captive*, given first at Covent Garden in 1803 and revived in 1881 by Ellen Terry, was entirely in this style. This "monodrama" was a dreadful concoction, its single character being a woman imprisoned in a dungeon and slowly going mad. The grueling performance was not repeated, which recalls *Nicholas Nickelby* and Mrs. Crummles' experience in her celebrated title role in *The Blood Drinker*. "Did it disagree with her?" asked Nicholas innocently, when told that she had to give it up. "Not so much with her as with her audiences," replied the lady's proud spouse. "Nobody could stand it. It was too tremendous."

Comic operas of the type noticed in Chapter XIV continued to be given through the nineteenth century in England, tending to approach melodrama more and more in character after 1800, and dropping the word "comic" from their descriptive titles. It is not always easy to draw a line of demarcation between the two forms. Vocalization and dancing can be as thick in melodrama as in comic opera; and plots, construction, character types and denouements follow a common pattern. Continental operatic libretti were often given as melodramas, *Les Huguenots*, *La Muette de Portici*, *Guillaume Tell*, *La Juive*, and others being popular all over London for decades in this form.

With the degradation of the drama, opera came to supplant tragedy with audiences of the better class in London, as it did in New York at this time. Gilbert à Beckett's jingle tells the story—

> When MUSIC, being all the rage,
> Usurped possession of the stage,
> The PASSIONS, flying in a hurry,
> Took refuge at the "Vic" and Surrey.

One hundred nights were devoted to the musical drama in the Drury Lane season of 1813–14, and in the thirties Alfred Bunn made it something like staple entertainment at Covent Garden, launching that house on its career as the English home of Italian opera, officially confirmed in 1847.

Balfe's *The Maid of Artois* (1836) is typical of native British opera. Bunn's libretto is worth glancing at. Isoline, the heroine, has been abducted by a marquis, the villain; and the hero, Jules, in attempting a rescue, is overpowered by the nobleman's servants and shipped off to the penal colony in Guiana. The intrepid Isoline eludes her captor and, in the second act, makes her way across the ocean disguised as a sailor boy. Arrived in the New World, she gains access to her lover in yet another disguise, that of a Sister of Charity, and thy escape together, after locking the brutal overseer in Jules's cell. In the denouement the fugitives are rescued by the marquis himself, a reformed man now, who confesses his fault and pleads for forgiveness.

The Maid of Artois, like the better-known *The Bohemian Girl* by the same composer, was a "comic opera"; that is to say, spoken dialogue rather than recitative provided the padding between the all-important arias as in *opéra comique*. However, on the Continent, particularly in France, not only this form but grand opera also, as it developed out of *opera seria* in the hands of Rossini and Auber, was becoming more and more melodramatic. Early in the century this traditionally aristocratic entertainment, part spectacle and part concert in composition and predominantly pastoral or mythological in theme, began to address itself to a wider public and to respond to more vital impulses in the life about it than it had previously done. Figures such as Cortez (in Spontini's work), William Tell, and Masaniello, many of them with revolutionary implications, tended to supplant Orpheus, Dido, and Iphigenia, who had been sufficient for Gluck and Piccini; and with new subjects the form took on a new character the better to enforce its strenuous moral: dynamic and exciting plots picturing virtuous innocence harried by malignant villainy. Rossini's *The Siege of Corinth* is an example. This stage of operatic evolution is usually lumped with Romanticism, but its affinities are really with humble melodrama.

It probably began with Beethoven, at least among first-rate composers. That great master's zeal for human liberty, his passionate participation in those humanitarian enthusiasms sweeping across Europe in his day, led him to strange sources in his long quest for suitable libretti for the operas he planned. His correspondence reveals various overtures to Kotzebue, of all people, the spurious "sensibility" of the author of *Rollas Tod* having apparently taken him in. For his *Fidelio* he finally selected Bouilly's *opéra comique, Léonore ou l'amour conjugal*, which Sonnleithner reworked for him (1805) after two other composers had set it to music—Caveaux in Paris, and Paër in Vienna. This play, originally written as a *fait historique* with songs (1798), is pure melodrama, all the essential elements being present: Florestan, the persecuted innocent, held in a dungeon by the villain Pizarro; the faithful Léonore, gaining access to her spouse in boy's disguise; the *reconnaissance* in the big third-act climax ("Another word and you are dead!"); the rescuing troops when all seems lost; and even the three-act form and the incidental comedy.

It was fully twenty years after *Fidelio*, that *La Muette de Portici* (libretto by Scribe) arrived, a work whose dumb heroine, to fix upon one element out of many, is eloquently expressive of melodramatic ancestry. Along with Auber came Rossini, famous for his musical storms and noisy crescendos; and finally that happy partnership, the prestidigitating team of Scribe and Meyerbeer, through which the melodramatic opera attained its apogee and melodrama itself got many a plot. Meyerbeer, as a matter of fact, admired and cultivated Pixerécourt, set *Marguerite d'Anjou* as an opera which was produced at the Odéon in Paris, and bespoke other libretti.[5] Weber's operas, different in their source from those of the Italian and French schools and more genuine in feeling than either, are not less melodramatic with their folklore demonology and their comic relief. Musically the affinity of Weber's work with melodrama is even more interesting. The passage which announces the entrance of the Black Huntsman in *Der Freischütz*—that memorable shiver of the violins accompanying the deeper tones of the clarinette and the sinister pounding of the drums—is merely the crude identifying motif of melodrama given new values by an artist. Wagner, who acknowledged his debt to Weber, was to do much more with this pregnant musical idea.

In 1824 Weber's masterpiece, which had its English premiere at Covent Garden, was the means of introducing one of the most popular themes in English melodrama and a type of stage effect more widely copied, perhaps, than any other in the whole range of the genre: the black art and the incantation scene. All London was held spellbound by that catastrophic second act which aroused only laughter in Paris: the sinister mountain defile where the action passes with its moonlight, its flapping bats and hooting owls; the apparition of the Black Huntsman (surrounded by blue fire) from a trap; the bargaining for a human soul while the demonic fire spits and glows; and the bloodcurdling climax when the final bullet is cast amid the flashing of lightning, the plunging of meteors, and the darting of flames from the bowels of the earth. It was this carnival of supernatural effects, rather than Weber's music—not heard in anything like its entirety until the third, or Drury Lane, produc-tion—that made *Der Freischütz* one of the most enduringly popular theatrical, in distinction to operatic, entertainments of the century in London.

Imitations came thick and fast; Devil's Glens or their equivalents and transactions with the Evil One became ubiquitous on English and American stages. Titles of plays given in the thirties and forties are revealing: Jerrold's *The Devil's Ducat*, Almar's *The Fire Raiser*, Fitzball's *Warlock Kennilston*, T. Dibdin's *The Sixes; or, the Devil and the Dice*, Peake's *The Evil Eye*, Amherst's *The Infernal Secret;*

---

[5] Pixerécourt, "Souvenirs de la Révolution," *Théâtre choisi*, Vol. II, p. iii.

or, the Invulnerable, Oxenford's *The Dice of Death.* Kindred to the *Freischütz* imitations were the gnome, spook, and monster plays. Here again German folklore frightfulness provided the material in a great many instances. At least one of the tales of E. T. A. Hoffman inspired an English melodrama, *The Devil's Elixir* (1829). *Faust* was made into a practicable stage play not fewer than twenty times in London before the middle of the century, and Fitzball's *The Flying Dutchman* was a famous success. This playwright–stage manager, with his genius for weird stage effects with blue fire and the like, became a specialist in supernatural, as he was in nautical, melodrama.

The English Opera House (later the Lyceum) in the Strand, which had been licensed by the Lord Chamberlain in 1809 for musical-dramatic entertainments and ballets, became a headquarters for the melodrama-cum-opera entertainments of the *Freischütz* type, even before Weber's work had its London premiere there. The repertory of this house drew heavily upon Teutonic sources. One of Lewis' early garnerings from this store, *One o'clock; or, the Knight and the Wood Daemon* (1811) was given here, as were Peake's *Bottle Imp* (1821), Buckstone's *The Death-Fetch; or, the Student of Gottingen* (1826), Fitzball's *Keolanthe; or, the Unearthly Bride* (1841), an opera, score by Balfe, and Planché's adaptation of Marschner's *Der Vampyr* (1820). Native genius was represented by dramatizations of traditional English ghost stories, including those about Herne the Hunter and the Lancashire Witches, and adaptations of *Frankenstein,* Mary Shelley's novel, which was presented twice on the London stage during 1823. Other nations contributed material to this theatrical Walpurgis Night: Ireland in Moncrieff's *Eily; or, the Banshee;* Scotland in dramatizations of those Highland legends given currency by Scott and Macpherson; and the Orient in a veritable swarm of magical plays and spectacles.

The English Opera House became an entering wedge for the penetration by the minor houses into the patent houses' very own bailiwick, Westminster, within whose limits the two great houses were protected from competition in a special way by their patents and by acts of Parliament. Music was to play a major part in the further encroachments by the independent theatres on the monopoly enjoyed by Drury Lane and Covent Garden. This story can best be told in connection with the history of the transpontine minors, which beckon us now from across Westminster Bridge.

XVII

The Rise of the Minors

I gape in Covent Garden's walls,
I doze in Drury Lane;
I strive in the Lyceum's stalls
To keep awake in vain.
There's naught in the dramatic way
That I can quite abide,
Except the pieces that they play
Upon the Surrey side.

—H. S. LEIGH

On the Surrey Side melodrama begins as pure pantomimic spectacle, taking the peculiar form of equestrian drama, which, as we have seen, the great houses were not above copying. This type of entertainment grew out of the riding schools and exhibits of horsemanship inaugurated by Philip Astley, an old trooper whose art had been admired by Marie Antoinette and Dr. Johnson, at his circus near the foot of Westminster Bridge in the 1770's and imitated by Charles Hughes, a strong man by trade, at his rival amphitheatre nearby, the Royal Circus, ancestor of the Surrey. In their original form these resorts consisted of open-air "horse rides" encircled by rows of benches under canvas awnings; toward the end of the century they were rebuilt in more permanent and pretentious style, with a roof, a gallery, boxes, and a stage at one side of the ring.

In the 1780's the transpontine horse shows took on the semblance of a plot often built around some triumph of British arms; *The Death of General Wolf* was one such and *The Destruction of the Bastille* another. This amalgamation of horsemanship and drama appears to have been the inspiration of Charles Dibdin the elder, who associated himself with Hughes when his amphitheatre was rebuilt lavishly in Blackfriars Road in 1782 and became the Royal Circus. Dibdin used the stage for his more intimate scenes with children as performers and shifted the action to the ring when the horses came into play, which was early and often. Patriotic, medieval, and oriental themes predominated in what we should perhaps call the scenarios; cruel tyrants, savage chieftains, gory pirates, distressed damsels, gallant knights, and jolly, dauntless tars were the characters; the action was forwarded by means of challenges, duels, pursuits, tournaments, assaults upon fortresses, and pitched battles attended by the most sanguinary slaughter; and figuring in the accessory embellishments were singing, dancing, trained quadru-peds, apparitions, military maneuvers, gunfire, and explosions and conflagrations ingeniously managed with fireworks. These composi-tions were interpreted in dumb show with occasional brief passages of dialogue bellowed to a vague, perfunctory musical accompani-ment as required at the minors by law. In the course of the performance the scrolls, or flags, of pantomime were displayed at intervals to assist an understanding of the business in progress. Vilely executed scrawls they could be at times with misplaced aitches and extraordinary orthography—"Leads her to the bridle halter" and the like. Titles were vivid and alluring: *The Blood-red Knight, Rinaldo Rinaldini; or, the Secret Avengers, The False Friends; or, the Assassin of the Rocks, The Fatal Prediction; or, the Midnight Assassins.*[1]

Dickens captured some of the delights of Astley's in his descrip-tion of the visit of the Nubbles family to this resort in *The Old Curiosity Shop.* Mr. George of *Bleak House* was another patron of Astley's; he shed honest ears at the distresses of the heroines. Thomas Dibdin, one of Charles's two sons,[2] who both followed their father's profession, was responsible for many of the scripts used at Astley's, among them being *Slaves of Barbary; or, the Bombardment*

[1] "The more terrific the title of a piece was, the more likely it was to attract."—Charles Dibdin the younger in his *Memoirs,* ed. Robert Speaight (London, 1956), p. 143.

[2] The elder Charles Dibdin (1745–1814) was a prolific playwright, an enterprising theatrical entrepreneur and England's best-loved composer of songs, especially sea ballads. The combined output of melodramas by Dibdin and his sons, Charles and Thomas, ran into several hundred, and their musical compositions were uncountable. Charles the younger wrote: "My Father, Brother and self have written more songs than not only three, but three score men put together,—some thousands, of which for public, private and various occasion, I have written nearer 5000 than 4000 . . ."—*Memoirs,* p. 46. The names of the elder Dibdin's songs gave titles to a whole library of nautical melodramas. In the first chapter of Thackeray's *The Newcomes,* the Colonel scored a famous triumph with his solo rendering of one of them, "Wapping Old Stairs."

of Algiers. In his *Reminiscences of a Literary Life* he recounts negotiations with the doughty centaur manager for the sale of a group of four. He received fourteen guineas for the lot, and the transaction was concluded with the understanding that the name of the illiterate impresario should appear on the bills as author. Astley defended his peculiar ideas on literary proprietorship by means of a similitude dealing with the purchase of a pair of boots. "You go into that 'ere shop," he explained, "and ask whose shoes they are. 'Mine, to be sure!' says Mr. Heath or Mr. Hobson or whatever his name. 'Ay, but whose make?' 'Mine, to be sure,' says Hobson again, when, zounds! sir, the fellow perhaps never made a shoe in his life. But he bought 'em, d'ye see, paid for 'em in the lump, or perhaps in lots of fourteen guineas' worth (as I buy these here things of you—and devilish slim some of 'em are for the money); and by that means they are his shoes, his make, and his all around the ring. Eh! just as these thingumbobs are mine; do you see that? Oho!"[3]

John C. Cross was another author; his *Sir Francis Drake and Iron Arm, Louisa of Lombardy, Julia of Louvain; or, Monkish Cruelty,* and *The Genoese Pirate; or, Blackbeard* thrilled many a crowded house at the turn of the century. Iron Arm is a ferocious cutthroat of a brigand who is pardoned by the Spanish governor of Carthagena on condition that he aid in defending that stronghold against the British fleet. In spite of the evil alliance, however, the besiegers triumph in a rousing engagement, the last scene showing the reduced town in ruins. Cross went to the Royal Circus as manager and part proprietor in 1789 after having served as stage manager and provider of afterpieces at Covent Garden, a post he relinquished to Thomas Dibdin. *The Genoese Pirate* and *The Round Tower; or, the Chieftain of Ireland* were given at that patent house as afterpieces.

Equestrian melodrama had a long history in England and the United States. It did not disappear with the general spread of more highly articulated stage melodrama from the second decade of the century on but achieved its greatest glory at the Royal Amphitheatre (as Astley's was called when rebuilt in 1804 after a fire) in the thirties with Andrew Ducrow as its premier interpreter. This riding manager, a veteran of the Cirque Olympique, has been described as a peerless horseman and a superb pantomimist; Christopher North sang his praises in *Noces Ambrosianae.*

[3] T. J. Dibdin (London, 1837), Vol. I, pp. 94–95.

After Ducrow, who died in harness in 1842, William Batty
assumed the management of the Royal Amphitheatre, introducing a
new scale of grandeur in spectacles like *The Wandering Jew* (with
real live beasts) and Fitzball's *White Maiden of California*, in which
the ghosts of Indian chiefs appeared mounted on milk-white steeds.
Shakespeare took to horse here when William Cook succeeded
Batty in the late fifties, *Richard III* and *Macbeth* among other plays
being converted into equestrian entertainments as they had been in
Paris. George R. Sims, who was born in 1847, recalls in his autobiography[4] a circus performance of *Romeo and Juliet*. Characteristically, however, the ring drama held to the patriotic battle piece.
All of England's famous victories for three-quarters of a century
were reproduced at the Royal Amphitheatre, the Napoleonic and
Crimean Wars supplying inspiration for many notable shows among
which *The Battle of Waterloo*, *The Burning of Moscow*, and *The
Battle of the Alma* particularly pleased the London populace. Tom
Taylor's *Garibaldi* was given in 1869. The last of the military
spectacles in the strict sense was *The Conquest of Magdala* in 1868.
    In 1871 the legendary Lord (his given name) George Sanger took
over Astley's. He completely rebuilt it and moved in with his
menagerie, transforming equestrian melodrama into the zoological
variety with circus animals. He, and his sons after him, carried on
for twenty-two years, adding new glory to the picturesque old
house and new magnificence to animal drama. True to Astley's
traditions, he wrote some of his own shows including the first one,
Lady Godiva. One of the most resounding successes of his management was *The Fall of Khartoum and the Death of General Gordon*
(1885). The Amphitheatre was demolished in 1893, but Sanger's
equestrian drama continued under canvas.
    The last glorious incarnation of the Houyhnhnm melodrama
belongs to the history of the American stage. For a decade and more
prior to World War I the huge Hippodrome in New York sheltered
a stupefying procession of colossal spectacles: *The Siege of Port
Arthur* by Owen Davis, *The Capture of Vera Cruz*, *Pioneer Days*,
Andersonville Raiders, *Marching through Georgia*, *Around the
World* and others, staged by Carroll Fleming and R. H. Burnside.
Productions of the same class given elsewhere were the perennial
Ben Hur (as dramatized by William Young and Charles W. Chase
in 1899) with its celebrated chariot race done many times since in

[4] *My Life* (London, 1917).

the films; *Quo Vadis* (standard version by Stanislaus Stange); and Edmund Day's *The Round Up*. And among tent-show derivatives were the Buffalo Bill shows and the opening spectacles of Barnum & Bailey's Circus: *The Last Days of Pompeii, Nero, Cleopatra,* and others.

In London, chiefly on the Middlesex side of the river, another species of spectacular melodrama flourished in the early nineteenth century, largely under minor house auspices. This was the tank drama, which took up its principal abode at Sadler's Wells (The Aquatic Theatre), Islington. Unlike its equestrian fellow, aquatic melodrama began probably at a patent house; *The Siege of Gibraltar,* an entertainment planned in imitation of the *naumachia* of the ancient Romans by its author, Charles Dibdin the younger, and given as an afterpiece at Covent Garden in 1802, introduced the mode for various water effects, fountains, pools, lakes, oceans, cataracts, and the like, into which the plot precipitated the characters for thrilling climaxes like those of *Timour* and *The Cataract of the Ganges*. The big scene of *The Siege of Gibraltar* represented the destruction of a Spanish fleet in an attack on the fortress; men-o'-war, carefully constructed in scale, were shown sinking, burning, and exploding as they moved across the stage in a tank. Dibdin's piece passed on to Sadler's Wells as *Timour* and *The Cataract* were to do also, where the management, availing itself of the proximity of the New River still open in those years, had installed for the season of 1804 pumps and two huge tanks behind the footlights, one at the level of the stage for bodies of water and the other above the stage for cataracts and falls generally.[5]

The Siege of Gibraltar was followed by a prolonged series of similar concoctions at Sadler's Wells: *The Invisible Ring; or, the Water Monster and the Fire Spectre* (1806), *The Ocean Fiend; or, the Infant's Peril* (1807), *An Bratach; or, the Water Spectre* (1805), *The Demon of the Ganges; or, the Tiger Tribe* (1834), *The White Witch; or, the Cataract of the Amazonia* (1808), *The Magic Minstrel; or, the Fairy Lakes* (1808), *The Council of Ten; or, the Lake of the Grotto* (1811), *Nerestan, King of Persia; or, the Demon of the Flood* (1823), and others. The greater number were from the pen of Charles Dibdin the younger, who was stock author and manager of the house for about eighteen years at the beginning of the century. His *The Wild Man; or, the Water Pageant* (1809)

[5] Charles Dibdin the younger, pp. 59–60.

illustrates some of the vagaries of aquatic melodrama. Poisonings, abductions, escapes, pursuits, combats, and attempted drownings provided the chief interest. Fully 20 per cent of the text of the typical aquatic melodrama was taken up with stage directions and descriptions of dumb show. According to George Colman the younger, Dibdin was the first man at any of the minors to engraft dialogue successfully onto the pantomimic spectacle.

As years went on, these primordial melodramatic entertainments tended to disappear. A pit was built over the horse ride at the Surrey when Elliston took over there in 1809, the mangers becoming dispensaries for solid and liquid refreshments; and the tank declined in dramatic importance at Sadler's Wells where melodramas ceased to be merely excuses for its employment, though aquatic dramas were given here until 1844 when Phelps acquired the lease and turned the house into a Shakespearean one. The Olympic Pavilion in the Strand, built by Astley in 1806 along the lines of his Surrey Side amphitheatre, was metamorphosed into a regular theatre in 1813 and licensed to perform burlettas or musical pieces. And when the Coburg was erected across the Thames to compete with the Surrey in 1816, no special provision was made for the horses, though this house did boast a tank as did the Adelphi and the Princess at the end of the century. Only at Astley's did equine actors continue to lord it over their human colleagues in dramatic importance. Nevertheless, the horse show had not quite died, for when the New Standard was rebuilt after a fire in 1865, it was so constructed that the stage could be converted into a ring by removing the boxes.

When the performers at the more important minors came out of the water and abandoned their mounts, they got into trouble immediately, running afoul of the patent houses. We have seen the difficulty with which the managers of these privileged institutions maintained their solvency, a feat at which they all eventually failed; and their feelings can be imagined when the unkempt and rowdy playhouses of the proletariat began to encroach upon their prerogatives and cut into their receipts. As long as the minors confined themselves to entertainments specified in their licenses—usually singing, dancing, and pantomime with no spoken dialogue—there was not much to be done about this competition. However, when the minors, chafing under the restrictions, began to present entertainments that here and there approached legitimate, or regular, drama, that was another matter. For this situation there were remedies provided to the metropolitans by their letters patent and by certain acts of Parliament passed during the middle years of the eighteenth century.

The patents were grants (1660) by Charles II to two royal favorites, Killigrew and Davenant, vesting them and their successors with the exclusive acting rights to the spoken drama. The companies at Drury Lane and Covent Garden became the repositories of these rights, which were extended by a special license to the Haymarket in 1705 covering the summer seasons when the big houses were dark. The so-called Licensing Act of 1737 prohibited the acting of plays in a theatre outside the city of Westminster, a prohibition which had the effect of sustaining the monopoly. The act also prescribed preproduction approval by the Lord Chamberlain of all plays. An act of 1751, made permanent in 1755, required the licensing of "places of public entertainment in the cities of London and Westminster" (Drury Lane and Covent Garden being exempted by name) and in an area of twenty miles radius thereof. This act was put forward as a police measure to facilitate the maintenance of law and order at public houses which offered entertainment. It designated the Lord Chamberlain to issue licenses in the innner zone, and local magistrates beyond. Under the act various minor theatres were licensed at various times in the eighteenth and early nineteenth centuries to give summer seasons in Westminster, among them the Adelphi, the Olympic, and the English Opera House (later the Lyceum), and in the outlying area Astley's, Sadler's Wells, the Coburg, the Surrey, and the Pavilion, Whitechapel.

Legally dubious, frequently violated, always unpopular and capriciously enforced, this corpus of restrictive law and precedent became a lively issue after Robert William Elliston took over The Royal Circus in 1810, changing its name to The Royal Surrey. An enterprising and audacious entrepreneur, this popular Drury Lane actor turned manager gave Shakespeare and classical comedies (*The Beaux' Stratagem* and *A Bold Stroke for a Wife*) and even an original blank verse tragedy, *Fazio*, by the Rev. Henry Hart Milman, Dean of St. Paul's. Elliston was promptly enjoined by the courts on the appeal of the patent houses, whereupon he resorted to the subterfuge of altering the titles of forbidden works, inserting songs here and there, and transcribing the text into rhymed doggerel, which he had his performers declaim to a musical accompaniment. As George Colman the younger describes the practice as it was followed at the Surrey and elsewhere, "they then made their recitative appear like Prose, by the actor running one line into another and slurring over the rhyme;—soon after a harpsichord was touched, as an accompaniment to the actor;—sometimes once in a minute, then once in five minutes;—at last—not at all;—till, in the process of time, musical and rhyming dialogue had been abandoned. . . ."[6]

Moncrieff's comedy, *Rochester; or, King Charles II's Merry Days*, given by Elliston in 1818 at the Olympic, to which house he transferred upon retiring from the Surrey, apparently was the first piece given at a minor theatre wholly unaccompanied by music,[7] though Charles Dibdin the younger, in his *Memoirs*, makes the claim that this innovation originated with him during his management of Sadler's Wells which dates from 1800 (p. 112). To resolve the hopelessly confused situation, the Lord Chamberlain was ultimately to simplify the official version of burletta to spoken dramas of not more than three acts, and containing not less than five songs in each act. It was never reduced to words, but this is what happened in practice.

Meanwhile melodrama in the formula of Pixerécourt, with its songs, its elaborate musical accompaniment to action and dialogue, and its three-act form, presented a ready-made solution to the problems of the minor house managers, and it was generally adopted. Charles Dibdin the younger wrote that in 1818 he had been the first to present melodramas in three-act form, adding rather cryptically that aquatic pieces of this length had been given prior to this. Actual French pieces appear to have been rather rare at the minors with the notable exceptions of the Dibdin-managed houses, the Surrey, and Sadler's Wells, one of the reasons being that a large number of

[6] *Random Records* (London, 1830), Vol. I, pp. 52–53. This writer, who had been both a practicing playwright and manager and later Examiner of Plays (1824–1836), was in a position to study the matter from both sides.

[7] See Moncrieff's introduction to the printed version of his *Rochester* in *Richardson's Minor Drama*, Vol. I, which incorporates his valuable testimony before the Select Committee on the drama appointed by Parliament in 1832 to report on the state of the drama. He writes that before *Rochester* was brought out, the dramas of the minors had been chiefly burlettas in rhymed doggerel, played to the tinkling accompaniment of a pianoforte.

successful plays by Pixerécourt and his countrymen were introduced at the patent houses, usually as afterpieces, and preempted
there by barefaced prescription. By and large, the bills of the
smaller houses in the field of melodrama did not differ much in
subject matter from those of their persecutors. Sprinkled thickly
through the repertoire were crude dramatizations of historical
legends including those of William Tell, Fair Rosamond, Guy
Fawkes, the Black Prince, Jane Shore, Wallace, King Arthur, and
Saint George; oriental extravaganzas inspired by the Irish poet
Thomas Moore (*Lalla Rookh*), Byron, and William Beckford's
Vathek; and adaptations of the works of Walter Scott, the border
ballads, and Ossian.

The story line of *Trial by Battle; or, Heaven Defend the Right,*
by William Barrymore, offered on the opening bill of the Coburg in
1818, is a good example of a minor house melodrama of this period.
The titled Falconbridge, having evil intentions toward the chaste
and beautiful heroine Geralda, makes overtures to a gang of smugglers with a view to having her carried off and her natural protector
slain. When the proposal is brought to these worthies in their cave,
a conscientious cutthroat among them demurs.

> SMUGGLER. As yet this band is ignorant of the crime of murder
> . . . to gain possession, then, of this female, loss of lives must
> ensue and some of ye may fall victims. Therefore I abjure the
> deed, nor will I longer belong to a band who, for the sake of
> gold, would sacrifice a helpless female at the altar of Lust and
> Infamy! (*Chord.*)
>
> OMNES. Stab him to the heart! (*Crash of music.*)

The conspiracy gets under way. Geralda is abducted in due form,
and during an attempted rescue her father is stabbed by Falconbridge. A companion of the old man is also struck—fatally—and the
villain attempts to fasten the crime upon the hero, Henri. This
young man demands trial by battle, no less, to clear his name, and in
a spectacular tournament scene in full medieval panoply with ca-
parisoned chargers and mailed knights he overthrows the villain's
champion and then slays that dastard himself.

Trial by Battle was based upon a curious case that had come up in
British courts a short time previously: a man accused of a crime
demanded this ancient legal privilege of vindicating himself by arms.
It was with plays of similar inspiration that the Royal Coburg

(renamed the Royal Victoria in 1833) was to attain a scandalous immortality through the *cause célèbre* melodrama. It was quite the handsomest and best-equipped of the minor theatres and was put up at the junction of the New Cut and Waterloo Road, South London, in 1816–1818 when expectations were brightest for a flow of prosperity from the Middlesex side of the river across the newly built Waterloo Bridge. These expectations were disappointed. The swamps and market gardens of the region did not transform themselves overnight into thriving marts of trade, nor did playgoers from the Middlesex side show any great eagerness to pay tolls and run the gauntlet of the footpads who infested the ill-lighted bridge from its beginning. Consequently the new playhouse with all its splendors— including a famous looking-glass curtain—had to reconcile itself to its fate as a neighborhood house. And what a neighborhood! Lambeth Parish was a suburban shantytown, and its population, transient and permanent, consisted of the ragtag and bobtail of the metropolis: apprentices on the loose, sailors, coal bargemen, navvies, costers, Chinamen, Malays, fishwives, peddlers, pickpockets, streetwalkers. They went to the play, crowding into the shilling gallery and two-shilling pit (these prices were subsequently cut in half), where, fortified with rations of porter, comestibles, and cut-plug, they settled themselves for the night, exchanging greetings with friends in remote parts of the house as the show proceeded, ragging unpopular performers, pursuing various private or community feuds if an opportunity presented itself, and stinking to high heaven.

Turning to the bills at this house, the modern reader is struck by the frequency with which Shakespeare was attempted, often with men like Kean, Macready, and Phelps to act it. There was nothing extraordinary in this. Aside from the circumstance that the south side of the Thames was Shakespearean earth, the plays were staple entertainment everywhere in those days and the chief criterion by which a serious performer was judged. To satisfy the demand for Shakespeare at the minors before 1843, managers either defied the authorities or presented the plays under various disguises, but throughout all the degradation of the stage in these years, the gigantic figure of Shakespeare is never anywhere for long out of sight; the influence of his dramas, for good and for ill, was an all-pervading one. We have observed it in the tawdry comic operas and the down-at-the-heels tragedies at the patent houses; it is no less apparent in melodrama. Courtroom melodrama may owe as much to *The Merchant of Venice* as to *Le Jugement de Salomon*, and

Richard III certainly cannot lightly be dismissed as a fountainhead of the eternal theme of black villainy persecuting juvenile innocence. Finally, in plot and incident, some of the worst excesses of the genre in England may be attributed to Shakespearean example: the sleep-walking, the witches, the sleeping draughts, the combats, the duels, the slaughter. And when melodrama was reproached for its dreams, its specters, and its mad women, apologists were able to point to the unimpeachable precedent.

In 1820, Glossop, a reformed tallow chandler then managing the Coburg, took a flier in Shakespeare, presenting Junius Brutus Booth (father of John Wilkes and Edmund) in *Richard III*, a tragedy calculated to touch patrons of that blood-pit in their weak spot. The engagement had a certain importance in the monopoly disputes and was not without effect on melodrama. Booth happened to be under contract with Drury Lane at the time, which constituted an additional grievance on top of infringement of the repertory, and made the venture fair game for the great house. The statute of 1755 was invoked, and Shakespeare across the river was promptly quashed once again. Glossop had better luck with melodrama, like Elliston before him. Caigniez's *Thérèse ou l'orpheline de Genève* had been given at Drury Lane in a version by the American John Howard Payne in 1821; after it closed there the Coburg manager proceeded to imitate it, that is, to copy it with a change of title from "Orphan" to "Maid." Another protest came from the injured patent house, followed by the usual legal steps; ironically, Elliston, now manager of Drury Lane, was the complainant. It was less effective this time. The suit was eventually dropped and the precedent established— later sustained in a ruling by the Lord Chamberlain—that imported pieces did not come within the scope of the monopoly. Adaptations from the French had, of course, been given at various minor houses before this, but they had either been disguised under new titles or were pieces not previously shown at the great houses. Now the last barrier separating the minors from the rich loot of French melodrama was removed.

As at the patent houses, the dog, bird, and monkey dramas were favorites at the minors and inspired numberless English imitations, the names of a few of which have been preserved: *The Cherokee Chief; or, the Shipwrecked Sailor and His Dog*, *The Smuggler's Dog; or, the Blind Boy's Murder*, *Jack Robinson and His Monkey*, *Philip and His Dog* (in which the canine hero drowns the villain and steals bread to give to starving farmers), *Caesar, the Watchdog of the Castle, The Planter and His Dog; or, the Slave's Revenge,* and so forth. Many of these were used as vehicles at the Coburg in the twenties and later in America by Barkham Cony who was one of a large tribe of perpatetic stage artists of the period classified in the profession as "dog Hamlets." They worked with a team of three—two humans, who played hero and villain, and a dog. The dog was by far the most important member of the ensemble. His prize contribution to the entertainment was to leap at the throat of the villain and tear open a carefully prepared sack of red ochre planted there for the purpose, the malefactor dying a horrible, bloody death on the stage.

That was the sort of thing they wanted at the Coburg—exciting combats, harrowing horrors, and buckets of blood—and that is what they got. Though after 1833 the house bore upon its portals the name of the irreproachable Victoria herself, symbol of British respectability, it touched new depths in spine-chilling melodrama. "Blood" or "murder" was usually to be found in the titles so that it came to be known as "The Bleedin' Vic." On its boards in 1819 T. J. Dibdin's homicidal Ruffian Boy, poniard in hand, pursued his fanatical vengeance on the lady who had rejected his advances; and Jack Sheppard and Sixteen String Jack began their prolonged theatrical careers of housebreaking, cribcracking, and brigandage. Here *Frankenstein* added a new dimension to monstrous stage criminality in Milner's version (1823) of Mary Shelley's shocker, and the body-snatching melodrama attained the proportions of a sanguinary plague. Melodramas of the deepest dye and coarsest texture were its staple commodity, according to F. G. Tomlins, critic for the *Daily Advertiser,* in 1840.

Crime, of course, was no novelty in drama, even in the style to which Coburg dramatists served it up; that is, in versions of actual atrocities. A *cause célèbre* was the source of *George Barnwell,* Lillo getting his plot from one of those broadsheet ballads hawked by London chapmen; and before that the authors of *A Yorkshire Tragedy* and *Arden of Faversham,* which Lillo rewrote, had used contemporary murders as the basis of their tragedies. In melodrama itself Pixerécourt used the newspapers more than once. He, however, was no lover of blood for its own sake. His plays deal with crime, true enough, but for the most part it is crime thrown into the background and partaking of the quality of legend. Both at the great houses and the minors, melodrama in the earlier decades had about it an exotic, storybook atmosphere which took much of the sting from its extravagant criminality. A glance at a few typical titles will make this clear: *Korastikan, Prince of Assassins; or, the Dreaded Harem* (Coburg, 1821), *The Savage Chieftain; or, Buried Alive* (Surrey, 1814), *The Demon of the Ganges; or, the Tiger Tribe.*

Coburg melodrama by contrast brought crime close and exposed it in clinical detail on the stage; the spotlight was thrown on the actual horrors. Instead of romantic conspiracies concocted in palaces and smugglers' caves and executed with swords against a background of oriental temples, Venetian lagoons and Alpine defiles, these journalistic pieces presented sordid smotherings and brainings of children and women in East End thieves' cellars, Fleet Street barber shops, and Norwich barns. They were vividly realistic projections in settings of contemporary reality—murder localized and authenticated.

Sweeney Todd and the awful fate of Maria Marten provided many an evening of gory delight at the Coburg and elsewhere both on the Surrey Side and to the north and east, for no one theatre or section of the metropolis enjoyed a monopoly on these exhibits. The latter piece was based on the "great Polstead murder case" which was the sensation of England in 1828.

Maria was a comely lass of Polstead, near Norwich, much given to being betrayed before she met William Corder, son of a prosperous farmer of the neighborhood, and "a young man who appears to have indulged an ungovernable propensity for forming intimate connections with females," in the words of a contemporary account. The liaison of these two produced a child, which promptly died under circumstances which gave rise to a suspicion of infanticide. Maria brought up with Corder the matter of regularizing their union, and appears to have been somewhat importunate. He finally consented to do the right thing and made an appointment with Maria at a certain red barn, promising to take her to London for the ceremony. Instead he murdered her, burying the body under a few inches of earth and setting fire to the barn. A few months later Maria's stepmother was troubled with dreams in which she professed to see the tragedy re-enacted. She went to the barn, rummaged about, and uncovered the body. Corder meanwhile had married a schoolmistress met through a matrimonial advertisement inserted in the *Sunday Times*. He was traced to London and arrested. He was tried and convicted and was executed at Bury, a crowd of thousands of witnesses fighting for bits of the rope. The

crime was horrible enough, but the melodramatists improved upon
it. Maria was shot according to the confession of Corder; but in the
stage versions there is a frightful struggle, in which the woman
wields a spade in her defense before being overpowered and stabbed
to death.

The style of delivery favored by Surrey Side audiences was a
rolling, sonorous one in key with the rough-house stage management; some of its distinguishing qualities are indicated in two
articles in *Household Words* both entitled "Amusements of the
People," written by Dickens after a tour of the principal transpontine palaces of the drama in 1850. "Ar-recreant, ar-wreatch,"
bawls the villain of *May Morning; or, the Mystery of 1715, and the
Murder* holding forth at the Vic; and a certain Michael the Mendi-
cant in the same play (a villain whose rough exterior conceals a
heart of gold) describes how he "ster-ruck down and fel-ed in
error" a just man many years before. Since then—"I have lived-er as
a beggar—a roadsid-er vaigerant, but no ker-rime has stained these
hands."[8] When his services are bespoke for a second job, he
exclaims: "What, more bel-ood!" Another abandoned creature, in
Eva the Betrayed; or, the Ladye of Lambeth, playing at a neighboring house, recounts a sad decline in his character thus: "There was a
tim-er when I loved my fellow-keretures, till they diserpised me;
now I live only to witness man's disergherace and woman's misery."
In another article Dickens pictures himself "laughing a hoarse laugh
in three syllables, and folding his arms tight upon his breast agree-
ably to most of the examples of glutted animosity that he has had
opportunity of observing in connection with the drama."[9]

The Surrey, bitter rival of the Coburg, was not behindhand in the
field of the *cause célèbre.* Frequently it stole a march on its
neighbor, notably with *The Gamblers; or, the Murders at the
Desolate Cottage,* based on the Thurtell and Weare case; this
production offered as props the actual sofa, chair, jug, and carriage
used by the murderers. It was for this house that the famous case of
Eugene Aram was first dramatized, in 1832, by Moncrieff, a case
which had already been the subject of Thomas Hood's poem and
Bulwer-Lytton's novel. The litany of murders recited in the titles
here parallels the Coburg's: *The Murderer; or, the Desolate Swamp,*

---

[8] "Amusements of the People," I, *Miscellaneous Papers from "The
Examiner"* (New York, n.d.), p. 129.

[9] "Bill Sticking," *The Uncommercial Traveller and Reprinted
Pieces,* 2nd ed. (London, 1964), p. 413.

The Murder; or, the Devoted Son, The Skeleton Witness; or, King's Evidence, The Shade; or, Blood for Blood. Surrey Side playgoers were given a wide choice in their favorite fare.

South London by no means had a monopoly on the Newgate drama; such cispontine houses as The Britannia, Hoxton, and the Standard, Shoreditch (two of the largest auditoriums in the metropolis), the Royal Pavilion, Mile End, The City of London, Norton Folgate, and The Queens, The Royalty, and Sadler's Wells all kept their bills well smeared with gore. These theatres were all rather fearsome dens, every bit as bad as the Coburg. The worst of the lot, by all accounts, was Sadler's Wells, that favorite resort of Mr. Jorrocks' Binjamin. Quite early in the century (1807) when it was still the Aquatic Theatre, the authorities had been forced to put it under restraint after a panic caused the loss of eighteen lives. The calamity arose from a quarrel. The word "fight" was mistaken for "fire" and so alarmed the gallery that everyone rushed for the doors at once—with the usual result. The peddling of liquor on the premises was thereupon stopped by the magistrates. Evidently John Barleycorn was ousted only temporarily, since in 1844, just before Phelps took the house over, the expiring management, in an attempt to stimulate interest in a languishing pickpocket drama, *Jack Ketch,* was able to advertise a pint of porter free with every ticket purchased for the pit. By that time the behavior of audiences had descended to the level of a beer garden. Dickens attended Phelps's premiere and wrote later that the place on that occasion "was entirely delivered over to as ruffianly an audience as London could shake together. . . . *Macbeth* was performed amidst the most hideous medley of fights, foul language, catcalls, shrieks, yells, oaths, blasphemy, obscenity, apples, oranges, nuts, biscuits, ginger beer, porter, and pipes. . . . Cans of beer, each with a pint measure to drink from (for the convenience of gentlemen who had neglected the precaution of bringing their own pots in their bundles), were carried through the dense crowd at all stages of the tragedy. Sickly children in arms were squeezed out of shape in all parts of the house. . . . Fish was fried at the entrance doors. Barricades of oyster shells encumbered the pavement. . . . Expectant half-price visitors to the gallery howled impatient defiance up the stairs, and danced a sort of *carmagnole* all around the building."[10]

[10] Dennis Arundel, *The Story of Sadler's Wells* (London, 1965), pp. 164–165.

In 1847 the celebrated *Sweeney Todd, Demon Barber of Fleet
Street* was first put upon the stage by William Dibdin Pitt at the
Brit giving rise to a whole cycle of Todd dramas that were in
demand for more than a half-century throughout the English-
speaking world. The playwright got his subject from a novel, one of
a whole library of immensely popular shockers of the period by
Thomas Preskett Prest which included *Varney the Vampire, The
Skeleton Clutch; or, the Goblet of Gore* and *The Death Grasp; or, a
Father's Curse.* Todd's racket was the murder of prosperous-looking
gentlemen customers for what valuables they had on their persons,
the victims being brought into his shop by a corps of juvenile
solicitors operating on the streets of the city. He would gently place
the unsuspecting patron in a barber chair, tuck an apron under his
chin, slosh a thickly lathered brush into his eyes to blind him, and
then cut his throat instead of his beard. The chair was rigged on a
trap-door, operated by a lever; his looting done, Todd would yank
the lever, and the corpse would take a header into the cellar,
where—according to many versions—his paramour-partner, Mother
Lovatt, would go about dressing the remains for pork pies, which
she sold in her adjoining shop. (Comic relief!) A shortage of raw
material for this delicacy led to the quarrel between the partners
which resulted ultimately in their detection and arrest. In other
versions feminine jealousy caused the trouble. The plot of the play
is constructed about the demon barber's attempts to add Mark
Ingestre, a stalwart British tar, to Mother Lovatt's larder.

In adapting actual crimes for the stage, melodramatists were not
meticulous in their regard for documentary fact. They whitewashed
culprits, gave unjustly condemned unfortunates the benefit of reprieves denied them in real life, distorted motives, invented villains,
suppressed material facts, and solved mysteries. Among the many
historical victims of judicial error who, in melodramatic resuscita-
tions, escaped the unhappy fate that overtook them in real life were
Annette, of *La Pie voleuse,* and *Eloi,* of *Le Chien de Montargis,*
both out of medieval chronicles. In the case of a frequently dramatized crime of more recent date, the famous robbery of the Lyons
Mail in the Forest of Lenhart during the Directory, first adapted for
the stage by Ducange, authors took different courses, some contriving the reprieve of the innocent man in the nick of time, and others
not. Agreement was lacking not only among various plays but even
within the same play in one instance; when the team of Moreau,
Sirandin, and Delacour came to treat the affair in what became the

standard version, *Le Courrier de Lyon* (1850), they wrote two different endings which were played on alternate evenings, so that Lesturques was sent to the guillotine for Dubosc's crime on Mondays, Wednesdays, and Fridays and returned to the bosom of his family a free man on Tuesdays, Thursdays, and Saturdays.

Throughout the nineteenth century and into the twentieth the sordid and sensational details of criminal prosecutions came to the aid of the faltering invention of melodramatists, the appeal of such matters on the stage being heightened by their flavor of contemporary scandal. In France the arsenic poisoning of a certain Lafarge by his wife in 1840 furnished the material for one of the most successful collaborations of Dennery and Anicet-Bourgeois, *La Dame de Saint Tropez* (1844); and in England Henry Irving appeared in one of the many dramatizations of the Tichborne impostor-heir case of the seventies. *Michel Strogoff*, by Dennery and Jules Verne, was a *cause célèbre*. Sir Charles Young's *Jim the Penman* (1886) was based on the career of the forger, James Townsend, and Jones's *Mrs. Dane's Defense* (1900) on the Osborn Pearl Case. Such fetching affairs as the Chelsea Trunk Murder, the Yarmouth Bootlace Murder, Wainewright's poisoning of his ballet-girl mistress, Madeleine Smith's teacup vengeance on her threatening French lover, and various "baby farm" scandals—from Mrs. Brownrigg onward— were appropriately celebrated by the dramatic art.

The minors had shown the way to the favor of the masses, progressing from their great spectacles of armed conflict, sieges, sea battles, and the like to the more orthodox melodrama overworked with threads of bloody realism. They could be counted on down through the century to transport their patrons with such edifying subjects as Dr. Crippen, burying in his cellar the remains of the wife he has murdered, or Jack, the Ripper, stalking his prey down mean Whitechapel alleys.

XVIII

Highwaymen and Housebreakers

It was a robber's daughter and her name was Alice Brown;
Her father was the terror of a small Italian town.
—W. S. GILBERT, "Bab Ballads"

After the shocking butcheries of *Sweeney Todd* and *Maria Marten*, there is something almost wholesome in the forthright felonies of those picturesque British highwaymen and housebreakers whose dramatized biographies begin in the 1820's to compete with horse opera, Whitechapel melodrama, and adaptations of Sir Walter Scott for the favor of transpontine audiences.

Theatrical fashions in freebooting change. The early generation of the profession in melodrama were ferocious, unreal ogres out of storybooks who foregathered in caves and gothic ruins in Bohemia, the Black Forest, or the Pyrenees and specialized in the abduction of heroines. Their aspect was romantic—even baroque; they wore extravagantly plumed hats with huge flapping brims, enormous yellow boots and gauntlets, green tunics over shining cuirasses, and magenta knee breeches held in place by great black belts into which were thrust a brace of formidable-looking pistols, a poniard or two, and a magnificent basket-hilted sword. It is possible to be thus precise in the matter of costume and gear thanks to the "tuppence colored" sheets of the toy theatre; the artists employed by West, Jameson, Hodgson, Skelt, and other publishers—Blake, both Cruikshanks, and John Flaxman among them—drew from living actors on the stages of the Surrey, Astley's, and the patent houses.

Contemporaneous to some extent with these primitive bad men were those preposterous humanitarian puppets sired by *Die Räuber* —melancholy noble men, for the most part, driven to a life of crime by the injustices of society. They have the fault of protesting too much. "I have done nothing but defend the weak against the vexations of the insolent and oppressing rich," says Roger to his son in *Victor ou l'enfant de la forêt*. "What has given you the right?" he is asked. "My love for humanity" is the old scalawag's reply. A high-minded bandit chief of this stripe was interpolated by Cobb in his adaptation of *La Femme à deux maris—The Wife of Two Husbands* (Drury Lane, 1803). A later example of this school of highwayman is Gilderoy, the Bonny Boy, in William Barrymore's play of that name (Coburg, 1822). He is a Highland "lifter" or "reiver," sworn foe of the law which, in the hands of his lowland enemies, has meant nothing but oppression to him and his Perthshire kin. "The richest booty would lose its value were I deprived of sharing it with the necessitous," he tells his sweetheart Jessie, by way of self-justification. His fine language and lofty sentiments do not impress that young lady, however. "Oh vile perversion of charity's true maxim!" quoth she. "In vain dost thou attempt to palliate a crime so hateful." She calls his oath of vengeance "a fatal vow choking the sources of contemplated bliss." It is a pretty debate.

Doubtless by this time the Gilderoys had become no more convincing with their audiences than with their sweethearts. In any event, the public enemy as represented on the stage began to undergo another transformation. He shed his neuroses and his primitive fierceness, trimmed his moustaches to a fashionable length and, renewing his wardrobe at the expense of some nobleman whom the chances of the road had committed to his tender mercies, stepped into his victim's coach and proceeded to town to keep various appointments in place of his victim at glittering palaces where lovely ladies' hearts and their escorts' purses found their way into his keeping. The picaresque rogue, in short, came to eclipse the humbug philosopher and social martyr. The process is already underway in Planché's *The Brigand* (Drury Lane, 1829) whose hero is a historical figure, Alexander Massaroni, the "Italian Robin Hood."

Louis Dominique Cartouche, a brazen and incorrigible Parisian scapegrace of the late seventeenth century, was another historical gangster. Thackeray recounts a malicious prank of his, played on a certain Abbé de Potter of Lille, a pompous and worldly prelate with whom Cartouche had an old score to settle. Ingeniously circulating the rumor that he had murdered the churchman and was travelling about impersonating him, the scamp had the satisfaction of seeing his enemy yanked from his coach, mauled by the police, and thrown into jail, where he was held for several days over his violent protests before the mistake was discovered. Hoaxes of this description abound in the melodrama, *Cartouche*, written by Dennery and Dugué in 1858.

There were various other Cartouche melodramas in France, one by Theodore Nezel and another by Victor Ducange (1827); several of them make the rogue out to be a sentimental as well as a comic hero, the victim of a certain "Red Judas." Quite a number were adapted for London use, as were various plays about Mandrin, another notorious French lawbreaker. Italy, always a freebooter's paradise, contributed at least two historical heroes to this type of drama in England besides Massaroni: Marco Sciarra, an Abruzzi brigand, and Michele Pezza, a Calabrian "insurgent," better known as "Fra Diavolo," under which *nom de guerre* Auber and Scribe introduced him in their comic opera. Although these foreign rascals frequently appeared in English translation, native sources were used for the great majority of the English rogue plays, supplemented by Spanish picaresque tales of an earlier period.

Sixteen String Jack was among the first of the Tyburn heroes to be glorified on the stage under the banner of melodrama, Leman Rede producing an arrangement of his exploits for the Coburg in 1823. This spectacle was rewritten and presented as a regular melodrama in 1841 at the height of the vogue for highwaymen plays. Like the Cartouche plays, it is rollicking comedy for the most part. To retrieve losses sustained at play with Beau Brummel, Tom Bullock, and Major Hangar, whose intimacy he has gained while impersonating a French count, Jack stakes five hundred pounds with these Regency bloods on the chance of their being robbed within twenty-four hours and then proceeds to make sure of his wager by doing the job himself with the assistance of his ruffianly crew. A disgruntled lieutenant "peaches," however, and our hero is taken shortly after the adventure and lodged in gaol. He promptly escapes in the skirts of his former sweetheart, a stock episode in the highwaymen plays, and hastens to a carouse with his cronies at "The Cock and Magpie" (all highwaymen are convivial), an occasion for introducing one of those "flash" songs or thieves' cants in which the low-life plays are rich. He is captured a second time in a raid on this resort, and in the final scene is discovered riding backward up Holborn Hill in the death cart. Jack does not pay the final penalty for his misdeeds, however. There is a last-minute reprieve, procured by the sportsmanlike Brummel and Hangar, and Jack takes his bow a free, and apparently a reformed, man.

Great lovers are exceptional among the knights of the road. Jack Sheppard, who after a life as a criminal celebrity became the darling of minor house habitués, was no Romeo; but when he died at the end of a rope, he left two "hempen widows." Neither Poll Maggot nor Edgeworth Bess was precisely a Juliet either, the two of them having amicably shared the rough favors of their hero. In his brief but exciting journey through life, Jack had little time for dalliance,

Besides, he had his public to consider; they expected something else from him. That public was a large one and embraced all classes. Wellborn ladies crowded in to stare at him in the dock; great men sought interviews; and the mass of Londoners, his worshippers, cheered him in the streets. Talent paid its homage also; Defoe and Gay visited Jack in Newgate, and Sir James Thornhill painted his portrait.

He deserved all this celebrity. Few felons have equalled him in versatility, fortitude, and resource; and certainly none put on a better show. A highwayman and second-story operator by preference, he could pick a pocket and rob a coach with the best of them while at escapes he was superhuman. No jail could hold him. His greatest exploit was his last—that classical achievement in which he battered his way through stone walls and ironbound doors and, with iron fetlocks on his ankles, clambered up a flue, over a high wall, and along the leads of Newgate to liberty. This feat was done full justice to in the plays written about him.

Jack's popularity on the stage was as great as it had been in life. One piece by Moncrieff, the most successful, was given at the Coburg as early as 1825, but the greater number (eight within one year) followed Ainsworth's novel, published in 1839. It romanticized the rascally apprentice unblushingly, endowing him with generous traits all too lacking in his historical character. He is not the nominal hero, however; that rôle is assigned to a dispossessed heir in the story, Thames Darrel, a youth gifted with all the virtues proper to a *jeune premier*. Darrel is the target of murderous conspiracies instigated by his villainous Jacobite uncle, Roland Trenchard, who had turned him over to be drowned in infancy and usurped his estates. Justice is eventually done, thanks somewhat to the loyalty and courage of Jack, who was raised as a fellow apprentice of Darrel's.

There were Jack Sheppard plays by Hatton, Buckstone, Webster, Tom Greenwood, Haines, and others in the second quarter of the century. Later (1859) when the Lord Chamberlain denied the boards to this particular hero, a clandestine cycle appeared, their subject disguised under such play titles as *Jack Ketch, The London Apprentice, The Stone Jug, The Idle Apprentice, The Boy Burglar, The Young Housebreaker, The Storm in the Thames, Thames Darrel, Old London,* and *Old London Bridge.* Ainsworth was usually followed, at least seven of the plays being based on his novel. New plots were devised, however, especially after the middle of the century. In J. B. Howe's *Handsome Jack and Scarlet Dick* (1861),

Sheppard is something of the lover, snatching the lady of his choice from under the very nose of a clergyman in the act of marrying her to another; and he becomes a dispossessed heir himself in other pieces. In France Dennery made his own dramatization of Ainsworth, a great success under the title, *Les Chevaliers du Brouillard*, at the Porte Saint-Martin (1857) with Marie Laurent in the breeches role of Jack. Mrs. Keeley had the title role in Buckstone's *Jack Sheppard*, the standard version, given at the Adelphi in 1839. Owen Davis wrote the last of the Sheppard plays in his "ten, twent' thirt' " days.

Prior to *Jack Sheppard*, Ainsworth had written *Rookwood* (1834), in which he whitewashed another notable gentleman of the road, Dick Turpin, the last of the great line of English highwaymen, hanged at York in 1739. In the story, and in the plays taken from it by Pitt and others, Dick is pictured as a fellow with a rich repertory of flash ditties and a whimsical philosophy of conduct by which he is able to justify his choice of a calling. "There's honor among thieves," he says, "or where else would you seek it, for it has left all other classes of society. Your highwayman is your true man of honor." Turpin was given more to the turnpike than the town; he was "the flying highwayman," thanks to the speed of his peerless mare, Black Bess, on whose back he was able to establish many a badly needed alibi. This made him a favorite in ring dramas at Astley's.

Bulwer-Lytton was a second writer of fiction whose quarryings from the rich lode of picaresque legend were utilized by playwrights. His *Paul Clifford*, dramatized by Webster in 1833, and by Fitzball two years later, betrays the sociological preoccupation of the serious novelist. The hero is the unacknowledged and abandoned natural son of an important public functionary, in this case a judge; and his various delinquencies are presented as a consequence of his upbringing and environment, ultimate responsibility being laid at the door of the derelict father. After the customary escapades on the road and in the tavern comes the big emotional courtroom scene in the last act which brings father and son together. Neither recognizes the other until the culprit at the bar has been condemned to die by the judge on the bench.

Other highwaymen of lesser renown, some of them historical, got into plays: Tom King, Captain Heron, Captain Hawk, Captain Maclean, Captain Spruce, Jerry Abbershaw, Ferdinand Count Fathom, and Nat Graves; and in addition to these were a numerous company of rapparees, tories, and the like, of whom the Irish

Captain Blood who stole the crown jewels from the Tower was the most spectacular.

Women were not unknown in the profession. Early in the nineteenth century Dibdin wrote *The Female Freebooter*, and there was an anonymous *Carline, the Female Brigand* in the same period and a *Female Mascaroni*, by Somerset. In the forties Margaret Catchpole's real-life adventures begot a cycle of melodramas, many of them deriving from Cobbold's narrative of this redoubtable lady's career. Sterling's version, given at the Surrey in 1845, was the first. Margaret's outstanding exploit was a ride that matched Turpin's famous one from London to York: forty miles on a stolen horse to keep a rendezvous with her smuggler-lover. She was a chronic offender and jailbreaker; ultimately the authorities got rid of her by shipping her off to a penal colony in Australia (as they did another melodramatized felon, George Barrington). Here the big third-act climax occurs in the plays. This is a desperate encounter of the heroine with the murderer of her lover; she hurls him over a cliff to his death.

At one time in the forties no fewer than six of these rogue plays were being shown in London. Concurrently crime began to increase at an alarming rate, and honest householders drew the natural conclusion that there was some connection between the phenomena. Protesting managers might point piously to the conclusion of the dramas, which invariably showed a repentant wrongdoer or a hanged one; yet these soiled heroes tasted retribution or turned over a new leaf only after three glorious acts of felonious sport. And if a rascal ever had his tongue in his cheek it was the highwayman in that final set speech bemoaning the evil of his ways and pointing a moral, a typical example of which occurs in Rede's *Sixteen String Jack:* "Henceforth I will endeavor . . . to be content with the proceeds of industry even though it be but a crust. I trust that all future delinquents will learn to profit by the example of Sixteen String Jack."

The sermons of Jack and his tribe fooled nobody, not even the Lord Chamberlain, and in the sixties the highwaymen plays were barred from the London stage. When the ban was finally lifted, the vogue for this species of melodrama had passed; a Sheppard play by James Hatton with Weedon Grossmith in the role of Jack failed at the Pavilion in 1898. A new type of rogue appeared to take the place of the highwayman on the stage in our own times—the urban desperado.

XIX

The British Tar as a Proletarian Hero

A British tar is a soaring soul,
As free as a mountain bird!
His energetic fist should be able to resist
A dictatorial word.
His nose should pant, his lip should curl,
His cheek should flame, his brow should furl,
His bosom should heave, his heart should glow
And his fist be ever ready for a knock-down blow.
—w. s. GILBERT, H.M.S. Pinafore

Popular as were the crime and highwayman plays, there was another type of melodrama which had an even stronger and more persistent appeal for London playgoers in the nineteenth century—the nautical. With Nelson remembered in the flesh and Cape St. Vincent still a vivid subject of personal reminiscence, this was to be expected. In the early years of the century indomitable British tars saved the day for old England in many a gory massacre in the ring at the Royal Circus and Astley's, and the same true blue boys of the bulldog breed rescued hard-pressed maidens by the score from a fate worse than death on the stage and in the tank at Sadler's Wells and elsewhere. At the patent houses of the same period, whimsical versions of the sailorman provided the comedy in numerous adaptations from the French, replacing the stock Savoyard or Gascon comics of the originals.

It was in this comic guise that the sailor made his bow in spoken melodrama of native manufacture, appearing in at least two plays which antedate *A Tale of Mystery*—J. C. Cross's *The Purse: or, the Benovolent Tar,* "a musical drama" (Haymarket, 1793) and Arnold's *The Shipwreck* (Drury Lane, 1797). Both Will Steady and Harry Hawser of these melodramatic comedies display virtuosity in manipulating that extraordinary nautical vocabulary which was to become as sacred a convention in the nautical plays as the flash jargon was in the highwayman plays, serving as a vehicle for expressing all the relations of life—a jargon for the beginning of which on the stage we would have to go all the way back to

Congreve's Ben in *Love for Love*. Cross's Will Steady exclaims "Shiver my timbers!" in and out of season; his wife is "a trim little frigate," as all of her successors are to be; and when this lady is reported as unfaithful to him, Will's incredulity takes a verbal form that will still be obligatory thirty years later when the supreme exemplar of the stage seaman, William of *Black Eyed Susan*, will find occasion to have recourse to it: "She ha'nt turned tail? She ha'nt put to sea under false colors?"

Though frequently forced and occasionally incomprehensible to a landlubber listener, this speech, like the thieves' argot, was at least preferable to the ornate style of diction favored by the straight characters in melodrama as a general rule. In any event, audiences liked it as they liked everything about this brave, forthright, jolly sailorman—his high spirits, his lurching sea-leg gait, his quid, his pigtails, and his outlandish oaths. Pit and gallery fancied him too much for him to be confined to a secondary role, and he is to be observed coming more and more to the fore during the twenties. As the Coxwain Long Tom Coffin, in *The Pilot* (1825), taken from Cooper's novel, he fairly stole the show; the gusto and easy familiarity of this gamey salt, born at sea and always uneasy out of sight of it, captivated audiences at the Adelphi. The success of Long Tom as portrayed by T. P. Cooke, a veteran of the Royal Navy, determined the career of Edward Fitzball, the adaptor, as a specialist in this type of melodrama. Dozens of nautical plays came from his pen in the years that followed.

After his triumph in *The Pilot* the comic seaman was ready to step into the role of official hero. He did this in Buckstone's *Presumptive Evidence* (Adelphi, 1828) and Jerrold's *Black Eyed Susan; or, All in the Downs* (1829). The latter, the most celebrated of all nautical melodramas, ran for four hundred nights at four London theatres in all during its first year—a record. The production restored the crumbling fortunes of the Surrey, undermined as a result of its long and ruinous competition with the Coburg, and established it as a nautical house, a character it was to retain until the end of the century.

William, the sailor-hero of *Black Eyed Susan*, is a comic, witty, frolicsome, hearty, and as handy at the double hornpipe as with a cutlass or a harpoon; but he is a heroic and sentimental comic, a comic with a soul—and a wife. The domestic instinct is strong in him, as it was in Will Steady of *The Purse* which was revived in 1827 and may have inspired *Black Eyed Susan*. He returns home after a three-year stretch of duty afloat to find his faithful Susan facing eviction at the hands of her grasping landlord Doggrass, a scoundrel who has almost persuaded her that William has perished at sea. There is a tender reunion, and Doggrass is properly disposed of; but greater tribulatons impend for the loving couple. A sea captain, in a carousing mood, makes an attempt on Susan's virtue, and William, arriving on the scene, plunges a knife into the villain without recognizing him. Alas! it is William's own captain, Crosstree, whom he wounds. William is arrested, put into irons, and shortly afterward tried and condemned to hang from the yardarm of his vessel, as the officer-hero of *The Pilot* had been. After long-drawn-out suspense and a pathetic scene of parting between husband and wife, William mounts the platform to die. The very noose is being adjusted when Crosstree—recovered and repentant now—rushes on crying, "Hold! Hold!"

> CROSSTREE—He saved my life; I had written for his discharge—villainy suppressed the document—'tis here, dated back. When William struck me he was not the King's sailor—I was not his officer.

Saved by a technicality! So the yellow flag comes down, the Union Jack goes up, Susan and William fall into an embrace for the concluding picture, and "all hands cheer." Nautical or supernatural, equestrian or domestic, melodramas—

> . . . nearly always end the same
> Upon the Surrey Side,

as W. S. Leigh sang.

At the conclusion of a long run at the Surrey, *Black Eyed Susan* was transferred to Drury Lane, where its success continued. Dickens, among other eminent Victorians, praised it as "a remarkable illustration of what a man of genius may do with a common enough thing," and the public at large could not get enough of it. Cooke played William 785 times, and he had imitators everywhere for fifty years. At the Haymarket in the eighties the Kendals appeared in a revised version of the old favorite, and McKay Rankin brought it out in the United States. The original play was revived at the Adelphi in 1897 with Will Terris as William.

William was an innovation as hero in more ways than one. He

was not only a comic, he was a commoner, an ordinary seaman, whereas Coffin had at least been a petty officer. The phenomenon of the plebeian hero is a phase of that democratization of the drama which, having begun toward the end of the eighteenth century in the peasant hero of Colman and the middle-class characters of Kotzebue, was proceeding through the nineteenth, chiefly in the people's theatre—the theatre of melodrama. The commoner rose in dignity, and the aristocrat showed a tendency to deteriorate. William Archer comments upon the phenomenon amusingly: "The baronet, degraded from the positon of hero, rapidly degenerated in character, and soon established that prescriptive claim to reckless villainy which he maintains to this day. The hopeless depravity of the baronetage has been for a century an uncontested dogma of stage sociology. You remember how in Gilbert's *Ruddigore* the virtuous young farmer Robin Oakapple, proving to be in reality the elder brother of Sir Despard Murgatroyd, at once becomes the nefarious Sir Ruthven Murgatroyd, while his faithful old servant, old Adam Goodheart, is instantly changed into the bold, bad baronet's wicked steward, and renamed Gideon Crawle."[1]

In high literary quarters there was outspoken censure of this growing practice of making heroes of common folks and villains of the highborn. Among the viewers-with-alarm were that weary rebel, Coleridge, and that unreconstructed Tory, Sir Walter Scott. The former specified "valiant tars" in his satirical catalogue of stage heroes of the day, along with "honest tradesmen, high-spirited half-pay officers, philanthropic Jews, tender-hearted braziers, and sentimental rat-catchers."[2] Scott was more solemn. "There is an affectation of attributing noble and virtuous sentiments to people least qualified by habit or education to entertain them," he wrote in his *Essay on The Drama*, "and of describing the higher and better educated classes as uniformly deficient in those feelings of liberality, generosity and honor which may be considered as proper to their station in life. This contrast may be true in particular instances, and, being used sparingly, might afford a good moral lesson; but in spite of truth and probability, it has been assumed upon all occasions by these authors as a groundwork of a sort of intellectual Jacobinism;

[1] *The Old Drama and the New* (Boston, 1923), p. 235.
[2] "Satyrane's Letters," *Biographia Literaria* (New York, 1926), p. 339.

consisting, as Mr. Coleridge has so well expressed it, 'in the confusion and subversion of the natural order of things.' "[3]

Pixerécourt could not have been charged with any designs on the "natural order of things." No leveller, he stuck to the grand style in his heroes for the most part, and when there is a noble villain in any of the plays, he usually cancels him out with a good man of the same or higher rank. Many of Pixerécourt's successors in French melodrama followed his example in this respect, Bouchardy and Dennery among them; but the influence of Romantic drama and the spread of democracy and socialism were damaging to the prestige of theatrical noblesse. The protagonists of the plays of Dumas are frequently commoners (Richard Darlington and Didier), natural sons and social rebels (Antony), actors who insult kings (Kean), and even lackeys (Ruy Blas). *Kean* is full of tirades directed against the privileged few, in one of which the man of the people is held up as necessarily virtuous and the nobleman necessarily base. Thackeray noticed the reflection of this point of view in the Boulevard plays. "The seducer or rascal of the piece," he wrote, "is always a wicked count or a licentious marquis."[4]

Herdsmen, coach drivers, fishermen, gypsies, bell ringers, locksmiths, ragpickers, and cocoa venders were the heroes of celebrated hits[5] during the thirties, forties, and fifties in Paris, many of them being revolutionary in tone after the pattern of *La Muette de Portici* which dealt with a seventeenth-century revolt of the fisher folk of Naples against their Spanish oppressors. A performance of this opera at Brussels in 1830 precipitated the revolution which won independence for Belgium. At times the class consciousness of melodramatic playwrights assumed such a bitter and belligerent form that suppression resulted; this was the fate of Emile Souvestre's *L'Enfant de Paris*, in which a virtuous workman is contrasted with a vicious aristocrat.

Revolutionary socialism as proclaimed in the Communist Mani-

[3] "Essay on the Drama," *Essays on Chivalry, Romance and the Drama* (London, 1887), p. 222.

[4] "French Dramas and Melodramas," *The Works of William Makepeace Thackeray* (London, 1886), Vol. XVI: *The Paris Sketchbook*, p. 271.

[5] *Lazare le pâtre, Jean le cocher, Gaspardo le pêcheur, Paris le Bohémien, Le Sonneur de Saint-Paul, Les Deux Serruriers, Le Chiffonnier de Paris, Le Marchand de coco, Le cocher de fiacre.*

festo, which was to flare up so violently in '48 and in '71 in the Commune, was already a formidable popular cause during the thirties and forties in Paris and other French cities. According to the gospels of these reformers, capitalism succeeded feudalism as the outworn institution which called for liquidation; and in the melodramas which preached their doctrines such as those of Félix Pyat and Brisebarre and Nus, the purse-proud banker replaced the marquis as the villain of the piece.

Romantic drama had little if any direct effect in a social way when given in England. Some of its more excruciating examples were adapted—*Lucrèce Borgia* (as *The Fiend of Ferrara*), *Angelo*, and *La Tour de Nesle* were given at the Coburg—but it was the horrors and the crimes which recommended them to managers and audiences rather than the politics or the poetry. Englishmen, however, were feeling the pinch of the same abuses which provoked the popular uprisings of 1830 and 1848 on the Continent, and their resentment was beginning to find a voice in melodrama as well as in such political movements as Chartism. Jerrold's plays as a whole are a case in point.

William of *Black Eyed Susan* is himself no radical—no railer, to use Dibdin's word.[6] He endures the injustices of his trial with true British pluck, never a whimper at authority escaping his loyal lips. But protest was put into words by more than one of the commoner heroes in the numerous imitations of Jerrold's play. Harry Halyard, in Haines' *My Poll and My Partner Joe* (1835), speaks his mind plainly in his heated denunciation of the press-gang which snatches him from his bride of an hour, Mary Maybud, in the first act of this enormously popular drama. Concerning this method of recruiting forces for the Royal Navy he says: "Fiends incapable of pity first gave birth to the idea, and by fiends only is it advocated. What, force a man from his happy home, to defend a country whose laws deprive him of his liberty? But I must submit. But oh! proud lordlings and rulers of the land, do you think my arm will fall as heavily on the foe as though I were a volunteer? No! I shall strike for the hearts I leave weeping for my absence without one thought of the

[6] To rancor unknown, to no passion a slave,
    Nor unmanly, nor mean, nor a railer;
He's as gentle as mercy, as fortitude brave,
    And this is the life of a Sailor.
            —Charles Dibdin the elder

green hills or the flowing rivers of a country that treats me as a slave." That harangue, if it makes sense at all, is a treasonable utterance. Yet Harry is no whiner by nature; he has described himself as "the happiest Dog on the Thames."

Harry merely protests. Another Harry, Harry Helm in *The Sea* by Somerset (Olympic, 1842), goes further; he mutinies in protest at barbarous treatment, as the North Sea and Channel Fleets had done resolutely but without violence at Spithead and the Nore in 1797. The captain has attempted to ensnare Harry's wife, Mary. The mutiny results in Harry's execution, and only a storm and shipwreck saves his widow from the captain's clutches.

In this piece the captain, a baronet, did not repent as did Crosstree; and after him few villains do. The brutal, lascivious nobleman, however, never became the stock symbol of wickedness he was for a while in France—the English nobleman, that is; the villain of *Paul Jones* has a title, but it is merely a Scotch one, and Sir Roland Trenchard in the Jack Sheppard plays is tainted with Jacobitism. Even the Irishman Boucicault stood in a certain awe of rank. When a village maid is seduced by a baronet or a viscount, in melodrama as a general thing it often happens that she is avenged and married by an earl or a duke. Occasionally, however, there are plays such as *The Duke's Victim; or, the Beguil'd One*, which tells its story in its title; they were frequent at houses patronized by the "lower orders," such as the Standard, the Brit, the Effingham and the Pavilion. At this last house, according to H. Barton Baker, hatred of the aristocracy was pronounced, and a silk hat, a black coat, and white Berlin gloves marked the villain every time.[7] The tastes of particular audiences ruled. As a general thing, the resentment of the poor in the English theatre was economic rather than strictly political or social, venting itself principally upon landlords, bailiffs, lawyers, and the like as will be seen in the chapter which follows dealing with domestic melodrama.

For nautical melodrama, however, the first choice for a villain was a pirate; here was a field where English playwrights really let themselves go. In contrast with the highwayman, their fellows on land, these marauders are rarely allowed any measure of humanity as portrayed on the stage. Fitzball's Red Rover in the play of that name from Cooper's novel is permitted to die nobly, and there are a

[7] *The London Stage; Its History and Traditions from 1576 to 1850* (London, 1889), Vol. II, p. 267.

few buccaneers of the heroic Byronic stamp such as Mavrongi, in N. B. Clarke' *Pirate of the Isles* given late in the century, and Clement Cleveland, in the various adaptations of Scott's *The Pirate*. Paul Jones was a sore problem for loyal British playwrights; Thomas Dibdin the younger grudgingly concedes the famous priva-teersman certain virtues in his version of Cooper's novel *The Pilot*. Jones, of course, is the hero; the villains are a Scotch laird and an outright pirate, a monster of the same breed as the slave-ship captain Black Brandon of Haines' *The Pirates of the Savannah, or, the Tiger Hunter of the Prairie* and Mark Andrews of Hazlewood's *Alone in the Pirate's Lair*. W. S. Gilbert's buccaneering crew—"all noblemen who have gone wrong"—those soft-hearted cutthroats with tender feelings for orphans, who reform *en masse* and marry the numerous progeny of Major General Stanley in *The Pirates of Penzance*, are less representative than some of the other stock melodramatic types travestied in the Savoy operas.

Fitzball crossed the nautical with the Freischütz theme in 1827, producing a hybrid that scored a big hit at the Adelphi and introduced a new type of amphibious villain. This play, *The Flying Dutchman*, was based upon the legend Wagner was to use though in a much ruder form; Heine had not yet come forward with the spiritual note of the redemption of the bemused wanderer through the power of a great love which was what appealed to the composer. Vanderdecken in the play is still a mere bogey, held in a spell by a submarine deity, Rockalda, from whom he hopes to purchase his release by luring a mortal maid to share with him his fate aboard his phantom ship, a crazy cutter which appears and disappears, always driving against the wind. The intrigue is built about Vanderdecken's attempts to pass himself off as a foreign suitor of a young English girl and abduct her. He is thwarted in the nick of time by the gallant young lover of the maid. The author's penchant for, and skill at, devising weird mechanical and pyrotechnical effects (which won for him the soubriquet, "blue-fire Fitzball") had full scope in this drama; Vanderdecken rises from the sea in flames, assumes the face and form of another at will, passes through solid walls, and vanishes in hissing smoke without leaving a trace. The pit loved it.

Scarcely less repugnant to right-minded audiences than pirates were wreckers, similarly inclined malefactors who worked closer inshore. A host of them were to be met with in melodrama from Arnold's *The Shipwreck* onward. Peculiarly odious specimens are Matt of the Iron Hand, in *Tom Cringle* by Fitzball from Michael

Scott's novel, *Tom Cringle's Log,* and Hans Hattrock, in the same author's *The Inchcape Bell.* The latter play was based upon an old legend which Southey had sung in one of his ballads. A warning bell placed by good monks near treacherous shallows to warn off mariners is removed by Hattrock and his fiendish crew, who pay for their crime by being crushed on the rocks themselves. The author added a thunderbolt to the climax—thunderbolts, conflagrations, and explosions being standard ingredients of transpontine melodrama.

Meanwhile the British tar hero, rather than the villain, remained the principal attraction of the genre. Wherever there are wrongs to be righted, innocents to be rescued, or villainy to be crushed, this favorite agency of a particular Providence is on the spot with a knockdown blow. He is irrepressible, unconquerable, indestructible, ubiquitous as he wields his cutlass, jigs his hornpipe, sings his ditties, cracks his jokes and mouths his big speeches on two hemispheres and the seven seas.

Only toward the end of the century does he begin to fade out. By that time gentility had cast its blight upon melodrama, even at the Adelphi and Drury Lane; and in such plays as *Harbour Lights* (by Pettitt and Sims, 1885) at the former house and *A Sailor's Knot* (by Pettitt, 1891) at the latter, the heroes are no longer proletarian Jack Tars but gentlemen and officers, played by such matinee idols as Charles Warner and Will Terris. The stage Irishman, as we shall see, was to suffer a like fate.

XX

English Domestic and Adelphi Drama

In tragic life, God wot,
No villain need be! Passions spin the plot:
We are betrayed by what is false within.
—GEORGE MEREDITH

Unlike the highwayman the British tar had a home life, rendered more romantic and affecting by its periodic character and the hazards to which the sailor's calling exposed him. The melodramatic use to which this fireside interest could be put is apparent from *Black Eyed Susan;* and after the success scored by that piece the so-called domestic drama was to be observed impinging upon the nautical in plays given all over London. The uxorious seaman became a convention; *My Poll and My Partner Joe* and *The Sea* furnish examples. And when a wife is lacking, the Dick Oakums and Mat Maintops of such plays have a betrothed in their home port, a dear old mother, or a noble, decaying father—usually all three—whose misfortunes supply that pathetic element so prominent in the appeal of the domestic dramas. As the curtain rises, these persecuted innocents are usually to be discovered, like Susan of Jerrold's play, on the threshold of the workhouse or the debtors' jail, and with no hope of a return of their natural protector from the sea; for in melodramas the foreign mails are in a continual state of demoralization and the mortuary columns of the newspapers veritable monuments of inaccuracy. Letters from wandering boys get lost as frequently as ships founder at sea; heroes are often erroneously reported dead in the first act.

Domestic melodrama, of course, was represented in the French importations. However, with the decline of sentimental humanitarianism in comedy, a school so effectively satirized through the character of Joseph Surface in Sheridan's *The School for Scandal,* this sort of thing did not flourish on the stage, and such works as *The Purse; or, the Benevolent Tar* and *The Adopted Child* can scarcely be said to have had any successors in native melodrama. Thus it is possible to argue that Douglas Jerrold's *Ambrose Gwinett* (1823) was a pioneer. Jerrold regarded himself as the inventor of domestic melodrama, without taking undue pride in the achievement; "a poor thing," he called it, quoting Touchstone, "but mine own." This writer stood somewhat apart from the run-of-the-mill dramatic hack of his day. Though humbly born and largely self-educated, he possessed a professional conscience and he revolted at the shabby traffic in French plays, refusing to write for Drury Lane on any other basis than as an original author. Virtually alone in his generation and with scant encouragement from the patent houses, he cherished the dream of a true national drama which would reflect the life of the times. In practice, it must be confessed, Jerrold fell somewhat short of his ideal. *Ambrose Gwinett* is a long way off from the realism implied in his program. It is a crime melodrama drawn upon the circumstances of an actual case in the reign of Queen Anne, the sensational feature of which was the reappearance after an absence of two years of a man supposedly murdered. In the play the hero, Gwinett, had been condemned to hang for the crime and was awaiting the gallows. The play has most of the vices of its type and period, but at least its characters are Englishmen with some flavor of plausibility—smiths, magistrates, sailors, tradesmen—and they are shown about their business in a little seaport town. A few other features of this primitive domestic drama deserve attention, among them the character of the villain, Grayling. He is not entirely the terrifying ogre of melodramatic tradition. At times he is a human, understandable sort of person, driven to conspiracy, murder, and false witness—which nearly sends an innocent man to his death—when a younger and handsomer suitor is preferred to him by the heroine. He fights the savage streak in his nature and suffers from remorse. The hero, on his part, does an extraordinary thing, refusing to fight when the villain insults his lady, consigning him instead to "the reproaches of his conscience." That was a daring thing for a playwright to do in the twenties, and at, of all places, the Coburg, where *Ambrose Gwinett* had its premiere.

After many rebuffs, Jerrold finally had a play accepted by one of the major houses and on his own terms—artistic terms, that is. *The Rent Day*, given successfully at Drury Lane in 1832 and all over England and America subsequently for years, was an original work, rural in setting, which gave a detailed picture of a characteristc aspect of English life. Though disfigured, like *Ambrose Gwinett*, by the usual melodramatic extravagances, it uses as the basis of its plot a credible situation growing out of the abuses of absentee landlordism and draws upon ordinary walks of life for its characters. Great stress is laid upon the pitiable situation of Martin Heywood, the victim of a concatenation of misfortunes perhaps unequalled in all drama. This distressed farmer recounts his tribulations to a sympathetic listener in the first act. He is "hunted by landlord, threatened by taxmen," and is without a shilling, without a home. His wife is starving; his "white-faced" children, with "withering limbs," are "crying for bread." On top of that he is arrested for conspiracy and illegal entry when he goes to the manor house to plead with the hardhearted steward of the estate for mercy, and there he hears that his wife, Rebecca, has betrayed him.

Of course, the report is false, being the invention of a villain who, as "the man in possession" at Martin's home, attempted to seduce and, failing in that, to rape the faithful Rebecca in her husband's absence. Circumstances tend to bear out the charge: the farmer finds his wife locked in a room with the steward. He will not listen to her explanation: that she came to the manor house out of common humanity to warn the steward of a plot against his life being hatched by the same blackguard who attempted her virtue and then slandered her, Silver Jack, and his pal, Hyssop, a precious pair who, having blackmailed the steward, Grantley, are planning a more vigorous stroke to get possession of a large sum of money which that functionary has embezzled and has about him. From this it will be seen that Jerrold did not rely too much upon fireside interest to put his play across. Jerrold's prescription was the standard one for domestic melodrama, a ha'worth of bread and an intolerable deal of sack.

Grantley is the principal heavy of *The Rent Day*. He is the new type of villain (Hyssop and Jack being survivals): the oppressor of the poor and the forecloser of mortgages, though the farm mortgage as a melodramatic device is ahead of the time with which this play deals. His ill-gotten hoard has been squeezed out of the unfortunate tenants committed to his tender mercies by the absent squire. Yet here again, as with Grayling, there are extenuating circumstances. It comes to light that the Squire's profligate father seduced Grantley's wife years before, and the steward's peculatons, by which he hopes to ruin his master, are by way of belated, vicarious revenge. Thus he becomes a sympathetic, understandable sort of villain, the type which will predominate in the repertory of Henry Irving, a transitional figure, in short, foreshadowing the decline and disappearance of melodrama; for when the proposition that villains are much like other folk comes to be accepted by theatrical audiences, the reign of classical melodrama will be over.

Farmer Heywood's luck turns in the last act. As the bailiffs are removing the furniture from his home, the back is knocked off an old chair, and out of it pour vast quantities of money hidden years before by Heywood's father. At the same moment the Squire himself appears for the first time in the play; he has been prowling about for weeks in the neighborhood in full knowledge of his agent's defection and has awaited this dramatic moment to come on and reveal his identity and his true character, which is a humane and even noble one.

Before Jerrold, John Baldwin Buckstone had worked this field of rural domestic melodrama. His *Luke the Laborer* (Adelphi, 1826) depicts a similarly distressed farmer and presents yet another villain not entirely devoid of human traits. Like Grantley, Luke has a grievance of long standing. Years before he was discharged by Farmer Wakefield for drunkenness and denied a "character," and, unable to obtain work as a consequence, he suffered greatly and saw his wife die of want. There is a note of genuine feeling in Luke's recital of his wrongs, expressed in simple, vigorous dialect. When the play opens, Luke has attained a degree of affluence and is pressing the same Wakefield, now impoverished, for repayment of a loan. He succeeds in having his hated debtor lodged in jail; and when the latter's daughter Clara procures her father's release by repaying the loan with borrowed money, the villain directs his attacks upon her. The squire in this play is a wicked one, harboring evil intentions toward Clara; and Luke abets him in decoying the girl to the manor house one night. Here the comic unwittingly upsets the nefarious scheme. Later, in a wood nearby, when the villains are pursuing the maiden after she has fled the house, a stout sailor man by the name of Philip, a stranger in the neighborhood, comes to the rescue and bludgeons Luke as he is about to seize his prey. Cheated thus again of his vengeance, the relentless old fellow falls back upon pistols and makes his way into Wakefield's house, murder in his heart. Once again the mysterious sailor thwarts him with the assistance of an equally mysterious old gypsy; and, as Luke is turned over for what the melodramists were wont to call condign punishment, the savior of the Wakefield family reveals himself as their long-lost son who had been carried off years before by kidnappers— more of Luke's work. The very agent who did the kidnapping is the mysterious gypsy of the earlier scenes; he comes forward at the climax to accuse the old man. There will be many another Philip in domestic melodrama, all of them showing his irritating disposition to conceal his identity; and many another Farmer Wakefield, with the same astonishing inability to recognize the child of his loins. The public loved the *reconnaissance* denouement, and playwrights were always complaisant in catering to their taste.

"Affecting scenes of real life" in its peasant and proletarian aspects after the manner of *Luke the Laborer* and *The Rent Day* took the fancy of melodrama audiences, and legions of such pieces appeared all over London. The home life of the poacher was exploited for its pathetic possibilities in Pitt's *Simon Lee; or, the Murder in the Five Field Copse* (1839); and one after another various types of city and rural workers came up for consideration on minor house stages. The titles of Jerrold's later plays reveal this increasing interest in the life of every day: *Sally in Our Alley, Martha Wills the Servant Maid, The Broken Heart; or, the Farmer's Daughter of the Severn Side, The Factory Girl.* Melodramas by other hands tell the same story in their titles: G. F. Taylor's *The Factory Strike; or, Want, Crime and Retribution;* Haines' *The Factory Boy; or, Love's Sacrifice;* Walker's *The Factory Lad;* Stirling's *Mary of Manchester; or, the Spirit of the Loom;* Roger's *Frank the Plowman; or, Love, Murder and Revenge;* Lemon's *The Sempstress;* Atkyne's *The Life of a Laborer;* J. B. Johnstone's *The Coal Mine;* Barnett's *The Merchant's Clerk;* Peake's *The Climbing Boy; or, the Little Sweep;* and anonymous pieces: *The Weaver's Wife; or, the First Crime; The Pawnbroker; or, the Saviour of a Sister;* and *Bertha, the Broom Girl.* All these were produced before the middle of the century.

One of the most widely acclaimed of the domestic dramas was Pitt's *Susan Hopley; or, the Vicissitudes of a Servant Girl,* an adaptation of a novel by Mrs. Catherine Crowe, one of the more popular female novelists of the Victorian era. After a prosperous run at the Vic in 1841, it continued to delight audiences in America and Australia as well as throughout England for decades. Susan is no heiress like Thérèse and so many of her other predecessors; she is a servant and remains a servant to the end, and she marries a lad of her own class. But what she lacks in glamorous station is more than made up for by the medieval character of the adventures which befall her. She sees visions, encounters highwaymen, and in the end leads a posse to the murder house where the villain is captured returning to the scene of his crime.

Domestic drama, inevitably, dealt largely with the wrongs of the poor. It was the practice of melodramatists to fix responsibilities for these wrongs upon the bad moral character of individual villains, rather than on structural defects in the social order—the Dickensian point of view, in fact. Certainly, great politicians and industrial bigwigs were usually exempt from castigation in melodrama. (Strikers are frequently treated with commiseration in the factory drama, but their leaders are usually portrayed as sinister villains.) The villains in this general class of play were predominantly lawyers, stewards, members of the squirearchy and of the minor nobility. The legal profession has been singularly prolific in the production of stage scoundrels. Baillie Mucklethrift, the "base-born chicaner" of *Guy Mannering*, was probably the first of the line; and after him came an uncounted company of pettifogging shysters who are to a man venal, cowardly, crafty, and cruel and always at the hire of the forces of evil. The names are significant: Claws, in *Sally in Our Alley;* Pounce, in *Fifteen Years of a Drunkard's Life;* Grubwig, in Pitt's *Marianna;* Snapfee, in *Tom Bowling.* Harry Halyard, sailor-hero of *My Poll and My Partner Joe,* "hates lawyers" (like Mr. George, of *Bleak House,* who "don't take kindly to the breed"), and the sentiment is shared by virtually the entire populace of English minor house melodrama. America seems to have felt the same way about members of the bar, as may be seen from Lawyer Marks of *Uncle Tom's Cabin* and a professional colleague, Cribbs, who is the chief villain of *The Drunkard.* Associated usually with the lawyer heavy is his minion, the bailiff, a character who is beaten up by the hero or the comic and pitched out of the house in the first act as a general rule.

Domestic melodrama enjoyed its greatest success in the proletarian houses, among them the Standard, the Brit, the Surrey, the Coburg ("so justly celebrated for its beautiful domestic dramas," in the words of one of its managers, Osbaldiston), Sadler's Wells, the Pavilion, and the Queens. It contrived to hold its own at theatres of a somewhat better class also, notably the Adelphi, where the Royal family kept a box. The company at this Strand resort was perhaps the ablest acting organization in London, numbering on its rolls at various times such players as Tyrone Power, Fanny Kelly, the Yateses and the Keeleys, T. P. Cooke, Webster, Buckstone, O. Smith, Reeve, Wright and Bedford.

Plays everywhere during these palmy days of repertory were written more or less with the special talents of particular companies in mind—the more so since the authors were commonly actors in the organization; but the practice of carpentering pieces to a company was developed to a higher degree at the Adelphi than elsewhere, a circumstance which helps to explain the peculiar constitution of the so-called Adelphi drama, at its most typical a form of domestic drama. The title part of *Luke the Laborer* was designed as a role for Yates, an early manager who acted; *The Bottle Imp* was adapted from the German because two of its characters were admirably suited to the abilities of Mr. and Mrs. Keeley; Boucicault had Webster in mind for the part of the old farmer in *The Willow Copse*. Comedy was given great prominence in the formula in order that justice might be done to low comedians like John Reeve and the famous team of Teddy Wright and Paul Bedford; and so popular a gift at interpreting villains as Smith's was not neglected.

In 1844 a French artist joined the Adelphi's company, a lady destined to become the chief attraction of the house, Celine Celeste (Elliott). Critics wrote of her half-savage nature, the plaintive charm of her impersonation of distressed heroines, and the sorcery of her personality. It was to exploit these qualities that Buckstone wrote *Flowers of the Forest* (1847) and *The Green Bushes* (1845), the two plays most closely associated with Celeste's international fame. Cynthia, gypsy heroine of the former play, is not a kidnapped heiress as so many of her predecessors in melodrama had been. She is real Romany. Years before the play begins, this beautiful damsel came upon Alfred, the English hero, in the Alps, where he had been wounded and left to die by outlaws. She nursed him back to health, falling in love with him though not allowing him to suspect it. When she encounters him again by chance in the first act, he is about to be married to an English girl—on the way to the church for the ceremony, in fact. Cynthia's devotion to Alfred is pure and unselfish, but she is an impulsive creature, and the sight of the man she loves about to wed another sweeps her into an indiscretion: she throws herself at his feet and declares herself. As a result of this performance, Alfred's early relations with the girl are misinterpreted; his marriage is broken off, and he is challenged by Hugh, his fiancée's brother. Forced into a duel, he fires into the air. Hugh falls dead, nevertheless, with a bullet in his heart; it comes from the gun of Lemuel, one of Cynthia's tribe, who, smarting from a whipping Hugh has given him, shoots from cover over Alfred's shoulder and escapes undetected.

Cynthia's father, Wolf, is an embittered man who saw his lovely young wife murdered years before by the gorgios; he hates the race and fears for the happiness of his child if she persists in her passion for one of them. The fatal issue of the duel presents him with an opportunity to dispose of Afred; he informs on him to a magistrate, charging him with the shooting of Hugh. Cynthia rushes into court. She has overheard Lemuel make a confession to his sweetheart, Starlight Bess; and she tells all to save the man she loves from the gallows. For this betrayal of one of her own people, Cynthia is cursed and turned out by Wolf and the tribe. Later, however, the father relents somewhat and offers to pardon her if she will stab Alfred, who, meanwhile, has been carried off by the gypsies. She sadly agrees, and with a dagger in her hand enters the tent where her lover is a drugged prisoner. There is a cry, and when the flap of the tent is drawn aside, Cynthia is discovered lying in a pool of blood, stricken fatally by her own hand, while Alfred is unharmed. The tortured gypsy girl has died for love.

In *The Green Bushes; or, Ireland as It Was*, adapted in part by Buckstone from the Irishman John Banim's novel, Celeste was cast as Miami, a half-Indian maiden who is impulsive, generous, vigorous —and a dead shot. The weakling hero, Connor O'Kennedy, a political fugitive from Ireland, meets the beautiful savage in the wilderness and goes matrimonially native, omitting to mention that he has a wife and child back home. Miami senses some mystery in his life and is troubled by it. Her misgivings are confirmed when Connor's wife, Geraldine, suddenly puts in an appearance, having come from Ireland in quest of her mate. Crazed by the discovery of Connor's treachery, Miami shoots him dead.

In the second act, which occurs two years later, the simple savage has become a great lady. Really the daughter of a French nobleman by an Indian mother, Miami has returned to Europe and assumed the position in society which is her right. She is discovered in her equipage travelling through Ireland, seeking the wife and child of the man she murdered in order that she may make restitution. When her coach breaks down in the mountains, she comes upon a mistreated waif whom she identifies by means of a locket as Evelyn, Connor's daughter. The child has been kidnapped by her father's faithless brother from the watchful care of Nellie O'Neill, foster-sister of Geraldine, to whom that lady entrusted her when she went abroad to seek her truant spouse two years earlier. Miami bribes the brutal peasants who have Evelyn in charge and takes the child to Dublin, where she endeavors to find traces of the mother.

Meanwhile the warm-hearted and devoted Nellie, disconsolate at the loss of the child, has been wandering footsore all over Ireland in search of her, singing always the verses from *The Green Bushes*, an old Irish "come-all-ye," which she knows Evelyn will recognize and respond to if she hears. This is a neat melodramatic device, which Wallack used in his gypsy play, *Rosedale*, Dennery in *Les Deux Orphelines*, and many another melodramatist in plays throughout the century. Evelyn, of course, finally does hear Nellie's song, and they are reunited. Geraldine appears also, and the little family is one again. The treacherous brother of Connor repents of his wicked deeds and restores the misappropriated property to the rightful heirs; and Miami dies, happy now at last that she has in some measure made amends.

Adelphi plays of this type, a great number of them written by Buckstone who was a member of the company, represent the top cut of native English melodrama of this period, a period which can be said to have come to an abrupt end with the passage of the act "for regulating theatres" in 1843 and the introduction into England of those new types of French melodrama spawned in the wake of Romantic drama, the so-called cape-and-sword pieces and the panoramic dramas of city life. Adelphi dramas are anything but conventional models of playwriting, considering their frequently pretentious and unnatural dialogue, their slapdash construction, their hokum, and their general air of improbability; yet they have many and real melodramatic virtues. Buckstone, overworked part-time hack that he was, possessed a theatrical imagination. Nellie's song is one sample of his creative use of it. In rummaging through his forgotten pieces, one occasionally encounters something more than mere melodramatic competence. The hesitation and bewilderment of little Evelyn at the kindness of Miami—something almost incomprehensible to her after the brutality of her keepers—is conveyed with delicate skill and understanding, and the primitive psychology of Starlight Bess, a minor character in *Flowers of the Forest*, comes through with startling truth. This gypsy girl is unable to reconcile impersonal British justice with her own instincts of right and wrong. When her lover Lemuel is convicted of his crime, she cannot believe that the judgment will be carried out. "Tell them," she pleads with her lawyer, "what a noble boy Lemuel is, how fond he is of me, and how he'd fight for me. . . . Let them see his handsome face and they'll never have the courage to harm him."

Finally, dramas like *The Green Bushes* and *Flowers of the Forest* differ from routine melodrama in not confining themselves exclusively to the theme of the persecuted innocent and its attendant ambuscades, pursuits, and conspiracies. There is action enough in all of them, it is true, but their chief interest lies rather in an internal struggle and a moral problem of choice or atonement—what the French designate as *cornélian*. The tendency is away from the sensational and the physical to a refinement of sensibility and a depth of feeling; the dilemma of Cynthia, the remorse of Miami point forward to *La Dame aux camélias* and *East Lynne*. This was the line Boucicault was to take in his best plays.

XXI

The Manufacture of Melodrama
and Theatre Economics

Since the drama is irrevocably related to the theatre, all the varied ramifications of the show business have their interest and their significance for students of the stage. —BRANDER MATTHEWS

Manufacture is a better word than creation for the process by which English melodrama came into being in the early nineteenth century—manufacture of a strictly standardized article. An author had merely to dump such material as he found in a novel, a ballad, a historical anecdote, a newspaper item, the Newgate Calendar, or what not, into the waiting mould of melodrama. A set of stock characters, a plot worked out in a sequence of exciting incidents and ringing the changes on the basic theme of persecution, songs and comic relief at intervals, plenty of sound morality, and a denouement in which poetic justice is satisfied: these were the ingredients, and they did not change much from the time of Lewis at the beginning of the nineteenth century to that of George R. Sims and Owen Davis at its end.

Melodramatic hacks early discovered the utility of prose fiction as a source of plots, and a "dramatist" could pick a novelist's pockets with impunity, copyright legislation being in an extremely primitive state. Dickens, who complained loudly of this abuse, adopted a plan which the Frenchman Frederick Soulié had hit upon before him to anticipate the pirating: he supplied adaptors with advance proofs of his stories for a consideration. Adaptations of novels for the stage were ineptly done in England, as a rule, particularly in the first half of the century. Scarcely ever, if we except Bulwer-Lytton, is there any evidence of the real skill that Pixerécourt showed, or that Boucicault was later to show, in such jobs. Usually a string of the more exciting episodes was transferred to the stage, the informative aside being worked for all it was worth to take up the slack in the plot which resulted from the compression.

The script was merely a beginning with melodrama. The success of a piece was usually made after it left the author's hands. The melodramatist wrought most happily in providing opportunities for overpowering scenic effects employing quadrupeds, real ships, real water, blue fire, explosives, and the like. No production was complete without its sensation scene, as it came to be called at the middle of the century. "New scenery" was enticingly described in luscious superlatives in the playbills—usually at the expense of the author who frequently was not so much as mentioned. The contrivances themselves often exhibited surprising ingenuity—and more than ingenuity. Colored silks and gauze were extended across the proscenium to get shadowy effects in fairytale and fog scenes; flats were unrolled from one perpendicular cylinder to another upstage (the diorama) to create an illusion of movement; experiments were made in contracting the proscenium to get intimacy in certain scenes, anticipating German innovations of later times; and as early as *Jonathan Bradford* (1833) we encounter the simultaneous, or divided, scene which, from the description in the printed text of the play, would appear to be an ancestor of the cut-away farmhouse of *Desire under the Elms* and other modern Broadway productions, including *Inherit the Wind* and *The Diary of Anne Frank*. The stage is divided into four apartments on two floors: two bedrooms above, the windows opening on a tile roof; and below a back parlor and a bar, separated by a hallway giving on the stage through a front door. The action goes forward in the several apartments, simultaneously or passing from one to the other. A divided scene had appeared before this on the melodramatic stage in *Venoni*, at Drury Lane in 1808; but *Jonathan Bradford* first exploited the rich dramatic possibilities of the device.

What was significant in all this activity was the tendency rather than the accomplishment, excellent as that could at times be. Concern with purely theatrical effects revealed the potentialities of a hitherto neglected factor in the playhouse, promoted a salutary redistribution of emphasis behind the footlights, and fostered a freedom of outlook and an adventurous, experimental spirit that were pregnant with possibilities for the future. The realistic, no less than the romantic, stagecraft of our times had its humble beginning in these often stumbling attempts of popular melodrama to create illusion, establish atmosphere—and attract customers. The innovations in mise-en-scène introduced by T. W. Robertson in his "cup and saucer" comedies at the Prince of Wales under the Bancroft management in the sixties derive largely from this playwright's previous involvement in melodrama, especially of the domestic variety.

The sensation scenes, the almost incessant action, and the

crowded stage in melodrama all called for more careful direction and more thorough rehearsal than the routine business of the traditional repertoire of conventional comedy and tragedy. This department of production in England was to be developed more fully somewhat later in the history of drama in the long-run individual productions of Charles Kean, Charles Fechter, W. S. Gilbert, Robertson, Boucicault, and Irving, though progress was more or less continuous through the first half of the century.

Under the conditions described, virtually anybody could write a play—and virtually everybody did. The ranks of regular playwrights were swollen by part-time recruits from the prompter's box, the managerial office, and the green room, as well as from trades and professions outside the theatre. Both the younger Dibdins, Elliston, Milner, Cross, Osbaldistone, Barrymore, Campbell, Arnold, Almar, Webster, Williams, Buckstone, Townsend, Somerset, Amherst, Moncrieff, Blanchard, Dillon, J. B. Howe, T. P. Taylor, and Boucicault were playwrights incidental to some other activity in the playhouse; and these names by no means exhaust the roll. Ducrow, virtually an illiterate like his predecessor Astley, put his name to more than one heroic spectacle, and Bunn, a manager, took pen in hand to supply the libretti for *The Maid of Artois* and *The Bohemian Girl*, in recognition of which literary accomplishment *Punch* referred to him always as "the poet Bunn." James Robinson Planché had a post in the Civil Service, Thomas Noon Talfourd followed the law, Douglas Jerrold and John Oxenford were editors, Joseph Sterling Coyne, Leicester Buckingham, and Bayle Bernard were critics, Tom Taylor had a half dozen careers, Henry Hart Milman was dean of St. Paul's, Albert Smith a dentist, Gilbert a Becket was a police magistrate, and Mark Lemon kept a pub. At the middle of the century, according to Boucicault, the man who wrote for the theatre and did nothing else—and made a living out of it—had virtually disappeared from the London scene.[1]

Needless to say, rewards were not fabulous. The earnings of playwrights had been good at the beginning of the century. Payments of a thousand pounds are recorded to the elder Charles Dibdin, Morton, and Colman, and Covent Garden paid Reynolds six hundred pounds for a melodrama, *The Exiles*, an adaptation at that. As the century wore on, important writers such as James Sheridan Knowles, Francis Talfourd, and Bulwer-Lytton continued to com-

[1] "Leaves from a Dramatist's Diary," *North American Review*, CXLIX (1889), 228.

mand as much as five hundred pounds at the great houses for their plays, and Coleridge got that amount for *Osorio* (performed as *Remorse*). This kind of remuneration, however, was exceptional. Three to thirty pounds was the scale in the twenties and later, according to Fitzball, for two-act afterpieces, under which head melodramas were usually classified at the theatres royal; Jerrold averaged twenty pounds at the Coburg in the same decade; and humbler houses paid less—two to ten pounds. Boucicault and Burnand recall fifty pounds as a good price for a three-act piece in the forties and fifties. Four pounds average was cited as the going price for a new play in London in testimony given at a Parliamentary inquiry in 1856. Buckstone, author of a string of hits, got sixty pounds, which was increased to seventy after much haggling with Yates, the Adelphi manager.

Dramatists had to whack out many plays in the course of a year in order to exist on such hire; and as a rule they were glad to sell themselves down the river as stock, or resident, authors at the various theatres for so much a week, turning out dramas as required. At the beginning of the century Thomas Dibdin filled this office at the Surrey, his stipend being fifteen pounds a week, for which he had also to act as house manager. Through a similar arrangement at Sadler's Wells commencing in 1800 his brother Charles received three guineas a week and two during the period when the house was dark, a payment which was ultimately increased to four and three guineas respectively plus benefit privileges worth from thirty to forty pounds.[2] Fitzball worked as this kind of resident playwright at the Surrey for a while in the forties for a pittance, and in 1829 at the same resort five pounds was as much as Jerrold could pry from the tightfisted Davidge. John Wilkins got thirty-five shillings a week at the City of London after the middle of the century, and Colin Hazlewood three pounds at the Brit. Is it necessary to mention that playwrights often died in the poorhouse? Morton and Moncrieff passed their last days at the Charterhouse.

The injustices of the system were flagrantly exhibited in the case of Jerrold, who, while gifted with no genius, was at least a sincere, honest craftsman who wrote his own plays instead of cribbing them from the French or from novels. *Black Eyed Susan* made a fortune (ten thousand pounds) for Elliston at the Surrey and later ran prosperously at Drury Lane with Cooke in the leading role collecting a salary of sixty pounds a week and receiving a benefit every

2 *Memoirs of Charles Dibdin the Younger*, p. 34.

three weeks. The author's receipts were sixty pounds, ten of which came from a bookseller for the printing rights.

Of course, only a few of the furnishers of British drama had legitimate grounds for complaint since the plays they offered over their own names were often stolen goods. The real sufferers were the novelists and French playwrights. But whatever the justification, the playwrights finally revolted at their lot and, joining forces, pressed for relief in Parliament under the leadership of Planché. Through their agitation, the Copyright Bill, or Dramatic Authors' Act of 1833, written by Talfourd, was passed. This promised some improvement, particularly in checking the depredations of piratical managers, of whom the provincials were the worst offenders. By the terms of the act, no play could be produced without the author's written permission. The Dramatic Authors' Society was formed at the same time to see to it that the law was enforced. Enforcement, however, presented insuperable difficulties; and later the play-wrights discovered that, when they sold the publication rights of a play to a printer (publisher), the acting rights went with them in the opinion of the courts—and they were as bad off as ever. Planché, who lost a decision to the bookseller Cumberland on this point, writes about the case in his *Recollections*.

In 1844 Dion Boucicault, then at the beginning of his career, received three hundred pounds from Madame Vestris, manager of the Olympic, for *London Assurance*, his first comedy hit. Subsequent essays by the young Irishman in the same field yielded considerably less—fifty to one hundred pounds. When he complained, Webster, manager of the Adelphi, explained the economics of the business to him. "Why should I pay 500 pounds for an original play which may fail," he asked, "when I can get translations of an assured Paris success for twenty-five?"[3] There was no answer, so Dion went to Paris, did his adaptations, and took his twenty-five pounds. But he was hurt in his pride and in his pocketbook—both sensitive points with him—and he resolved to do something about it.

They ordered these things differently in France, he discovered. In Paris an author was assured of a fair, if not a princely, return for his work, a condition which undoubtedly had much to do with the superiority of French over English melodramas. Forty-two years prior to the passage of the Dramatic Authors' Act, a French law had

[3] "Decline of the Drama," *North American Review*, CXXV (1877), 243. See also "Early Days of a Dramatist," *North American Review*, CXLVIII (1889), 591.

clearly established the rights of playwrights in their property, and it was an effective law. A decree of the National Assembly, June 13, 1791, required the formal, written consent of authors to the representation of their plays. This, however, proved only a beginning in the fight for amelioration of the dramatists' lot. The principle had to be implemented.

The decree confirmed existing arrangements between the Français and living authors or authors recently deceased, but it did not undertake to lay down procedures to be followed at the many new theatres which had sprung up at the Revolution except to the extent that its application was extended to the Odeon in 1807. French playwrights, in the main, remained at the mercy of niggardly managers. Early in the century both Pixerécourt and Caigniez, among other melodramatists, were made the victims of hard bargains. Corsse, at the Ambigu, paid the latter only nine hundred francs for *Le Jugement de Salomon*, on which he made three hundred thousand.

The crux of the problem was the lump-sum payment, and to this the playwrights addressed themselves soon after banding together in what was probably the first authors' trade union, the Comité des Auteurs (1806).[4] Pixerécourt was a leader in this group and from him came the suggestion of the sharing agreement or percentage plan as a remedy. It was not an entirely new idea. Remuneration in this form had been paid as early as 1653 to Quinault by the players at the Hotel de Bourgogne; and shortly afterwords it was adopted as standard practice by the Français, replacing the outright payment. The actor-proprietors of the foundation, however, saw to it that the playwrights never got too much profit from the arrangement, devising all manner of exemptions and deductions. These abuses were corrected to some extent toward the end of the eighteenth century through the heroic exertions of Beaumarchais, who gained a fortune from his *Mariage de Figaro*, but at the debacle of the Revolution the new theatres apparently made individual bargains with authors without reference to the existing practice at a higher level.

In their campaign to establish standard rates of payment the

---

[4] In the 1780's Beaumarchais had brought dramatic authors together at regular intervals to formulate plans and agree on terms in their war with the Français, but no permanent organization was formed.

authors had recourse to organization and negotiation rather than legislation. By maintaining a solid front, first in the Comité des Auteurs and later in its successor, the Société des Auteurs—more alert and aggressive bodies than the English Society of Authors— they finally succeeded in imposing their demands on all theatres, in the provinces as well as in Paris. Under the negotiated arrangements, the Boulevard houses began by paying a stipulated sum each night. This plan was retained only at the Cirque, where forty francs per night were the terms. When Boucicault was in Paris, 10 per cent was the rule at standard melodrama houses, the Porte Saint-Martin, the Ambigu, and the Gaîté. At the Française, the playwright drew one-twelfth of the gross for five-act plays; at the Opéra Comique, one-sixth to one-eighth; and at the Vaudevilles, the Gymnase, the Variétés and the Palais Royal, 12 per cent.[5] Royalties continued during an author's lifetime and for a period of ten years after his death, payable to his heirs. Besides royalties, playwrights were entitled to a certain number of passes, which they had the privilege of selling through the box office. The collections and disbursement of all royalties, fees, and perquisites were made through a board on which the playwrights were represented.

Caigniez died poor, but after him few popular French dramatists did, unless through speculation or improvidence. Pixerécourt had his magnificent library, his city apartment, and his country house at Fontenay-sous-Bois, until a fire in 1835 at the Gaîté, of which he was part owner, ruined him; Anicet-Bourgeois, who was a half-starved notary's clerk when he began writing plays, ended as a gentleman of leisure in a sumptuous chalet on the cliff at Étretat; Dennery was a munificent patron of charities; Sardou lived regally at his château at Marly and his villa at Nice on his annual income of 250,000 francs from the theatre. Drama paid better than fiction at the middle of the century and later in France; it was in play form, and not as novels, that *La Dame aux camélias* and *La Vie de Bohème* (*Scènes de la vie de Bohème*) made fortunes for their authors. Dumas's receipts from one hundred performances of the former at the Vaudevilles totalled sixty thousand francs. Even such a popular romancer as Jules Verne found playwriting more profitable than the writing of novels.

[5] Admission prices ranged from fifty centimes to five francs at the Boulevard houses. All these figures are Charles Hervey's, from his *Theatres of Paris* (Paris, 1846), published in English as a sort of tourists' guidebook, pp. 357–358, 361 ff.

Back in England, Boucicault took a job as house author at the
Princess with Kean at fifteen pounds a week and set about enlisting
his fellow-slaves in a campaign to wrest from managers concessions
like those which had been won in France. In London, as in Paris,
there was a fairly ancient precedent for the percentage plan which
here took the form of the author's benefit. This institution began in
Shakespeare's time and was revived at the Restoration. At first the
author received the receipts of one performance, the third; during
the eighteenth century the number was increased to two and then to
three. However, at the end of the century, when house charges and
other deductions had mounted to a considerable figure especially at
the patent houses, playwrights, when given their choice in the
matter, came to prefer an advanced guarantee in the form of a fixed
payment to the doubtful benefits of speculation on the drawing
power of their works and the uncertainties of the weather. Thus the
way was opened for a return to the lump-sum arrangement of
earlier times. Such payments were nearly universal in the nineteenth
century in England, certainly at the minors. A few instances of
royalty or percentage payments are recorded. Tom Robertson got
ten pounds a night from the Bancrofts at the Haymarket after he
attained fame; Macready paid Browning twelve pounds a night for
the first twenty-five performances of *Strafford* at Covent Garden
(1837) and ten thereafter; and on a lower level George A. Sala
collected twenty-five shillings a night from Shepherd in the fifties at
the Surrey for an adaptation of *The Corsican Brothers.* In the
United States, Boker collected 5 per cent on his poetic tragedies,
and Barras seventy-five dollars per night on *The Black Crook;* and
in 1879 Bartley Campbell had an arrangement with Palmer whereby
he got ten dollars per night for *My Partner.* Incidentally, Boker
and Boucicault were instrumental in obtaining the first legal protection of the playwright in the United States: an act of Congress
passed in 1856 which outlawed the theft of play titles.

Boucicault's campaign among British playwrights failed, owing to
the selfishness of a few members of the Authors' Society who put
their individual profits above the interests of their profession. Dis-
gusted, he washed his hands of the affair. Thereafter he confined
himself largely to working for his individual interests. A dramatist
with a knack of giving the public what it wanted, a shrewd
bargainer, a brilliant showman, and a courageous fighter, he was
well equipped to fight single-handed the battle for the emancipation of the playwright.

In 1860 came the opportunity for which he had been waiting.

Returning from America with an assured hit of his own composition in his pocket, *The Colleen Bawn*, he went ahead with his own production in partnership with Webster at the Adelphi, hiring a cast himself and arranging for all other details. The play ran for 360 nights in London, the Queen herself returning twice to weep over the woes of the heroine, Eily O'Connor. The author-producer then proceeded to organize and tour his own road companies (three of them) instead of selling the rights to provincial managers—a plan he had experimented with in America to forestall pirating—and made another handsome profit. He followed the same procedure with his later plays, losing fortunes occasionally as well as making them. In every case, however, according to an article he wrote, "the author was starred, and his importance recognized."[6]

Boucicault's independence and his success made many enemies for him among London managers; in 1864 a cabal used all the power at their united command to jockey him out of a sharing agreement he had entered into with Vining at the Princess for the production of *The Streets of London* (which had been *The Poor of New York* in America). He prevailed in spite of them.

The Colleen Bawn speculation had far-reaching consequences. The individual production, the long run, the touring production (one, two, and three companies in England), and typecasting in the Boucicault manner came more and more to the fore in the English and American theatres, ultimately shouldering out the traditional repertory or stock organization and opening the way for the syndicate of the twentieth century. Following the success of *Hazel Kirke* in New York at the Madison Square in 1880, road companies of the play were sent out, two of them managed by Charles and Gustave Frohman who were to take the lead in developing and extending the new system; and later in the same decade *The Lights o' London* and other London melodramas were handled in the same way on this side. In the United States, travelling companies, or combinations, which Joe Jefferson encountered for the first time in Michigan during 1869,[7] numbered one hundred in 1876–77; they had increased to three hundred by 1880 and to five hundred by 1900.

The sharing agreement likewise made headway, though slowly.

[6] "Leaves from a Dramatist's Diary," *North American Review*, CXLIX (1889), 232.

[7] *Rip Van Winkle: the autobiography of Joseph Jefferson* (London, 1949), pp. 49–50.

All authors did not have a *Colleen Bawn* to proceed on, nor were
many of them endowed with the practical abilities to turn a play to
such good purpose as Boucicault. (Bartley Campbell drove himself
insane from overwork attempting to emulate the Irishman's feat of
producing his own plays and organizing and managing road companies). Through the sixties and seventies dramatists continued to
be shortchanged in their dealings with managers. Taylor got only
150 pounds for *The Ticket-of-Leave Man*, a greater money-maker
than any of Boucicault's works, and thirty-five pounds was as much
as Charles Reade could get for many of his plays. Steele Mackaye
did not share in the distribution of the million dollar profit from his
Hazel Kirke beyond a five thousand dollar annual salary as manager
of the Madison Square. As late as 1897 William A. Brady was able to
buy *Way Down East* outright, and during the same decade Clyde
Fitch disposed of his *Frédérick le Maître* on this basis. Nervertheless,
times were changing, for which Boucicault must receive most of the
credit. In 1865 Vining entered into the same arrangement with
Reade on *It Is Never Too Late to Mend* as he had with Boucicault
on *The Streets of London* a year earlier, and the playwright told his
biographer, John Coleman, that his share from the receipts of the
first eighteen nights amounted to more than all he had received for a
period of eighteen years from his other plays. It was at Boucicault's
suggestion that Francis Cowley Burnand[8] insisted upon a percentage
plan of payment which brought the author two thousand pounds
instead of 150—the regular price for a West End burlesque in that
decade. Ten years later, again in the columns of *The Theatre*,
Burnand was urging upon London managers the adoption of a
standard royalty agreement.

Straitened finances at the Royalty had brought the management
to accept Burnand's proposition, and the same condition induced
Wilson Barrett to offer George R. Sims an interest (10 per cent of
the gross) in *The Lights o' London* in lieu of a flat price when he

---

[8] "I think Mr. Dion Boucicault, as author and manager, let in the
light on the relative position of author and manager. It was he who
explained to me the just and equitable arrangement of percentages."
—"Francis Cowley Burnand: an Autobiography," *The Theatre* (London) I (Feb. 1, 1883), 107. This judgment was confirmed by George
Augustus Sala, who wrote: "Boucicault invented the royalty payment."—*The Life and Adventures of George Augustus Sala*, Written
by Himself (London 1895), Vol. I, p. 93.

was putting on that play at the Princess in 1882—and a highly remunerative interest it proved. Paul Meritt was the beneficiary of a similar spur-of-the-moment compromise offer by Wilmot at the Queens for his *The New Babylon*, a smash hit at the same time as Sims's play. Two years later, for the first time in an English-speaking country, an author made a fortune on royalties from a single play. He was Henry Arthur Jones, and his play was the melodrama, *The Silver King*, from which he collected eighteen thousand pounds in his lifetime. George Bronson Howard matched the feat in the United States in 1889 with his *Shenandoah*. Others grew rich writing for the theatre in the eighties and nineties; Henry Pettitt, a furnisher of Drury Lane melodrama, who had gotten five pounds at the Pavilion for his maiden effort, left an estate of fifty thousand pounds. Meanwhile, leaks in the copyright laws were plugged and international agreements concluded (1887–1891) which ended the nuisance of unauthorized importations and brought royalties from foreign performances. Augustin Daly paid Sardou $9,500 for the American rights to *Odette*.

The improved financial status of the playwriting profession attracted a better type of author, who, writing superior plays, drew better-class audiences—people of means and the fashionable world. Stalls, which had made their appearance in better-grade London theatres at the middle of the nineteenth century, encroached more and more upon the pit, as the carriage trade flocked to see such "Mayfair dramas" as *The Second Mrs. Tanqueray* and *The Dancing Girl*. Bars were removed from the premises and admission prices raised. The whole tendency proved disastrous for melodrama in the end. Jones, with the proceeds of his melodramas in his pocket, was free to devote his time and energy to the sort of plays he really desired to write, serious studies of modern English life. Slowly but surely the old-fashioned drama of action and scenic spectacle was driven back whence it had come—to the East Ends and Boweries of the world where the movies were ultimately to supplant it.

All this, however, was in the future. At the middle of the century melodrama had decades of prosperity to look forward to. This prosperity was to arise chiefly from the introduction to the English stage of thrilling new themes discovered—or, at least, most effectively developed—by the French in the wake of Romantic drama, and presented in the form of the cape-and-sword dramas and the panoramic plays of city life. In this enterprise, Dion Boucicault was a leader.

XXII

Boucicault and the Stage Irishman

LARRY. *Mr. Keegan: If you are going to be sentimental about Ireland, I shall bid you good evening.* —JOHN BULL'S OTHER ISLAND

No melodramatist at all comparable to Pixerécourt appeared in England until after the death of that French pioneer, and when one did appear he proved to be not an Englishman at all but an Irishman with the extraordinary Gallic name of Boucicault derived from a Huguenot ancestor. Dionysius Lardner Boucicault's plays, his ideas, and his projects were ubiquitous from the middle of the century onward; two continents felt his influence, often profound, as actor, adaptor, stage director, manager, and *régisseur*. He invented the first fireproof scenery; originated the terms "sensation scene" and "sensation drama" and brought to perfection the sort of thing they were used to describe; discovered Henry Irving and brought him to London; initiated the young David Belasco, who was his amanuensis for a while, into the secrets of his art; showed his colleagues how to handle stage crowds before the Meiningen troupe was so much as heard of in England; gave Joseph Jefferson a lesson in acting which was to profit that great American comedian in building up all the flavorful characterizations associated with his fame; abolished "half time" and its attendant evils by the prestige of his example; and did as much as any one man to domesticate the French cape-and-sword and city-life melodrama in England and the United States. John M. Synge, Bernard Shaw, Sean O'Casey, Brendan Behan, and the American James A. Herne have acknowledged a debt to him as playwrights. Henry Miller told his biographer, Frank P. Morse, that he owed most of his skill as a director to Boucicault. In the third quarter of the century he was the most prolific, the most prosperous, and the most widely imitated playwright of the Anglo-Saxon stage, if not its most important single figure. His decisive contribution to the establishment of the long run, the touring production, and the royalty system is described in the preceding chapter.

During his four-year stay in Paris (1844–48), a period of the greatest importance in his development, Boucicault turned to what was to be his *métier*—melodrama. He began with adaptations. The cape-and-sword plays were the principal novelty in the French capital then, and he did a version of *Don César de Bazan* for Webster in 1844. Then, after a rendering of *La Closerie des genêts* (*The Willow Copse*) for the Adelphi, came *Pauline* (from Dumas), *The Broken Vow* (*L'Abbaye de Castro*), *Genevieve; or, the Reign of Terror* (*Le Chevalier de la maison rouge*), and others.

In 1850 he found a berth at the Princess as stock author for a while during Charles Kean's management, an important period in the annals of the old Oxford Street house. At this time Macready was retiring, and the patent houses, where he and all the other great tragedians before him had made their bid for fame, were giving up the pretence of being any longer the special custodians of legitimate drama. Such people of taste and intelligence as still went to the theatre were turning elsewhere, and the son of the great Edmund in his own house naturally attracted many of them. The elaborate and beautiful mounting of the plays there, if not the quality of the star's acting, soon earned for the Princess a place as the accepted successor of the degenerated nationals. The queen herself became something like a sponsor for the new actor-manager.

Kean, like Boucicault, had been in Paris, where he had seen and admired the melodramatic tragedy of Casamir Delavigne and the new Romantic melodrama of Dumas at the Théâtre Historique. He was ambitious to emulate the French actors Ligier, in *Louis XI*, and Fechter, in *Les Frères corses*, and he arranged for English productions of these dramas. To Boucicault fell the work of adaptation. *The Corsican Brothers* was given first, and it proved a tremendous success, not a little of it owing to the effective management of the vision scenes, in which the adaptor had a hand. Numerous examples of the cape-and-sword school followed at the Princess, one by Boucicault, *The Vampire*, in which the adaptor appeared in the role of the monster, and others by various hands: John Oxenford (*Pauline*), Bayle Bernard (*Mount Saint-Michel; or, the Fairy of the Sands*, from a novel of medieval Normandy with supernatural touches, by Paul Féval); Palgrave Simpson (*Marco Spada*, a bandit melodrama of the romantic type, from Scribe's libretto for Auber's opera); and Charles Reade (*The Courier of Lyons*).

At the termination of Kean's ten-year period at the Princess the cape-and-sword melodrama was firmly established on the English stage. It triumphed completely in the sixties, when the brilliant Charles Fechter appeared at the Lyceum, the Princess, and the Adelphi in a fuller repertory which included *Ruy Blas, The Duke's*

Motto (John Brougham's version of *Le Bossu*), *The King's Butterfly* (from Paul Meurice's *Fanfan la tulipe*), and *The Watch Cry* (*Lazare le pâtre*), as well as *Don César, The Corsican Brothers, Monte Cristo*, and *Bel Dominio* (Brougham's version of *L'Abbaye de Castro*). In 1867 Fechter took these plays to America, where for a few years he charmed the ladies with his fancy French lovemaking and his bouncing heroics.

When Boucicault left Kean as the sequel to a quarrel and came to the United States in 1853, he put Romanticism—at least of the Dumas brand—behind him. He worked in New York and on the road for several seasons getting a firsthand impression of audiences from the excellent vantage point of the actor; and on the basis of this experience he turned to new themes, new settings, and new appeals in his plays. "The actual, the contemporaneous, the photographic," were what the public wanted, he decided; and he proceeded to give it to them.[1] No writer has ever been more sensitive to popular taste or more complaisant in catering to it.

The first application of his theory came in 1857. This was a panic year, and he set to work on a panic play. A French original lay ready to hand, *Les Pauvres de Paris*, which had already been done at least once in English without attracting any wide notice. Boucicault's version, *The Poor of New York*, was a triumph and held the stage for thirty years and more. It is easy to see why. It is the Second Bank of the United States which closes in the prologue (Nicholas Biddle's famous institution of that name in Philadelphia had closed in 1837, the period represented); the captain is a Yankee captain; the scene is New York, not Manchester and London as in the other adaptation, the sets representing Union Square near Tammany Hall, Fifth Avenue outside the Brevoort, Five Points, and Brooklyn Heights; and the dialogue is pitted with piquant references to the Astors and the Livingstones, the new Croton Reservoir and the Academy of Music, the Maison Dorée and the Union Club, the *Herald* and even *The Police Gazette*. The thing was as spicy and topical as the *Herald* itself.

In the same year India was shaken with the Sepoy Mutiny, and the papers were full of the trouble. Boucicault fixed upon that for his next subject and, using an actual occurrence for a starting point, wrote *Jessie Brown; or, the Relief of Lucknow*, which succeeded not only because of its timeliness but because of its intrinsic merit as

[1] "Leaves from a Dramatist's Diary," pp. 229 ff.

a melodrama as well. He had by now served his apprenticeship in the good school of French adaptation; this effort, an original play, can be called his masterpiece. It was a masterpiece by a less special and technical definition. The ear for easy, natural dialogue, the sharp eye for surfaces of character, and the sense of dramatic situation with which he seems to have been endowed in his cradle were never exercised with more telling effect. The people in the play are real people, by the one-dimensional standards of melodrama, sketched with a sure hand: Cassidy, the comic Irish private, thoroughly enjoying a bloody scrimmage with the heathen and unable to repress a joke at the most solemn and perilous moments; Sweeney Jones, five-foot-two of real soldier and reliable as a terrier; Blount, the parson, whose clerical conscience bothers him grievously as he wields a ramrod to excellent purpose in the defense of the fort (can Shaw have got his Rev. Mr. Brudnell, of *The Devil's Disciple*, from his Irish predecessor?); Geordie, the coward who finds himself when the real test of his mettle comes; and little Scotch Jessie Brown, a heroine from humble life, staunch, simplehearted, heedless of self, jealously proud of her stalwart Highland race, and real woman to the core. Completely commercialized and utterly cynical as he was and freely admitted himself to be, Boucicault nevertheless had the secret of a potent magic for bringing homely, unspoiled folk like Jessie alive on the stage.

Closer to home for Americans in the fifties was the question of slavery; and with one eye on *Uncle Tom's Cabin* Boucicault wrote *The Octoroon* in 1859. Irish luck persisted; the play opened at the Winter Garden within a week of the execution of John Brown and was the usual success in spite of an unhappy end. After a highly exciting evening, Zoe, the mixed-blood heroine of the title, finally kills herself rather than allow the white hero, who loves her, to marry her and thereby incur social ostracism and the loss of his ancestral estates in Louisiana, which may be saved by his union with her generous rival, Dora. Supporting the fable was the usual battery of surefire accessories. There is a mute in the cast of characters, the Indian boy Wah-no-te (Boucicault's rôle) falsely accused, like Pixerécourt's Eloi, of murder; a mortgage foreclosed on the old homestead by the villain; a dramatic slave auction, at which the same viper outbids the magnanimous Dora for Zoe, whom he covets; a threatened lynching, averted only at the last minute and by inches; a river boat in flames shown moving across the stage at the back; and a fight to the death with knives.

The play was "contemporaneous" and "actual" and in one detail literally "photographic." Daguerreotypes were then a novelty, and Boucicault contrived to introduce a camera into his action in an episode lifted from a recent novel. The villain murders the Negro boy Paul, a mail carrier, to get possession of a letter the delivery of which will wreck all his schemes. Apparently there have been no witnesses. The crime, however, is recorded—caught by an amazing camera "without the agency of human hands," thanks to a "self-developing" fluid with which the plates are prepared, and to "the blessed sun of heaven," which, "looking down, struck upon this plate the image of the deed," as the hero explains it in the big scene wherein the villain is unmasked.

One more journalistic play may be mentioned, *The Long Strike* (1866), an ingenious dramatization of two novels by Mrs. Elizabeth Gaskell, *Mary Barton* and *Lizzie Leigh*. From a theatrical standpoint one scene laid in a telegraph office was masterly. An innocent man is about to be convicted of the murder of a mill owner. The only person who can establish an alibi for him is a sailor, already at Liverpool, one hundred miles away, and aboard his ship, which is sailing for America in the morning. The sweetheart of the accused prisoner comes on to send a telegram in an attempt to reach this valuable witness. The office is closed, however, and the clerk tells her the station is dead for the night. At her vehement appeal he consents to send a flash. It is tapped out on the practicable apparatus used in playing the scene, and all wait tensely. Minutes pass and no answering signal is heard. The young woman, in despair, turns to go, when suddenly through the theatre the instrument is heard to click; the line is open and the message can go through!

In 1859 Boucicault was working at Laura Keene's Theatre, after having quarreled—there were always quarrels—with his associates at the Winter Garden. Here was given the premiere of *The Trial of Effie Deans*, a version of *The Heart of Midlothian*. Two scenes in it were highly spectacular: the trial, with the author in the role of advocate for the defense, and the storming of the Tolbooth by a howling mob, which battered down the huge doors of the prison and swarmed onto the stage.

In March Miss Keene unexpectedly found herself with a failure on her hands, Boucicault's comedy, *Vanity Fair*, and she appealed to her aide for something which might be used to tide her over the several potentially prosperous weeks of the season remaining. He had no play ready, but he undertook to provide one. Oh his way home from the theatre he dropped into a tiny basement shop on lower Broadway and stuffed his pockets with paperback fiction bought from the little Italian proprietor—who happened to be the original Brentano—and at his lodgings off Union Square he sat up late that night working over one of the novels, *The Collegians*, by another Irishman, Gerald Griffin. In the morning he was able to dispatch this cheering message to Miss Keene: "I send you seven steel engravings of scenes around Killarney. Get your scene painter to work on them at once. I also send a book of Irish melodies with those marked I desire Baker to score for the orchestra. I shall read one act of my new play tomorrow; we rehearse that while I am writing the second, which will be ready on Monday; and we rehearse the second while I am doing the third. We can get the play out in a fortnight."[2] He was as good as his word; the play was produced on schedule. It was *The Colleen Bawn*, the earliest and one of the most popular of those Irish dramas which were Boucicault's supreme contribution to melodrama.

The Collegians (1829), a vigorous and original novel, is a somber psychological study, almost naturalistic in tone, of a possessive and imperious mother love and its disastrous effects upon its object, a well-meaning but weak young man, an only son. The tragic plot is unfolded against a background of Irish provincial manners closely observed and set down with no glossing over of the drunken violence and cold-blooded brutality of gentry and peasantry alike. The hero—if he can be called that—Hardress Cregan, an impoverished Kerry squire, loves a beautiful and uncultivated ropemaker's daughter, Eily O'Connor. He marries her in an uncanonical ceremony performed by an unfrocked priest and carries her off from her widowed father to an isolated retreat on the Lakes of Killarney. He keeps the marriage secret fearing the effect upon his mother, an ambitious, strong-minded woman, who has other plans for her boy, including particularly an alliance with a mild, pleasant gentlewoman-heiress of the neighborhood, Ann Chute. Under the relentless prodding of his formidable parent, Hardress neglects, then quarrels with, his still unacknowledged bride; and finally, after he has actually pledged himself to Ann, he instigates his faithful boatman, Danny Mann, to drown the unhappy Eily as the only way out of his terrible dilemma. Overwhelmed with remorse and half maddened by what he has done, Hardress vents his feelings upon his agent

[2] *Ibid.*, pp. 231–232.

Danny, beating him savagely when they meet for the first time after the crime. Danny revenges himself by informing, and the police descend upon Castle Chute at the very hour of Cregan's wedding to Anne.

This strong meat became so much mush and molasses in Boucicault's play. No dramatist since Pixerécourt had so thoroughly distorted a work of literature in preparing it for the stage; Gerald Griffin, a conscientious artist, must have certainly turned over in his grave at the result. Throughout, however, it was distortion in the interest of good melodramatic theatre; the job from end to end was an excellent example of Boucicault's skill at reconstructing a work in a way that would go down with the mob. "I despoil genius to make the mob admire it," he confessed.[3] He tampered with the motivation, changed the mood, substituted a happy end, and added and suppressed with a ruthless hand. The marriage is performed by a priest in good standing; Eily's marriage lines—the papers—are dragged into the plot to provide two dramatic scenes, a particularly effective one being the curtain for the first act, in which Father Tom puts the girl upon her knees and makes her swear on her mother's grave that she will never part with them; Ann is metamorphosed into a horsey soubrette making jokes in the manner of Lady Gay Spanker of *London Assurance*—the same jokes at times; Moll of the Reeks, a drunken, brazen, fighting harridan, becomes the tender, motherly Sheelah; a villain is invented, holding a mortgage which he threatens to foreclose unless the widowed Mrs. Cregan accepts him for a husband—an addition to the original story which furnishes a generous excuse for the son's bigamous overtures since it is to save his mother that he undertakes to marry for money; Danny does not deliberately betray his master; and Hardress becomes an entirely innocent party to the drowning—which finally turns out to be no drowning at all, Eily being hauled dripping out of the lake in the nick of time by Myles-na-Coppaleen and eventually reunited to her repentant spouse.

It was this rescue scene and this character Myles and possibly Ann as well—all Boucicault's creations save for the slightest of suggestions—which made *The Colleen Bawn* the record-breaking hit it became. The whole stage picture and all the business were got up and directed with a cunning hand: the marine cave, realistically

---

[3] Townsend Walsh, *The Career of Dion Boucicault* (New York, 1915), p. 73.

reproduced, with the moon seen through an opening at the back; Eily thrust from the boat in spite of her touching pleas for mercy; the shot which fells Danny; and the sudden appearance of Myles, who, crawling down the rocky cliff, catches sight of Eily and dives spectacularly into the water to save her.

At least one such sensation scene figured in each of Boucicault's plays: the flaming river boat in *The Octoroon;* the hanging of Achmet in *Jessie Brown;* the burning of the house in Five Points in *The Poor of New York;* the storming of the sponging house in *Formosa;* the horse races in *The Flying Scud* and *The Jilt;* the sinking ship in *Daddy O'Dowd;* and the escape of Shaun in *Arrah-na-Pogue; or, the Wicklow Wedding*, a scene in which the prison wall is turned inside out so that the audience first sees the captive in his cell and a moment later coming through the window and climbing up the ivy of the wall to freedom. Beginning in 1868 with *After Dark (Les Bohémiens de Paris)*, which had a scene representing London's new underground, Boucicault increased the number of sensation scenes to three and four in his plays. "Sensation is what the public wants," he told William Winter, "and you can't give them too much of it."[4]

Myles was the celebrated stage Irishman in all his glory. As such, he was no novelty, of course; droll, jaunty, devil-may-care Hibernians had capered and joked in English comedy and comic opera prior ever to Sir Lucius O'Trigger of Sheridan's *The Rivals;* and during the first half of the nineteenth century comedians like Tyrone Power and the first John Drew made a business out of interpeting them on both sides of the Atlantic. As depicted by Boucicault, however, who knew this character in his native habitat and had studied him from life, the stage Irishman assumes new traits and radiates new charm. What differentiates him particularly is that he develops as a personality in the course of the action. In the early scenes he is presented in a minor key as a purely humorous character, such as he had been in previous drama and as he is in *The Collegians* where Myles remains a subordinate figure, a sly, impudent scapegrace in rags and tatters, addicted to poteen and venial deviltry, broad of brogue, invincibly good-natured, and liberally endowed with mother wit and the Irish peasant's inborn faculty for fluent and quite bewildering tergiversation. As the play proceeds, Boucicault brings this character along slowly, adding touches here

[4] William Winter, *Other Days* (New York, 1908), p. 140.

and there and working up to a sudden fortissimo, one of those gratifying surprises of character which count so heavily on the stage: Under the pressure of an emergency, the latent fineness of the likable ne'er-do-well rises spectacularly to the surface in a deed of heroism or self-sacrifice—usually as the curtain to the second act—to bring the drama to its climax, a moment nicely timed to fall in with the sensation scene. Such a moment was the rescue of Eily. The comic, in short, becomes the comic hero. Boucicault did for the genial peasant what Fitzball and Jerrold had done for the British tar a generation earlier. The nominal, wellborn straight hero, with which all the Irish plays are provided, a colorless figure at best, is thrown completely into the shade.

The success of *The Colleen Bawn* set imitators to work almost at once. The play had scarcely closed at the Adelphi when Edward Falconer, another Gael and creator of the role of Danny Mann, opened at the Lyceum with *The Peep o' Day Boys*, which had a sensation scene closely patterned after Boucicault's marine cave. Other "ould sod" dramas followed in close order by Falconer, Brougham, Hazlewood and others; they can be counted by the score. There were several dramatizations of the career of that favorite Irish hero, Robert Emmett, one by Brandon Tynan (1902) and another by Frank Marshall. Marshall's play, written for Henry Irving in 1883, was banned by the Lord Chamberlain. It was given its premiere by Boucicault in Chicago in 1884. American playwrights contributed their quota of Irish drama. James A. Herne wrote *Garry Owen* for Tony Farrel and Maggie Cline in the nineties; Bartley Campbell turned out *My Geraldine* for Boucicault's first wife, Agnes Robertson, an ideal Irish heroine though Scotch by birth, and *Friend or Foe* for William J. Scanlan; and even a Native American agitator such as Harry Watkins of early Bowery fame put his name to an Irish piece, *Trodden Down; or, Under Two Flags.*

After Boucicault the authors didn't matter greatly, especially in the United States; what the audiences came to see was the star. Billy Florence, born Conlin, and his brother-in-law Barney Williams, founder of the Shriners, were popular stage Irishmen; and somewhat later several performers specialized in this line, often appearing in nothing else, among them Tyrone Power, W. J. Scanlan, Joe Murphy, Andrew Mack, and Chauncey Olcott.

Ireland, as James Joyce has pointed out, is a land of song; and plays needed to have plenty of tunes in them to please this race of ardent playgoers on both sides of the Atlantic. Boucicault rewrote

"The Wearin' of the Green" and sang it in *Arrah-na-Pogue* causing a near riot at the Princess in London on the opening night in 1864; and ballads are thick in all the plays given in America, where the Irish drama became an established industry in the eighties. A fruity tenor voice was an indispensable requisite in a star. It was Scanlan's rendering of such things as "Mavoureen," "Molly O," and "The Old Countree," quite as much as his acting or the plays he appeared in (*Mavourneen, The Irish Minstrel, Myles Aroon, The Minstrel of Clare*, etc.), that made him the gallery lion he was. He "composed" all his songs himself, though he was unable to read a note of music. Olcott, who inherited his mantle—though excitable partisans of Andrew Mack would never concede it—introduced some of the greatest of Ernest Ball's song hits including "Mother Machree," "I Love the Name of Mary," "A Little Bit of Heaven," and "When Irish Eyes Are Smiling," beside many equally popular numbers of his own composition such as "My Wild Irish Rose." The plays themselves showed a sad falling off from the high standards set by Boucicault, for which the star system can in part be blamed. *O'Neill of Derry, Barry of Ballymore, A Romance of Athlone*, and other items in the Olcott repertory, written for the most part by Augustus Pitou who was his, and had been Scalan's, manager were pretty thin soup. Significant of the decline is the circumstance that the star invariably played the part of a genteel hero, a fine gentleman.

Boucicault followed up *The Colleen Bawn* with *Arrah-na-Pogue; or, the Wicklow Wedding* (1864) and *The Shaughraun* (1874). These plays were even more cordially received than the earlier one, as they deserved to be since they are better jobs. *Arrah-na-Pogue* is particularly good and the first two acts of it are as fine a piece of genre comedy writing as was done in the whole English-speaking theatre in the nineteenth century. These were original dramas, based upon the uprising of '98 and the Fenian troubles, factual events in Ireland's eternal fight for freedom. Perhaps the finest thing about them is that incomparable speech which Irish playwrights find so easy to write because they have merely to put down on paper what they hear all about them. A generation before Synge caught the singing rhythm and poetic imagery of this language from his loft in a peasant cottage in Wicklow, Boucicault, his generally despised predecessor, had in some degree done the same thing. "I was filled with sudden death," says a character in *The Colleen Bawn*, meaning that a sudden rage overwhelmed him. Father Tom's recipe for punch, in *The Colleen Bawn*, and Shaun's account, in *The Shaugh-raun*, of how he came to steal—or, rather, be stolen by—Squire Foley's mare in the midst of a fox hunt are two of many examples of richly humorous dialect writing. Men of unimpeachable literary taste have expressed their admiration for Boucicault's dialogue.

Boucicault's note to Miss Keene promising her *The Colleen Bawn* reveals the speed at which he wrote, his attention to incidental detail like music and stage settings, and his methods of work; and the analogy to Pixerécourt is apparent. Like his great French prede-cessor, the Irishman scribbled his plays in close contact with the playhouse, accepting the suggestions of actors and rewriting much at rehearsals; and he made himself a nuisance back stage by his exacting demands, earning the lasting enmity of many of his co-workers. His productions were models of effective theatre, distin-guished by that speed and precision of tempo which was to become the outstanding virtue of our American melodrama of later years.

Boucicault was probably the greatest of the classical melodrama-tists, certainly in English, and he was nearly the last, passing in 1890 from the scene he had done so much to enliven. He outlived the greatness of the form, and when a new type of drama, represented by the problem play, captured a new type of theatre goer, he could not, or would not, adjust himself. His hits grew fewer and fewer as the seventies passed into the eighties. Many of his later Irish plays failed to draw. His last success was *The Jilt*, a horse-racing comedy given in 1885; but Daniel Frohman, visiting him at his lodgings a few days before his death, found him scribbling away at new plays, and full of projects.[5]

[5] Daniel Frohman, *Memories of a Manager* (New York, 1911).

XXIII

The Fine Art of Plagiarism

It was a Victorian school boy who defined a plagiarist as a writer of plays. —VINCENT STARRETT

Boucicault was indebted to the French for more than his themes ("the actual, the contemporaneous, the photographic" were largely of French inspiration), his formulas, and the plots of the early plays he did for Webster, Kean, Vining, and Wallack. Throughout his career he was continually borrowing—to use a charitable word— characters, sensation scenes, situations, and whole dramas, and omitting to mention the fact. *Janet Pride* was announced as his own composition, and the claim fooled even such an experienced play-goer as Henry Morley, famous critic of the London *Era*, who did not know of *Marie-Jeanne* from which it was taken; and there was no acknowledgment in the printed version of *Le Vampire* that the plot owed anything to Dumas. These are two instances out of many which might be cited. Some of the Irish plays themselves, especially the later ones, first entertained audiences at the Gaité, the Ambigu, and the Porte Saint-Martin in slightly different dress: *The Dublin Boy* had been *Le Gamin de Paris; Danny O'Dowd, Les Crochets du Père Martin; The Amadan, Le Crétin de la montagne;* and *Kerry, La Joie fait peur.*

Boucicault's chief competitor in this import line of business and in the manufacture of English melodrama generally in the mid-Victorian era was Tom Taylor, whose period of active production extends from 1844 to 1878. He was dubbed "the great godfather of French drama" by Thomas Purnell, dramatic critic for the *Athenaeum*, in a magazine article which led to a prolonged exchange of incivilities on the subject of plagiarism.

It was a moot subject, plagiarism, and with good reason. These two playwrights were merely the fugelmen of a numerous company of dramatic pirates who provided the bulk of theatrical entertainment for the British public in the third quarter of the century. Widespread as had been the practice of unacknowledged adaptation from the French before the passage of the Theatre Regulation Act in 1843, it increased after it. Fitzball noticed this when he was setting down his memoirs in 1859. Where three or four versions of a play by Pixerécourt or Caigniez had been exceptional, five and six were common of a Dennery or Bouchardy success. In the course of the single season of 1844 *Don César de Bazan* was to be seen at no fewer than eight houses in London. Three versions of *Belphegor* appear on the list of productions given during 1851 at the ten leading theatres of London as set down by Charles Reade in *The Eighth Commandment;* of the pieces listed, perhaps seventy-five in all genres were French, twenty of them being melodramas. On Easter Monday of 1852, two rival productions of *La Dame de la halles,* by Masson and Anicet-Bourgeois, were presented in English on London stages, neither being credited to the French authors. William Archer, recalling his salad days as a London critic in the early seventies, describes the scenes in the lobbies of London theatres on first nights when journalists crowded about James Mortimer, who had wide knowledge of the Paris stage, in the hope of his dropping some hint as to the French play from which the "new" play of the evening had been "conveyed." That it was not the brainchild of the man signing his name to it on the playbill was taken for granted.[1] John Oxenford, another critic of the day, estimated that four out of five adaptations were not acknowledged as such. An industrious adaptor himself, Oxenford was in a position to speak with authority on the subject.

A curious phrase is to be encountered in playbills of the day: "a new and original drama." This is to be understood in a Pickwickian sense; to explain it is to reveal the trickery practiced on the public by even the most eminent and respectable authors. A drama was "new," these casuists asserted openly, when it had not been previously produced in England—hence the otherwise tautological "original." In 1879 a Robert Reece brazenly sued *The Theatre* (London) for damages when that journal reprinted a *Manchester Guardian* review questioning his claim in a program note that a play of his was "new." The basis of this plea was that he had not stolen his piece from another English work, as the defendant maintained, but from a French one! Palgrave Simpson, John Hollingshead, and Taylor were called as witnesses for the plaintiff to sustain the nice distinction. Taylor contributed some unconscious humor to the proceedings. When it was asserted by counsel that a play could be described as consisting of a trunk, branches and leaves, representing

[1] *The Old Drama and the New,* p. 32.

respectively the plot, the characters and the dialogue, Taylor interrupted indignantly: "Sir, you forget the sap!"[2]

Actually, on the basis of English law, Reece had a good case,
copyright protection being in the state in which it was, especially in
the field of the drama. International copyright statutes had been
enacted in 1838 and 1844, and in 1851 a treaty was entered into
between England and France (a "literary convention") which
became a law in England through an act of Parliament, May 28,
1852. This gave full protection to books, but the section on plays
contained a joker not eliminated until 1875. "It is understood," read
the act, "that the protection stipulated by the present article is not
intended to prohibit fair imitations or adaptations of dramatic works
to the stage in England but is only meant to prevent piratical
translations." And further: "The question whether the work is an
imitation or a piracy shall in all cases be decided by the courts of
justice of the respective countries, according to the laws found in
each."

How ineffective the statute was rendered by these limitations may
be seen from the case described by Charles Reade in *The Eighth
Commandment*. This writer made an honorable arrangement with
Brisebarre and Nus for the English rights to their *Les Pauvres de
Paris* and produced it in London as was required by law to establish
proprietorship. His version was immediately pirated at another
London theatre. Repeated attempts to obtain redress at law and
establish a principle cost him large sums of money and endless
expenditures of time and ultimately came to nothing.

In spite of this and other similar discouraging experiences, Reade
continued to deal contractually with the French authors of plays he
adapted, as did a few other English and American playwrights and
managers. Palgrave Simpson paid French authors one-half and one-
third of the fees he received for adaptations, and Madame Celeste
was scrupulous in this respect while she was manager of the Adelphi
(beginning in 1844) and at the Lyceum and elsewhere later. In New
York, Wallack turned down Boucicault's pirated version of *Une
Cause célèbre* in 1878 when he learned that another producer,
Palmer, had bought the American rights from Dennery. Augustin
Daly, another leading New York manager in the period after the
Civil War, also paid royalties to foreign playwrights.

[2] "SAP," by A Man of the World, *The Theatre* (London), n.s.,
II (1879), 237–240.

Taylor and Boucicault, if they did not always fully acknowledge the French sources of many of their plays or reimburse the authors, did frequently transform what they borrowed; the sap, at times, was impressive. Perhaps the most intelligent job of this kind was Taylor's *The Ticket-of-Leave Man* (1863), from *Léonard*, by Brisebarre and Nus. This is a free and genuinely creative adaptation in which characters, background, and comic relief are all convincingly English. It was a famous hit; audiences liked it better than any other play of the day, original or adapted, with a few possible exceptions such as *East Lynne* or *The Two Orphans*. Henry Neville, who created the role of the hero Bob Brierly in England, played it 2,000 times, and Billy Florence 1,500 times in the United States.

Bob is introduced in the first act as a young greenhorn from Lancashire having his fling in London on a small legacy left him by his parents. He is taken in hand by a team of counterfeiters or "coiners," Jem Dalton and Walter Moss, who use him as their "pigeon" or fall guy. One night at the Bellevue Tea Gardens, a smart West End music hall where the entertainers are Negro minstrels, he is caught in the act of passing one of the homemade twenty pound notes. The arrest is made by Hawkshaw, the detective who has been shadowing the gang. Bob is sentenced to Portland for a three-year stretch.

While frequenting the Bellevue, Bob had struck up a sentimental friendship with a singing girl at the place, May Edwards, a sweet, wholesome creature, orphaned and quite alone in the world. May knows that this kind, generous country boy is innocent, and she writes him regularly while he is doing his time. These letters enable our hero to keep a grip on himself through the ordeal. Mutual sympathy and friendship ripen into love via the post, and May, now employed as a seamstress and lodged frugally with her pet canary, Goldie by name, husbands her pennies with a view to matrimony. Finally Bob is released on parole and May procures work for him under an assumed name in the establishment of her employer's husband, a Mr. Gibson.

The path of a ticket-of-leave man, or paroled prisoner, is a rough one, especially in melodrama. Dalton and his crew reappear upon the scene and recognize Brierly in his new situation. It is a stroke of luck for them; they have a little project in mind with respect to Mr. Gibson's strong box, in the furtherance of which their onetime fall guy can be of great use. He will hear none of it, however, and for his honesty he is denounced to Gibson by the villains as a ticket-of-leave man. That upright merchant, horrified, immediately dismisses Bob—and May at the same time—the blow falling on the very day of their marriage for a very doleful third-act curtain.

Bob is in low spirits when encountered again in the fourth act at the Bridgewater Arms, a rowdy East End music hall where he is making a last desperate attempt to get honest work from the foreman of a gang of laborers who are seen being paid off in the place. Dalton has picked up his trail again; and after Bob has been hired for the gang, the villain and his confederate Moss appear and inform on him again with the usual result. Believing that he now has his victim in a position where he will listen to reason, Dalton broaches new plans for the deferred raid on Gibson's strong box. This time the young man pretends to fall in with the scheme. Moss and another character exit temporarily. The hour is late; the barroom is closed and locked. A single loiterer remains in the place, a drunken navvy to all appearances. He seems to be asleep as he sprawls across the table.

> BOB. Now's the time. (*seizes the pen that stands on the bar, and writes, reading as he writes quickly*) "To Mr. Gibson, Peckham. The office will be entered tonight; I'm in it to save the property and secure the robbers—R. Brierly." But who'll take it?
>
> HAWKSHAW (*who has got up and reads the letter over his shoulder*). I will.
>
> BOB. You?
>
> HAWK. (*pulling off his rough cap, wig and whiskers, and speaks in his own voice*). Hawkshaw the detective. (*gives a pistol*) Take this—I'll be on the lookout . . . (HAWKSHAW *lets his head fall as* DALTON *reappears beckoning at the door, and* MOSS *reappears from the trap. Closed in*)

After that, Mr. Dalton's goose is cooked. The denouement occurs in a graveyard behind Gibson's office, where the malefactors are taken in a desperate fight. Bob, wounded (slightly) and in the embrace of his faithful May, administers a well-deserved rebuke to his suspicious ex-employer as the curtain falls:

> BOB. Mr. Gibson, you wouldn't trust me, sir, but I was not ungrateful. You see, there may be some good left in a TICKET-OF-LEAVE man after all.
>
> *Tableau*

Taylor's melodramas, original and borrowed, form a diversified exhibit. Among them are *Arkwright's Wife*, a biographical piece about the inventor, written in collaboration with Steele Mackaye, an American; *Plot and Passion*, constructed about a political intrigue in the Napoleonic era and introducing Fouché; *The Antipodes; or, the Ups and Downs of Life*, which mixed the thrills of an Australian gold rush with those of English horse racing; *Garibaldi*, a ring drama for Astley's; adaptations of *Faust*, *The Vicar of Wakefield* (his first melodrama, 1850), *Uncle Tom's Cabin*, and novels by Ainsworth, Mary Elizabeth Braddon, Dickens (*A Tale of Two Cities* as a play was written in collaboration with the author), and other novelists of the day; many historical dramas; and what is perhaps the first of the murder mystery plays, *The Hidden Hand*, based on a French original which will be examined in detail in Chapter XXXIV. He wrote several typical Adelphi dramas (*Two Loves and a Life*, 1854, in collaboration with Reade, and *Helping Hands* in the following year) and other pieces with the familiar Adelphi stamp upon them done for other houses, including the very successful *Mary Warner* (1860) and *Henry Dunbar* (1865).

Taylor rivalled Boucicault in number of successes (his plays totalled more than seventy) but not in profits taken or in scope and variety of activities in the theatre. He had scarcely time for much administrative or directorial work (he did not act professionally), being occupied at various times in numerous other fields. The list of his professions and avocations is so formidable as to appall an ordinary lazy mortal: practicing barrister, editor of *Punch*, art critic, fellow of one of the Cambridge colleges, professor at London University, poet, and officer of the London Board of Health.

He cultivated comedy, and here he was fully Dion's match. There are still people alive who remember *Our American Cousin* with its quasi-immortal Lord Dundreary, a character who, as created by the elder Sothern, gave his name to a highly decorative cut of side whiskers. It was at a performance of this play by Laura Keene's original New York company at Ford's Theatre in Washington that John Wilkes Booth shot Lincoln.

Probably Taylor's most stirring writing as a Romantic playwright is in *Lady Clancarty; or, Wedded and Wooed*, based on the Assassination Plot of 1696 and derived from a tale retold by Macaulay in his *History of England*. Its plot was envied him by no less eminent a novelist than George Meredith. It was an immediate hit as first played by Henry Neville and Ada Cavendish at the Olympic in

1874, and it proved a highly successful vehicle later for the Kendals, Belle Pateman, and Lily Langtry.

A frequent collaborator with both Boucicault and Taylor was Charles Reade, better known as a novelist than as a playwright. Like them, he adapted freely from the French, but he was conscientious about doing the right thing by the writers whose plays he used as has been indicated above. Reade also drew upon contemporary English novelists for plots—Mrs. Frances Hodgson Burnett and Anthony Trollope, to mention two—and here he was not so scrupulous. However, he also relied extensively upon his own unaided invention. After beginning his literary career as a dramatist with an adaptation, he passed on to writing original plays. In this category belongs his first success, *Gold* (1853), probably the earliest of the Australian gold rush dramas.

Reade put his talents at the service of reform, following in the footsteps of Mrs. Gaskell, Mrs. Trollope, Dickens, Bulwer-Lytton, and Disraeli. His *Free Labor* (adapted from his novel, *Put Yourself in His Place*, but produced in 1871 before that work was published) dealt with the "rattening," or terrorism, by labor unions during the so-called Sheffield outrages of the middle sixties.[3] In spite of his humanitarian reputation, he took sides in this play against the workers and their unions as melodramatists in this era generally did however much their sympathies were aroused by the inhuman conditions prevailing widely in industry at the time.

Reade attributed his success to a capacity for taking pains; he was a herculean worker, a systematic reader, and an indefatigable researcher. The exhaustive documentation of his various works gives them a value which their often extravagant melodrama and puerile characterization do little to sustain. The treatment of prisoners in English and Australian jails engaged his crusading energies in *It's Never Too Late to Mend* (1864), which was got up with his usual meticulous care, all of the background and incidental detail being based on blue books and personal investigation of the gaols at Durham, Reading, and Oxford. The result proved much too grimly realistic for British playgoers. Two scenes in the play, one of a gang of convicts being worked on a treadmill and another showing a young inmate hanging himself after a flogging, were so harrowing that there was an outcry at the opening performance at the Princess.

[3] Ernst Toller's expressionist drama, *The Machine-Wreckers*, a very different piece of work, is based on the same affair.

The two offending scenes were suppressed and the piece went on to score a great success which was also a financial success for the playwright.

Hard Cash (1853), like Wilkie Collins' *The Woman in White*, took for its theme abuses prevalent in private lunatic asylums; and *Foul Play*, dramatized in 1868 under its own title and again nine years later, with Boucicault collaborating, as *The Scuttled Ship*, attacked a form of marine commercial racketeering. The spendthrift villain falsifies papers, manipulates cargoes, and arranges with a confederate to scuttle a ship in midocean, expecting a handsome return on the operation at the expense of the underwriters. The wide ranging action of Reade's sensational plots reminds the reader of Jules Verne; *Foul Play* begins in Australia and concludes in England, with episodes on shipboard and on a desert island. A favorite situation with romanticists of the Rider Haggard school was used probably for the first time in this novel, and, according to Joseph Knight, critic of the *Athenaeum*, with excellent effect in the play: a beautiful young woman, cast away on a uninhabited island in the company of a man she hates and mistrusts but whom she comes to respect and love after he proves himself innocent of the crimes she suspects him of and saves her life.

Around this time the French drawing-room melodrama or problem play offered a whole new cache of material for the English adaptors. It was theirs for the taking, but in mid-Victorian England the new emphasis on the sexual aspects of the plot and some of the circumstances and passages in the dialogue were highly dubious from the standpoint of English morality. In order to use this material the adaptors had to be very careful to tone down or expunge anything that might arouse the Lord Chamberlain or antagonize the British public.

Tom Taylor in particular may be considered a pioneer in the domestication of the problem play in England, and his *Still Waters Run Deep* (1855), adapted from Charles Bernard's story *Le Gendre*, was probably the decisive item in launching the popularity of this form of melodrama not only in England but also in the United States. In spite of his care the play did not escape censure. Nevertheless the production was a hit and the young Henry James hailed it as a laudable attempt to bring drama into line with contemporary life.[4] The drawing-room melodrama was on its way.

[4] *The Scenic Art,* p. 152.

XXIV

Girls Who Took the Wrong Turn

I shall see my dear husband once more—ask him to forgive me—and then I shall have done with life. —Lady Isabel, *East Lynne*

Seduction, attempted or accomplished, was not unknown in early continental melodrama, as may be seen from *Le Jugement de Salomon*, *Valentine*, and much of Kotzebue, whose works were adopted into the melodramatic repertoire. However, abduction was preferred in matters of this kind, being more exciting and less liable to forfeit sympathy for the heroine, who was expected to be impregnable to the wiles of the most plausible of Lotharios—as careful as she was good. Moreover, the straitlaced authors of melodrama of the first generation shrank from anything like the exploitation of sex.

With Romantic drama came a change. After *Tour de Nesle* and *Le Roi s'amuse*, heroines of melodrama here and there are given to indiscretions—and worse. This tendency never became general in popular melodrama, but simultaneously with the urbanization of melodrama, a process underway in the thirties, the girl who takes the wrong turning and the wife who forgets her marriage vows become familiar puppets. They are sympathized with and wept over, but their offense is not condoned.

In the beginning, death or madness are the wages of sin for girls who go away without a wedding ring. In Ancelot's *Henriette ou deux ans après* (1829, Ambigu), the heroine succumbs to the blandishments of a titled lover and is undone. Part of her punishment is to see her father executed for a crime committed by her lover. In a drawing-room denouement two years later the two sinners meet by chance and die of the shock. In Marc Fournier's *Les Nuits de la Seine* (1852, Ambigu), Hortense, the erring wife, has her oldest child torn from her arms, is pitched into the Seine, and later goes mad. She recovers her wits only at the closing moments of the last act when a heaven-sent beam falls from the ceiling and cracks the skull of the villain. Lucille, of *La Closerie des genêts* (1843), by Frédéric Soulié, is spared the extreme penalty but she pays and pays for her surrender to her well-intentioned lover, prevented by cruel circumstances from doing the right thing by her.

Through adaptations of such pieces as these the seduction drama became acclimated in England, the Adelphi playing an important part in the process. Madame Celeste's peculiar endowments made her an ideal interpreter of wronged females. It was she who created the roles of Henriette and Lucille in London. Seductions are an important element in such novels as *Clarissa Harlowe*, *The Vicar of Wakefield*, *Heart of Midlothian*, and *David Copperfield*, all of which were dramatized frequently on melodrama stages. The approach, however, in almost every instance, was the typically English one, described by Hippolyte Taine: "When you venture on a seduction, as in *Copperfield*, you do not relate the progress, ardors, intoxication of love; you only depict its miseries, despair and remorse." Obviously Professor Taine was not a patron of the "Boulevard du Crime."[1]

When the question arises in a play whether or not a woman has done wrong when she has violated the Sixth Commandment, it ceases to come under the classification of authentic classical melodrama, French or English, but *La Dame aux camélias* has had such a widespread effect on our genre that it must be at least noticed in passing. Mounted first in Paris in 1852, this classic drama of the lost woman could be performed in England up until 1880 only in Italian with music or in James Mortimer's bowdlerized version, *Heartsease* (1875), used by Modjeska, which concealed Marguerite's means of livelihood by referring to an "engagement"—an achievement in understatement comparable to the subtitle of the first American version, by John Wilks, introduced by Jean Davenport, *Camille; or, the Fate of a Coquette*. In 1860, however, the technically bad woman with a good heart who redeems her scarlet past with generous and noble acts of repentance had made her Anglo-Saxon stage debut in Boucicault's *Formosa; or, the Railroad to Ruin*.

At the proletarian level, the traditional English point of view on sex remained unshaken. Maids' melodramatic tragedies of original composition proved popular at various outlying houses in London, where they took a characteristically violent form and emphasized the class aspects of the stock plot. Harrowing details were laid on with a trowel at the Standard, Shoreditch, the City, the Brit, Sadler's Wells, the Pavilion, and the East London, and the seducer was almost invariably of the upper classes, his trusting victim

[1] Hippolyte Taine, *History of English Literature*, trans. Adolphe Laun (Philadelphia & Chicago [1908]), Vol. IV, p. 451.

being the daughter of a poor, aged, toilworn farmer or laborer, and his only consolation. In *Lucy Lisle, the Cottager's Daughter; or, the Maid, the Mother and the Maniac* (that subtitle alliteratively indicating the successive steps of the heroine's downfall), poor Lucy is shot down by her betrayer, Osmond, when he learns that she is not, as he has been led to believe, the heiress to the fifty thousand pounds. Lucy dies forgiving him. The Maria Marten case was often squeezed into this frame, as in Langdon's version at the City, where Corder appeared as a squire in red coat and riding boots which he was given to tapping with his riding crop, according to form. Maria, considerably whitewashed, is an unsuspecting country virgin, lured into the primrose path through the connivance of a sinister fortune-telling gypsy, who, like Wolf of *Flowers of the Forest*, nursed a grudge against all gorgios.

East End and suburban playwrights occasionally skirted *lèse majesté* in their choice of villains for these pieces. No less a dignitary than a Lord Chief Justice is the deceiver in *Agnes Primrose* (City, 1859)—probably the same plot as in Pitt's *The Wreck of the Heart; or the Story of Agnes Primrose* (Vic, 1841) and evidently based on a *cause célèbre*. In the big concluding scene the Justice pronounces the death sentence on the girl he has foully wronged—the mother of his child! And not only the judiciary but the highest ranks of the peerage were represented among these heartless stage monsters.

Two of the most famous items in the whole English-speaking melodramatic repertory deal with the theme of the erring wife: *East Lynne* and *Lady Audley's Secret*, both dating from the mid-sixties. In each, the treatment is the familiar English cautionary one. *East Lynne*, taken from a novel by Ellen Price Wood, was billed "a great moral sensational play" even in the American hinterland and for fifty years the grievous calamities of Lady Isabel, as portrayed by a long line of emotional actresses, wrung tears from millions all over the Western world. *East Lynne*, of which there were numerous versions,[2] belonged in the same surefire category as *Uncle*

[2] The first adaptation of Mrs. Wood's novel, *Edith; or, the Earl's Daughter*, was mounted at Niblo's Gardens, New York, in December, 1862; the first English one at the Queens in 1863. Audiences at the Effingham saw it in 1864. Belot and Nus produced a version in Paris, worked up on the basis of a summary of the plot given them orally by an English actress. It became *Miss Multon* in a New York

Tom's Cabin, Camille, and *The Ticket-of-Leave Man:* They could be relied upon to draw audiences when all else failed, at all levels, particularly the lower ones.

Strictly speaking, *East Lynne* is not a melodrama at all, even of the modified Adelphi variety. Nobody is shot or kidnapped and the audience learns of the one murder only by report; there are no missing heirs or stolen wills; and a sensation scene is lacking as well as a happy end. It is, indeed, the native equivalent of the contemporary French drawing-room melodrama, and probably the first example.

The heroine, Lady Isabel Vane, a daughter of the nobility married to a gentleman commoner, imagines she has a rival for the affections of her spouse, and her jealousy is played upon so effectively by the villain, Sir Francis Levenson, a baronet, that she consents to elope with him. He proves to be an unprincipled brute—even a murderer; and the betrayed and betraying woman, after a disastrous adventure, returns to her old home, brokenhearted. She has forfeited her position there, of course, and hence cannot return openly. Posing as a governess in a disguise which includes a pair of blue spectacles, she obtains employment in the household where another woman has now taken her place as wife; and after her child has died on her breast, she dies also as her husband stands by, weeping for the past and for her, forgiving at last when it is too late.

In the final quarter of the century Lady Audley ran Lady Isabel a close second as the most popular sinning female on the English-speaking stage in many adaptations of a novel which sprang from the same pen that gave *Aurora Leigh* and a long shelf of similar compositions to the world. The author, Mary Elizabeth Braddon, belonged to the class of writers called by Charles Reade "obstacles to domestic industry."

In *Lady Audley's Secret* Lucy Graham, a poisonous beauty of the Becky Sharp school, has put a marital adventure behind her without the formality of a divorce, when she is introduced in the first act and is now Lady Audley, wife of Sir Michael, an elderly, widowed, worthy, and entirely wooden stage nobleman whom she bewitched into matrimony while serving as governess to his children. She has taken appropriately melodramatic measures to obliterate all traces of

---

adaptation for Clara Morris in 1876 and enjoyed a long career on the American stage. Other versions came from Oxenford, Hazlewood, and T. A. Palmer.

her past; a tombstone bearing her true name is to be found in a convenient graveyard. As for husband number one, George Talboys, he is safely exiled in India, or so she has persuaded herself.

Robert, nephew to Sir Michael, brings a visitor one evening to dinner; it is George himself, back from India and very melancholy over the discovery of his wife's tombstone. He and Lucy meet in a big scene; and upon recognizing him the guilty creature "shudders and remains petrified" (Suter's version), one of the many exciting emotional performances of this extraordinary woman. When she returns to normal, she manages an aside to George, making an appointment for the lime walk in the garden. She picks this spot because it is near an old well which is in a bad state of repair. Getting the superfluous mate there, she draws a poniard (that favorite weapon of domestic tragedy) from her bosom, maneuvers George toward the well, stabs him, and pushes him into the crumbling masonry, which gives way, carrying him with it into the well. So much for George.

This crime by no means ends Lucy's difficulties. A servant has witnessed the assault, and he is willing to forget what he saw only in consideration of a tidy sum of money which will enable him to marry the woman of his choice and set up as a publican. Meanwhile Robert, smelling a rat, is prosecuting an inquiry into the antecedents of his missing guest and his newly acquired aunt. Lucy contrives to get both these characters into the same inn one night and sets it afire. The blackmailing servant is roasted, but Robert escapes. He and George, who has meanwhile been fished out of the well half-dead and nursed back to health, hunt down the murderess together and confront her with her crimes. She feigns madness, then takes poison and dies.

A performance of Lady Audley that kept pace with the stage directions of William Suter's adaptaton, the earliest English one, must have been something to watch. In the intervals between stabbing gentlemen and pushing them down wells and setting fire to inns, Lucy utters "wild cries" and "wild shrieks," laughs "wildly," tosses her arms (again, "wildly") over her head, presses her hand upon her heart, staggers and falls senseless, dashes herself to the ground, and "falls over backward." Only the peculiar hardihood of a stage villain could stand for very much of that business. The falling over backward, in fact, was a heavy's trick. There was a special technique for it, writes William A. Brady, in his reminiscences, *Showman*—"elbows stiff, spine rigid, then fall over backward square on the back of your head." "We all practiced it," Brady goes on, recalling his days as an urchin gallery god on the Bowery, "and we valued villains in direct proportion to the stiffness of their falls. When J. B. Studley, a fine old-time actor, started doing villains at the old Bowery and tried dying like a human being—a natural, sprawling collapse—the whole house came right over the footlights at him with hisses and cat-calls and roars of protest. They wanted a real fall."[3]

Marguerite of *La Dame aux camélias* or Camille, as she was to be known across the Atlantic, was a courtesan, but she was presented in a romantic and highly favorable light, and many of the heroines of these plays belonged in the same general category. This was the basis of much of the criticism that was aimed at the problem plays in England. The severity of the criticism, however, did not discourage native playwrights from imitating their French confreres. *Formosa; or, the Railroad to Ruin*, an otherwise old-fashioned melodrama by Boucicault, which had a long run at Drury Lane in 1869, offered as its central character a fancy lady who was reputedly drawn from a familiar figure in contemporary London life. In Wilkie Collins' *The New Magdalen* (1873), a reformed prostitute marries a high-minded English clergyman and is completely rehabilitated. It was a big success and mildly handled by critics.

As years went on and public opinion underwent a fundamental change with respect to such matters, they aroused less and less indignation. Through the eighties and nineties, Frank Harvey, a playwright-manager of London, ground out a whole series of gripping emotional melodramas with such titles as *John Jasper's Wife, Married, not Mated, The Wages of Sin, The World against Her,* and *Shall We Blame Her?* In W. G. Wills's *Forced from Home* (1880), the heroine, disowned and cast out by her father, goes to live under the roof of a gentleman not her husband. In the new century at Standard, Shoreditch, and the post-Irving Lyceum came *The Worst Woman in London, The Girl Who Wrecked His Home, The Bad Girl of the Family,* and many more in the same vein by Walter and Frederick Melville.

The hussy was on the way to becoming the heroine in melodrama of the declining years of the nineteenth century, and the villain was becoming a kind of hero—another aspect of that transvaluation of values which is characteristic of our age. The transformation of the villain can best be investigated in the repertory of Henry Irving.

[3] *The Saturday Evening Post*, Jan. 11, 1936, p. 6.

XXV

The Villain and Melodramatic Acting

> Soul, disregard
> The bad, the good;
> Be haughty, hard,
> Misunderstood
> —JOHN DAVIDSON

At the hub of the typical melodrama was the villain, at his best a superman of crime, tireless in inquity, implacable in vengeance, inexhaustible in evil resource. Around this monster's treasonable ambitions, his sinful loves, his base grudges, the plot revolved; his ingenuity, his energy, and his sublime persistence kept matters in that headlong whirl which made these dramas what they were. Melodrama would have been impossible without him.

The audience, being thus obligated to this personage for their evening's entertainment, tacitly admitted his importance and paid him the compliment of their loathing. It *was* a compliment; the hisses he inspired, the often quite frightful language which greeted his words and his deeds—what were these but unwitting tribute, a sort of inverted approbation? It was in this light that the villain himself regarded them; that raucous din from the gallery was music to his ears, confirming what his soul told him, that he was a man apart, superior to the slave morality of the crowd—a Nietzschean hero.

Whether hissed or applauded, the villain was noticed, a circumstance which made these rôles desirable from the professional point of view. In France Revalard, Jenneval, and Lemaître scored some of their greatest triumphs in villain roles. England boasted a line of celebrated stage rascals: N. T. Hicks (called "Bravo" Hicks on account of his skill in portraying those picturesque Renaissance gangsters whose stage popularity dated from adaptations of Cooper's *The Bravo of Venice*), T. P. Cooke, John Richard Smith, Bob Heritage, and Jack Bradshaw, a famous Guy Fawkes. At one time or another all of these strutted on the historic boards of the

Vic being of that goodly company which Henry S. Leigh lauded in
one of his *Ballads of Cockayne*

> If I could choose a fresh career,
>   If Fate would let me have my pick,
> I'd say, well, Destiny, look here,
>   I'll play the villains at the Vic.

Chief among them was Smith, who became "O. Smith," even on
the printed playbills after a memorable early impersonation at the
Surrey of a certain Obi, or Three-fingered Jack, "The Terror of
Jamaica," the Caribbean pirate-villain of Fawcett's nautical drama of
that name. Smith in his proper person was the mildest and most
inoffensive of mortals, who painted watercolors and collected
butterflies; but his peculiar histrionic talents condemned him to play
bloodstained wretches, natural and supernatural, all his acting days.
Every species of stage deviltry came within his scope. His counsel
prompted a father to lead his own son into crime in *Grace Huntley;*
his hand slew the rightful heir in *Peter Bell, the Waggoner;* his hell-
inspired cunning lured good ships to their doom on the rocks in
Inchcape Bell. Atrocities were his ordinary occupation. As Jonathan
Wild in *Jack Sheppard* he hacked the fingers from the hand of
Trenchard, his accomplice, sending that nobleman plunging to his
doom to the accompaniment of the famous tag line, "You have a
long journey before you, Sir Roland"; as Guy Fawkes, he plotted
with the foreign foe to blow up king and parliament; as the monster,
he crushed a child to death in *Frankenstein.* He was by turns
counterfeiter, blackmailer, incendiary, assassin; night after night he
abducted maidens, cheated orphans, stole millions, and betrayed his
country. It was in German *diablerie* drama that he reached the
heights, however; as the vampire, coming terrifyingly to life under
the restoring rays of the moon on the mountainside after having
been stabbed to the heart; as the Bottle Imp, in a skintight costume
of green scales and demon's horns and wings, dragging Nicola
offstage to hell in the last act to the line: "Parricide, thy hour is
come. Thou art mine—ha! ha! ha!"; or, finally, in his greatest
triumph, as Zamiel, bursting forth from a rock in the Devil's Glen in
Der Freischütz, surrounded by blue fire and accompanied by
convulsions of nature. He was the incarnation of fire and brimstone.

Smith had a formidable assortment of terrifying tricks in his bag;
a half-crazed look and manner, a stealthy step, a hollow voice, and a
piercing eye; and he was a master of gruesome makeup. His trump
card, however, was his laugh, a taunting, deliberate basso profundo

effect in three syllables that never failed to start pleasant tremors down the not particularly sensitive spines of transpontine addicts of blood-and-thunder drama. That laugh was widely imitated in the profession and became a convention in the interpretation of villain roles.

Turning to domestic drama one finds those bankers, lawyers, baliffs, stewards, and squires who distrain for rent and lay traps for milkmaids to be a mean-souled lot, with little that is glamorous or awe-inspiring in their makeup. It was in this type of play that disquieting symptoms made their first appearance: a decline in that primitive integrity of evil, which distinguished the villain in his prime, and the emergence of an incipient moral sense that spelled decadence. This tendency in the villain to have a heart and a conscience is already afoot in Adelphi drama. In Buckstone's *Presumptive Evidence*, an early melodrama with an Irish setting, the murderer weakens and confesses in time to save the life of his enemy, the falsely accused hero. Black Ralph, of the same author's *Dream at Sea*, ends a wicked life with a good deed, baring his own guilt to save an innocent person. In *Flowers of the Forest*, Wolf, the gypsy king, is a man who has suffered a great wrong at the hands of Englishmen, which gives his thirst for vengeance a certain excuse.

It was in the form of an evildoer of this general type, a man the audience is disposed to feel sorry for, that toward the end of the nineteenth century the villain made a reconquest of the center of the stage in England through the agency of Henry Irving. In the sixties this actor was a reliable heavy who had acquired a modest reputation as an interpreter of "bad men in good society," such as Compton Kerr, the sleek, shakedown artist of *Formosa*, and Rawdon Scudamore, of Boucicault's *Hunted Down*, the rôle in which Boucicault discovered him at Manchester. Irving was intelligent, gifted, ambitious, and persistent; he patiently awaited his opportunity to do bigger things, meanwhile perfecting his art. The opportunity came in 1871, when he was in the company at the Lyceum. Matters were going badly with H. L. Bateman, the American manager of the old house at that time, and as a forlorn hope he allowed Irving to persuade him into a production of a French play of Alsatian life by Erckmann-Chatrian, *Le Juif polonais*, which had already been done unsuccessfully at another London theatre, though it was a great draw in Paris at the Cluny in 1869 with Tallien in the principal role. The sequel is theatrical history. *The Bells*, as the play was called in this version by Leopold Lewis, was the event of the season. In the role of Matthias, Irving revealed himself as an actor of the first rank, a supreme interpreter of melodrama.

Matthias is an old burgomaster-innkeeper of a little Alsatian town. Forty years earlier, to save himself and his family from ruin, he murdered a peddler, a Polish Jew who had been his guest, for his bag of gold, waylaying him on a lonely road as he left the town and hacking him with an ax. He burned the body in a limekiln and covered his tracks so well that suspicion has never touched him. Thanks to the fresh start which the Jew's hoard made possible, he has accumulated a modest fortune through the years, meanwhile earn-ing a reputation as an honest tradesman, a model citizen, a good husband, and a devoted father. Remorse for his single crime, how-ever, and fear of detection have never ceased to gnaw at his soul. The image of his victim haunts him wherever he turns. He fancies that he hears bells, the bells of the sledge in which the Jew came to his door asking shelter and invoking a blessing on the house; their jangling recurs impressively through the scenes in which he appears.

The play as Irving interpreted it was a somber psychological study of this guilty soul under the pressure of an accumulation of circumstances which bring the crime up vividly before him. The melodramatic action is almost entirely in the past; Matthias relives his crime in a dream scene on the eve of his daughter's wedding, and in another dream in the last act he finds himself accused at the bar of justice and forced by a mesmerist to confess. At the climax of this scene, a big opportunity for the actor, he plunges from the bed upon which he has been lying, staggers across the stage and falls dead, as the assembled wedding guests crowd through the door in alarm, attracted by his cries. His guilty secret goes to the grave with him.

Though various forms of melodrama were represented in the vehicles of Henry Irving during his brilliant quarter of a century at the Lyceum, of which he became manager in 1871, this was the type that dominated his repertoire: a character like Matthias, sin-haunted, remorseful; a villain with something fine, something tragic about him; a good man stained with a single crime. Here is the roll call: Faust; Robert Landry of Watts Phillips' *The Dead Heart*, the plot of which closely resembled *A Tale of Two Cities;* Eugene Aram (the Hood-Bulwer-Wills Aram), a scholar and schoolmaster whose idyllic romance is engulfed in the backwash of a passionate tragedy of his youth; Falkland of *The Iron Chest*, Colman's tragedy from *Caleb Williams,* a noble nature poisoned by an accusing conscience;

Werner (*Werner*), the man under a curse, believing himself a parricide; Louis XI (*Louis XI*), a king haunted by the fear of death; Ravenswood of *The Bride of Lammermoor;* Robespierre in *Thermidor,* the play Sardou wrote for Irving; and Vanderdecken, doomed to beat about on a stormy sea until Judgment Day as penance for an impious oath. In *Vanderdecken,* the Wills–Percy Fitzgerald redaction of the Flying Dutchman legend which Irving used, there is a significant transposition: the terrestrial and normal pretender to the hand of the heroine has become a jealous, greedy villain, while Vanderdecken, presented as a pathetic wanderer yearning for love and human sympathy, is transformed into a senti-mental hero.

These sinister and melancholy figures were chosen by a sure instinct. They furnished the tragedian with unique opportunities for the exercise of his special gifts as an actor and a producer, oppor-tunities he might have sought in vain among the stumbling experi-ments of the rising generation of realists, whom he is often accused, somewhat impertinently, of having neglected. In playing them he did pretty much as he pleased with his parts, so that the finished portrait as it appeared behind the footlights frequently had as much of Irving as the playwright in it. Coquelin complained to Brander Matthews that Irving's Matthias was "not in accord with the intent of the author . . . who had drawn a far simpler and less tragic figure," an outright scoundrel, bluff and hearty in manner, who fears nothing but discovery and is untroubled by moral qualms.[1] That was the way Paulin Ménier played him in a later (1884) Paris revival of *Le Juif polonais.* No one knew this better than Irving himself. What he did, sometimes by discreet editing of the text of a play but more often by creative interpretation on the stage, was to communicate new depth and substance to parts that in themselves were not infrequently thin, crude, shadowy, trivial. He took these puppets and spiritualized them, raising them, as Jules Claretie, a director of the Française, put it, to his own level; his Adams became Othellos, his Matthiases, Macbeths, his Ravenswoods, Hamlets.

Melodramatic acting was acting to music; and music, with its regular and accurate time divisions, makes for definiteness and a certain patterned quality in gesture as well as in speech, however unconscious the performer may be of its influence. Gordon Craig

[1] Brander Matthews, *These Many Years* (New York, 1917), p. 197.

has written that a performance by Henry Irving was "a song and dance." He "pranced and glided, twinkled and pirouetted." "His movements were all measured. He was forever counting—one, two, three—pause—one, two—a step, another, a half, a faintest turn, another step, a word . . ." "When he came to melodrama, he realized that a good deal more of a dance would be needed to hold up these pieces—and then it was that, putting out all his skill, he wiped up the floor with his role and danced it like the devil."[2] Craig has the gift of eloquence; his re-creation of Irving's first entrance in *The Bells*, in which he writes of "figure after figure of exquisite pattern and purpose . . . unfolded and then closed, and ever a new one unfolded in its wake," is surely as illuminating a piece of comment of its kind as dramatic criticism in our language has to offer; the spell of great acting has rarely if ever been communicated so movingly in mere words.[3]

The music was steadily diminishing as the end of the century approached, and Romanticism on which the art of Lemaître and Irving had been nourished was giving way to realism in the theatre. Acting reflected these changes. Such men as E. S. Willard in England, and Steele MacKaye, James A. Herne, Belasco, and Gillette in the United States were experimenting with a quieter, more restrained style, more in keeping with the new melodrama of city life which came to prevail in their lifetime. (See Chapter XXXII). Critics frequently objected. The *Dramatic Mirror* in its review of *Sherlock Holmes*, which opened in New York in October, 1899, referred to what it called "the stolidity and dry reticence" of Gillette's acting style and went on: ". . . to be inanimate is to be natural. An occasional sign of life and force, would materially improve his performance."[4] Gillette usually surrounded himself with a company in which ranters of the old school were heavily represented, according to Elizabeth Marbury, in *My Crystal Ball*.[5] In contrast with this turbulence his own low-keyed method stood out the more prominently.

Outside the Lyceum, particularly in theatres of the better class, the villain found the times turning against him. He disappears in whole plays during the eighties and nineties, even those given at

---

[2] *Henry Irving* (New York, 1930), pp. 73–74.
[3] *Ibid.*, pp. 51–58.
[4] *The Dramatic Mirror*, Nov. 18, 1899.
[5] (New York, 1923) p. 90.

houses of proletarian patronage, for example, *The Trumpet Call*, an Adelphi drama (1891) by Sims and Buchanan. His eclipse was even more pronounced across the Atlantic. There are many melodramatic elements in the plays of Herne, but, save in the case of the early *The Minute Man*, the old-style villain is not among them. Steele Mackaye's *Hazel Kirke*, which established a long-run record when it played at the new Madison Square Theatre in 1880, offered a sinning female without a seducer. And the "villains" of *Held by the Enemy* and *Secret Service* are honorable, patriotic gentlemen.

Extinction was by no means imminent for the picturesque puppet, however. In this same decade of the eighties he asserted himself again with some of his old vigor in a plague of East End atrocities which ensanguined the last days of melodrama's reign as an important dramatic form in England. This was the so-called Drury Lane, or London, melodrama, whose chief stage was Drury Lane under Harris and Collins. In these loud and spectacular pieces he is the villain of tradition insofar as his moral character is concerned, but he has acquired social polish and a good tailor. His accent is faultless, his long, elegant fingers are carefully manicured, and his hard eye gleams from behind a single eyeglass. He is handsome, suave, and scornful, twirling his black moustache—the dark-complexioned (black-a-vised) villain has been obligatory in the Anglo-Saxon theatre since Elizabethan days, in contrast to the blonde one of French tradition—or languidly tapping a silver cigarette case as he lifts a contemptuous eyebrow at the howling gallery—howling still in the eighties at Drury Lane and the Princess no less than at the Surrey and the Vic. He leads a double life, dining with duchesses (whose pearls he deftly lifts between epigrammatic compliments) and then hurrying off into Seven Dials toward morning to keep rendezvous with a gang of low-life ruffians, his tools. The last of a noble line, he by no means disgraces it.

XXVI

The Twilight of the Gallery Gods

Rags are royal raiment when worn for virtue's sake. —BARTLEY
CAMPBELL, *The White Slave*

For the present generation the association of Tom and Jerry suggests a cat and mouse cartoon or a mellow potation of the toddy
family associated with Christmas cheer. In the early stretches of the
last century, however, these homely English praenomens, thus
linked, had other and more virile connotations. They were a sort of
symbol of all that was gamey in London life during the sparking
days of the Regency: its goatish humors, its boisterous camaraderie,
its ruttish animal spirits, and its genius for raising hell.

It all began in a novel from the pen of Pierce Egan, a sporting
character of the day whose authoritative knowledge of blood
horses, game cocks, fox hounds, pugilists, women, and other diversions of the "blood" of the period made him the idol of undergraduates and the associate of gentlemen. *Life in London,* published
in 1821 with hand-colored illustrations by George Cruikshank (a
collector's item today), dealt in lively detail with metropolitan
existence as exposed in the course of an exhaustive tour of its more
disreputable attractions undertaken by "Corinthian Tom"[1] to complete the education of Jerry, his green but far from feckless cousin
from the country. All the more notorious places were looked in
upon—the bagnios, the pothouses, the promenades, the routs, the
jails. They visited Westminster Pit for a dog-and-monkey fight; the
Saloon at Covent Garden for an appointment with the Cyprians; the
"Sluicery" for a swallow of its celebrated gin, "blue ruin," and the
White Horse Cellar for something more palatable in the way of a
dram; a Bow Street police court; and Fleet Prison. In the course of
their rounds the two roisterers upset a sentry house on its occupant,
the "charley," or watchman; took a hand in a lusty street brawl
between the "kids" and the swells; and were taken in custody and
lodged for the night in gaol.

[1] "Corinthian" was the term for a type known earlier as a "Maca-
roni," and later as a "swell."

In spite of the outcry of the moralists—or, possibly, because of it—the book enjoyed a tremendous vogue; and it was promptly dramatized by Moncrieff, the first of seven stage versions produced in London. *Tom and Jerry*, as it was called on the stage, was even more popular than *Life in London*, and the little Adelphi was hard put to accommodate the crowds which, for nearly three hundred nights, gathered to enjoy the show. It became *The Beggar's Opera* of its day, and was revived again and again for half a century. There were sequels also: *Tom and Jerry in Paris*, *Tom and Jerry in Edinburgh*, *Nautical Tom and Jerry*, and even a *Tom and Jerry in New York* (given at Brougham's theatre there); and among the various imitations were the celebrated Mose the Fireman plays in America.

Tom and Jerry was a burletta, or musical farce, but it introduced a milieu which was to be widely adopted in melodrama, the metropolitan panorama, with emphasis on various picturesque aspects of city low life. The first melodramas of this type shown on the English stage, however, were French. Frequently these were merely translations, with Parisian locales and sometimes with the very titles retained as in the case of Dillon's *Mysteries of Paris* (1844) and Stirling's *The Bohemians; or, the Rogues of Paris* (1843); again, a London setting would be substituted, the characters retaining their French names, as in Moncrieff's *Scamps of London; or, the Crossroads of Life* (1843), another version of *Les Bohémiens*.

In the sixties the genre began to acquire prestige through elaborate productions of plays by Tom Taylor, Boucicault, and others. French sources continued to be used for the most part, though by this time they were overhauled more thoroughly in the process of adaptation with English slang, manners, and atmosphere mortised into the parent structure. *The Ticket-of-Leave Man* was one of the earliest of these and the most successful. Only less popular were Boucicault's adaptations, among them *The Streets of London* (1864) (the same as *The Poor of New York*) and *After Dark; A Tale of London Life* (1868). The last, perhaps more completely than any of its predecessors, stimulated "the emotion of recognition" in audiences through its spectacular reproduction of sights well known to Londoners: a Rupert Street "silver hell," Blackfriars Bridge, a music hall, and the recently completed underground shown with a steam train rushing through it. *Formosa*, given at Drury Lane in the following year, is of the same pattern, the plot concerning itself with the schemes of a gang of blackmailers and thieves in high society who try to fix the Oxford-Cambridge boat race, among other ambitious speculations.

Though the French influence was incontestable, native comedy and fiction including *Tom and Jerry* contributed to this English city melodrama. The sixties saw T. W. Robertson's charming and enormously popular "tea-cup and saucer" comedies at the Prince of Wales with their literal realism of mise-en-scène and their piquant character sketches of recognizable London types, such as Eccles of *Caste*. Dickens was being adapted on every hand. What is often called the first of the London melodramas proper, Andrew Halliday's *The Great City* (1867), was a version of *Great Expectations*. It offered a sensation scene in which the ex-convict Magwitch tears down telegraph wires to assist his escape, and a concluding tableau in a railroad station (similar to the opening scene in *After Dark*) in which the villain is seized by the police as he attempts to board a train.

Original plays were to be encountered more frequently in the late sixties and early seventies, among them Watts Phillips' *Lost in London* and *On the Jury*, Travers' *The Darker Side of the Great Metropolis*, and H. J. Byron's *Haunted Houses* in which a house collapses on the villain. London melodrama reached its meridian in the eighties, when a whole tribe of writers came forward to specialize in it: George R. Sims, Henry Pettitt, Paul Meritt, Sutton Vane, Benjamin Landeck, Arthur Shirley, George Conquest, Henry Arthur Jones, and many others.

The Grecian, City Road, Hoxton, was a cradle for the best of this talent. Its manager at this time was George Conquest (the younger), playwright, adaptor, actor, and ingenious contriver of mechanical stage effects. Educated in France as a schoolfellow of Coquelin, he kept in close touch with that nation's melodrama, accumulating an extensive collection of Parisian successes in the library of his theatre where he and his pupils were wont to retire when wooing the muse. It was under the tutelage of this all-around man of the theatre that Pettitt and Meritt learned their palpitating art before moving out to conquer the West End. The 'prentice work of this prolific team (Conquest himself often lending a hand) included *Against the Stream, Snatched from the Grave, British Born, Sentenced to Death, Dead to the World, Brought to Justice, The Sole Survivor, The Missing Witness*, and *Velvet and Rags*. The titles tell volumes.

Meritt's *The New Babylon*, given at the Duke's in 1879, announced the emergence of the school into a wider sphere. The virtues of this drama were described thus in a "powerfully worded" advertisement: "the Most Attractive Drama Ever Written. Suits All Classes. The Collision in the Atlantic; Tattersall's with its Sale of Horses; Cremorne with its Dancing Platform and 10,000 Lights; Goodwood on Racing Day; the Thames Embankment with its Electric Witness; and Seven Dials by Night are Pictures of Real Life which Must Attract." A critic called the production "a mixture of *Tom and Jerry* and *Formosa*."

In the same year Augustus Glossop Harris, a grandson of the tallow chandler–impresario of the old Coburg, began his historic management of Drury Lane with a Shakespearean production, and in 1880 he presented *The World*, by Pettitt, Meritt, and himself. It was the first of the spectacular "autumn melodramas" by means of which this able and energetic showman succeeded in doing what so many of his predecessors had failed at, namely, putting the old house on a permanent paying basis. Thanks to him and Arthur Collins, who succeeded to the management in 1897, these shows became as much an institution as the Christmas pantomime itself; Londoners would not have thought of missing either. *The World* was a tremendous triumph. Besides making a fortune for Harris, it earned a clean half-million for the purchaser of the American rights. The plot intrigue, like that of any one of the melodramas of this school, was extremely complicated, piled high with terrific incident, congested with characters, and fairly bulging with high-powered climaxes. Customers always got their money's worth in action, variety, and excitement at a Drury Lane melodrama.

In 1882 at Drury Lane came *Youth*, by Meritt and Harris, which offered an elderly villainess avenging herself upon a man, now a vicar, who years before had betrayed and deserted her. She pays him back through his son, bringing upon the youth all manner of indignities and misfortunes. Other "sensational and domestic dramas," as they were billed, followed *Youth* at the Lane, the series continuing well into the present century: *Pluck, a Story of £50,000, The Millionaire, A Million of Money* (stakes were always high), *Freedom, Human Nature, A Run of Luck, Pleasure, A Sailor's Knot, The Prodigal Daughter, A Life of Pleasure, Floodtide, Hearts Are Trumps, The Great Ruby, The Prince of Peace, Paul Kauvar* (by the American, Steele Mackaye), *The Sins of Society, Sealed Orders, Stolen Orders*, and others. For a decade or so in the beginning they were chiefly the work of Meritt and Pettitt; in the nineties Henry Hamilton and Cecil Raleigh took over the job of writing them. In their finished form, however, they were to a great extent the creation of Harris. Besides acting in a few of the earlier ones, "Druriolanus," as he came to be known to Londoners, helped in the writing, his name usually appearing on the bills as collaborator. The staging was almost entirely of his devising, and this was supremely important; what drew Londoners in hordes to the old house each year in the autumn was the promise of scenic and mechanical wonders as much as anything else. There was always plenty to gape at and gasp at on the huge stage. In *The Whip* (1909) the villain crawls along the running board of a moving train to uncouple the car in which the hero's horse is being shipped to Newmarket; in *The Sins of Society* (1907) a huge transport sinks foot by foot on a stage shrouded in fog, a steam siren screeching meanwhile and a wireless crackling and sparking while the hero grabs a Union Jack, moves down center, and bellows: "Let us all die like men!"; two trains collide and a bank is sacked by an enraged mob in *Pluck* (1882); *The Prince of Peace* (1900) showed Parliament in session, a wedding in the Abbey, and a yacht crushed by a steamer; the Alhambra promenade was reproduced in *A Life of Pleasure* (1893); *The Great Ruby* (1898) featured a duel to the death in a balloon; *Hearts Are Trump* (1899) presented a flower fete at the Botanical Gardens and an Alpine avalanche; and in *The White Heather* (1897) were to be seen the stock exchange in session and a submarine duel between hero and villain, with the possession of the former's marriage papers at stake.

In *The Prodigal Daughter* (1892), the first race with real horses was staged at Drury Lane, and *The Derby Winner* (1894) brought them back. The sporting plays here owed their famous technical accuracy to Cecil Raleigh, son of the renowned Fothergill ("Foggy") Rowlands, gentleman-rider and proprietor of a training stable at Epsom. In various other plays of this type—*The Sporting Duchess* (inspired by Caroline, Duchess of Montrose), *The Whip* (which ran through two seasons, 1909 and 1910, and held the boards for years on tour and in America), and others—there were boxing contests, boat races, fox hunts with real hounds, gymkhanas, and polo games. Boucicault, always on the alert for novelty, had been the first to utilize sport sensationally in melodrama, introducing a horse race in *The Flying Scud* (1866) and boat racing and boxing in *Formosa*, produced three years later.

Turf dramas were numerous on both sides of the Atlantic in the closing years of the nineteenth century and the early years of the twentieth: *The English Rose,* by Buchanan and Sims; *Sporting Life,* by Raleigh and Seymour Hicks; Wilson Barrett's *Nowadays;* Hamilton's *Newmarket;* Dazey's *In Old Kentucky;* dramatizations of Mary Holmes best-selling novel, *Lena Rivers;* Henry Blossom's comedy, *Checkers;* Paul Armstrong's *Blue Grass;* Neilson Burgess' *The Country Fair;* and J. R. Young's *Macushla,* a vehicle of Chauncey Olcott's. Cyril Maude made his stage debut in Gilbert Hastings Macdermott's *Racing* at the Grand Islington in 1887, and Lillian Russell displayed her undulating charms in *Wildlife,* by George Broadhurst and George V. Hobart.

Crooked gamblers, aristocratic but impoverished owners, incorruptible old trainers, hocussed jockeys, doped horses, and droll bookies people these animated spectacles; the clamor of the betting stall, the jangling of the saddling bell, and the thunder of the home stretch echo through them; and, of course, they all build up to the big scene on the track in which the all-important jockey, seeing through the villain's schemes, or throwing off the effects of the drug that has been administered him, goes on to win—or even better, the scene in which the heroine herself (looking very fetching in silks) leaps into the saddle when all seems lost and rides the race of the century (in violation of Jockey Club rules), bringing in her estranged sweetheart's gelding a nose ahead of the field.

Early in his management of Drury Lane, Harris was offered a play by a novelist of the day, George R. Sims, and he rejected it, as did every other London manager in fact. Finally the persistent author found a man willing to gamble on it, an actor newly launched as manager at the Princess, Wilson Barrett. The play, *The Lights o' London,* was given in 1882, and it made manager as well as playwright, becoming a greater sensation than *The World* itself and the very model of London melodrama. The latter half of this play gave off the very stink of the teeming, noisome London slums, one scene in particular being masterly in its realism: a fight in the streets of the Borough outside a pub on a Saturday night, costers, navvies, ragged urchins, and Belcher-like females milling about, and a barrel organ whining a cheap tune above the hubbub of cries and screams.

Here was a milieu of which Sims was a student. His second play, *Romany Rye,* went into it more systematically and exhaustively, earning for itself, and for London melodrama generally, the epithet, "The Gospel of Rags." Adapted from its author's novel, which bore the happy title of *Rogues and Vagabonds,* it marshalled a numerous and picturesque battalion of derelicts and malefactors onto the stage of the Princess in 1881: drunkards, juvenile thieves, wharf rats, bums, gypsies and evil old hags, not to speak of white-collar swindlers, usurers, and rascally attorneys.

It was at the Princess also that the best of the London plays was given in 1894. This was *The Silver King*, by Henry Arthur Jones and Henry Herman. It tells a story of regeneration. The hero, Denver, is a man tormented by remorse, believing himself a murderer. Under the lash of his conscience, he is transformed from the drunken gambler and weakling of the first two acts to the sober humanitarian and resolute man of action of the last three. It was the best London melodrama could do, and it wasn't bad. Matthew Arnold, writing in the *Pall Mall Gazette*, permitted himself to grow enthusiastic about the play. Within the limits of the old melodrama formula, it achieved something like mastery. But the inadequacies of that formula at its best are flagrantly evident: the obvious manipulation of entrances and exits, the roundup of characters for the recurring climaxes, the preternatural cynicism of the villain, the incredible fortitude of the heroine. The venerable aside lingers on, reaching the height of absurdity in this play in a scene wherein two characters, having the stage to themselves, spout confidences alternately across the footlights—the footlights, now, of the modern picture-frame stage!

At the Princess in the eighties melodrama put forth another shoot, akin to the city-life spectacle in its reliance upon elaborate scenic and quadruped accessories: those religious and pseudo-classical spectacles associated chiefly with the Barrett management. *Claudian*, by Wills and Herman (1883), belongs to the same school as *The Last Days of Pompeii*, *Ben Hur* (1899), *Quo Vadis* (three New York productions of which were mounted in 1900), and *The Wandering Jew*. *Clito*, by Grundy and Barrett, which followed three years later at the same house, was laid in ancient Greece and had for its central figure a beautiful hetaira. Sardou's archaeological dramas doubtless gave the authors more than one suggestion for this piece and for a later one of their compositions, also presented at the Princess, *The Daughter of Babylon*. However, not long after Barrett's triumphs there, the Princess was pronounced unsafe and converted to a warehouse.

At Drury Lane the last of the melodramas was *Good Luck*, by Seymour Hicks and Ian Hay, put on in 1923, the year in which Collins retired. Hicks brought the playscript to the manager, who asked, "What is it about?" Hicks replied: "The heroine rides the horse to victory in the last act." That was enough for Collins. It was a grand success. The Drury Lane shows were classical melodrama's swan song; when *Good Luck* concluded its run, the genre belonged to history. The theatre became a musical house featuring big American operettas.

At the Lyceum, a last stand was made by the Melville brothers, Walter and Fred, who moved in from the Standard, Shoreditch, to take over the property in 1909, and produced melodramas of their own composition for a period of thirty years—*Married to the Wrong Man*, *The Bad Girl of the Family*, *The Girl Who Wrecked His Home*, *The Midnight Wedding*, *The Sins of London*—along with works by other authors, including Edgar Wallace. This was no longer the historic building of the Irving regime, which had been demolished and replaced by a new structure in 1903–4.

Across the Thames and in the East End, and to the north and west, it was the same story. The Vic closed down in 1871 and remained dark for the greater part of a decade, never again figuring as a melodrama house. The Surrey, where two generations of Conquests presented a long series of famous thrillers from 1881 through 1904, fell idle and lay empty for many years, finally being torn down in 1955. The Elephant and Castle, rebuilt in 1902, took over for a while but did not survive long. Sanger's Amphitheatre (Astley's) disappeared in 1895 and its very site was obliterated in a street improvement of 1903.

In the East End, portents of extinction appeared as early as the 1860's when the City of London succumbed to the Yiddish drama, followed by the East London (previously the Effingham) in the following decade. This was ultimately to be the destiny of the Pavilion, Mile-End, also, but not until it had made history in the second half of the century, under the management of Morris Abrahams and Isaac Cohen. The Theatre Royal, Stratford, a late-comer in the ranks of East End playhouses (1884), after having served intermittently as a refuge of the debilitated blood-and-thunder repertory, gave up the struggle after a disastrous attempt at a comeback in 1935.

From being largely self-sufficient, with their own acting organizations, production staffs and even their own stables of playwrights, these and other outlying theatres of the metropolis, including the West London (once the Marylebone), came at the end of the century to depend upon the reversion of West End successes through the medium of touring productions, and when these sources diminished and disappeared, they closed their doors as playhouses of the living theatre. New plays were not to be had, and the old ones lost their magic. The Brit, the last to maintain its own stock company, dispersed it in 1899 upon the death of the legendary Mrs. Sarah Lane, who had guided the destinies of the house for a half century. It passed to other hands and eventually settled down as a cinema. Sadler's Wells also descended to films and later was demolished and replaced (1930) by the present structure dedicated to loftier ends.

If the Drury Lane shows were melodrama's swan song, its last gasp was *Young England*, a Drury Lane type show first put on at Victoria Palace in 1934. The tremendous box office success which this play scored was small comfort to the aged man from the provinces, Walter Reynolds, who wrote it. Crowds flocked to see the show through 278 performances, enjoying it hugely, but their enjoyment was all at the expense of the sadly outdated heroics of the plot and the faded purple of the dialogue. The villain was derisively, if good naturedly, hooted, and the hero, a noble-souled scoutmaster, boisterously cheered as he struggled manfully against unjust accusations and turned over the money collected for his defense to pay gambling debts contracted by his scalawag pater, the earl, to save him from disgrace.

By this time, melodrama had become a polite diversion housed in the West End. It specialized in two peculiarly modern types closely related to each other: the murder mystery and the psychological study of criminality. William Archer's tour de force, *The Green Goddess*, given first in 1919 at the Walnut Street Theatre in Philadelphia and at the St. James's, London, in 1923, is the closest approach the modern carriage-trade theatre has made to the old classical melodrama formula; the sensation scene of the airplane landing and the sinister oriental villain, the Rajah of Rukh, played by George Arliss in the American production, are pure Surrey Side. Archer's thriller, however, would never have passed muster at the Surrey before a bonafide melodrama audience; its heroine is a married woman in love with a man not her husband. Popular melodrama was moral to the bitter end.

III
AMERICA

XXVII

American Primitives

The dramatic productions of this country . . . are of so limited a number and quality that the task we have undertaken seems as one scarcely worthy the notice of a historian . . . —JAMES REES (1845)

American melodrama in the early nineteenth century was an unimpressive product, scanty in volume and poor in quality. Plays in this genre were rarely produced abroad and made little impression when they were. *Uncle Tom's Cabin* marked a turn of the tide. The shockers on American themes to be encountered on London or Paris playbills prior to the middle of the century were usually the work of Englishmen or Frenchmen such as adaptations of Cooper's novels, beginning with *The Pilot*. Of English manufacture were the London versions of *Nick of the Woods* (by J. T. Haines, Vic, 1839) and *Jack Long of Texas; or, the Shot in the Eye* (by J. B. Johnston, Vic, 1847), both from American novels of the same names, the former by Robert Montgomery Bird (1837), the latter by Charles W. Webber (1844) and both independently dramatized in the U.S.A.

In America itself American melodramas were but a drop in the bucket of blood served across the footlights. The ratio of imported to native drama was perhaps as great as fifty to one for a great part of the century if pieces written by foreigners in the U.S. are included; the theatre remained a colonial appendage of the mother country with scarcely greater independence than the York or Manchester circuits. Only topical spectacles celebrating some national victory or the like seem to have been turned out in any quantity.

To cite the shows given at the two leading houses of the country during the first quarter of the century, the Chestnut in Philadelphia and the Park in New York, would merely be to repeat the repertory of Drury Lane and Covent Garden. Melodramas were numerous: *The Voice of Nature, A Tale of Mystery, Alfonso of Castile, Children in the Wood, The Mountaineers, The Hunter of the Alps, Adelgitha, Tékéli, The Maid of Paliseau, The Bandits of Calabria, Christopher Columbus,* and others. Quite early *Timour the Tartar, The Cataract of the Ganges,* and other horse operas became American, as they had been English, favorites; and each successive phase of the sensation drama made its way across the Atlantic. Included were *diablerie* pieces; the Scott, Bulwer, and Ainsworth adaptations; and the minor house repertory of highwayman, nautical, and domestic dramas. To be encountered everywhere on the American stage were *Black Eyed Susan*, *The Flying Dutchman*, *Aladdin*, *Thirty Years of a Gambler's Life*, *Theresa*, *Orphan of Geneva*, *Jack Sheppard*, *The Rent Day*, and *Richelieu*. *The Purse* and Arnold's *The Shipwreck*, those forerunners of nautical drama, were given as afterpieces at the Park immediately following their premieres in London.

Adaptations of foreign plays usually arrived in versions by Englishmen but not always. John Howard Payne contributed many French plays which he adapted in the course of several sojourns in Paris, particularly an extended one in 1822. Eighteen Americans prepared versions of French plays in the period from 1714 to 1830 according to Frank Pierce Hill.[1] William Dunlap, active in the early management of the Park, may have gone to the sources for his numerous German adaptations, but internal evidence suggests that he availed himself to some extent of Thompson's *German Theatre*, in six volumes and containing nineteen staple items, which went through three editions before 1812. The German influence diminished early in the century in the United States as in England.

When the Bowery and its environs evolved into a pleasance for New York's proletariat, managers there turned frequently to Coburg and Surrey successes for their bills: bandit and crime plays such as *The Idiot Witness; or, a Tale of Blood*, *The Skeleton Witness*, *Jonathan Bradford; or, the Murder of the Roadside Inn*, *Michael Earl, the Maniac Lover*, *The Robber of the Pyrenees*, *Dick Turpin*, *Margaret Catchpole*, and the dog, ape, and horse shows. Amherst from Astley's did a land-office business at the National in the thirties with Cook's Circus in *St. George and the Dragon*, *Gulliver in Lilliput*, *Lodoiska*, *Mazeppa*, and other items from his Surrey Side repertory. From 1835 onward, Barkham Cony, assisted by Master Edward Blanchard, filled many prolonged engagements at the Bowery and similar houses in his transpontine thrillers.

Tastes along the frontier did not differ materially from those in

[1] *American Plays Printed, 1714–1830* (Palo Alto: Stanford University Press, 1934). Pixerécourt, Bouilly, Caigniez, and other French playwrights are represented. See pp. 121–133.

the cities of the eastern seaboard. From the reminiscences of Noah Ludlow and Sol Smith,[2] two actor-managers who toured the hinterland before the Civil War, we learn of the plays that found favor along the Ohio, down the Mississippi, and across the south from the Atlantic coast to New Orleans. Prominent among them were *Pizarro, The Castle Spectre, The Secret, Adelgitha, The Lady of the Lake, The Miller and His Men, Three-fingered Jack,* and *The Lady of Lyons.* Later, when the frontier had been pushed onward to the West Coast, touring companies doing the gold rush towns confined themselves largely to imports. Belasco's early work as a play hack in California consisted almost exclusively in dramatizing the novels of Dickens, Reade, Ouida, and Wilkie Collins, and in adapting Paris and London successes.

English plays found their way to the American market through various channels. John Miller, an American bookseller who had a shop in London, functioned as an agent-fence in procuring acting versions, and English actors brought plays in their baggage.[3] There was little emigration westward of acting talent early in the century, and even this little was reduced further by the war of 1812. Since performers were in such short supply in America, managers made trips to the British Isles to recruit them following the Peace of Ghent in 1815. The first to do so were Stephen Price, lessee of the Park, and his stage manager and partner, Edmund Simpson. These operations were to have enduring consequences in delaying the emergence of a vigorous native American melodrama. The ease with which foreign plays of tested appeal could be obtained produced a competitive situation which did not encourage native playwriting talent. The professional playwright can hardly be said to have existed, a condition which must be attributed to the financial precariousness of the trade.

American plays, such as they were, came largely from hack journalists, actors, and theatrical handymen—and amateurs. Their deficiencies frequently were not only literary and grammatical but orthographical as well, particularly as exposed in melodramas. Always these writers imitated European models, and prevailingly

[2] Noah Ludlow, *Dramatic Life as I Found It,* (St. Louis, 1880); Sol Smith, *Theatrical Management in the West and South for Thirty Years* (New York, 1868).

[3] Philip H. Highfill, "Edmund Simpson's Talent Raid on England in 1818," *Theatre Notebook,* XII, 4 (1958), 85.

they used European themes. Foreign novels were dramatized whole-
sale and American works also. Besides Cooper, thirteen of whose
stories reached the stage beginning with *The Spy* in March 1822,[4]
plays were made from the fiction of less known writers: Robert
Montgomery Bird, George Lippard, Joseph Holt Ingraham, John P.
Kennedy, and Samuel Woodworth (who wrote "The Old Oaken
Bucket"). Lippard was an eccentric Philadelphia writer and editor
who made a sensation with his contemporary gothic novel, *The
Quaker City; or, the Monks of Monk Hall* (1844), which owes
much to Ainsworth. His *Blanche of Brandywine* was produced by
Laura Keene (1858), Joseph Jefferson collaborating on the adaptation. This was a drama of the Revolutionary War, crowded with
characters taken from history including Washington and Lord
Howe. Louisa Medina Hamblin, actress-wife of an early manager of
the Bowery, was an industrious adapter. Mordecai N. Noah and
Benjamin Judah wrote original dramas such as *The Grecian Captive*
and *Rose of Aragon*, and solemn, bearded Philadelphia burghers
ground out gimcrack tragedies on approved classical themes, as well
as "noble savage" Indian plays, chiefly as vehicles for their fellow-
townsman, Edwin Forrest.

Prior to the middle of the century—when *Uncle Tom's Cabin*
and various plays by Boucicault lent prestige to melodrama of
American theme—the native product consisted of primitives in the
fields of city and rural life, patriotic war dramas, and the first
interesting shoots of what was to develop into the most characteristic form of American indoor and outdoor melodrama, the Wild
West show.

In the main American dramatic authors in the early days concentrated on a species in which they had little or no alien competition,
the patriotic war play. These works—by Miss Medina, Bannister,
Richard Emmons, Richard Penn Smith, Clifton W. Tayleure, G. C.
Foster, H. P. Grattan, Harry Watkins, and others—had little to
set them apart from the English and French pieces of the same class
save for place names, the appearance of Indians, Negroes, and Yankee
comics in the *dramatis personae*, and, of course, the flag under which
the military rush on at the last moment to save the day. As a general
rule they contained the familiar sentiments, the familiar character
types, the familiar situations, the familiar sight and sound effects,

[4] George C. Odell, *Annals of the New York Stage* (New York,
1927–1949), Vol. III, p. 22.

and the familiar patriotic rant. The villains are craven, double-deal-
ing Tories or heartless, overbearing Britishers; the heroes, dauntless
sons of Uncle Sam, capable of demolishing a half-dozen foreigners
in any circumstances and continually bragging. "Lie there, where
every mother's son of ye English wolves ought to be—under an
American freeman's foot," roars the comic hero of C. W. Tayleure's
Horse-shoe Robinson (1836), adapted from John P. Kennedy's
novel of the same name; the whole affair is as jingoistic as an old-
fashioned text book.

John D. Burk's *Bunker Hill; or, the Death of General Warren*
and William Dunlap's *The Glory of Columbia* were two of the
more popular plays of this variety. Oddly enough, the most successful of the lot was one entirely free of jingoistic violence, Bannister's
Putnam: The Iron Son of '76 which ran one hundred nights when it
was first given in 1847 and continued in the repertory for twenty-
five years. Its British soldiers, especially Cornwallis, are depicted
throughout as chivalrous foes, and the rôle of villain was assigned to
a renegade Colonist. The play is further differentiated from type by
having a good Indian among its characters.

As the wars with England receded into the past, and the passions
associated with them cooled, another theme, one that was uniquely
and inalienably American, emerged in American playwriting: the
frontier.

XXVIII

The Wild West

The Indian plays have become perfect nuisances. —JAMES REES
(1845)

A strange homicidal maniac, "Nick of the Woods," roamed the wilderness of Pennsylvania in Colonial days. He was a sort of Jekyll-Hyde character as border legend portrayed him. When it suited his purpose, he played the part of a misanthropic Quaker recluse, the butt of frontier ridicule because he would never fight; and so well did he carry it off with his madman's cunning that none suspected him of being "bloody Nathan," a fleet and powerful killer who prowled along the border slaughtering every Indian who crossed his path and marking the carcasses with knife-slashes in the form of a cross on the breast. The tribes which suffered at his hands regarded him with superstitious horror; to them he was "the Jibbenainosay," or walking spirit.

A tragic history lay behind Nick's aberration. In his youth, when he was Reginald Ashburn, his bride and all his kin had been scalped before his eyes by the Shawnees, and from that day forward he had pursued his fanatical vengeance on the whole breed of red men without respite and without mercy. As Robert Montgomery Bird retold the story in his novel, *Nick of the Woods*, Nick's special hate was reserved for the chief who had committed the outrage, Wenonga, "the Black Vulture of the Shawnees." He has stalked this brave for years, and, for the climax of the story, hunted and hunter are brought together in titanic combat.

The novel was as widely read at home and abroad as any of Cooper's had been and shortly after its publication in 1837 it was dramatized all around the country if we are to believe James Rees, a contemporary theatrical chronicler. Louisa Medina Hamblin, wife of an early actor and manager in New York, wrote the standard version, which became the most successful American melodrama of the first half of the century. Mounted first at the Park in 1838 under the title of *The Jibbenainosay*, it was still being played year after year in the sixties and seventies by Joseph Proctor and W. G. Coggswell, and there were later productions. Corse Payton revived it in 1906. Nick was the subject of a Currier and Ives print, sure indication of popular appeal.

The most thrilling moments in the play are provided by Nick's spectacular entrances. One of these, at the end of the second act, has him precipitated down a cataract in a canoe of fire. As a rule his arrival is nicely timed to frustrate some redskin deviltry aimed at the lives, the fortunes, or the sacred honor of Roland and Edith, "genteel" characters straight out of Cooper. Such emergencies occur often enough; the plot fairly rocks with ambuscades, raids, and abductions, accompanied by incendiarism, tomahawking, knifing, and the promiscuous discharge of firearms. For a final smashing climax there is an engagement of the whites and the Shawnees, the Indians getting the worst of it amid great slaughter; and as the curtain descends, the wigwams of the savages are seen burning.

Bird was a playwright as well as a novelist. His work for the stage comes under the head of the Philadelphia school. This school confined itself largely to blank verse tragedy of a wholly European and degenerate pattern and hymned the sagas of remote and quasi-legendary characters including Jack Cade, Spartacus, and Pelopidas (Pelopidas of Thebes, out of Plutarch). Native subjects were not ignored. Here and there the hero would be a Sassacus, a King Philip, or a Metamora (this last in John Augustus Stone's play of the same name, given in 1829); in these circumstances he would wear pictur-esque feathered headdress and carry a tomahawk but would be otherwise undistinguishable from his classical fellows. Whether a noble Roman or a noble Wampanoag, he was addicted to the same flatulent declamation (designed to exercise the robust lungs of Edwin Forrest) and the same calculated heroic attitudes. The Philadelphia school flourished from 1825 to 1840.

The Cooper Indian found his way onto the stage in numerous dramatizations of the *Leatherstocking Tales*. Typically he is the "noble savage," in a tradition which goes back in melodrama to *L'Héroïne américaine* of Boulevard pantomime and to Major Robert Rogers' *Ponteach; or, the Savages of America*, the first American Indian play, never produced. What set *Nick of the Woods* apart from *Metamora*, which preceded it, and other dramas of the type and what entitles it to be considered the first authentically indige-nous Wild West melodrama, is the absence from it of this "noble savage."

Early in his career (1829) Bird wrote a conventional Indian play,

King Philip; or, the Sagamore (never printed), from which Stone was accused of having extracted the plot of *Metamora*. Later Bird visited Kentucky. His sojourn there altered his opinion of Indian character, as well it might. No romantic or literary sentiment colored the Kentuckians' opinion of the aborigine. In their eyes he was a dirty, drunken, treacherous, murdering scoundrel, a varmint on a par with the painter and the rattler and to be dealt with accordingly: good Indian, dead Indian. The nostalgic, poetic warrior of Cooper could be villainous on occasion certainly, as witness the Sioux, Wencha, and the Huron, Magna, and the whole breed of Mingoes; but this realistic Indian of the frontiersman's world was universally unregenerate—the villain of the piece. This point of view was set forth in Bird's *Nick of the Woods* possibly for the first time in a work of fiction having serious literary pretensions. The author himself seems to have been aware that he was pioneering; he wrote in his preface that he was "exhibiting the Indian in darker lines than are naturally employed by painters of such figures."[1]

The convention of the bad Indian prevailed over that of the "noble savage" in melodramas written around the ever receding frontier, becoming noticeable in the forties. The Indian is not always the chief villain. Mexicans dispute his primacy during the Texas troubles, and Anglo-Saxon and half-breed outlaws later; but almost invariably the red man is in league with the forces of evil as instigator or agent when he is not the principal actor. In Augustin Daly's *Horizon* (1871), the very children of the Cherokees showed marked traces of that congenital depravity attributed to the whole race of Indians in the frontiersman's creed. The various plays concerning Daniel Boone, Kit Carson, General Custer, and Buffalo Bill all conform to type in this repect. Recurring Indian troubles are doubtless accountable in some measure for this stubborn enmity of the American for the race he had dispossessed. From 1869 to 1875 more than two hundred pitched battles were fought between Indians and the U.S. Army.

Upon those occasions in *The Jibbenainosay* when Nick is not waiting poised in the wings—or in the flies—to swoop to the rescue of beleaguered innocence, that office is assigned to another colorful personage in the cast, Ralph Stackpole. Ralph is the bucktail—a long-legged, rawboned gimlet-eyed, weather-beaten woodsman and

[1] Robert Montgomery Bird, *Nick of the Woods; or, The Jibbenainosay* (London, 1837), Vol. I, p. xii.

scout, outfitted from his native habitat in buckskin clothes and a coonskin cap and accoutered for every border contingency with long rifle, powder horn and bowie knife. He is no Cooper idealization—no Leatherstocking—but a bellowing, rampageous roughneck and playboy, and even a hoss thief, though he insists that it is only injun mounts that he steals. Afraid of nothing that walks, crawls, swims, or flies, he never wearies of telling the world about it. He crows like a cock, neighs like a horse, and delivers himself of speeches such as this: "Who's for a fight? Where's your old 'coon can claw the bark off a gum tree? Where's your wolf of the rolling prairie? Here's a man for you, Tom Bruce; same to you, Jimmy Big Nose, and to all of you. Ain't I the old snag to shake off a saddle—can go down Old Salt on my back and swim up the Ohio! Hurraugh for a fight!"

"Roarin' Ralph, the ring-tailed screamer," as he calls himself, is "no portrait drawn from the imagination," wrote his creator. "The history of this wild scape-gallows, his prowess in the pinfold and on the battle field, his adventures in the beech tree and his escapes from the meshes of the law . . . are recollections still cherished in some parts of Kentucky and made the theme of many a gleesome story."[2] In short, like Mike Fink the river boatman, put into a play for the first time by James Rees in the thirties at New Orleans, and like Paul Bunyan and Pecos Bill, Stackpole was a folk hero—a folk hero, incidentally, whose eccentricities it was possible to corroborate by men of already legendary renown still alive in the thirties, especially Davy Crockett and Simon Kenton (who was to appear in his proper person in two famous American romances published at the turn of the century, *Alice of Old Vincennes*, by Maurice Thompson, and *The Crossing*, by Winston Churchill).

James K. Paulding was accused, and with reason, of having used the future hero of the Alamo as model for his Captain Nimrod Wildfire, who, as the principal character in *The Lion of the West*, a farcical comedy written in 1830 for James Henry Hackett, was perhaps the first representative of the type on the legitimate stage. It was in this kind of play, it may be said, rather than in straight melodrama, that the bucktail appeared most persistently during his long career as a character in American drama.

The homespun backwoods bravo is the first character cut from the whole cloth of American life at its richest, gamiest, and most

[2] *Ibid.*, p. xiv.

characteristic as it manifested itself along the frontier, and he was properly appreciated as such. From his earliest appearance on the stage, in 1822 at New Orleans in *The Hunter of Kentucky*, a song and dance skit by Noah Ludlow, he was recognized as the real McCoy and hailed with delight wherever he appeared. His gusto, impudence, cocksureness, high spirits and good-natured combativeness, his low-comedy antics and racy verbal extravagances endeared him to plebeian audiences and qualified him for the role of favorite comic hero of the assertively democratic American masses, particularly of the Jacksonian generation; he became the transatlantic equivalent of the jolly British tar. On the Bowery as well as in his native Mississippi and Ohio valleys, he remained the typical Western hero for two generations, or until the arrival of the soberer Buffalo Bill, a character who nevertheless (in his theatrical representations) retains many of the same traits. Kit Redding, the Arkansas Traveller, in De Walden and Spencer's melodrama of that name, was to be his continuator in the seventies and eighties.

The frontier, as it pushed westward during the nineteenth century, was rich in the materials of which melodrama is made. Savage Indians were everywhere; bandit gangs as incredible as any that Pixerécourt had imagined plied their trade along the desolate stretches of the great traces; lynch law and personal combat took the place of orderly processes of justice; massacre became a kind of custom.

Richard M. Coates, in *The Outlaw Years*, has vividly retold the story of the bad men of the old Natchez Trace, a dreadful company of scoundrels far surpassing the Turpins and the Sheppards in audacity, ambition, and ferocity. These Murrels and Harpes gambled, caroused, and brawled in the river towns, made themselves up as circuit riders and passed their "queer" money at Methodist revivals, stole horses, abducted Negroes and sold them on a big-business scale, waylaid travellers, robbed the mails, wrecked and looted river boats, and killed from sheer habit. Among them were morons, sadists, madmen, clowns, embittered outcasts at war with society, and even dandies—faultlessly mannered and elegantly turned out in Bolivar coats and Philadelphia beavers. One of these fop-desperadoes, Murrel, "The Land Pirate," who had a spark of genius in his perverted soul, organized henchmen in a far-flung secret brotherhood, projected a vast slave rebellion, and dreamed of a grandiose robber empire extending throughout the Southwest.

A few of the more formidable of these gangs found their way

into ephemeral theatrical pieces. A play billed as *The Harpes*—the title being all that survives of it—played at Louisville and Cincinnati in the late forties; and Barrington's *Murrel, the Land Pirate*, which had Ichabod Crane for its comic, was given successfully in various parts of the nation after it was introduced in New Orleans.[3] However, the legend of these ruffians never attained the renown on the stage that it would seem to have merited. American bandit drama, when it came into its own toward the close of the nineteenth century, dealt with lesser men: Deadwood Dick, Jesse James, Billy the Kid, and their kind. These gentry—road agents, train robbers and gambler-killers—pursued their various vocations along the lines of the newly built railroads, in the cattle towns along the border, and in the mining camps of the far west. This milieu, however, was to be associated in the theatre less closely with its villains than with its heroes, a glamorous roll at the head of which stands that demi-god, Buffalo Bill.

It was Ned Buntline, pen name of Edward Zane Carrol Judson, the most prolific and successful of Beadle's dime novel authors, who persuaded Cody to turn play-actor in 1872. In four hours' time one hectic afternoon in a Chicago hotel, the dime novel specialist wrote *The Scouts of the Plains* for Cody and his pal Texas Jack Omohundro, rehearsing it overnight and presenting it to the public the following evening with "Indians" recruited on the streets of the city. The greenhorn stars got through the evening thanks principally to heroic assistance from Buntline himself, who, doubling as an actor, went on with his protégés, fed them their lines, and covered up their lapses by ad-libbing. The crowd overlooked all the many shortcomings of the performance. They had paid their dollars to see Buffalo Bill in person; and if he hadn't spoken a line, it would hardly have made any difference to them.

After a triumphal progress through the country in *The Scouts of the Plains*, which played for two seasons, Cody appeared in a succession of other pieces, all meeting with a similar reception. In 1876 he abandoned the footlights temporarily to join the punitive Army expedition sent into the Sioux country to avenge the Sixth Cavalry. Upon his return, he was presented in *The Red Right Hand; or, Buffalo Bill's First Scalp for Custer* (by J. V. Arlington, an actor). The action in this piece included the star's widely

[3] James Rees, *The Dramatic Authors of America* (Philadelphia, 1845), p. 35.

publicized single combat with Yellow Hand. *May Cody Lost and Won*, by Major A. S. Burk, an Army man, followed. Later vehicles were *The Prairie Wolf, Life on the Border*, and *Buffalo Bill, King of the Border*, and there were others, the greater number of them from the pen of a dime novel writer, Prentiss Ingraham.

Cody's career was a treasure trove for melodramatists. He had faced every kind of Western peril and dealt with every species of Western bad man—red, white, and mixed. Such real adventures, however, did not suffice for Buntline, Ingraham, and the other playwrights who set about endowing their hero with superhuman powers and exposing him to the most extravagant hazards. When Bill's trusty rifle or six-shooter barked, not one but two or three redskins were apt to bite the dust; wrongs awaited him to be righted in every scene, maidens to be rescued, villains to be foiled; and romance beckoned him from behind every property tree and in the depths of every canvas gully. Mrs. Cody, in her memoir of her husband, records the amazement of that plain man at the things he was called upon to do, and the language that was put into his mouth.

The Buffalo Bill Show, Cody's own venture, which dates from 1882, was a more faithful transcript of the stirring days of the old West. In these exciting outdoor spectacles, herds of real buffalo were driven across the ring, cowboys roped steer and rode bucking bronchos, and authentic Indians, veterans of Little Big Horn among them, galloped madly in pursuit of the actual Deadwood Coach of history. For a quarter of a century this spectacle toured the country annually, and in Europe the show enjoyed triumphs no American stage play could hope for. In England Gladstone saw the show six times, and Queen Victoria herself, accompanied by the royal princes, took a ride in the Deadwood Coach.

Aside from the dime novel, the most important influence on Wild West melodrama insofar as the written word was concerned was Bret Harte, laureate of the gold rush and its literary godfather. Harte himself had no knack for drama though he attempted it several times. Other hands were more successful in turning Harte's material into dramas. *M'liss*, adapted many times (by Clay M. Greene and E. F. Goodrich, among others) and always with lavish garnishings of murder, lynching, and arson, was one of the best-liked plays of its day, especially as a vehicle for Anne Pixley and Annie Russel. T. Edgar Pemberton successfully dramatized *The Judgment of Bolinas Plain* under the title *Sue* (1896), and in 1907

Paul Armstrong's *Salomy Jane* made money for George Tyler on Broadway.

Virtually every writer of gold rush plays from the seventies onward used the stock Harte character types and aped the famous Harte brand of sentimentality: Joaquin Miller in *Forty-Nine* and *The Danites in the Sierras;* Bartley Campbell in *How Women Love, The Vigilantes,* and *My Partner;* and Augustin Daly in *Horizon.* Loder, in Daly's play, is a ruined wastrel who atones for an ill-spent life by dying heroically to save the waif-heroine. Campbell's plays are filled with tomboy-waifs, fancy ladies who turn out to be model wives, comic Chinese cooks, slick gamblers, evil dive-keepers, and rough old miners with hearts as soft as women's. *The Danites* which Miller wrote with the assistance of P. A. Fitzgerald, a Philadelphia playwright, deals with the massacre of a party of Mormons by a band of "gentile" emigrants and with the tracking down and destruction of the guilty ones by the "avenging angels" (Danites), the militant arm of the Mormons. It was one of the major hits of its era and, when it was taken to England in 1880, marked the first time a completely American company played in an English theatre.[4]

Plays of the Beadle dime novel school—the cycles of Buffalo Bill, Jack Harkaway, Deadwood Dick, *et al.*—were all what might be called heroic in temper; that is, they were largely brag, slaughter, and low comedy. The Harte derivatives, by comparison, were excruciatingly emotional situations replacing in some degree the old-fashioned roughhouse and clowning; and these qualities tended to commend Western melodrama to audiences of more fastidious tastes. In this new, refined manner was Frank Hitchcock Murdock's *Davy Crockett* (1874), played so long and with such great success by Frank Mayo. *The Girl of the Golden West,* which edited the gold rush dramas for Broadway dress circles of a later generation, chose its ingredients judiciously from both the Davy Crockett sort of thing and the Bret Harte school. This masterpiece among Western melodramas will be examined in a later chapter.

The cowpuncher brings up the rear of the pageant of the old West as it files across the stages of melodrama. He dates from the era of the great cattle drives up from Texas which began after the Civil War. Really a shaggy hired hand doing a routine job and

[4] M. M. Marberry, *Splendid Poseur; Joaquin Miller, an American Poet* (New York, 1953), pp. 164–165.

bearing not too good a reputation, he was shamelessly romanticized in fiction and drama. The dime novel discovered him (*circa* 1885), and his numerous stage representations in the proletarian theatre stemmed from this source. In the early years of the present century, writers such as Clyde Fitch, Owen Wister, Stewart Edward White, and Augustus Thomas took him up and gave him literary and social caste. Theodore Roosevelt's Western adventure probably had much to do with this rehabilitation; Wister, author of the often dramatized classic, *The Virginian* (first production in 1904), had been T.R.'s classmate at Harvard and his companion later on the range. Here and there the cowboy hero in the Broadway plays by these writers appears as a technical (in distinction to, or in combination with, a natural) gentleman. Fitch's *The Cowboy and the Lady* (1897), an emotional drama with a big courtroom scene, offered a dude rancher who had been at Harvard. Jim Carston, of *The Squaw Man*, is out of Burke's *Peerage*. Lieutenant Denton, of Thomas' *Arizona* (1899), is an officer who resigns his commission to become a cowboy after he has chosen disgrace for himself rather than allow his beloved captain to learn that his young wife was on the point of eloping with the villain. The climax of this stirring and well-constructed Texas play is precipitated by the shooting of the villain when the hero is alone with him. At the inquest, Denton is exonerated when an examination of the caliber of the fatal bullet proves it to be from the weapon of Tony, the Mexican *vaquero* comic, whose sweetheart has been seduced by the villain.

Edmund Day's *The Round Up* (1907) was a throwback to the naïveté of early days with its spectacular staging, its juvenile heroics, its real horses, and its pitched battle with the Apaches. The production made its annual round of the circuits of the country for a decade or more as a sort of winter substitute for the Buffalo Bill show. *Pioneer Days* by Carroll Fleming, which played 298 times at the Hippodrome in 1908, was a spectacular of the same vintage.

The suggestion of racial, regional, and class problems further modified the Western of Broadway in *The Squaw Man* (1905), by Edwin Milton Royle, and *The Great Divide* (1907), by William Vaughn Moody. A reaction to this etherializing tendency was the he-man school represented by such writers as Jack London, Richard Harding Davis, Alfred Henry Lewis, and Rex Beach, whose novels were frequently dramatized in the first decade of the century. These strenuous sagas—in adaptations by Paul Armstrong, Willard Mack, and others—introduced new settings, among them the Canadian Northwest with its highly advertised Mounties, Alaska of Klondike gold rush days, and revolution-wracked Central American republics. Original plays competed with adaptations: Eugene Walter's *The Wolf* (1908) and *Rio Grande* (1908), William de Mille's *The Northwest Mounted* (1908), and George Scarborough's *The Heart of Wetona* (1916)—the last written in collaboration with, and produced by, Belasco.

Meanwhile, an even more primitive formula, deriving from the dime novel school, was being used profitably by producers at the level of the proletarian theatre, under the aegis of "ten, twent', thirt'," favorite heroes being Billy the Kid, the James Brothers, the Daltons, and other recent Western bad men. *Billy the Kid*, by Walter Woods, first put on at the Star in 1906, toured for twelve years and was advertised (*circa* 1913) as having been seen by six million people. Star of the original production was a youngster later to become a leading man in Broadway musicals, Joseph Santley.

In our own generation, two brilliant attempts have been made to construct a play of ideas on the cadre of the Western: Robert E. Sherwood's *The Petrified Forest* was a success of the season of 1934–35 on Broadway, with Leslie Howard and Humphrey Bogart in leading rôles; and *The Survivors* (1948) by Peter Viertel and Irwin Shaw, an eloquent sermon on the futility of war, was an undeserved failure.

XXIX

The Delirium Tremens Drama

The stage offers the quickest, the most direct and continuous means of action upon the masses.—C. A. SAINTE-BEUVE (1849)

In early drama the souse was a farcical figure. Douglas Jerrold's *Fifteen Years of a Drunkard's Life*, a domestic melodrama given first at the Coburg in 1828, elevated him to the dignity of a pseudo-tragic hero. This play was obviously patterned after Ducange's *Trente Ans ou la vie d'un joueur* (Chapter VIII), which had received its English premiere a year earlier at the same house in a version by Milner, *The Hut of the Red Mountains*. Even the title of Jerrold's play is imitative, though it is worth noting that, while gambling required thirty years to bring about the ruin of its victim, booze does the job in half that time.

Like Georges in the Frenchman's tract, Jerrold's hero, Vernon, has a devoted wife, an angel-child, and a false friend. This villain, Glanville, is the miscreant who, with devilish subtlety, lures Vernon to his destruction, chiefly by getting him drunk and swindling him. Both Georges and Vernon are well-meaning but weak gentlemen who bring misfortune and death upon those they love as well as upon themselves.

Vernon is continually swearing off and continually backsliding; "he never takes an oath but he settles it with a bumper." The sight, or even the mere promise, of a drink has a demoralizing effect upon him. Glanville describes his case to an accomplice, the lawyer Pounce. "At our first meeting," he reports, "he swelled a little and glared sullenly. I mentioned wine—and as the serpent's eye brings down the fluttering bird within its venomed jaws, so at the very sound his mounting spirit drooped—and now, look! see where 'tis drugged within him." (*Throws open door in flat and discovers* VERNON *on the floor as if slid from the chair, on the rail of which his head is yet resting.*) "See where the image of noble, ambitious, god-like man—the master of the earth and all its beings—the creature that binds the elements to his will—that tempts the billows in their wrath and blunts the lightning—the gifted soul that would read the will of fate within the star-lettered front of heaven—see where he lies, gorged to the throat with wine, the mockery of life, the antip-odes of reason."

Even the villains preach in the booze plays; Glanville rises to his peroration like a practiced temperance lecturer: "Habitual intoxica-tion is the epitome of every crime; all the vices that stain our nature germinate within it, waiting but a moment to sprout forth in pestilential rankness. When the Roman stoic sought to fix a damning stigma on his sister's seducer, he called him neither simple rebel, blood-shedder or villain—no, he wreaked every odium within one word, and that word was—drunkard."

Not for a pint of porter could the costers, navvies, and fishwives who crowded the Coburg's pit and galleries have explained what half those magnificent words meant, nor could they so much as have understood what Glanville was talking about. But mouth-filling rhetoric was a consecrated ingredient of classical melodrama; and speeches like this, if they did not run on too long or occur too frequently, went over almost as well as murders. Certainly neither audience nor management at the Coburg could have been suspected of any sympathy with Jerrold's edifying thesis. Many of the minor theatres of London, and American houses of the same class, were able to carry on only by virtue of a subsidiary "wet business." Nearly all of them had at least one bar on the premises, and porter and gin were liberally dispensed up and down the aisles in the course of the performance along with miscellaneous foodstuffs, helping to sustain the customers through the long evening of entertainment which ran from six thirty until midnight and later.

In the forties Cruikshank, Dickens' illustrator, published a series of drawings called *The Drunkard's Progress*, which had an enor-mous sale. Number 1 is entitled, "The Happy Home; the Bottle Is Brought Out for the First Time," and others portray with a wealth of harrowing detail the gradual degeneration of the tippler. He loses his job, his family is reduced to want, his children turn to crime. Finally he murders his wife (with a bottle) and goes mad—"The Bottle Has Done Its Work." These pictures were realized in numer-ous dramas, the artist himself directing the production of Thomas Prochis Taylor's version, *The Bottle*, given in 1847. The second generation of this distressed family was then placed upon the boards as *The Drunkard's Children* in several adaptations, one by Taylor and another by Thomas Beer Johnstone.

Many of the British dipsomania plays were given in the United States, and their popularity inspired a vigorous native growth. The year 1844 saw what is probably the first of these, *The Drunkard; or, the Fallen Saved*, "a moral domestic drama," by W. H. Smith, an actor, and "a gentleman of Boston," who chose coyly to remain anonymous. The piece had its premiere at the lecture hall of Barnum's Boston Museum, and enjoyed a long run (130 nights), thanks to the wiles of old P. T. himself, who hornswoggled the temperance people into beating the drum for his show. *The Drunkard* owed much to the English dramas, but certain significant departures from the familiar formula are to be observed. The drunkard is reformed, a dead set is made at "the traffic," and *delirium tremens* makes its bow as a melodramatic device.

Edward, the hero, shows all the pathological symptoms of the drink habit as standardized by Jerrold, and his excesses give rise to the same train of disasters as in the English play, namely, a dissipated fortune, a ruined home, and a starving family. Like Vernon, Edward is mulcted by a sober, calculating villain, the lawyer Cribbs, and he also deserts his family, heading for New York. In the second act he is discovered in that metropolitan sink of iniquity, staggering along Broadway, carousing in a tavern, and getting himself jailed for brawling. Next we see the faithful wife, Mary, who has followed Edward; she is discovered in a "bare, wretched attic," sewing shirts by candlelight to earn a crust of bread for her starving child, who is shown shivering with cold on a bed of straw. At this "effect," writes the editor of French's edition of the play, "it was no uncommon thing to see men and women weeping like children."[1]

In the midst of this touching scene the villain enters. Cribbs, like all his breed, is a scoundrel through and through—craven, treacherous, thieving, libidinous, brutal. (He beats a poor idiot girl in an early scene.) After traducing Edward, whom he has ruined, he makes a dishonorable proposal to Mary, for whom he cherishes an adulterous passion. She spurns him. "Nay, proud beauty," cries he, "you shall know my power. 'Tis late, you are unfriended, helpless"— and he attempts to have his wicked way with her by force. It is a tense moment; the child, rudely awakened from her innocent slumbers, cries out in terror; Mary struggles in the embrace of her persecutor. Heaven, however, is watching over female virtue. The door is flung open and a savior strides in; he is William Dowton, the sturdy Yankee comic of the piece. He hurls the viper to the floor,

[1] *French's Standard Drama*, Vol. LXXXVI, p. vi.

denounces him as "the most contemptible of earth-born creatures," and thrusts him out at the door ("noise of falling downstairs").

The next scene, laid in a stable, offers the *pièce de résistance* of the evening, a realistic imitation of that exciting affliction known variously as the horrors, the rams, the jimjams and *mania à potu*— Edward being the sufferer. Virtuosity in this piece of business was highly esteemed by audiences, and the enduring popularity of plays like *The Drunkard*—which was still being played in the eighties— can be attributed in some measure to the ambition of performers to have a go at it. Charles Warner, a celebrated lead at the Adelphi in the seventies, virtually made his reputation through a similar opportunity in *Drink*, Charles Reade's adaptation of Zola's *L'Assommoir*. "The final scene," writes Errol Sherson of this performance, "was a masterpiece of acting that made men and women gasp and want to get away . . . and the effect on [Warner] could be seen in the gasping, shaking figure that came before the curtain to take his call."[2]

The Drunkard probably established a persistent misconception of the symptoms of the rams. "Those snakes," roars Edward, in the midst of his convulsions; "how they coil round me. Oh! how strong they are—there, don't kill it, no, no don't kill it, give it brandy, poison it with rum, that would be judicious punishment, that would be justice, ha, ha, justice, ha, ha."

After his attack, Edward attempts to take poison but is restrained by a distinguished stranger who enters in the nick of time. He is Mr. Rencelow, "the princely merchant, the noble philanthropist, the poor man's friend, the orphan's benefactor"—himself a reformed sot. "I administer the pledge of sobriety to those who would become an ornament of society," he explains. Heeding the advice of this evangelist, Edward turns from drink, and in due course becomes an ornament of society, rejoining his wife and recovering his fortune from the despicable Cribbs.

Franklin, in *Fifteen Years*, asks the more or less rhetorical question, what is to be done about a person like Vernon? Dogrose, a minor character, ventures the answer: "Destroy all the vineyards, demolish all the distillers, and cry down the trade of brewer as wicked and unlawful." Such an ambitious program, however, was not taken seriously by English playwrights. It was left for our own

---

[2] *London's Lost Theatres of the Nineteenth Century* (London, 1925), pp. 167–168.

countrymen, with their peculiar intrepidity in grappling with moral questions, to undertake it. Edward sounds the tocsin; when a tavern-keeper asks him what brought him to his present pass, he replies: "You. Rum. Eternal curses on you! Had it not been for your infernal poison shops in our village, I had still been a man—the foul den where you plunder the pockets of your fellows, where you deal forth death in tumblers, and from whence goes forth the blast of ruin over the land, to mildew the bright hopes of youth, to fill the widow's heart with agony, to curse the orphans, to steal the glorious mind of man, to cast them from their high estate of honest pride and make them such as—me!"

Ten Nights in a Bar-room, the *Uncle Tom's Cabin* of the prohibition movement, translated this bullyragging into more posi-tive terms of propaganda. The tavern-keeper, who had been a minor figure in *The Drunkard,* here becomes the second heavy; and the *raisonneur,* Romaine, comes down stage and harangues the house for votes. "If you would save the young, the innocent," he says, "we must cover them from the tempter, for they can no more resist his assaults than the lamb can resist the wolf. They are helpless if you abandon them to the powers of evil. Let us, then, one and all, resolve this night that the traffic shall cease in —— County. A large majority of the people, I am convinced, will vote in favor of such a measure."

Slade, the saloonkeeper, had been an honest, respected citizen while he was a miller, but when he changed his trade, the audience is told, his moral fiber deteriorated rapidly. "Decency died when you exchanged the pick and facing hammer for the bottle and the shaker," he is reminded one night by Joe Morgan, one of his drunken customers and the horrible-example hero of the play. The remark provokes a quarrel, and Slade, urged on by the first heavy, the gambler Green, hurls a tumbler at his insulter. Joe's agility does not appear to have departed with his sobriety; he sidesteps nimbly and the missile whizzes past him. It strikes an innocent bystander, sweet little Mary Morgan, Joe's angel-child, who has come on her nightly errand to plead with her parent and sing the ditty:

> Father, dear father, come home with me now;
> The clock in the steeple strikes twelve.

Her injury proves a fatal one, and through several scenes she dies lingeringly—and eloquently, quoting improving moral poetry at Joe to the very end.

Poetic justice is accomplished in Slade's fate. He succumbs to the stuff he deals in and, drinking up the profits, descends to squalid poverty and is finally slain by his own son, who has become a drunkard tending the parental bar.

Mary's death brings about a great change in Joe. He emerges from his sorrow a chastened man, a teetotaler. In the concluding scene he and his beaming spouse are seen in the elegant parlor of their now prosperous home "forming a picture" with Romaine and other characters.

MRS MORGAN. Words cannot describe the joy I feel, to see you thus redeemed. I could have knelt above your grave and blessed Him who took you from me, rather than had you continue in your old habits. How day by day have I looked forward, with a shuddering and dread at my soul, as I have seen you sinking day by day away from me! But that is past. You are now free once more, and able manfully to stand up and breast the temptation with which the coming years are crowded. There will be no more hindrances, no more hands stretched out to drag you down. If love can shield you, you are safe; for my heart will, for your sake, ever prove constant.

ROMAINE. Yes, years in happiness are in store for us all. And the results of the past few years will serve always as a beacon to warn us of the dangers and temptations that constantly beset the pilgrim on his voyage through life.

MORGAN. Restored once more to happiness, let us hope that others may learn a useful lesson from our past experience, and that none will regret deducting from the calendar of their lives the

TEN NIGHTS IN A BAR-ROOM

As some poor stranger wrecked upon the coast,
With fear and wonder views the dangers past,
So I with dreadful apprehension stand,
And thank the powers that brought me safe to land;
A drunkard now no longer—that is o'er,
Free, disenthralled, I stand a man once more.

Ten Nights in a Bar-room was written by a William W. Pratt, Esquire. It would be more accurate to say that it was compiled by him, since he was not above literary larceny when it suited his pious purposes. Romaine, Mrs. Morgan, and Green all quote *Fifteen Years*

of a Drunkard's Life (the Roman stoic speech, among other items)
and omit to credit Jerrold; and Joe has an attack of the rams, seeing
snakes as Edward saw them. The plot and the principal characters
were taken from a narrative tract written by T. S. Arthur, a Philadelphia Sunday School novelist and publisher of the middle of the
century. Only the dismal comics are the playwright's own, and even
they are no more than stock Yankee types, familiar from scores of
melodramas and farces of the period.

Given first at Purdy's National on the Bowery, the play enjoyed
several prosperous runs in New York and other eastern cities. Its
greatest triumphs, however, were scored in the sticks. For a full half-
century it maintained its popularity in the American hinterland, and
in the present century the resolute cohorts of the Anti-Saloon
League and the Women's Christian Temperance Union contrived to
keep it alive until the fight for prohibition was virtually won.
Productions persisted after the Eighteenth Amendment and later.
The last straight revivals were those put on by Robert Downing, a
reformed drunkard who died in 1944 in Milwaukee where he was on
the faculty of Marquette University.

The Drunkard and *Ten Nights in a Bar-room* dominated the
American temperance drama, but there were many other examples.
One from an eminent hand was James A. Herne's *Drifting Apart*
(1888) which dealt with the ravages of drink among Gloucester
fishermen.

In the course of the Boston run of *The Drunkard*, two members
of the original cast, Caroline Fox and George C. Howard, were
married. This professional couple, with one of their offspring,
Cordelia, born in 1848, went on to participate in the premiere of
another notable item on the roll of reform propaganda dramas, a
play which was to become the first, and the greatest, international
triumph of American melodrama, *Uncle Tom's Cabin*.

XXX

Uncle Tom's Cabin

Uncle Tom's Cabin with Miss Adah [*Menken*]; *there is a show of which one dreams!*—PAUL VERLAINE

As became a pious Christian woman whose husband, father, grandfather, and seven brothers were all New England clergymen, Harriet Beecher Stowe viewed the playhouse askance and refused to give her consent to the dramatization of her masterpiece. Copyright laws being what they were, however, shortly after the publication of *Uncle Tom's Cabin; or, Life Among the Lowly* in book form (March, 1852), it was pounced upon and converted into a theatrical entertainment by others, none of whom every paid her a penny of the profits. These profits, in aggregate, were colossal; *Uncle Tom's Cabin* became the world's most successful melodrama as well as the world's most successful novel. Certainly it stands alone among American stage pieces in popularity, in longevity, and in influence. On the occasion of its revival by the Players' Club in 1933, a spokesman for that organization estimated that it had been given before 362,922 audiences in the United States alone.

It is surprising to discover that the bitter and prolonged abolitionist controversy produced no more melodramas than it did, particularly in view of the distinctly journalistic and polemical bias of the American popular stage in the nineteenth century. There were anti-embargo, anti-Masonic, and anti-bank plays, but this vastly more momentous question would appear to have been carefully avoided. Horace Greeley was one who chided the theatre for its indifference to the great humanitarian crusade for the emancipation of the Negroes. Boston itself was remiss, this center of the movement having but a single stage work to its credit championing abolition, *Neighbor Jackwood*, a fugitive slave drama from a story by J. T. Trowbridge, given at the Boston Museum in 1857—"to mixed applause and jeers."

England did better than this, though human servitude had ceased to be even a colonial issue with her as early as 1833. Back in the eighteenth century, George Colman the younger had written a bitter antislavery musical, *Inkle and Yarico*, put on with much

success at the Haymarket and frequently revived. Morton's sentimental comedy, *The Slave* (used by Macready as a vehicle), was
given in 1816; and Shirley Brooks' *The Creole; or, Love's Fetters* in
1847. In the latter a white man is shown in love with a woman of
mixed blood (as in *The Octoroon*). This situation is reversed in a
later play, Wilkie Collins' *Black and White* (1868), wherein the
man is a West Indian slave's son. As for France, E. C. van Bellen
mentions that not fewer than eleven pieces protesting against
slavery and the oppression of subject races received production in
Paris between 1828 and 1841.[1]

Perhaps the strength and aggressiveness of antiabolitionist feeling
in important cities of the North discouraged treatment of the
subject on the stage; meeting halls were stormed and burned, and
the homes of abolitionists sacked by mobs in Philadelphia and New
York. The mobs were theatregoers, and managers doubtless felt that
they had troubles enough with audiences as it was, without provoking them with propaganda on this incendiary theme. *Uncle Tom's
Cabin* itself (the play) was denounced by the *New York Herald* as
"an insult to the nation."

Abolitionist sentiment *per se* probably played no more than a
minor part in the success of the play on the stage. Indeed, it may be
said that a too earnest and exclusive concern with Mrs. Stowe's
message condemned the earliest Broadway version of the novel to
failure. The adaptation by C. W. Taylor, given at Purdy's National
(New York) in August, 1852, confined itself to the persecution of
Cassy and George Harris, neglecting those model slave-owners, the
St. Clair family and George Shelby, the better to enforce the
humanitarian moral. I daresay this concentration of interest resulted
in a better play from the standpoint of construction than the
scattered, episodic version which was to become the classic one; but
we have only to mention that little Eva was missing in order to
reveal what the technical superiority cost in terms of heart appeal.
Not even the happy end which Taylor tacked on was able to save
matters after that. (Tom recovers from Legree's beating and is
brought back to Kentucky for a happy reunion with George and
Eliza, and all are set free with the privilege of remaining on the old
plantation.)

When actor-playwright George L. Aiken prepared his adaptation,
the definitive one of history, he avoided Taylor's mistakes. Little

[1] *Les Origines du mélodrame* (Utrecht, 1927), p. 176.

Eva is there larger than life, and as sentimentally appealing—a golden-curled "angel-child," dispensing sweetness and light, singing Methodist hymns, dying prettily, ascending to heaven behind scrims, and returning to bless the dying Tom from atop a property cloud (or astride a milk-white dove in many adaptations) at the heartbreaking finale. It was this rôle, in fact, which influenced George Howard to mount the play at his Troy Museum in Troy, New York, in September 1852, as a vehicle for his four-year-old daughter Cordelia, the "infant phenomenon" of the company.

Along with Eva virtually all the rest of Mrs. Stowe's overpowering appartus from the novel were crammed into the six acts, thirty scenes, and eight tableaux of the final Aiken version. The original production, in four acts, confined itself to the New Orleans episodes of the novel and concluded with the death of Little Eva. During the Troy run, a four-act sequel was produced, dealing with the Red River episodes and including the deaths of Tom and Legree. By the time the show went into New York City, the two plays had been combined into a single play of six acts, constituting a full evening's entertainment by itself, something new in the theatre of that day. It was given thus, without benefit of curtain raiser or afterpiece—an innovation which was destined to have historic consequences. No other play ever offered a richer assortment of surefire melodramatic hokum. In every act were memorable situations, unforgettable lines: the sensation scene of the ice-filled Ohio River, across which Eliza, her infant at her breast, makes her way perilously to safety; the fight in the hills, in which the slave hunters pursuing the fleeing George Harris are routed and their leader Loker thrust over the edge of a cliff by the imperfectly converted Quaker. Phineas Fletcher ("Friend, thee is not wanted here"); Eva's death; the slave auction; the whipping of Tom and the old Negro's noble defiance of Legree ("You may own my body, but my soul [pointing upward] belongs to God"); Legree himself, that very pattern of a villain; and, on the lighter side, that incomparable gallery of comics—Topsy and Miss Ophelia, and Aiken's additions, Deacon Perry and Gumption Cute.

It is easy to be superior about it today: the monstrous shapelessness of the plot; the weird Negro dialect, taken over from the novel; the lush sentimentality, reaching its bizarre climax in Legree's attack of remorse, when he recalls that he, too, had a mother, one with golden locks; Eva's apotheosis. But of what avail is such sour judgment in the face of the overwhelming verdict of a half-million audiences in every part of the world during more than a half-century?

Uncle Tom's Cabin; or, Life Among the Lowly, billed as a domestic drama, was a smash hit at the Museum, running one hundred times, the first of many records it was to set. The company moved on to Albany for a short engagement and then went into New York City, setting up at Purdy's National, where Taylor's version had run briefly eleven months before. It opened on July 18, 1853. Here it ran for 325 performances, another record.

People who had never been in a playhouse before flocked to the National to see Aiken's *Uncle Tom*, many of them attracted by the encomiums of reformers and clergymen reproduced in a lobby display. Prices were increased three times in the course of the run without any noticeable diminution in the size of the audience. All were welcome; an advertisement published toward the end of the engagement announced "a neat and comfortable parquette for accommodation of respectable colored persons." They were segregated, of course, and required to use a separate entrance.

Before Aiken's version had completed its run, H. H. Conway's was mounted at Barnum's Museum, meeting with a favorable reception; and a Bowery version also appeared. Thereafter no season was complete without at least one producton somewhere in New York. At one time during the Civil War the play was to be seen at no fewer than four houses in the metropolis. From New York the Howards proceeded to Philadelphia and other cities in the East, and in 1858 they visited Chicago, where Annie Marble's version, given six years earlier, had introduced the play to the Middle West. Early in 1860 the Howards returned in triumph to New York; *Uncle Tom's Cabin* had become a career for them.

In Europe as well, audiences stormed theatres everywhere to see *Uncle Tom*. Two versions were got up hurriedly in Paris in 1853, one by Dumanoir and Dennery and the other by Texier and De Wailly. In England there were dozens of productions, if not scores. One English playwright, Fitzball, prepared three versions for as many London theatres in the course of 1852. There were eleven versions exhibited in that city before 1853, according to Clement Scott, noted London critic; the Vic production ran for 111 performances, most unusual for that era. Fifteen years later five productions reached the boards in one season. Other countries in western Europe saw the show, as did Armenia, Russia, and South Africa, to mention only the more remote. What may be called a private performance for the edification of the King of Siam, put on by Anna Lenowens, the English tutor of his children, was to become the inspiration a century later for perhaps the most charming of all redactions of the saga: Jerome Robbins' *The Small House of Uncle Thomas*, the ballet interpolated in the Rodgers and Hammerstein musical, *The King and I*, in 1952.

Virtually every member of the original Howard cast became a celebrity, and the honors that came to them were not confined to the playhouse. When the company visited England, the Negro clergyman then playing Uncle Tom was received in a special audience by the Queen. By that time Cordelia Howard had retired from the theatre, after having played Little Eva continuously for eight years. In 1886 her parents were still professionally occupied in their original parts.

Few performers of that generation or the two succeeding ones missed playing in the classic. Thomas D. ("Jim Crow") Rice, first of the blackface comedians, appeared in the first Bowery Theatre production in 1854, introducing his musical specialties. Mrs. Fiske's first rôle was Eva, and Otis Skinner's, Tom. Other Evas were Madge Kendal, Maude Adams, Annie Russel, and Mary Pickford; other Toms, David Belasco, Lawrence Barrett, Wilton Lackaye, De Wolf Hopper, and heavyweight boxer Peter Jackson. Fay Templeton, Lotta Crabtree, Mrs. John Wood, Lizzie Weston, Rose Kline, Fanny Herring, and Billie Burke all played Topsy. Performers could not well escape the piece, played as it was at every town, hamlet, and crossroads north of the Mason-Dixon Line. It was given in opera houses, dime museums, hotel dining rooms and beer gardens, on vacant lots and river boats, under canvas and even on wheels—in Ben Welch's Wagon Show. "Uncle Tomming" became a profession in itself—even a hereditary profession like tumbling, children following in the footsteps of their parents. As many as two hundred companies at one time were occupied in presenting the show to the American public.

There were innumerable versions, with a bewildering number of variations and embellishments, the Aiken script usually being employed as a base. Minstrel specialties and sensation scenes such as river steamboat races were often added, and old playbills enumerate such subsidiary attractions as "a trick donkey," jubilee singers, real slaves, and so many head of horses, mules, oxen, ponies, etc. When Peter Jackson appeared as Tom he always sparred a few rounds with Joe Choyinski, another old boxer, playing George Shelby in

the company. As likely as not John L. Sullivan might well be starring down the street as Simon Legree in a counterattraction. Sullivan toured in his own Tom company from 1896 to 1902.

The dogs were a comparatively late addition to Tom shows,
making their bow in a New York production of 1879 according to
Wesley Winans Stout.[2] These canine performers, which were
elaborately advertised and placed at the head of the parade from the
railroad station to the theatre when the show hit town, were often a
problem: dewlapped, pendulous-eared bloodhounds, with their
peculiar air of wretchedness and preoccupation, could at times be
very unconvincing languidly pursuing the fleeing Eliza across the
ice-filled river. Managers were given to substituting larger and
fiercer looking beasts, described on the playbills as "ferocious
Siberian [or Alaskan] bloodhounds," but really Great Danes. Odell
refers to an advertisement announcing that alligators would assist
the hounds in a Tom show at the Windsor on the Bowery in 1891
(Vol. XV, p. 75)—alligators on the ice-choked Ohio!

When the appeal of the entertainment in its orthodox form began
to wane, there came the more lunatic transmogrifications: the all-
child companies; "mammoth double companies," with TWO Evas,
TWO Topsies, TWO Uncle Toms, and TWO Legrees which
throve in the eighties; the operas, swing versions, and musical
comedies, one of which was *Topsy and Eva*, starring the Duncan
Sisters; and finally—a desecration which Mrs. Stowe, mercifully, was
spared—*Uncle Tom* as a burlesque show!

The Tom show industry probably reached its zenith in the mid-
eighties. Decline was well under way at the turn of the century,
when the tent companies had dwindled to twenty. The depression
of the thirties finished off the few surviving stragglers. *Uncle Tom*
was not in the repertory of "ten, twent', thirt'," the syndicate
organizations which virtually took over popular entertainment in
the field of straight comedy and melodrama in urban centers from
about 1902 onward. Productions of the classic on Broadway grew
fewer and fewer, especially after the elaborate William A. Brady
revival of 1901. When a hit was scored by the Players' revival of
1933, using a version prepared by Augustus Thomas based on
Aiken, it was a surprise for everybody concerned. Since then *Uncle
Tom* has failed to make a successful New York comeback.

[2] "Little Eva is Seventy Five," *The Saturday Evening Post*, Oct.
8, 1927, p. 192.

Mrs. Stowe wrote a second slavery story, *Dred, a Tale of the Dismal Swamp* (1856), which was only less popular as a novel and as a play than *Uncle Tom's Cabin* itself. There were six dramatic versions of it, all forgotten today, as are the other dramas by numerous hands which, somewhat belatedly, addressed themselves to the subject of the downtrodden black man. Some slight interest attaches to a few of these: *Ossewatomie Brown*, by Mrs. J. C. Swazey (1859), dealing with that passionate abolitionist zealot, better known as John Brown; Bartley Campbell's *The White Slave;* and Herne's *The Reverend Griffith Davenport* (1899), a serious study of a Southern abolitionist clergyman torn between loyalty to his people and steadfastness in his principles.

XXXI

Virtue in the Country, Crime in the Town

O, Zarathustra, here is the great city; here hast thou nothing to seek and everything to lose. —NIETZSCHE

The growth of an autochthonous American melodrama was not immediately encouraged by the invasion of our shores throughout the nineteenth century by a horde of foreign actor-authors and actor-managers, the greater number of whom became permanent guests and proceeded to take over the leadership of our theatre. These immigrants—virtually all of them from the British Isles—included the Wallacks, the Booths, William E. Burton, and John Brougham in New York; the actor-manager Laura Keene in New York and later in Philadelphia, where Mrs. John Drew had preceded her; Charles Fechter, chiefly in Boston; and Boucicault everywhere. With characteristic insularity, the Britishers adhered closely to their national repertory. I can, for instance, find only one serious American play on an American theme given by Miss Keene though that single piece was, according to Lawrence Hutton, an American critic of the day, of unusual merit, *Love in '76*, a comedy, by Oliver B. Bunce. And Mrs. Drew, at her famous Arch Street Theatre in Philadelphia, kept the flag of classical British comedy flying.

Lester Wallack (nephew of Henry and son of James W., whom he succeeded as manager of Wallack's in New York), an American by the accident of birth, became the bellwether of his spiritual compatriots. The most stiff-necked of the lot, he set himself to hold the stage in thrall to the nation of his extraction. His company was usually 100 per cent British, and the repertory at his famous theatre at Broadway and Fifteenth Street from 1861 to 1882 consisted chiefly of Robertsonian comedy, Dickens and Scott adaptations, Adelphi drama, and new pieces by Tom Taylor, Reade, Boucicault and Brougham. Wallack did his own Dumas adaptations and also dramatized a few English novels. One of these, *Lady Lee's Widow-hood*, presented as *Rosedale* (1863), made an excellent melodrama of the Adelphi school. It had a famous scene reminiscent of one in *The Green Bushes:* the sergeant-hero, seeking his kidnapped child in a gypsy camp at night, moves stealthily from tent to tent humming a lullaby which he knows the youngster will recognize.

John Brougham, like Boucicault, was Irish, and hence more open-minded and adaptable than his English colleagues. Both these actor-playwrights were quick to turn to subjects suggested by their new home. Brougham's best efforts were in the field of historical bur-lesque—*Pocahontas, Hiawatha, Columbus E Filibustro* and others—though he also turned out melodramas, at least one of which, *The Lottery of Life* (1867), had a New York setting.

Boucicault became the foremost melodramatist of his day in America, as he was in Britain. *The Poor of New York, Belle Lamar,* and *The Octoroon* are all important American melodramas, at least in the historical sense, and served as models and inspiration to native authors disposed to treat the domestic scene on the stage.

The Poor of New York broke no new ground insofar as its subject matter is concerned. There had been New York plays long before 1857, the year in which this piece had its American premiere, and in sufficient numbers to warrant their being called our first indigenous school of melodrama, with the possible exception of the Wild West variety. *Life in New York* was written in 1834 for "Jim Crow" Rice, the first of the really successful black-face comedians. Eight years later came *The New York Merchant and His Clerks,* "a domestic drama by the author of *Satanas*," which ran only four times, in spite of such attractions as "new scenery representing the Battery, Wall Street, Chatham Square and the Lunatic Asylum." The forties witnessed the first of the many plays built round the volunteer fireman, a hero who came into his own as Mose in Benjamin Baker's *A Glance at New York* in 1848. This impudent, cock-sure, jaunty, devil-may-care hooligan, always accompanied by his gal Lize, became the darling of the gods in the 12½ cent galleries, as portrayed by Frank Chanfrau, a New York favorite, who had been born on the Bowery at Pell Street. Mose reappeared monotonously for decades in a succession of plays comparable to the *Tom and Jerry* cycle, one of them being *The Mysteries and Miseries of New York,* an adaptation by H. P. Grattan of a story by Ned Buntline. *The New York Fireman and the Bond Street Heiress* is a piquant item of 1850, reported by Odell in his *Annals of the New York Stage.*

The scope of the city plays widened in the next decade, as may be seen from a few of the titles: *The Dry Goods Clerk of New York* (1851), Purdy's *The Ship's Carpenter of New York* (1856), Buntline's *The New York Printer* (1851), *Katy, the Hot Corn Girl* (1854), G. C. Foster's *New York by Gaslight* (1856), Cornelius Matthews' *Broadway and the Bowery* (1856), *The Rich of New York* (1856), and *Gotham, or Daylight and Gaslight* (1857).

Like *Tom and Jerry*, these compositions were predominantly farce. Moreover, their representation was confined almost entirely to the plebeian houses of the Bowery and its estuaries, the Chatham, the National, and similar resorts. Boucicault took a different line. Following his French models—actually using French plots in *The Poor of New York* and *After Dark*—he constructed his plays around a serious theme and introduced plenty of pathos and sentiment. In addition, he saw to it that they were mounted with elaborate realism and, through his prestige and connections, procured their production at first-class Broadway houses. *The Poor of New York* had its premiere at Wallack's.

The immediate results of the success of this play were not impressive insofar as encouraging native playwriting was concerned. But a precedent had been set, and ten years later the young Augustin Daly was able to make a place for himself in the Broadway theatrical world with his *Under the Gaslight*, a lively chromotype of postwar Gotham in its low-life and high-life aspects, done in the Boucicault style. Daly's success was not repeated. He had two disastrous failures with American plays in 1877, *Ah Sin*, by Mark Twain and Bret Harte, and his own *The Dark City*. He lost his theatre in consequence, which may explain his failure to experiment further in this field. When dramas of city life ultimately became accepted at theatres such as the Union Square, Wallack's, and even Daly's own house in the eighties and early nineties, it was in the form of imports—*Lights o' London*, *Hoodman Blind*, *The World*, *Youth*, and similar London melodramas.

Meanwhile at humbler resorts the New York plays continued to reproduce themselves. In the sixties, seventies and eighties stage-manager playwrights such as Foster, Gaylor, Arthur, and Watkins sponsored them by the score: *New York after Dark*, *New York in 1860; or, a Hit at the Times*, *New York and Brooklyn; or, the Poor Sewing Machine Girl*, *The Burglar; or, Wedded by Moonlight*, *The Gunmaker's Bride; The Ups and Downs of City Life*, *Out of the Streets*, *Life in Brooklyn, Its Lights and Shadows*, and *Bertha, the Sewing Machine Girl*.

Odell, in his *Annals of the New York Stage* for the season of 1875–76, comments that "Bowery lads preferred to have their plays deal with crime in big cities or with hair-raising adventures in the rich heart of the west" (Vol. X, p. 43), and he cites a few offerings at the Bowery by way of confirmation: *Dick the Newsboy*, *Si Slocum* (a Western), *Streets of New York*, *The Waif of New York*, *Unmasked*, *Terror of the Plains*, *Wild Bull; or, Life on the Border*, *A Glance at New York*, and *The New York Fireman*.

In 1887 came the greatest of all the fireman plays, Joseph Arthur's *The Still Alarm*, which, like *Under the Gaslight*, was as big a hit in England as in the U.S. The enthusiasm with which it was received everywhere was principally a tribute to the minute realism with which the author and producer re-created on the stage the whole exciting spectacle of a firehouse when an alarm comes in. Arthur wrote a number of sterling dramas of situation and action which later proved successful in the "ten, twent', thirt'" era; his plays and others like them, as given at the Fourteenth Street Theatre, the Grand Opera House, and other proletarian houses in the eighties, served as a transition from the Bowery drama to that of the Star and the American after the turn of the century.

Boucicault's *The Octoroon; or, Life in Louisiana* did for the rural backwater what *The Poor of New York* had done for the city as a background for American melodrama; and here again Daly took a page from the Irishman's book. The scene of Daly's *The Red Scarf; or, Scenes on the Aroostook* (1868) is the timber regions of Maine, and *Horizon* (1871) is laid on the frontier—the debt to Boucicault here being equally a debt to Bret Harte. The rural-life play, however, no less than its urban fellow, had preceded the arrival of Boucicault on our shores. An early example of this is Charles H. Saunders' *Forest Rose; or, American Farmers* (1825), labelled "a pastoral opera." It is an adaptation of a novel by Samuel Woodworth. A characteristic note is sounded in this piece, one which was to persist in American rural drama: distrust of the city slicker.

There was no politically privileged landed gentry in the United States—certainly not in the North, where virtually all the playwriting was done—and no acute agrarian distress arising from the greed or social isolation of a great class of hereditary landlords. Hence for the villain's role in the American rural domestic play some substitute had to be found for the squire or lordling of the English plays of this type. For the intensely parochial and resentfully rural nation that America had already become in the 1840's, the city smoothie filled the bill nicely. With his dandified attire, his cane and his moustache—that badge of the sissy in the eyes of all right-thinking patriots—this figure was a symbol of the hatred and mistrust with which the rustic viewed the growing wealth and power of the cities. Usually the slicker wears European clothes and affects European speech and manners, and his cynical principles and turpitudinous conduct are traceable to the influence of that decadent continent. Here and there he is an actual foreigner, in which case he is made out a swindler, an impostor, and often a half-wit into the bargain; if anyone is disliked more heartily than the smart city chap it is the alien. *Fashion*, Mrs. Mowatt's melodramatic comedy of manners produced in 1845, eloquently expresses the Andrew Jackson brand of 100 per cent Americanism, setting off the blunt, honest old farmer, Adam Trueman, against the slimy Count Jolimaitre, "a fashionable European importation."

Probably the first full-blown American rural melodrama is *Rosina Meadows; or, Temptation Unveiled*, a seduction drama adapted from a novel by William B. English, which was happily described by an admiring critic as "a tale of a fair blossom untimely nipped." The villain was labelled "a city spark" in the playbill of the first production, in 1843 in Boston.

The conflict of the city and the country persisted in American drama; toward the end of the century it may be observed in Denman Thompson's *The Old Homestead*, and in that later classic, *Way Down East*, written by Lottie Blair Parker and Joseph R. Grismer and produced by the firm of William A. Brady and Florenz Ziegfeld.

Poor Anna Moore in this play is tricked into a mock marriage by the aristocratic English-mannered Harvard quarterback, Lennox Sanderson, who deserts her shortly after the first kickoff. Her mother dies of a broken heart, and her newborn child follows the old lady to the graveyard on the hill. Penniless and scorned, the victim of a rich man's lust wanders to another part of the country, where she finds work as a housemaid with the Bartletts, a typical New England rural melodramatic family. A guest arrives at the Bartlett home while Anna is there; he proves to be Sanderson, coming to court the fresh and blooming daughter of the house—with the usual bad intentions. Chancing to encounter his discarded love, he abuses and threatens her. Meanwhile the tongue of a village gossip brings the story of Anna's past to her employer's ears. Old Bartlett, a good but hard man, seeing his duty, drives the scarlet woman out into the night with appropriate Biblical objurgations, while a blinding stage snowstorm rages.

In this, her darkest hour, our heroine finds a champion. Bartlett's son, David, the homespun hero, denounces the unfeeling conduct of his sire in a fine-sounding speech (as Stéphany had done a century earlier in *Cœlina*), declares his love for the frail little slavey in spite of her past, and dashes from the house to follow her and find her. He overtakes the fleeing girl, saves her from a horrible death in a frozen river, and brings her back to be his honorable bride. The old man, like Dufour, relents and bestows his blessing.

This show never did much business in New York, but it made two hundred thousand dollars for Bill Brady on the road. Meanwhile the bucolic note had been sounded in melodramatic comedy, loudest and with tenderest quaverings, perhaps, in that durable tear-jerker on the theme of the prodigal son, *The Old Homestead* (1878), with its carefully worked up central figure of old Joshua Whitcomb, the father. There was some such gnarled rustic in all the "b'gosh" dramas, as they came to be called: Uncle Nat, in *Shore Acres* (1882); Uncle Sam'l, in *Hearts of Oak* (1879); Squire Tucker and Colonel Moberley, of *Alabama*; Colonel Dolittle, in *In Old Kentucky*; and Mrs. Barnaby Bibbs, a feminine version of the type, in Neilson Burgess' *The Country Fair* (1889). These sundry gaffers and beldames fairly oozed quaintness and barnyard charm; contemporary audiences were reminded of honeysuckle and new-mown hay. One of the most flavorful of such roles, David Harum, in the play of that name, adapted by R. and M. W. Hitchcock from Edward Noyes Westcott's novel (1900), was played successfully by Will Rogers, and the character became the backbone of a seemingly interminable radio serial.

Herne's later plays, with the exception of *Margaret Fleming* and *The Reverend Griffith Davenport*, are "b'gosh" comedies crossed with melodrama, the plots being propelled by a series of accidents—bank failures, foreclosed mortgages, shipwrecks, pension awards, unexpected returns of long absent sailor-husbands supposed dead, and the like. This writer suffered from a complaint which would have proved fatal in an outright melodramatist—a costive invention. He either borrowed plots and situations or employed over and over again the few that were of his own contrivance. His importance for melodrama, and for the theatre at large, lay in his experimentation with quieter and subtler methods of writing, acting, and directing, in which Belasco and Gillette were his pupils.

The superb conclusion of *Shore Acres* (1883, Boston Museum) (which, like *Sag Harbor*, produced in 1899, is a kind of sermon on the evils of land speculation) sounded the knell of that hoary device, the grand finale featuring the full strength of the company "forming a picture" or tableau—a piece of business which French melodrama had introduced to the stage.

(UNCLE NAT *stands looking after* MARTIN, *his face lighted up by an inner glow of peace and happiness. His thoughts are reflected in his face, but not a word is spoken. The scene is played in absolute silence.*)

(*He sinks into the rocking chair close by with a sigh of content and satisfaction. He settles himself comfortably, with his chin resting in his right hand as he thinks.*)

UNCLE NAT (*He thinks this*). Well, everythin's all right again. (*He nods his head approvingly.*) I wonder how long Nell 'n' Sam's a-goin' to stay? A month 'r two anyway. (*Then a soft, tender smile creeps slowly into his face at the thought of the baby.*) Bless that baby! I wonder what the young uns'll say in the morning? It'll be beeter 'n a circus here when Mills sees thet baby. (*He chuckles softly at the thought, then suddenly he scans the door, wondering if he locked it. He rises slowly, easing himself on the arms of the chair, and plods to the door; he tries the lock, then tucks the doormat snugly against the sill to keep the snow from drifting in. Then he goes to the window, rubs the pane to clear the frost from it and peers out*) Gracious, what a night! (*He stoops down, and looks up to find the lighthouse beacon. He nods his head.*) Ol' Berry's all right—Tim's here. (*As he turns from the window shrugging his shoulders and shivering a little.*) Snow'll be ten foot deep in the mornin'. (*He goes to the stove and sets the kettle back, lifts one of the lids and looks at the fire. A thought strikes him.*) By George, it's a-goin' to be pooty hard work to git the ol' farm inter shape again. (*He shuts the damper.*) Well, hard work never skeered me. (*He goes to the woodhouse door and fastens the bolts, coming down to the door, softly pushes it open and stands there for a moment, looking off. He smiles to himself as he thinks.*) I wonder what the young uns'll say in the morning? (*For a moment he is lost in thought; his right arm slowly relaxes. Then he turns and starts to climb slowly up the stairs, his heavy footfall echoing through the empty rooms. The wind howls outside; the sharp snow tinkles upon the window-pane. The stage darkens slightly. He reaches the top of the stairs and goes off, closing the door after him. The stage is left in darkness except for the firelight flickering through the chinks of the stove. The cuckoo clock strikes twelve and the curtain slowly descends.*

END OF THE PLAY[1]

That sort of effect became commonplace in the theatre, but in the nineties Herne had to struggle against the hidebound conservatism of managers and critics at every step in order to be allowed to attempt it.

The season of 1889–90 marked the turn of the tide in the fortunes of native drama, at least on the New York stage. "Something was happening," writes Odell; "the old order was changing" (Vol. XIV, p. 57). Four American plays led the field; they were *The Old Homestead, The Charity Ball* (by Belasco and Henry de Mille), *The Country Fair,* and *Shenandoah.* In the following season *Blue Jeans* joined the ranks of top hits. It is worth noting that these were predominantly rural plays. Three of the five—all the rural plays— were given at houses catering to the poorer classes downtown, such as the Union Square, the Academy of Music, the Fourteenth Street (formerly the Lyceum) and Proctor's. However, rural melodrama was soon to make good on the level of the so-called two-dollar theatre of Broadway but not until these theatres had first fallen before the assault of the native drama in the form of the Civil War play.

[1] James A. Herne. *Sag Harbor and Other Plays* (New York, 1928), Act. V.

XXXII

Melodrama Comes of Age

Belasco and Gillette

The theatre can benefit from slick production of popular plays as well as the production of literary masterpieces. —ERIC BENTLEY

At the level of Broadway, the New York theatre remained indifferent to native drama. In the seventies and eighties Lester Wallack continued pointedly to prefer English plays—and English players. Upon removing to his new house at Thirtieth Street in 1882 he did, it is true, bring himself to give a play by the young Belasco and Henry de Mille which was, however, nothing more than a rehash of two London successes.

Wallack's two American-born peers in the triumvirate which dominated the New York theatre of Broadway during these years showed scarcely greater cordiality than he toward the dramatic writings of their countrymen, particularly in the field of melodrama. A. M. Palmer specialized frankly in French drama and melodrama of the type of *The Two Orphans* and *A Celebrated Case;* Campbell's *My Partner* (1879) was one of the few American plays given either at the Union Square or later at the Madison Square, to which Palmer transferred his activities in the same year in which Wallack moved uptown. Daly became an important producer early in the seventies with *Frou-Frou, Alixe, L'Article 47* and other "reigning Paris sensations," as he advertised them, and some examples of London melodrama.

A change came in the late eighties. Palmer, who was friendly enough toward American comedy as written by Bronson Howard, William Gillette, Bartley Campbell and Augustus Thomas[1] sponsored Gillette's Civil War drama, *Held by the Enemy* (1886), a successful venture; but Bronson Howard's *Shenandoah* was really the turning point. The history of this work illustrates the timidity of producers in dealing with American melodrama. The play had

[1] Gertrude Elliott Forbes-Robertson, *My Aunt Maxine* (New York, 1964).

gone begging for fifteen years before Montgomery Field finally put it on at Boston in 1888. Several important theatrical men made the trip up from New York to attend the premiere, but they were no more favorably impressed by the performance than they had been by the manuscript and allowed the venture to die on Field's hands. One young man saw possibilities in this panoramic drama of the Civil War; he was Charles Frohman, then striking out on his own as a manager. He bought the rights of the play when it closed, commissioned Howard to make certain revisions, and presented it the following year in a spectacular production at the Star in New York. It was a smash, packing the house for a full season; at a single stroke it made rich men of both author and manager.

The lesson was not lost upon Broadway, and soon a parade of similar plays got under way, continuing until World War I. Prominent in it were *The Girl I Left Behind Me, The Heart of Maryland, Alabama, Secret Service, Arizona, Richard Carvel, Cumberland '61, Nathan Hale, Barbara Freitchie, Pierre of the Plains, Alice of Old Vincennes, The Girl of the Golden West, Rose of the Rancho, Rio Grande, The Warrens of Virginia, Janice Meredith,* and *The Bad Man.* All these were offered by the best managers and commanded the services of the most expensive talent, players such as Maxine Elliott, Margaret Anglin, Nat Goodwin, Mary Mannering, Julia Marlowe, Robert Edeson, Maurice Barrymore, John Drew, Kyrle Bellew, Viola Allen, Mrs. Leslie Carter, Blanche Bates and Frances Starr.

Unlike the cape-and-sword dramas, which shared the glory of this century-end romantic renaissance, these plays were almost without exception written directly for the stage and not adapted from novels. They were, moreover, competently written and theatrically apt compositions for the most part. As a group they represent American melodrama at its best. Indeed they are probably the finest body of work that the genre as a whole has to show. Several among them were received with popular and critical favor in England—a fairly severe criterion of merit when one considers their purely national subject matter and the traditional coolness of the British toward American plays. William Archer called *Secret Service* "the best drama of adventure and situation in the English language."

The contemporary drama of the war, almost exclusively a Bowery product, had been of the overheated patriotic variety, being disposed to concentrate all courage, virtue, and right on the side of the boys in blue. Charles Gayler's *Bull Run; or, the Sacking of*

Fairfax Courthouse, given at the Bowery in 1861, was probably the first. Among the others were *Shiloh, Hatteras Inlet, The Federal Spy; or, Pauline of the Potomac,* and *The Union Prisoner; or, the Patriot's Daughter.* All these given in the early sixties in New York. *Belle Lamar,* written by Boucicault for Murdock in 1874, struck a deeper note. The husband-hero of the play is a Union officer, and his wife, who has divorced him, is a Virginian intensely loyal to her state. Love and patriotism come to grips in the ensuing drama, and, as usual, it is love which proves the stronger with the woman. This is the basic situation in virtually all the Broadway Civil War plays that followed, beginning with *Shenandoah.* Barbara Freitchie, in Fitch's fine play of that name, picks up a rifle and fires point blank at an infantryman wearing the uniform of her own beloved South when he goes to shoot Captain Trumbull, the Yankee officer whom she loves; and later, when the Captain lies dead behind the shutters, she unfurls the stars and stripes defiantly from her verandah as General Stonewall Jackson and his army march through the streets below. In *Shenandoah,* Gertrude Ellington, another Virginia belle, gives up her own horse to General Sheridan, thereby enabling him to make his famous ride; Edith, of *Secret Service,* hands a commission to Captain Thorn in order to save his life, knowing full well that he is a spy and may use it to do irreparable injury to the cause which means so much to her. Over all these plays hovers the spirit of reconciliation. *Secret Service* became popular in the South itself, and Col. Henry Watterson told Augustus Thomas that *Alabama* did more than all his long efforts as an influential Kentucky editor to heal the wounds of the war.

Shenandoah is still close enough to the old blood-and-thunder school to be funny. The platoon of characters includes two pairs of straight lovers and two pairs of comic lovers; a conventional ne'er-do-well who wipes out the disgrace he has brought upon the honored name he bears by volunteering and, fatally wounded, bringing back the precious papers; and the father of this wayward son, a general who in addition to all the responsibilities of his command has to contend with the highly erratic behaviour of various love-sick subordinates and the apparent infidelity of his beautiful young second wife. This woman is the entirely innocent victim of a concatenation of misunderstandings involving letters, handkerchiefs, lockets, and the like. The scandal which links her with the equally high-minded hero is owing not a little also to the machinations of a villain who is a coward, a spy, a traitor, and a home-wrecker. The sensation scenes, however, had most to do with putting the show across. Sheridan's ride was done in glorious style; the full strength of the company, men and horses, fought back and forth across the stage; the wounded hero rose from a sickbed and dashed onstage to stem a retreat; rockets flashed, artillery boomed, and rifles puttered from one curtain to another.

To this climacteric chapter in the history of American melodrama the contribution of Belasco and Gillette, as authors and directors, was decisive. In 1893, in collaboration with Franklin Fyles, drama critic of the *New York Sun*, Belasco wrote *The Girl I Left Behind Me*, a frontier play which had a run comparable to that of *Shenandoah;* and two years later he established himself brilliantly as an independent manager with another play of his own composition, *The Heart of Maryland*, which had a Civil War background. From that triumph he moved ahead steadily to a position of leadership in the American theatre, his progress being marked by a succession of melodramas celebrating the national saga in its more strenuous and colorful aspects.

In a theatre coming rapidly under the control of commercial speculators divorced from the writing and acting phases of the profession, Belasco enjoyed certain obvious advantages over his competitors. He belonged to the old school; indeed, he was to be its last survivor, with the possible exception of William A. Brady. During his youth and early manhood in California he had filled every post open in the playhouse, including those of "infant phenomenon," callboy, prompter, copyist, barnstormer, advance agent, scene painter, stage manager, playwright and adaptor. As an actor he proved quite as versatile, and as an author not fewer than one hundred plays came from his pen before he was twenty-five: farces, spectacles, "society melodramas," shockers, dramas, and a passion play. An even greater number of plays by others took shape under his guiding hand while he served as Maguire's stage manager at San Francisco. Herne was his associate in various projects; Boucicault dictated *Led Astray* to him at Virginia City in 1873; and during his early years in New York when he slaved as stage manager and play doctor for the Mallorys and Daniel Frohman, he had for collaborators the foremost American playwrights of the day, Bronson Howard and Steele Mackaye. This unique apprenticeship told in his work. He wrote plays well, cast them expertly, and above all mounted and directed them brilliantly.

His mise-en-scène set a new standard on Broadway for magnificence and verisimilitude and went as far as mere literal realism could go in the projection of atmosphere and the evocation of mood. Those who saw them could never forget the stage effects he created: the shadowy passage to heaven of the myriad-souled Yo-San and her lover in *The Darling of the Gods;* the desolate seacoast and the mountain gorge in *Under Two Flags*—the one swept by a blinding sandstorm and the other shaken by a furious tempest; the frontier saloon of *The Girl of the Golden West;* the mission garden in *Rose of the Rancho.*

More impressive than the stage pictures themselves was the directorial craft by which Belasco brought his scripts alive on the stage. In his early days on the West Coast, in the manner of Boucicault, he had put on his battles and conflagrations with a wealth of sensations. In his Broadway period he discarded these extravagances in favor of no less elaborate but more delicately conceived effects. His art grew in finesse. As he matured and studied audiences in the East, he learned the use of pause, the potency of suggestion, the dramatic force of understatement. At no time in *The Girl I Left Behind Me* were the Indians brought upon the stage for showy mass effects of the old style; yet by means of their yells, the rumble of their war drums, the glow of their fires, and the clatter of their horses' hooves the audience was never permitted to forget the menacing presence of the savage horde. With greater sublety in *Madame Butterfly* an uncanny effect of the passage of a whole night was achieved, dusk fading into darkness, night brightening into dawn, as poor Cho-Cho-San wanly waited in the window for the white, unworthy lover who came too late.

In the second act of *The Girl of the Golden West,* action came to a standstill while Belasco, *régisseur,* stepped in and took the play out of the performers' hands to give it a tremendous dramatic fillip by the manipulation of stage accessories. It is night in the solitary cabin in the Sierras; the Girl and Johnston have suddenly declared their love and are locked in a first surrendering embrace. Outside, a blizzard rages; a high wind, soughing in the pines, whips the snow against the window panes. An outer door is heard to slam in the draft; the bed curtains flap wildly; a basket blows down from a wardrobe; a flower pot topples over with a crash; blankets hanging from the loft stir; the oil lamps flicker perilously. Finally, after minutes have elapsed, the wind is heard to subside and a clock sounds the hour of two from the mantel. All this happens slowly, naturally; meanwhile not a movement comes from the lovers, in each others' arms downstage. Far more tellingly than any word or gesture this inanimate pantomime conveys how utterly these two are lost in each other.

Belasco's directorial technique took many other ingenious forms. In the scenic prologue to this same play a painted canvas scene, rolled vertically on drums, presented a moving, map-like panorama of the whole picturesque area where the action unfolds; first, the heights of Cloudy Mountain in the moonlight with the Girl's cabin perched aloft and a steep footpath winding down the walls of the canyon to the settlement below; and next, the little camp itself, shown at the foot of the path, the miners' cabins huddled about the Polka Saloon, through the windows of which drifts the muted din of rough revelry—the rattle of poker chips, the strains of banjo and concertina, and masculine voices raised in a chorus of "Camptown Races." This is erased suddenly in a blackout, and a moment later the lights come on full to reveal the interior of the saloon, where a shindig is in full swing—the music continuing meanwhile and serving to bind the two scenes together.

In accomplishing effects like these Belasco had something to work with which his great predecessors, Pixerécourt and Boucicault, had lacked; namely, fluid, dynamic, powerful, and perfectly controlled light. If he did not exhaust the myriad potentialities of this magical new resource in the playhouse, he at least used it with imagination and taste—even with brilliant originality at times. He was a close student of, and a tireless experimenter in, new illuminating methods, particularly after he had his own theatres, which, in their electrical equipment, were the most advanced of their day. Colors of his own mixture were made for lamps when he could find none on the market that suited him; a portable light bridge above the proscenium and a portable switchboard were two of his inventions; light rehearsals formed an important part of the meticulous routine in preparation for a show; twenty-four electricians, instead of the customary two or three, accompanied his more elaborate productions on tour; every square foot of his stage was covered by artfully disposed strips, chasers, bunches, and spots; "baby spots" followed various characters about the stage—a practice which he probably introduced—and detailed light-plots assisted the action at every turn, like an elaborate musical accompaniment.

In acting, beginning with his work for the Mallorys at Madison Square Theatre, Belasco became identified with a subdued, colloquial style, which his critics derisively dubbed "milk and water."

New lighting equipment had much to do with this reform, which Gillette and Herne were pursuing independently, and, according to the interesting theory advanced independently by Daniel Frohman and Brander Matthews, with the disappearance of the aside in playwriting as well. On stages illuminated by candles, oil, or even gaslight,[2] particularly the stages of the larger houses, the communication, otherwise than orally, of anything in the way of delicate shades of feeling was out of the question insofar as a greater part of the audience was concerned; hence the orotund conventions of the old school of acting, and those little confidences thrown across the footlights as "asides." The elimination of this disfiguring anachronism dates from the period at the end of the century. Present in the London melodramas of Pettitt, Meritt, Jones, and Sims in London, and in *Shenandoah*, the aside fades out in *Held by the Enemy* (1886) and *Alabama* (1891) and has disappeared entirely in *Secret Service* (1896), *Arizona* (1899), and *Barbara Frietchie* (1899). American melodrama, by reaching its majority when it did, became the beneficiary of this advance in technique—a circumstance which helps keep many of these plays comparatively fresh and modern-sounding even today, whereas English melodramas of the same date have about them the quaintness of museum pieces.

Belasco, Gillette, and Thomas modernized melodrama, making it plausible, adult, and even intellectually respectable, and giving it the benefit of the same careful writing and conscientious construction which the realistic play had been receiving. After 1895 the kidnapped orphans, the ghosts, the papers, the foreclosed mortgages, the providential accidents, the disguises, the rescuing comics, the missing heirs, and even the *reconnaissance* itself went into discard. Violence became confined to act-ends, when it was resorted to at all; the rhetoric was brought under control; and the sentimentality was tempered. This was purely an American achievement, since, by this time, the form had ceased to be written by British playwrights of any merit. After overhauling, however, it was still melodrama in its essentials. Startling situation and striking stage effect remained

[2] Irving never used electricity at his Lyceum, and gas was laid on only very late in his management there. He did make extensive use of the calcium limelight, which had been invented by Thomas Drummond in 1825 and introduced on the stage in 1837 at Covent Garden by Macready. It was used regularly by Charles Kean in the fifties at the Princess.

the basis of appeal in the plays at the Belasco theatres. Heroes continued to be high-minded and heroines of unimpeachable moral character—at least until the years around World War I—and persecuted innocence lost none of its old prestige as a theme.

The Girl I Left Behind Me had as much incident as a Buffalo Bill play though it was conveyed in a different way. The big scene was the climax of the third act. The leader of the uprising, Scar Brow, an Indian educated by the white man, warns General Kennion, commander of the army post, that he is giving the order to storm the stockade, and that when it is taken all the men will be slaughtered and the women saved for a worse fate. The General's daughter, Kate, overhears the threat. True melodramatic heroine that she is, this beautiful creature prefers death to dishonor; and she exacts a solemn promise from her father that he will shoot her when all hope is gone. When the horrific yells annnounce the final assault, the old man sadly prepares to go through with his pledge. The lock of his rifle is heard to click off, and father and daughter begin the Lord's Prayer together. They have got along as far as the phrase, "Thy will be done," when the girl cries out suddenly, raises her head to listen, and thrusts the muzzle of the rifle aside. The General fears she is losing heart, and he brings the weapon up to fire, when again— "Wait!" cries the girl. What she has heard now grows loud enough for the audience to recognize; it is a bugle call—the U. S. Cavalry is galloping to the rescue, the hero at their head. In *Jessie Brown*, from which Belasco evidently got his scene, it had been bagpipes.

Belasco's next Western play, *The Girl of the Golden West* (1905), was a labor of love in which he embodied his affectionate recollections of his own early experiences in mining camps. It is the carefully wrought product of his maturity. He had by this time rid himself of the Boucicault influence, and emerged as a major melodramatist in his own right. The play, for all its apparent echoes of Bret Harte, is an original effort, full of accurate observation and faithful to the peculiar mores of the makeshift, masculine communities which it depicts. It is simple in its action, plausibly motivated, and persuasive in its portrayal of character. The dialogue, with some exceptions, has a directness, a freshness of idiom and vocabulary, which lifts it far above the level of the studied dialect effects of Campbell and Joaquin Miller. Altogether the play is the best drama of the gold rush that we have.

Belasco wrote or collaborated on the writing of several other Western plays, but none of them was in the same bracket as *The*

Girl of the Golden West. Rose of the Rancho (1906), principally if
not entirely the work of Richard Walton Tully, has the same theme
as Helen Hunt Jackson's *Ramona:* the exposure of the aristocratic
old Spanish landowners of Monterey to the tender mercies of
Yankee land-jumpers after the Mexican War. *The Heart of Maryland* was Belasco's single contribution to the drama of the Civil
War, at which so many of the romantic American playwrights of
this era tried their hands.

Like Belasco, William Gillette was an actor and director who
knew his trade thoroughly and used his professional knowledge at
every turn in the writing of his fine plays. If one virtue more than
another stands out in them it is their theatricality—a legitimate
utilization of every resource of the stage. This is in evidence
everywhere in his plays, in *Sherlock Holmes* (the lighted cigar in
the dark Putney Gas Chamber, is one example), and in his early
Civil War melodrama, *Held by the Enemy;* but it is to be seen at its
best in the climax of *Secret Service.*

Thorne, the hero, is a Union spy operating in Richmond. In the
third act he is on the verge of being exposed and arrested in a
military telegraph station where he is preparing to send out flashes
which will result in the withdrawal of Southern troops at points
where the Union Army plans to attack.

Edith Varney, his Confederate sweetheart, comes to his rescue
with a commission which she procured for him before she suspected
his true status. Her intervention saves him, and she goes off in the
company of the Confederate officer who has been interrogating
him. At the door she turns and observes that Thorne has gone back
to the instrument and is tapping out the message which may mean
the defeat of the South. She had proffered the commission in order
to save his life, and he is using it to betray her.

Throughout the play, Gillette, playwright, has been skillfully
adding stroke by stroke to the picture of a people giving everything
for a cause. Edith's father is at the front; her youngest brother has
left to join him; another brother lies dying from his wounds in their
home. Everything that a country can mean to a woman, the South
means to her. The sudden and overwhelming realization of all this,
Gillette, actor, in the rôle of Thorne, succeeds in conveying in those
few moments while he stands motionless over the telegraph instrument facing rigidly front, his jaw clenched on a cigar and his hand
poised above the transmitter. It is a situation superbly imagined and
superbly played—melodramatic theatre at its finest.

Finally Thorne drops his arm; his mind is made up. He tells a subordinate to countermand the orders he has sent and leaves.

Simultaneously with the rise of American melodrama to the status of two-dollar entertainment under the banners of Belasco and Gillette, the separation of middle-class and popular melodrama, which had been widening year by year, became absolute divorce. Between 1900 and 1910 the cheap popular theatre emerged as an independent industry, self-sufficient in every department; it had its own repertory, acted by its own companies in its own houses, across the country as well as in New York. Melodrama dominated this final chapter of the popular theatre in America. Its story—a brief, colorful, and spectacular episode—is the story of "ten, twent', thirt'."

XXXIII

"Ten, Twent', Thirt' "

Rather than do what you say, Remington Hallowell, I will starve in the gutter. —AN OWEN DAVIS HEROINE

In the late nineties Terence McGovern was an obscure bantam-weight who, for the sum of three dollars, cash, could be engaged to batter, and be battered by, any able-bodied male of the same weight whom a matchmaker saw fit to turn loose with him in the so-called prize ring. At a Greenpoint sporting club one night his talent at assault came to the attention of Sam S. Harris, then a young small-time entrepreneur as yet uncommitted to the theatre. Harris was impressed, and seeking out McGovern he arranged to take over his affairs in the professional capacity of manager.

The partnership prospered. McGovern won three titles in short order, and Harris got the inspiration of putting his talents to work in a new field. It was an era of exploitation of celebrities outside of the acting profession on the melodrama stage for their publicity value. The People's Theatre on the Bowery could not hold the crowds which gathered in 1894 to witness Steve Brody re-enact, in *On the Bowery* (by R. H. Stevens), his famous leap from Brooklyn Bridge, an exploit which the playwright edited into a thrilling rescue of a beautiful maiden from a watery grave.

Prize fighters were especially in demand, and they were usually available. Among them were John L. Sullivan, Bob Fitzsimmons, and James J. Corbett. As a class, these decaying pugilists were the world's worst actors. Corbett was an exception. He carved out a second career for himself in cheap melodrama and later as a mono-loguist in big-time vaudeville. He made his stage debut in *After Dark*, sponsored by William A. Brady, his manager, and the pair made big money with *Gentleman Jack* by Brady and Charles T. Vincent, *Brother Bill, A Naval Cadet,* and other plays.

The grand climax of all the boxer melodramas, naturally, was the big fight. Sometimes this was a formal affair with gloves in a ring, like the bout at the Orleans Club devised by Brady in *Gentleman Jack*, a spectacular stage effect which "Druriolanus" Harris himself admired in London when the show was given at Drury Lane in

1894. The galleries, however, preferred an irregular encounter under more romantic circumstances, with some slimy bully getting his deserts with bare fists. The one in *A Naval Cadet* is a classic. The scene is a Houston Street cellar, and the heroine lies prostrate, at the mercy of Shad Sanders, the villain, a prognathous thug in a red flannel undershirt. All seems lost when a crash is heard from above, and down the rickety stairs two at a time dashes a well-knit, manly form in evening clothes: Ned Cornell, naval cadet. Shad, furious at the interruption, advances on the intruder, a knife between his teeth. "So you've come for the Gal," he says with a sneer. "You think you can take her from me, eh? Well, you're up against the hardest game you ever tackled, see?" Cadet Cornell nonchalantly removes his immaculate white gloves, deposits them with his silk hat on a convenient barrel, and goes for the villain. The chief requirement in a villain for this species of entertainment was the ability to take it, and the portrayer of Shad Sanders certainly got it in the exciting moments that followed.[1]

Terence McGovern wasn't a heavyweight and certainly he wasn't an actor, but his well-publicized prowess as "Terrible Terry," holder of three titles, and his extracurricular capers in barrooms and dance halls made him a prime box-office attraction, which the knowing Harris was not slow to cash in upon on the melodrama stage. A vehicle was hastily thrown together and launched on its way, *The Bowery After Dark*. It stood 'em in the aisles at theatres in New York and across the country; actor and manager returned East with their pockets bulging.

This ten-strike determined the career of Sam Harris. He went definitely into the business of theatrical producing, specializing in what he described as "melodrama of the better class." In this enterprise he had two partners. One was New York City politician "Big Tim" Sullivan's brother Pat who had $1,500 to invest, and the other was a go-getting alumnus of the ushering personnel of Miner's Bowery Theatre. At the moment, the latter was advance man for a sensational melodrama, and "known to be the best man in show business to draw a big opening to a bad play," in the words of Owen Davis.[2] He was Alfred W. Herman, in the process of becoming Al W. Woods.

---

[1] Alvin Harlow, *Old Bowery Days* (New York & London, 1931), p. 459.
[2] *I'd Like to Do It Again*, p. 75.

Harris and Woods were representative of a new generation of the genus showman which, seizing control at this period from the hands of the old professional type of manager, worked profound changes in the American theatre on all its levels of legitimate drama, vaudeville, burlesque, and popular melodrama. (The Theatrical Syndicate was organized in 1896.) Gifted organizers, adroit financiers, born gamblers, and keen, unsentimental students of popular taste and psychology, they standardized the product they dealt in, promoted it sensationally and marketed it efficiently on a nationwide scale. And made it pay as it had never paid before.

The rise of these new men coincided with a phenomenon of some sentimental interest: the eclipse of the Bowery as the home base of English-speaking melodrama for the people. During the nineties the two surviving temples of the genre, the Windsor and the Peoples, succumbed to the Yiddish drama, as did the old Bowery, which had been a German-speaking house since 1879; and about 1900 Miner's Bowery abandoned its traditional two-part bill, on which a melodrama often found a place on toward midnight. Melpomene, packing her trunks and gathering her retainers about her, betook herself to other quarters of the town, leaving the "livest mile in Christendom" to its medical museums, its shooting galleries, its penny arcades, its burlesque shows, its rescue missions, and its dives.

Certain types of plays, such as the city-life, rustic, and Wild West creations of dime-novel extraction, had been native to this East Side rialto; but otherwise melodrama here had not differed greatly from that offered at more elegant New York theatres. Season after season, Broadway companies and Broadway stars had visited various Bowery houses as regular ports of call on their annual tours: Billy Florence in *The Ticket-of-Leave Man*, Lester Wallack in *Rosedale*, Boucicault in *The Shaughraun*, the Chanfraus in *Kit, the Arkansas Traveller*, Kate Claxton in *The Two Orphans*, Booth and Barrett in *Richelieu*, James O'Neill in *Monte Cristo*, Clara Morris in *Camille*, Anne Pixley in *Mliss*, and the Union Square and Madison Square companies with their repertoires.

A different policy was pursued by Sullivan, Harris and Woods, Davis and William T. Kehoe, H. R. Jacobs (pioneer of "ten, twent', thirt'"), Stair and Havlin, the Blaneys, James H. Wallick, the Mittenthaler Brothers, Mark E. Swan, Jacob Litt, Higgins and Company, and other firms of the same class, in plays showing in New York at such popular theatres as the Third Avenue, the Academy of Music, the Star (Lester Wallack's old house), the Manhattan Opera House (Brooklyn), and the American where the forces of melodrama rallied and reformed their ranks for one brilliant last stand before the cinematic deluge. The policy called for original dramas written by stock authors and played strictly by melodrama companies. Popular melodrama became a distinct business, emancipated from Broadway and following a well-standardized pattern. The stock company was not unusual, but the characteristic setup was the touring production and the circuit. The prevailing admission scale was ten, twenty, and thirty cents, though at Proctors' it was twenty-five cents to seventy-five cents, and twenty-five cents to a dollar at the eleven Blaney houses. The phrase, "ten, twent', thirt'" was coined by an expansive medicine-show personality of the era, Corse Payton, who organized stock companies which, like the Subway Circuit of later years, specialized in revivals of Broadway hits a few years after they had ceased to draw in the big time.

Prominent among the new writers corralled as stock authors by Sullivan, Harris, and Woods was Theodore Kremer. He worked closely with his producers, as the other authors were to do. There was a fairly well-fixed routine: Woods would dream up a snappy title, the posters would next be designed and printed, and finally the play would be written and rehearsed. Prolific like all his kind, Kremer ground out scores of dramas for this and other managements. His masterpiece, and Harris' greatest hit, was *The Fatal Wedding*, given in 1901. It filled the old Grand Opera House for months at one dollar top, and there were five road companies, the star of the second one being Mary Pickford. The plot dealt with a nefarious conspiracy by the villain and his paramour to wreck the peace of a happy home by means of false accusations against the blameless wife, leading to a divorce.

Kremer wrote plays of various types, including *Fast Life in New York*, *Slaves of the Orient*, *The Triumph of an Empress*, *The Power Behind the Throne* (a Graustarkian romance), *Queen of the Convicts* (a reconstruction of the checkered career of Queen Draga of Serbia), *A Race for Life*, *The Great Automobile Mystery*, *A Desperate Chance* (the jailbreak of the Biddle brothers), and *The King of the Opium Ring*. However, his output consisted predominantly of the sort of thing illustrated in the plot of *The Fatal Wedding* and suggested by such titles as *Wedded and Parted*, *For Her Children's Sake*, *For Her Daily Bread*, and *Fallen by the*

Wayside. The broken home was his favorite theme, as mother-love was the favorite theme of Hal Reid, another highly successful author of "ten, twent', thirt' " and the father of Wallace Reid, star of the silent films.

The domestic pathos, realistic accessories, and contemporary milieu of these plays did not exclude melodramatic treatment of the good old blood-and-thunder kind, any more than similar qualities had excluded it in *La Femme à deux maris, Rent Day, Susan Hopley, The Drunkard,* or *Rosina Meadows.* Some idea of the thrills provided can be got from a press agent's release for *No Mother to Guide Her:* "A secret marriage," he reported, "a bank robbery and a murder enliven the first act." Bertha, the Sewing Machine Girl, in the play of the same title, is kidnapped, thrown into a lake, put to torture in the villain's den, and finally trapped in a burning house, from which she and her blind sister escape by jumping into a fireman's net from an upstairs window, a famous sensation scene. The villain of *Why Girls Leave Home* is caught up and smothered in a Murphy bed in the very act of pursuing the heroine around her boudoir—hoist by his own petard. They were domestic dramas in the heroic style.

Frequently the pathos and action were infused with a timid but insistent suggestion of sex; the good old theme of "the girl who took the wrong turning," and "the wife who forgot her marriage vows," to quote play titles, became a standby of "ten, twent', thirt'." The impression prevailing generally today of old melodrama, that it was concerned exclusively with attempts on the virtue of farmers' daughters and poor working girls by city slickers and millionaire-employers, arises from the profusion of such fables in this class of play. Lillian Mortimer, author of *No Mother to Guide Her,* special-ized in this line; the plays she wrote as starring vehicles for herself included *Her One False Step, A Girl of the Streets,* and *A Man's Broken Promise.*

Actually, however, the sex angle was handled very cautiously; the titles had a trick of promising more than the fables fulfilled. "There must be no temporizing with 'the wages of sin are death' slogan," wrote the greatest of the "ten, twent', thirt' " authors, Owen Davis. "In all my experience I have never seen it defied."[3] "We entertain millions with clean plays only," boasted the Blaneys in their the-

---

[3] *Ibid.,* p. 102.

atres.[4] The hero could go wrong, succumbing to drink and even to drugs; the prodigal son theme was a favorite one. But the woman, whose conduct was the touchstone in melodrama's morals, had to die if she slipped—or, rather, if she fell. Usually a heroine was held fearfully over the edge of the abyss for three acts and yanked back dramatically to safety before the final curtain.

Among girls who yielded to temptation and paid the awful penalty, the Queen of the Highbinders, in Kremer's play of that name, was prominent. She was one of that regal sisterhood which took so well on the three-sheet posters—those queens of the white slaves, of the bigamists, and of the opium rings. The Highbinders, originally a blackmailing secret society of Chinese nationals whose activities in melodrama consisted principally in luring beautiful white females into noisome opium dens and abducting them for immoral purposes, brings us to a theme which no history of "ten, twent', thirt' " can overlook: the Yellow Peril. This bugaboo was agitated wilily by the yellow press of the day, for which it proved as great a bonanza as the Spanish-American War itself; and it was taken up by the playwrights of the popular theatre in the middle nineties. Sinister Orientals slink in and out of *While Frisco Burns* and *Across the Pacific,* and their heinous conspiracies provided material for a whole cycle of Chinatown thrillers—*Queen of the White Slaves, The Chinatown Trunk Mystery, The Queen of Chinatown, Midnight in Chinatown, Drugged, The King of the Opium Ring, Slaves of the Orient, Rescued from Highbinders,* and dozens more. In the process, the amiable comic Chinee of Bret Harte ancestry was completely sunk; the queue, the opium pipe, and pidgin English became as much the badge of a villain as silk hat, white gloves, and cigarettes.

In 1902 Sullivan, Harris, and Woods acquired as an author Owen Davis, who, though still in his twenties, had already made his mark as a playwright for the gallery houses. Five years earlier Davis had come to New York, a stage-struck greenhorn not long out of Harvard, and had learned his trade by making a scientific study of the popular drama from the vantage point of the ten-cent gallery of the theatres up and down Eighth, Third, and Tenth Avenues. He writes about it in *I'd Like to Do It Again:*

[4] Ruth W. Sedgwick, "Those Dear, Dead Days of Melodrama," *The Stage Magazine* (New York, XII, 11 (August, 1935), p. 39.

"When the very hard-boiled gentleman who sat next to me wept or laughed or applauded, I wasn't at first always sure of his reason, my duller mind not at that time responding to the sentimental, dramatic or comedy cue as quickly as his trained intelligence, and I made a point of falling into conversation with my neighbor in an effort to share as fully in the delight of those present as was possible for an unfortunate inhibited by a Harvard background.

"One of the first tricks I learned was that my plays must be written for an audience who, owing to the huge, uncarpeted, noisy theatres, couldn't always hear the words, and who, a large percentage of them having only recently landed in America, couldn't have understood them in any case. I therefore wrote for the eye rather than the ear and played out each emotion in action, depending on my dialogue only for the nobel sentiments so dear to audiences of that class" (pp. 36–37).

It is all curiously reminiscent of Pixerécourt's apprenticeship on the "Boulevard du Crime"; and the parallel between the first and the last of the great melodramatists of the classical tradition is seen to persist as the inquirer turns to the details of Davis' formula and examines the working methods which he adopted on the basis of what he saw and heard in these professional slumming expeditions. The plots ring the changes on the theme of persecution: virtue, after surviving a cycle of moving accidents by ford and flood, is rewarded in the end; villainy, which never reforms, gets its just deserts. Romantic love scenes are out of order. The comic relief is of prime importance, and a sensation scene provides the climax of an evening full of hair-raising thrills.

There are eight essential characters: the hero, who can be either very poor, which is preferable, or else very young and very drunk (if sober and wealthy he becomes automatically a villain); the heroine, by preference a working girl (cloak model, "typewriter," factory girl, shopgirl, etc.) and practically indestructible; the comic —Irish, Jewish, or German—played usually by the highest paid member of the company; the soubrette, "a working girl with bad manners and a good heart," devoted to the heroine; the heavy man, identified by a moustache, silk hat, and white gloves; the heavy woman, a haughty society dame or an "unfortunate"; the light comedy boy; and the second heavy, "just a bum, a tool of the villain—it was usual to kill him along toward the middle of the second act" (Davis, p. 105).

The interrelations of these puppets, like their several moral characters, were as fixed and unchanging as the laws of the Medes and the Persians. Villain and heavy woman always had an understanding; heroine and hero paired off, as did soubrette and comic boy—and the last always assisted the heroine in her tribulations. Any departure from routine was fatal. Davis records that once he tried to have the comedy boy in love with someone other than the soubrette, but he had to rewrite the play; "the audience got too bewildered."

The immediate models of "ten, twent', thirt'" were cockney melodramas, especially the repertory of the Melville brothers, which were quite as popular in the U.S. as in England, and American plays imitated from them, such as Arthur's *Blue Jeans, The Still Alarm,* etc. The construction of model and copy was identical: more or less elaborate big scenes alternating with "oleos," or front scenes, the latter typically short and providing some belly laugh to cover the racket of striking and setting up behind the drop. Davis' plays ran to fifteen or sixteen scenes as a rule, "the end of each being a moment of perilous suspense or terrifying danger. This gave the playwright rather more than seven minutes to instruct his audience, to prepare his climaxes, to plant the seed for his next scene, and to *reach* his climaxes."[5] The aside flourished. The plays were nearly always in four acts. The big scenes and mechanical effects occurred in the third act.

Much thought and labor were lavished on the title (Davis estimated that 50 per cent of the drawing power of a piece depended upon this element), the posters, and the sensation scene wherein stage carpenter, mechanic, playwright, and director conspired to achieve some overpowering effect. An idea of what these effects were can be gotten from surviving twenty-four sheets. The one for Davis' *The Lighthouse by the Sea* shows a rocky seacoast lashed by a furious storm, with plenty of gaudy lightning in evidence. In the background a noble ship is foundering; and a lighthouse, its beacon darkened, is up right. Down right three men on shore are beating one another furiously; down left, on a rock, a fisherman in oilskins is pointing a pistol at the villain, who is hanging by his hands from a cable which runs from the shore to the lighthouse. Far out over the water is the heroine, tight-roping it heroically to the rescue, a

[5] Owen Davis, "Why I Quit Writing Melodrama," *American Magazine,* September 1914, p. 126.

lighted torch in her grasp. Across the bottom is the line, "You shall not light the lamp tonight!"

The stunts of earlier melodrama were revived—the real animals and reptiles as performers, the collisions on land and sea involving ships and trains with automobiles for a special novelty as the new century began, the horse races, the drownings in real water, the opened floodgates and towering cataracts, the fights on rafts, the buzz-saw murders, the collapsing walls, the conflagrations, the electrical storms, the landslides, explosions, and earthquakes; and combined with these in countless permutations were new scenic and mechanical contrivances, some of them worthy of Rube Goldberg.

"One of the striking features of *Deadwood Dick's Last Shot* is the raising of an American flag by an educated horse to signal an attack that saves the heroine from being burned at the stake," reads a press agent's release. The hero of James H. Wallick's *The Queen of the Highway* was hauled in the nick of time from a gulch of fierce gray timber wolves into which he had been pushed from a cliff. One of the hazards survived by Terry McGovern in *The Bowery after Dark* was a cellar full of "ferocious snakes." Ramsay Morris' *The Ninety and Nine,* inspired by Sankey's revival hymn of that name, offered a prairie fire and a locomotive with a train rushing through it. This was one of many railroad dramas. "A wall of fire" moved across the stage in *While Frisco Burns,* a drama of the catastrophe of 1906. In Lincoln J. Carter's *The Eye Witness* which concluded with "a destructive cyclone," an automobile vaulted to safety from a half-opened drawbridge.

Carter, a playwright-producer who worked out of Chicago, managed this sort of thing with consummate skill. His first show dates from 1888. In his *The Heart of Chicago,* he got a vividly realistic illusion of an onrushing train by constructing his property locomotive and cars like an accordion and pulling them out slowly, wheels spinning, pistons driving, bells clanging, steam engine swishing, and a magnesium headlight cutting out through the darkened auditorium. For a Niagara Falls scene he played floodlights with mediums on a shiny oilcloth floor and released live steam to counterfeit mist. Many standard devices still in use in the theatre began with Carter. He substituted a bull drum for the old thunder box and thunder curtain, and scraped together a piece of carbon and a file connected with an electric current to get realistic lightning. He was the first to use braziers of lycopodium for "conflagrations," and later, when real flames were barred by fire laws, he introduced red silk streamers agitated by electric fans.[6]

Carter was a prolific author. He, Davis, Kremer, and many others embraced in their melodramas all phases of human activity, from a domestic misunderstanding to a major international conflict like the Russo-Japanese War. "Everything was fish that came into our net," Davis has written. "If a particularly horrible murder excited the public, we had it dramatized and on the stage usually before anyone knew who had been guilty of the crime. Frequently I have had a job of hasty rewriting when it became evident that my culprit from real life was an innocent and perfectly respectable citizen."[7] Kremer's *A Desperate Chance* was written around an escape of the notorious Biddle brothers from a Pittsburgh jail—an affair in which the warden's wife, mistress of one of the prisoners, conspired. Davis' *The Chinatown Trunk Mystery* was a version of the murder of Elsie Segal, school teacher and missionary worker. The Harry Daw of *The Millionaire's Revenge* was the murderer Harry Thaw, and the fleeing lovers of *Caught in Midocean* were Dr. Crippen and his mistress, the first fugitives whose capture was effected by wireless. *Kidnapped in New York* was a lurid rewriting of the Martha Clarke snatch.

In addition to current wars, the Yellow Peril, the depredations of modern outlaws (the James Brothers, the Daltons, and Billy the Kid), the Dreyfus Case (*Devil's Island*), the Russian Revolution of 1905, the flight of the Dowager Empress of China, various industrial troubles such as the Pennsylvania coal strikes, and the Molly Maguires, Black Hand, and Mafia outrages were all given the "ten', twent', thirt' " treatment. The muckraking plays of Broadway were echoed in scores of hard-hitting dramatic preachments on the malefactors of great wealth (*The Wolf of Wall Street*) and the wicked trusts. There were detective plays (*King Brady, Secret Service Sam* and that personal favorite of Sam Harris, *The King of Detectives*), mining camp plays (*At Cripple Creek*), Klondike plays (Scott Marble's *Heart of the Klondike*, at the Star in 1897, was the earliest), racing plays, battleship plays, department store plays, military plays, Mormon plays, and newspaper plays (*The Power of the Press*).

[6] Arthur E. Krows, *Play Production in America* (New York, 1916), pp. 221, 228.
[7] *I'd Like to Do It Again*, p. 85.

The performers included many whose names were later to glitter in lights on Broadway: Laurette Taylor, Fiske O'Hara, George Sidney, Lottie Williams (in *Only a Shopgirl* and *The Factory Girl*), Richard Bennett (his first professional role was Tombstone Jake in *The Limited Mail*), Bert Lytel, and Joseph Santley. Lillian Gish made her debut at the age of five in *Her One False Step*—in the rôle of the false step.

The processed product of these play-mills was promoted and distributed with a genius equal to that which went into the manufacture. Circuits of theatres owned or leased by the promoters were built up in various regions of the country, and a full schedule of productions made the rounds with machine-like precision each season. Harris had as many as twenty-three companies on the road at one time, each netting from $100 to $300 weekly. (Salaries were $40 to $100.) Woods split off from Sullivan and Harris, setting up for himself and taking Davis with him. For eight years, Woods and Davis, as the producing team of Stair and Havlin, supplied a "wheel" of theatres from Boston to Kansas City with a continuous stream of high-powered entertainment that gave delight to millions. Davis wrote from seven to thirteen plays a season meanwhile doing dozens for other producers on the side; these and a like number of pieces, some old favorites among them, constituted the firm's annual output. In addition, he had charge of casting, rehearsals, scenery, costumes, and lithography. It took about a month to get a play off the belt and that included the writing which required the least time of all. *Her Marriage Vow* was turned out in three days.

Woods often contributed a title, but his specialty was the business and promotion end of the operation. An experienced and resourceful advance man, he knew the commercial theatre from the ground up and had a Barnum-like flair for beguiling simple souls. He was fertile in exploitation stunts. Three bums dressed in convict stripes and manacled together moved about in lockstep up and down the streets in the neighborhood of the theatres where *Convict 999* was appearing; bootblacks gave free shines to ticket-holders for *Tony the Bootblack*.

Competition was keen in the "ten, twent', thirt'" field, and producers extended themselves to outshine their rivals. Out of this condition arose the superproductions—larger companies, richer costumes, bigger and better sensation scenes. The first of these was *Nellie the Beautiful Cloak Model,* and it turned out to be Stair and Havlin's greatest hit. Other producers followed suit. The result was disaster. If the superproduction could make a lot of money, it could lose a lot too if it flopped; and most of them flopped. One after another the various firms came to grief or got out from under when the pinch came. One Sunday in 1904 Sam Harris met George M. Cohan at an outing of the Words and Music Club on Staten Island, and before the day was over a partnership was projected and *Little Johnny Jones* slated as its first Broadway production. Three years later Al Woods followed them to Broadway, and meanwhile the Proctor houses surrendered to vaudeville. The Blaneys stuck it out for a while, and here and there stock companies carried on. But the movies, which specialized in the very type of show that was the standby of "ten, twent' thirt'," did a far better job. The millions who thrilled to *The Great Train Robbery* on the screen were able to compare it with the stage play, and its superiority was obvious. The old theatres were transformed into nickelodeons, and on their bellying sheets were to be seen such soul-stirring matters as Pearl White thrown from cliffs by the villainous Paul Panzer in *The Perils of Pauline;* Grace Cunard hounded and harried week after week in *The Broken Coin;* and Broncho Billy Anderson riding to the rescue of imperilled damsels on the payroll of the Essanay Company. Flesh and blood entertainment was no match for this new competitor.

XXXIV

The Murder Mystery
and Psychological Melodrama

Who cares who killed Roger Ackroyd? —EDMUND WILSON

Émile Gaboriau's *L'Affaire Lerouge* (1866) and Wilkie Collins' *The Moonstone* (1868) are usually considered pioneers of the full-dress murder mystery in novel form. Antedating both these works is a French play which in many respects anticipated the murder mystery in its dramatic form, *L'Aïeule*, given for the first time in Paris in 1863.

In this melodrama by Charles Edmond and Dennery, a beautiful young girl, Blanche, is slowly wasting away. Her case perplexes physicians, who can discover no trace of any specific malady that might account for her condition. The Commander, one of the guests at the chateau where the action takes place, is an amateur physician and chemist; he secretly analyzes the drinking water left for the girl each night at her bedside and discovers traces of an unspecified poison (Tom Taylor and Horace Wigan made it arsenic in their English adaptation, *The Hidden Hand*, given in 1864).

Suspicion points at first, horribly, to Blanche's own mother, the Duchess, who has allowed herself to become infatuated with Gaston de Montmarcy, a young man of wealth and position in love with her daughter; and the question of her guilt or innocence is not cleared up until it has contributed heavily to the suspense and supplied material for several highly dramatic scenes. Here is the first faint fragrance of that red herring whose exhalations will pervade all modern detective drama and fiction.

One character is definitely not suspected, the dowager of the title, and for the excellent reason that she has been stricken recently with paralysis and cannot stir from her chair. This old woman, mother of the Duke's first wife, now dead, is an extraordinary person—strong-minded, passionate, proud. A fanatical partisan of her own kin, she is violently jealous of her daughter's successor, the present Duchess, whom she considers an interloper in her ancient but impoverished family, and of Blanche, who is the Duchess' child by a previous husband. All the affection in her nature is concentrated upon her grandchild Jeanne, the Duke's only child, fruit of his first marriage; she is aggressively, even morbidly, devoted to the girl.

De Montmarcy, loving Blanche and secretly loved by the Duchess (an infatuation of which he is entirely unaware), is really the official fiancé of Jeanne through a match arranged at court, a match highly gratifying to the dowager. Jeanne, however, loves the Commander, and she feels no resentment over the romance which has sprung up between De Montmarcy and Blanche, who is her close friend. Not so the old grandmother; she is furious at this development which threatens to wreck her fondest hopes.

By the time the final scene of the last act rolls around, the engagement of Jeanne and De Montmarcy has been cancelled, and the decision has been reached in family council that Blanche shall marry that much-sought-after gentleman. Blanche is packing to leave the château to escape the still unidentified poisoner, being urged thereto by the Duke and by Jeanne. Meanwhile dreadful doubts have begun to trouble Jeanne concerning her grandmother. For the climax she is suddenly presented with an opportunity to resolve these doubts, and she seizes it at the risk of her own life. All the characters are assembled on stage for a police interrogation. Blanche asks for a drink of water. The old lady has a tumbler by her and offers it. Before Blanche can drink, Jeanne snatches the glass from her and puts it to her own lips. At this, the supposed paralytic springs from her invalid's chair with an agonizing cry and wrests the glass from her grandchild, convicting herself as the poisoner. The glass contains a lethal dose of the poison; she drinks it herself and dies.

Though a murder is not consummated in *L'Aïeule,* and though the police inquiry and detectives figure only negligibly in the action, the play is nevertheless clearly entitled to be called the first, as it is one of the best, of the murder-mystery melodramas, since it depends for its peculiar interest on the tracking down of an evildoer of whose identity the audience is kept more or less in ignorance until the concluding moments of the final act, when she betrays herself in a highly dramatic climax.

This point of departure was a distinct novelty for melodrama in the sixties. In the conventional crime play—*Le Chien de Montargis, Fuàldes, Maria Marten, Jonathan Bradford, Lady Audley's Secret*—there is no major mystery to be solved, however many minor ones there may be. Almost invariably, from *Cœlina* onward (and backward, for that matter), the villain is presented in his true colors at the very outset; he communicates his heinous intentions across the footlights in monologues, plots his manifold crimes with confederates on the open stage, and actually commits them in full view of the audience. That he should do so was virtually obligatory in the nineteenth century.

L'Aïeule remained an exception—a sport; though it was extremely popular in two languages, the play inspired no imitations. A full half-century elapsed before the murder mystery became a popular dramatic form.

If the murder mystery was a novelty on the stage in the mid-nineteenth century, the detective was not. The dramas concerning Vidocq, chief of detectives in Paris, which promptly followed the publication of his *Mémoires* in 1820, introduced him as a character; and he reappeared frequently in the low-life dramas of the forties and succeeding decades which derived from *Les Mystères de Paris*, among them the elder Dumas' *Les Mohicans de Paris* and Paul Bocage's *Les Puritains de Paris*. In England a Bow Street Runner (policeman) arrests Corder in *Maria Marten*. Another one plays an important part in *Sweeney Todd*—Major Bounce, a jolly fellow and something of a humorist, who worms his way into the good graces of Mother Lovatt and presents himself to the Demon Barber as a customer in order to get evidence against him. Tom Taylor employed a plainclothes officer Gimlet (another droll wag) in his drawing-room melodrama, *Still Waters Run Deep* (1855), and eight years later in *The Ticket-of-Leave Man* gave to the world the dependable Hawkshaw, probably the most renowned of his line.

Hawkshaw's principal resources were a mastery of disguise and an impressive, if largely unexplained, ubiquity. There was nothing brilliant, dashing, subtle, or exotic about him; he was a plain, honest, and rather kindly policeman who tracked down wrongdoers, snapped handcuffs on them in the last act, and marched them off with a few well-chosen words at the final curtain. He owed his immense and lasting popularity to his very commonplaceness and, of course, to his creator's talent for theatrical arrangement; audiences, particularly plebeian ones, warmed up to him because he was such a familiar and reassuring embodiment of retribution—a sort of *deus ex machina* in a plug hat.

As the century wore on, the conventional stage detective, straight man or comic, reappeared frequently in melodramas: Taylor's *Mary Warner* (1869), Boucicault's *After Dark*, *The Long Strike*, and

Rescued, Byron's *Haunted Houses* (1872) and *Lancashire Lass* (1868), Watts Phillips' *Lost in London* (1867) and *Maude's Peril* (1863)—which offered probably the first Scotland Yard man in drama—and many others. London melodramas of the eighties and nineties, dealing largely with urban crime, inevitably found plenty of employment for the durable and indefatigable gumshoe; as Baxter, he is an important character in *The Silver King,* and he wanders in and out of the stirring action of *Romany Rye* and other cockney pieces at Drury Lane, the Princess, the Adelphi, the Surrey, the Brit, and elsewhere.

Many crime and detective plays were based upon popular fiction. In France various low-life novels by Paul Féval, more or less imitated from Sue, supplied Dennery and other playwrights with material for successful pieces. Among them were *Les Marches de Londres, Les Mystères de Londres* and *Les Habits noirs;* and *Les Misérables,* with its memorable figure of Javert, was often dramatized. Wilkie Collins turned his own novels, *The Moonstone* and *The Woman in White,* into dramas; Dickens' various novels of mystery and crime detecton—*Our Mutual Friend* (frequently given as *The Golden Dustman*), *Barnaby Rudge, Hunted Down, Bleak House,* and the unfinished *The Mystery of Edwin Drood*—all found their way onto the stage; and Reade's *Foul Play* was given in two distinct versions.

Crime and police novels were being adapted for the stage in America also. Bowery dramatists were kept busy from the early seventies onward transcribing for the theatre the interminable adventures of such dime novel detectives as Old Cap Collier (the earliest of them), the Old Sleuth,[1] Old King Brady, and the indestructible Nick Carter (created by John R. Coryell) who shone brightest in Chinatown raids. At least one play featuring Carter was translated into French and given at the Ambigu—Alexandre Bisson and G. Livet's *Nick Carter* (1910). Mark Twain's *Pudd'nhead Wilson,* wherein fingerprints help solve a murder for the first time in fiction, was a Broadway hit of 1894 in a version by Frank Mayo,

---

[1] Harlan P. Halsey, author of *The Old Sleuth* (and some six hundred other novels), was the first to use the word "sleuth" for detective. He attempted unsuccessfully to have it copyrighted. This definition was so effectually impressed on the American people that few among them today are aware that the word was originally short for sleuthhound.

who starred in the production; and Anna Catherine Green's *The Leavenworth Case* was given in an adaptation by the author in 1892.

Pudd'nhead Wilson was a lawyer, but as a general thing the crime-solvers of the novelists, like those of the playwrights, were run-of-the-mine coppers, often with their comic value emphasized in the tradition of Gimlet, Buckett, Bounce, and Jules Verne's Mr. Fix. For all the native shrewdness and criminological competence that they at times give demonstration of, they were predominantly (Bowery characters excepted) comic figures—socially inept and grammatically fallible. Nevertheless, their shrewdness and competence are at times extraordinary; Sergeant Cuff of *The Moonstone* and Inspector Buckett of *Bleak House* are vulgar policemen of genius. Such characters were by no means wholly imaginative creations, as so many of their successors in fiction and drama have been; Cuff was a kind of portrait of Chief Inspector Whicher whose theory in the Road Hill House Case, a famous Victorian mystery, was eventually sustained by a confession after it had been rejected by the authorities at the Yard; and Dickens' sleuths are obviously a by-product of their creator's extensive association with the constabulary.

Sherlock Holmes was not a commonplace figure like Hawkshaw, nor a semicomic one like Buckett, whatever his eccentricities. He was picturesque and romantic, and he had that attribute of mystery so desirable in a melodramatic hero. Furthermore, he was a gentleman, the first in his profession if we except the shadowy Dupin, Poe's ratiocinative abstraction. However, in spite of their hero's eminent fitness for stage purposes, Doyle's narratives never became really successful plays though there were numerous productions based on the stories. William Gillette's *Sherlock Holmes* (1899), a hit in England and America for years, is an adaptation only in the loosest sense. The playwright merely borrowed a few of Doyle's characters and incidents, inventing a plot of his own and developing his action not along the lines of the Doyle formula with its concentration on detection and its surprise ending, but according to time-honored melodramatic practice. That is, the cards are laid on the table, face up, quite early in the play; and the interest centers upon Holmes' resolute and cunning campaign to outwit the plainly labelled villains and rescue the unfortunate and misguided Alice Faulkner (a sterilized version of Irene Adler of *A Scandal in Bohemia*) whom they have in their clutches.

Perhaps Doyle's stories, like Poe's Dupin "trilogy" (Baudelaire's term), were too much the intellectual stunt, too exclusively the mathematical puzzle, to admit of ready adaptation to the physical, dynamic medium of conventional melodrama; their very virtues were a handicap. Holmes's near infallibility presented difficulties, also. Although Watson alludes briefly to failures, Doyle makes only one the basis of a story, *The Yellow Face*, and here the failure is only in the preliminary diagnosis. No unfortunate consequences follow from this false start; suspicion is not directed at an innocent and sympathetic character who is made to suffer thereby. And upon those few occasions in the stories when the posture of circumstances or the limitations of the official police give rise to such suspicions as in *The Beryl Coronet*, *The Silver Blaze*, and *The Crooked Man*, no effort is made by the author to work up sympathy for the falsely accused one. In short, the good old melodramatic device of the persecuted innocent is almost entirely neglected.

This, for melodramatic purposes, is almost fatal, as Owen Davis pointed out in *I'd Like to Do It Again* without mentioning Doyle specifically. "The author must not only create an interest in who committed the crime," writes this expert manipulator of the modern murder-mystery formula on the stage, "but, if he hopes for success, he must make them fear that some one character dear to them is guilty. In other words, the mystery play in which one hasn't gone deep enough into the emotions to make the audience care who committed the murder is never successful, no matter how mysterious it may be" (p. 164). The distinction is between the intellectual puzzle or guessing game on the one hand, and the emotional story or human drama on the other.

Gaboriau avoided this mistake (a mistake, of course, only from the standpoint of the stage), and accordingly it is to him and not to Doyle that Davis pays tribute as the inspiration of the modern American murder-mystery play. The Frenchman's detectives are fallible enough (Holmes calls Lecoq "a miserable bungler"), and as a consequence the reader is given plenty of reason to feel sorry for the falsely accused heroes. Until late in *L'Affaire Lerouge*, each scrap of evidence collected by the indefatigable Father Tabaret tends to sustain the case the police have built up against the generous, high-minded young viscount; in *La Corde au cou*, Lecoq is powerless in the face of the net of circumstantial evidence which enmeshes a similarly sympathetic character; and again in *Le Dossier*

No. 113, Lecoq makes but slow headway in extricating the likable young bank cashier, Prosper Bertomy, from his difficulties.

By naming Gaboriau as the inspiration of the modern murder-mystery play, however, and stopping there, Davis is saying either too much or too little. Granted that the theme of the wrongly but plausibly suspected sympathetic character is common to his stories and the plays that followed them, there are yet many vital differences. Gaboriau's stories and their imitations, which include *The Mystery of a Hansom Cab*, *Pudd'nhead Wilson*, and *The Leavenworth Case*, offer elaborate plots with many romantic and melodramatic ramifications, the detection playing a minor part in the whole involved proceedings. This is true also of the stories of those two English plot specialists, Dickens and Wilkie Collins, and of the modern Frenchman Simenon. Furthermore, though the detective in the stories may be kept in the dark as to the explanation of the mystery until late in the narrative, the reader is not, since he is supplied with clues which make the identification of the guilty one fairly easy halfway through the book. Turning to the plays, we find the Poe-Doyle straight-line course followed rather than the meandering one of Gaboriau, and the solution is reserved for the denouement, as might be expected in a generation brought up on Sherlock Holmes.

Now the playwrights were able to stick close to the trail and preserve their secret in a play of full three-act length only because of a device hit upon by another Frenchman without whose contribution the modern detective novel, no less than the modern detective play, might never have been evolved. This Frenchman was Fortune Hippolyte August du Boisgobey, a disciple of Gaboriau's, who struck out on a new path in his novel, *Le Crime de l'opéra* (1880), contriving his story in such a way that instead of one or two persons being suspected there are six or seven. Here was the perfect means for protracting the problem without cluttering up the action with matter not strictly germane to the mystery. At the same time, the device intensified the suspense and enhanced the fascination of the guessing game, so important an appeal in the modern mystery play and in the modern mystery story. Philip Barry and Elmer Rice burlesqued the convention in their gay *Cock Robin*.

The technically excellent formula of the modern Broadway murder mystery was developed gradually during a period roughly contemporary with World War I. An early contribution was made by *The Argyle Case* (1912), the work of Harvey J. O'Higgins and Harriet Ford, assisted by William J. Burns, head of a private detective agency. The play begins after the crime has been committed (a new approach), and the involved exposition is skillfully fitted into the development, which, under the guiding hand of the detective (who is the romantic hero), is directed toward breaking down the *prima facie* case against the innocent, appealing heroine and fixing the guilt upon the real culprit, mastermind of a counterfeiting gang which has been blackmailing the murdered man, an uncle of the girl. In other details the procedure remains rather primitive. The murderer can be pretty well identified in the second act, and the interest of the succeeding action resides in the various stratagems employed by the detective to get evidence. The episodic treatment as used in the detective plays from the Vidocq days down to and including Gillette's Sherlock Holmes persists; the action embraces a period of several days, and the scene shifts from place to place. The climax is old-fashioned melodrama. It is played out on a double stage representing the attics of adjoining houses, a device which goes back to *Jonathan Bradford* and *Les Pauvres de Paris*. In one is the counterfeiting gang, and in the other, spying on them by means of a dictograph, a group of detectives, who crawl over the roof and through the windows for the arrest.

In the work of men like Owen Davis and Bayard Veiller, the murder mystery crystallized into its standard form, a form which, curiously enough, is a return to the classical unities. Characteristically the framework is the police interrogation at the scene of the crime or the courtroom trial, not utilized in the novel until *The Bellamy Trial* in 1927. After suspicion has been directed at one character after another, a confession is finally extorted by psychological means from the least likely person by a detective of the intuitional type (the murder-mystery business has an elaborate nomenclature) usually not connected with the police and often a woman.

In matters of detail, authors owed much to the cross-examination scenes and other realistic legal and police procedures in the muckraking dramas, to the admirable third act of *Mrs. Dane's Defense* in which a skilled advocate maneuvers a woman into a full confession, and to the imbroglio of farce, particularly the "mystery farce," of which Augustin McHugh's *Officer 666* (1912) and *Seven Keys to Baldpate* (1913) are examples. In the latter, dramatized from Earl Derr Bigger's novel of the same name, the adaptor, George M.

Cohan, took a large group of characters and for three acts kept them in a state of lively and continuous melodramatic agitation. The time is a winter's night, and the scene throughout is the lobby of an isolated summer resort hotel in the Catskills. To this deserted retreat comes a popular novelist from New York, Bill Magee, seeking absolute seclusion and quiet for the writing of a novel which he has undertaken to complete in twenty-four hours on a wager. He locks himself in with what he has been assured is the only existing key to the place and goes to work. Upon his solitude there intrudes, one after another, an astonishing assortment of characters, each with a key and all bent upon some secret and usually sinister errand having to do with certain papers concerning a transit franchise which are locked in the office safe. In an atmosphere of mystery and suspense as lights flash on and off, there are surprise meetings, confrontations, violent scenes of challenge and recrimination, struggles in the dark, pistol shots, thefts, abductions, and finally a murder. All is managed with that combination of speed and violence which is the peculiar virtue of American stage direction. The play concludes in what is perhaps the first of the trick endings, or at least the first of the modern trick endings, since much the same sort of thing was attempted in Loaisel-Tréogate's *Le Château du diable*, back in eighteenth-century pantomime. The whole situation proves to be nothing more than the externalization of the plot of the shocker which Magee is grinding out to win his bet.

Elmer Rice's *On Trial* (1914) is one of the earliest of the courtroom mystery-melodramas. It was peculiar for its use of a device borrowed from the silent films; various pieces of crucial testimony are re-enacted by means of flashbacks, managed with blackouts and a revolving stage instead of being merely recounted by witnesses. Critics thought highly of the novelty at the time, but it did not catch on although Rice used it again five years later in *For the Defense*. Other playwrights were content with the inherent drama of the courtroom—the clash of opposing counsel, the appearance of surprise witnesses and the trapping of unwary ones, and impulsive confessions—eked out at times by a second or even a third and fourth murder committed on the scene as the trial or inquest proceeded.

In one of the best of these plays, *The Trial of Mary Dugan* (1917), Veiller got along without the supplementary crime—without virtually any physical action in the melodramatic sense, in fact. The production carried realism of atmosphere to the limit. The intervals between acts were cleverly arranged to seem like recesses in the court's sessions; the single set used throughout represented the courtroom, and the audience represented the jury with the judge and counsel directing their remarks across the footlights. A wealthy man, Edgar Rice, has been fatally stabbed in the New York apartment of Mary Dugan, a Follies alumna whom he has been keeping. The murder occurred immediately after a violent quarrel of the lovers in the course of which the girl had threatened Rice's life. Mary is on trial as the play begins. Her defense is that she had left the apartment for a few minutes and returned to find Rice dead. Conviction appears certain, and the girl is being urged by her attorney to plead guilty. This gentleman happens to be her immediate neighbor in the apartment house, and he was the first person to have appeared on the scene after the murder.

Mary has a brother, Jimmy, younger than herself, whom she has put through law school in a distant city, where he was not likely to learn of the source of the money which paid his way. At the climax of the trial this young man appears in court. After observing the proceedings for a while, he approaches his sister and induces her to discharge her attorney and turn the case over to him. His first move as her counsel is to change her plea back to not guilty; then he wades in. He puts his predecessor as counsel on the stand as a witness and draws one damaging admission after another from him, until he finally traps him into the confession that, while Mary was out of the apartment, he had killed Rice, against whom he nursed a grudge. The idea is a variation of one first used by Gaston Leroux in that detective play classic, *Le Mystère de la chambre jaune* (1912) (imitated in *The Crimson Circle* and *The Bat*), in which the detective on the case turns out to be the murderer.

In Veiller's *The Thirteenth Chair* (1916) a miscellaneous company of guests in a New York drawing room sit in on a "fixed" seance which has been arranged by one of them, Wales, in an effort to discover the murderer of a close friend who had relations with all those present. When the lights are out and the circle is closed, Wales is stabbed to death in the same manner in which his friend had been. A police inspector is summoned, and he conducts the investigation on the spot. He draws out testimony highly damaging to Helen O'Neil, the beautiful fiancée of the hostess' son, a poor girl who has been "educated for a lady" by a devoted old Irish mother. The mother happens to be the very woman Wales employed as medium for the seance. The inspector is on the point of arresting Helen when the old lady, acting on a hunch and bringing into play some of the tricks of her profession, terrifies the guilty one into a confession.

The suggestion of the occult was used delicately and artfully in *The Thirteenth Chair*, which is more than can be said of the flock of "spook" mystery-farces which drove overworked property men and electricians to distraction in the early twenties—compositions designated "fright-wig" melodrama by George Jean Nathan. Clutching hands, hairy monsters, homicidal maniacs, terrified comic Negroes, howling winds, mysterious moans in the night, and gloomy old mansions furnished with trapdoors, secret rooms and sliding panels: these were their stock in trade, and their chief criterion of success was the hysteria they were able to induce in audiences. *The Gorilla* and *The Cat and the Canary* were of this type. These productions toured the country for years, scaring people by the millions and taking their money for it.

Summing up the American murder-mystery play, it can be said that, like the American murder-mystery story, it was content to rely for its interest on its neat construction, its surface excitement, its incidental comedy, and its suspense. Its triumphs were largely triumphs of ingenuity: new methods of murder (the revolver discharged from the radio set in Albert C. Fuller and Clyde North's *Remote Control*, 1929), novel settings (the El of Eva Kay Flint and Madge Madison's *Subway Express*, 1929, and the vaudeville theatre of *The Spider* by Fulton Oursler and Lowell Brentano), and new types of alibis (the phonograph playing in the death chamber of Daniel M. Rubin's *Riddle-Me-This*, 1930).

It has remained for the English, who turned to the form rather late in the day, to demonstrate that it was capable of providing adult entertainment. *The Bat* and *The Thirteenth Chair* were big successes in London, and the first phase of British-made murder-mystery melodrama was imitation, illustrated in such plays as Edgar Wallace's *Criminal-at-large*, a hit on Broadway in 1932. Even in the beginning, however, it was imitation with a difference. Wallace restored the prestige of the Scotland Yard man, which had suffered greatly from the Sherlock Holmes stories; and in eliminating the amateur as detective he also eliminated the amateur's method of esoteric clues and highbrow deduction, a sacred convention in the mystery field since Poe and Gaboriau. The technique of Wallace's operatives, is, indeed, that of Hawkshaw, being a kind of prescience and ubiquity made possible by the organization and system of which he is a part.

After Wallace, other British playwrights, including A. A. Milne and Patrick Hamilton, took up the detective play, as novelists G. K. Chesterton, E. C. Bentley, and Dorothy Sayers had taken up the detective novel; and these able writers gave the form the benefit of high literary competence with the happiest results. A. A. Milne's *The Perfect Alibi* and Patrick Hamilton's *Rope* are admirable plays, as *The Nine Tailors* and *Trent's Last Case* are admirable stories, aside from the murder-detection problems around which they are constructed. Ingenuity and originality are not confined to the contrivance of the crime puzzle in these English pieces. A whole new dimension in criminal types and motivation is introduced; and the dialogue has grace and wit, qualities which are sadly lacking in the mechanically slick productions of our Broadway artisans. In Hamilton's *Rope* (1929) two thrill-hungry psychopathic undergraduates strangle a companion for "motiveless" Nietzschean reasons and invite the victim's father to a dinner, served off the chest in which the boy's body has been stowed. In *The Perfect Alibi* (1929) the chatter of the juveniles has a nimbleness and spontaneity which would become any of the sophisticates of Noel Coward or Evelyn Waugh, and the chief murderer is a personality not unworthy of standing alongside that other fat villain, Count Fosco of *The Woman in White*.

In one important particular the British departed radically from their American models: they threw the guessing game out at the start, "blowing the gaff," in the English phrase. In *The Perfect Alibi*, Anthony Armstrong's *Ten-minute Alibi* (1933), and *Riddle-Me-This* (1930), the crime is committed early in the play before the eyes of the audience, and an alibi is carefully rehearsed in full view on the stage. The loss entailed in this sacrifice of the surprise ending proves trifling and the gain immense. The thrill of the chase is no less keen for the quarry's being known, and the opportunities for characterization are vastly enlarged.

A later phase of the murder-detection melodrama, developed by the British and imitated—not too successfully—by our own playwrights, is seen at its morbid best in Emlyn Williams' *Night Must Fall* (1936), Hamilton's *Angel Street* (1939) which broke a Broadway long-run record set by *The Bat*, and Edward Percy and

Reginald Denham's *Ladies in Retirement* (1940)²—a class of play in which *Rope* properly belongs also. Danny, the jaunty, cunning, wheedling bellboy of *Night Must Fall* merrily whistles "Mighty lak a Rose" as he moves about, a woman's severed head in his bag; and each of the other plays of the same school which have followed it (*Love from a Stranger, Hangover Square,* and dozens more) has some such homicidal maniac, often the bright star of a constellation of psychotics, as in the case of the American play, *Uncle Harry* (1942), by Thomas Job, which Eva la Gallienne and Joseph Schildkraut did so well on the stage.

These villains—and villainesses—are not wicked but neurologically ill, in the patter of the psychiatrist, and hence not responsible; the warrant of the moral law does not run here. As Evelyn Waugh phrased it, "The modern 'psychological thriller' has, properly, no villain, for the crimes are not acts of free will."³ The ultimate twist of psychological melodrama was probably reached in *Arsenic and Old Lace* (1941), written by Joseph Kesselring and produced by Russel Crouse and Howard Lindsay. The two sweet and charming, but hopelessly mad old ladies of this piece make a career out of enticing homeless derelicts off the streets and poisoning them for their own good. In the wake of this hilarious travesty, which was a prolonged hit in New York breaking the long-run record set by *Angel Street* and was equally popular on the road, the straight article seemed to lose some of its fascination for theatre audiences.

² The dates are those of the New York productions.
³ The Jesuit Who Was Tuesday," *The Commonweal,* XLV, 23 (Mar. 27, 1947).

XXXV

Melodrama Went Thataway

"Talk" is poison to a Western. —REX POLIER

As the films moved in, live melodrama, after finding a brief refuge in stock, retreated into the hills and led a gypsy life in the tent shows. Uncle Tom apparently died for the last time under canvas near Wilkes Barre, Pennsylvania, toward the end of 1930 and went to heaven, and simon-pure melodrama died with him. But it is as idle to speak of the death of melodrama, as of its birth. The blood-and-thunder drama has a hard core that is ageless and indestructible.

The triumph of the films was more of a disaster for the popular theatre than it was for melodrama. For melodrama it was no disaster at all, certainly not from the standpoint of survival. What melodrama did when the crisis came was simply to drift over into the ranks of the enemy, taking along its gaudy accoutrements, its raffish side-show manners, and its bag of tricks. The bag of tricks was to prove an even more valuable property than the actual plays themselves, which were no small windfall for a new and ill-regarded art that had to scrounge for its raw material. The tricks were dramatic techniques of such an order as to be of unique utility to a medium which had not learned to speak.

The popular melodrama theatre had a tolerance for the spoken word, but it was scarcely more than a tolerance, especially in England and America. Basically this theatre worked with building blocks other than verbal ones. These included animated business and dumb show; a stage whose limits were extended by traps, elevated platforms, and the ambient air up into the fly loft; manipulable properties and lights; and a pattern of almost continuous movement contrived to mesh at climaxes with an elaborate and frequently gimmicky mise-en-scène. Dialogue was an ingredient of the mixture, to be sure, and conspicuously so in the form of the harangue, beloved of ham actors, which melodrama had taken over from the tirade of tragedy; but the talk was accessory to the central business of hubbub and spectacle. By word count, stage directions in a printed melodrama could run to 20 per cent of the text as a whole, not including the descriptions of costumes and scenery which were always extensive.

The rôle of the author, generally speaking, was functional, and he provided a continuity rather than a play. What he worked in was no longer a writer's theatre,[1] an actor's, or even an actor-manager's except peripherally. The man in control—whether he was called manager, house manager, stage manager, "contriver," or whatever[2] —foreshadowed the motion picture director in diversity of activity and might be described as a ringmaster. A playwright or actor frequently assumed this rôle as did Fitzball.

What the best of these men were unconsciously working toward was nothing less than a dynamic new way of telling a story on the stage. Ingenious craftsmen of the theatre, they invented and refined one device and effect after another tending toward this kind of creative theatre. William Hazlitt recognized what was going on without being impressed with the artistic quality of the results. In a review of *The Conquest of Taranto*, by Dimond and Kelly, given at Covent Garden in 1817, he drew some general conclusions: "A dramatic author does not profess to provide entertainment at his own expense, but contracts with the manager to get up a striking, impressive exhibit in conjunction with the scene painter, the scene shifter, the musical composer, the orchestra, the choruses on the stage, the lungs of the actor . . . The author loses no opportunity in playing the game into the hands of his theatrical associates, so that they may supply his deficiencies and together produce a perfect piece."[3]

The substance of Hazlitt's comment recurs in a summary by an observer of melodrama more than a century later. Marguerite

[1] When the Adelphi management celebrated the 100th performance of *The Pilot*, in 1826, with a dinner for one hundred guests, the author was "overlooked." Fitzball, the author in question, tells the story in *Thirty-Five Years of a Dramatic Author's Life* (London, 1859), pp. 162–163.

[2] The "acting manager" in the early nineteenth-century English theatre was really business manager, in charge of the front of the house. In 1824 the proprietor of the Surrey engaged Charles Dibdin the younger as "acting manager, author and *contriver*." The italics are Dibdin's, in whose *Memoirs* the passage occurs, p. 142.

[3] *The Complete Works of William Hazlitt* (London & Toronto, 1930), Vol. V, p. 367.

Courtney, looking back to the productions of her father, Charles A. Taylor, a typical author-contriver-manager of "ten, twent', thirt'," writes that "Character, plot and dialogue were rigging for physical heroics and mechanical effects."[4] Managers, or "contrivers," were stimulated to creativity in the theatre of action by the shape (or shapelessness) of the early nineteenth-century English play, especially melodrama, and by a physical peculiarity of the English stage of the period. The plays used an early point of attack and episodic development in a straight line, a form subserved by the system of grooves and sliding wings and flats, which made scene changing easy. Short scenes on the forestage alternated with more or less elaborate scenes embracing the full stage, the intervals running to as many as twenty-four; and managing the transitions became a challenge. Experimentation with a view to bridging the gaps smoothly and rapidly was materially advanced by the introduction of gas, laid on for the first time in a theatre at Covent Garden in 1817 and in use soon afterward at most other houses in London. The new illuminant could be perfectly controlled from a single source, and it soon became the practice to "fade" scenes in and out and even to simulate something like the "dissolve" of motion pictures. Gas also permitted the darkening of the auditorium during the performance, though this does not seem to have been done with any consistency before Henry Irving's tenancy of the Lyceum late in the century.

Within scenes, effects were developed by various means to maintain pace, make things lively, and diversify the picture. The panorama came into use as a scenic background creating the illusion of movement, as of a shoreline viewed from a moving ship. Vision and dream scenes were spotted behind gauze on platforms well up on a darkened stage, and similar tricks were borrowed from the pantomime. The treadmill was used in horse race scenes and otherwise. And in the famous multiple scene in *Jonathan Bradford* (Chapter XXI), which many subsequent plays were to copy, simultaneity was achieved. All the strands of this continuous tinkering were gathered up in the work of the old master, Boucicault. Dozens of examples could be cited from his melodramas. Two of the most representative occur in the Irish plays, *Arrah na Pogue* (1864) and *The Shaughraun* (1874), in each of which a political prisoner

---

[4] *Laurette* (New York, 1955), p. 540. Mrs. Courtney's mother was Laurette Taylor, who played heroines in her husband's melodramas on the West Coast long before she became the toast of Broadway.

batters his way through a stone wall in an English jail and climbs a wall to freedom with the help of confederates and complicated stage machinery.

From approximately 1908 through 1915, experimenters in the new medium of the screen were moving steadily toward a goal to which stage melodrama aspired but which it was prevented from attaining by reason of the refractory materials with which it was condemned to work in the sticks-and-stones theatre. The goal was a kinetic new theatrical art form which the magical powers of light, harnessed by a mobile motion picture camera, were destined to bring to reality. As new doors opened in the progress of the film, particularly sound, and as the medium matured as an art, these techniques, which at least had their inspiration in stage melodrama, lost their utility and were demoted or displaced by newer and better ones. By that time melodrama had got into the bloodstream of its new host and no longer needed this kind of factitious reinforcement in order to maintain itself in the organism.

The treasure in the form of plays which the films took over from the hoard accumulated by nineteenth-century melodrama served them nearly as well as the techniques they derived from the same source, and they were to have a similar history in their new incarnation. After performing their mission they were superseded in large part and retired from service. The traditional repertory proved invaluable during the toddling age of the new and then lightly regarded art. The old plays represented usable scripts of tested audience appeal. They were tailor-made to the requirements of a still silent screen, and they were mostly in the public domain. The early films made free of this store, particularly after the switch to increased footage of three and four reels and more provided room for a story narrative to turn around in, which was about the year 1910. Griffith made the first four-reeler, *Judith of Bethulia*, in 1913. A random glance at the "retake" record is revealing. *Monte Cristo* was first filmed in 1913, with James O'Neill in the rôle with which he had been identified for seventeen years in the live theatre; there were to be eleven retakes before 1937. In 1964 a handsome French movie, *Les Mystères de Paris*, acclaimed in Paris, was the ninth version of that material to be done. Reviving the old favorites did not always work out, but a whole library of items appears to have been well received. Among them were *The Ticket-of-Leave Man*, Boucicault's Irish plays, *The Lady of Lyons*, *Under Two Flags*, *Enoch Arden*, and adaptations of Scott and Dickens novels, including *Ivanhoe, Oliver Twist,* and *A Tale of Two Cities. Under the Gaslight,* a London melodrama of the type of *The Lights o' London* and the Drury Lane repertory, flourished. *Way down East* (1920) and *Orphans of the Storm (The Two Orphans)* (1922) were to be done by Griffith, who based *The Birth of a Nation* on *The Clansman,* a Broadway melodrama of 1906 from the novel of the same name by Thomas Dixon, Jr.

As the sources of popular stage melodrama dried up in England and America and the studios came to rely on their own stables of writers, the films continued to ransack the old plays for odds and ends, using situations, scenes, and lines over and over again when they proved effective. A cotter pin was removed surreptitiously with felonious intent from the wheel of post chaise, diligence, or stage coach for the first time—but far from the last—in *The Cedar Chest; or, the Lord Mayor's Daughter* by Almar, given at Sadler's Wells in 1834.

The Biblical epics survived all phases of filmic evolution—*Ben Hur, The Sign of the Cross, The Ten Commandments*—as did their secular equivalents in the archaeological field, including *Cleopatra.* Besides the Biblical, the melodrama categories which negotiated most successfully the leap from stage to screen were the monster fantasies and the horse operas; and the Civil War spectacles attained stature under the guiding hand of D. W. Griffith after having had a successful stage career beginning with Boucicault's *Belle Lamar* in 1874 and Bronson Howard's *Shenandoah* in 1888. These types are of unimpeachable melodramatic provenance. The bloodlines of horse opera run back to the Paris Cirque and the Surrey Side ring shows of the late eighteenth century, and the monster strain is of like antiquity, descending from the gothic school, which got its start on the stage in the same era. Frankenstein's monster, the vampire, the hunchback of Notre Dame, and the phantom of the opera, with their macabre kith and kin, as galvanized by such bloodcurdling talents as Lon Chaney and Boris Karloff, did all right on the silent screen, but the sound track lent new resonance to their enormities, commencing in 1929 with the first all-talking picture, *The Terror,* with Conrad Nagel. Science fiction, in its more lunatic manifestations, and the monster theme formed a fruitful alliance (*King Kong, The Thing from Outer Space,* etc.), the scientific binge of our generation contributing to the size of their public. Simultaneously various romances of Jules Verne, often dramatized on the stage, were transferred to the screen.

Griffith has become typed as the pictorial chronicler of the War Between the States as well as the first authentic American artist of the screen, but he had a hand in the evolution of the Western also. His superb handling of great masses of horsemen in the cavalry scenes of *The Birth of a Nation* conferred prestige on this typically cinematographic—and melodramatic—effect and thereby helped powerfully to promote the Western into the select classification of the two-dollar-audience picture.

The Western, of course, is coeval with the movies from their very birth and has continuously proved an asset beyond price to the industry. *The Great Train Robbery*, written and produced by Edwin S. Porter around the turn of the century, was a Western; and cowboys and Indians early became a standby of the nickelodeon one-reelers. Max Aronson ("Broncho Billy" Anderson), who had the lead in the Porter classic, created the first cowpoke film hero in 1908, and from that year until 1915 he turned out four hundred of these sagebrush saddle thrillers for different producers, making a million dollars. In 1907 the form broke into three reels, with Paul Panzer's *The Life of Buffalo Bill*. Beginning about 1910, the place of the Western was assured in all studio schedules. In the years from 1910 to 1915 the movie palace sprang up all over America and Thomas H. Ince was the man who made the breakthrough for the Western. His pioneering enterprise as a producer and director assured that the glamorous figure of the cowboy would soon be riding around the world.

The advantages of location shooting for this type of picture had been demonstrated in *The Girl from Montana* in 1908, and with this lesson in mind, Ince launched his operation in a big outdoors way. In 1911, he hired Miller Brothers' 101 Ranch Wild West Show en masse, Indians and all, and put it down on twenty thousand acres he had leased at Santa Barbara. Before the year was out he released *Across the Prairie*, which introduced the first full-dress Western. High in the saddle, the hero in chaps was ready for top billing, and the actors to do the job were available: William S. Hart, who worked for Ince, and Tom Mix. They established the image of the cowboy at home and abroad. As Rio Jim, Hart, the strong, silent man, won the lasting affection of the French. Western buffs of that nation still remember him with nostalgia.

In the subsequent aggrandizement of the legend through the twenties, the Western got into definitely historical territory by way of "big" pictures. James Cruze, who also worked for Ince, made

The Covered Wagon in 1923 and John Ford followed with *The Iron Horse* in 1924. These and other releases of similar scope and caliber raised the silent Western to its highest point of achievement. The intrusion of sound at the end of the decade threatened a check, disturbing King Vidor and other exponents of the Western, but it was back on the trail with *In Old Arizona*, 1929, its documentary potentialities enhanced. Sound also added to the appeal of the string music and cowboy tenor of Gene Autry, Bill Boyd, and Roy Rogers, who probably added more fans to the ranks of Westerns than all the more solemn interpreters put together.

The spread of television after World War II posed difficulties which had repercussions on motion picture melodrama including the Western. These were ultimately resolved by creativity and negotiation. The loss of audiences stimulated the development of the wide screens, which was nothing less than a godsend for the Western, permitting the projection of the breathtaking landscapes of the monumental mesa country as background for the kind of heroic action and sweeping movement of the great films of the Southwest done in the forties, some of them by John Ford and frequently starring John Wayne. The competition of TV and the films was to be regularized by various top-level deals. The former settled for the serial or episodic pattern in Westerns which was exactly right for its rating and advertising problems, and movie moguls opened up their vaults and turned over their mountainous accumulation of old films to the rival medium for a consideration. The coaxial cable had corralled another market and another audience for the already immense Western product. The packaged serial featuring frontier characters from Daniel Boone on through the era of the shooting sheriffs and the post-Civil War period consistently outscore other types of programs and consume much of the prime time on all networks year after year.

The Western hero of the films owes little except in broad outlines to any single stage prototype, being a composite of the Crocketts, the Boones, the Buffalo Bills, and the Natty Bumppos of the nineteenth century with a touch of the cowboy imparted by such Broadway creations as the hero of *Arizona* and *The Virginian*. The man in chaps whom the film was to glorify is an independent synthesis, and within the pattern the type ranges the spectrum from extreme volatility to a rigidity that resembles mummification, the variations being determined by the audience.

In the early tintypes, the psychology is reduced to a few elementary notations. The moral character is vintage melodrama. Here is a man of action who shoots straight and rides magnificently and who does not know what it is to falter or be afraid. He does a lot of shooting, but his targets are all bad guys. Lochinvar and Robin Hood are in his professional ancestry. Sex plays no part in his strenuous, dedicated life; and the aura of the female is generally absent even in legitimate contexts.

Within this category, bifurcation occurs early. Hart characteristically was "The Good Bad Man," a phrase that was the title of one of the Douglas Fairbanks' pictures. Often a technical outlaw and a fugitive from justice, he drinks strong liquor and can be impulsive with his shooting irons. He was, authorities say, authentic Old West. The Tom Mix equivalent was more antiseptic—straight eagle scout. His code was impeccably middle class except for a few regional variations. He shoots people only when absolutely necessary, preferring to use his fists. He is Old West touched up for domestic consumption. Subsequent cowboy heroes inclined to this formula. Hoot Gibson, Ken Maynard, Buck Jones, Hopalong Cassidy, and the banjo strummers generally speaking are never a bad example for any mother's son. After World War I this unexceptionable character became routine in the oater, which draws its public from the regional areas and the big city neighborhood movie public. But in pictures zeroed on more metropolitan markets, the mixture became enriched.

Sex erupts flagrantly in the fifties, with pictures like *The Outlaw* and *Duel in the Sun*. And along with sex, sociology, psychiatry, Sartre, and even foreign affairs (allegorically) infiltrate the milieu. Characters like Billy the Kid are exposed like clinical smears on a slide; heroes have hesitations and misgivings, and the Indian is presented as the white man's victim rather than an unregenerate savage or a squalid comic. Plots become allegories, and critics begin to talk about myth and symbol.

The Western melodrama of the films, thanks to vast improvements in scripts and directors, has been able to assimilate all this heterogeneous material. It has become a frame on which may be draped a backwoods feud or the future of mankind, and sometimes both in the same story. Beneath the sheriff's badge and sombrero may be Everyman. In its most refined and most reverberating effects, the Western can be, as it was in the beginning, wordless:

A lonely, troubled man, prudently shunned by good folk and very scared, has got to go forward alone and do what he has to do.

Words like justice and law and order—or any words at all—sound like an impertinence when used to describe the thing that moves Gary Cooper out from cover into the open, down the long, long street of the shabby frontier town, and into the sights of the two killers' Colts. Through the tense, prolonged sequence there isn't a human sound except for the eerie, offstage ballad voice droning a muffled chorus in dialect. The words don't register very clearly and they don't matter; that droning voice is a signal from a distant drum.

Thus in 1953 with *High Noon* melodrama got back again to doing what it had always wanted to do, if half unconsciously—get along without the spoken word. And without it the people out front in the dark watching the screen were able to see a little deeper into the human heart and the human herd.

Bibliographical Notes on Plays

A surprisingly large proportion of the immense production of nineteenth-century writers of melodrama in France, England, and the U.S.A. was printed and is accessible; and a similarly vast corpus of English and French plays survives in manuscript, largely in the censorship archives of those two nations. Also extant are examples of the primitive, circus-like melodramas performed at Surrey Side minor theatres in London at the close of the century (*see* CROSS*).

Nineteenth-century melodrama in print falls into three main categories by type of publication: copies in pamphlet form vended at theatres; hardbound copies, both separate plays and collected editions of individual authors, intended chiefly for reading; and professional, or acting, copies, also in pamphlet form. In addition there were private printings for restricted professional use.

At only a few of the theatres, including the Ambigu in Paris and Drury Lane in London, plays were offered for sale and then only early in the century. Hardbound publication was rare also; PIXERÉCOURT (collected edition) is the only French melodramatist who attained this distinction, if we except writers for the carriage-trade theatre, such as Sardou, late in the century. In England hardbound publication was confined to a few writers of literary attainments or pretensions such as BULWER-LYTTON, JERROLD, TOM TAYLOR.

The great bulk of the melodrama output consisted of professional editions of individual plays published primarily for sale to provincial managers and late in the nineteenth century to stock companies. Publication for this market of plays in series (often called editions or libraries) constitutes by far the largest single segment of the whole, and it is in this form that melodramas have survived and are most generally available today. In England and the U.S.A. plays in series were usually numbered individually, sometimes being issued in monthly or weekly numbers, or were gathered in numbered volumes.

In virtually all printings in pamphlet form the cast of the original metropolitan production was given and frequently also a description of scenery, properties, costumes, etc., in greater or less detail. Diagrams for more elaborate scenic effects were occasionally added for melodramas by BOUCICAULT and others at the middle of the

* Names CAPITALIZED are to be found in General Bibliography.

century, when sensation scenes were the rage, and later. The composer of the incidental music and the designer of the scenery were credited with their contributions during the first generation of melodramas and occasionally later in Paris and less frequently in England. Sometimes they were famous—or to become famous— names: Daguerre, Piccini, Bishop. Documentary introductions and footnotes were not unknown; before HUGO, PIXERÉCOURT prefixed essays to plays (*Charles le Téméraire, Le Chien de Montargis*) justifying his use of history and citing authorities. Plays in Cumberland's editions were preceded by commentaries signed "D-G." (GEORGE DANIEL) which are full of valuable contemporary data, including descriptions of the production, acting, etc. MONCRIEFF wrote introductions for Richardson's Minor. In the serial publications an illustration of a scene from the play was common, woodcuts being used in the beginning.

France

All the stage works of Pixerécourt from 1797 onward were issued by J. N. Barba (successor, Tresse) at Paris, as were plays by many of his contemporaries; other publishers were Dabo, Pollet, and Quoy. The imprint of the Ambigu appears on editions put out at the theatre in connection with the play of the evening at this Boulevard house. These individually issued plays were typically octavo in brochure form, tending to quarto size in the thirties.

Serial publication of plays, including melodramas, was already flourishing in the twenties, Barba, Dabo, and Pollet being in the field. In the thirties, *Magazin Théâtral*, published by Marchant, had cumulated to twenty-one volumes with from seventeen to twenty-one plays in each, many melodramas among them. *Théâtre contemporain* and *Théâtre contemporain illustré*, published by Michel Lévy Frères (later Calmann-Lévy) appear to have dominated the field at the middle of the century. Sixty to one hundred *drames* (melodramas in this case) were listed on the back of the brochures as being in print during the sixties and seventies. Delamain, Boutelleau et Cie., originally Tresse & Stock, apparently took over and by the new century had established a monopoly in their Librarie Stock. In the 1920's this house was advertising itself as "furnishers of all pieces for the theatre published in France." As recently as 1928 Stock was announcing as many as a hundred melodramas.

The Georges Donay collection at the Bibliothèque de l'Arsenal at Paris, containing forty thousand printed pieces, embraces almost every printed French play, melodramas included. This collection is reported by GILDER and FREEDLEY as having been catalogued. I have not seen it.

Only Pixerécourt, among French melodramatists, has received any attention in a bibliographical way (see VIRELY). I know of no general bibliography of melodramas except one in VAN BELLEN, where three hundred titles are listed, with publication dates (the entries are incomplete in this respect), theatre, and date of production. It is not a complete list and is limited to the period 1790–1820. WICKS, *The Parisian Stage*, designated merely as a list and not a bibliography, is a list of plays performed in Paris from 1800 to 1830 based on advertisements of performances as they appeared in the Paris press. There is a comprehensive collection of French melodramas at the New York Public Library. Pixerécourt's *Théâtre choisi* is at Columbia University in the special collections in the Nicholas Murray Butler building.

Manuscripts

Censorship of the theatre was in effect in France until the establishment of the Third Republic, except for a few brief interludes coinciding with changes of regime. The manuscripts submitted to the Department of the Interior for approval are preserved in Paris. According to ALBERT (*Les Théâtres des Boulevards*, p. 285), manuscripts of all pieces played in Paris theatres 1815–30 were transferred to the Archives nationales; and the same writer (p. 88) locates those of pieces performed during the Revolution in the collection of the Bibliothèque Carnavalet.

England

The Hand-Lists of Plays in NICOLL are invaluable—and unique; nothing comparable has been done for the French or the American theatres. In these compilations, along with date and theatre of original production, basic bibliographical data is supplied for each item, separate and serial publication being indicated where there has been such publication.

Various precursors of melodrama, including sentimental comedy, historical and middle-class tragedy (by Lillo, Moore, et al.), and comic opera of a romantic and exotic cast, are liberally represented in Bell's *British Plays* (1777), consisting of ninety-five plays in a like number of volumes; Dodsley's *Select Collection of Old Plays* (1744) in twelve volumes; *The British Drama* in two volumes (1824–26); and Inchbald's *British Theatre* (1808), one hundred plays in twenty-five volumes. Gothic drama and native melodrama of the transitional period at the turn of the century (by Cobb, CROSS, Arnold, and others) and imported French and German pieces (*A Tale of Mystery, The Stranger, Pizarro,* etc.), as given at the patent houses, are in the twenty-six volume, one hundred play *London Theatre* (1815–18), edited by T. J. DIBDIN, and in the four volume *London Stage* (1824–27) which offers 172 plays. Meanwhile *The German Theatre* (1800–11) appeared in six volumes, translated by BENJAMIN THOMPSON.

The rapidly expanding minor house repertory, in which melodrama was a staple, began to come into its own in *Richardson's Minor Drama* (1829–31), four volumes, prefaces by MONCRIEFF; *Cumberland's Minor Theatre* (1826——); and others. B. N. Webster, long associated with the Adelphi as actor and manager, edited *Acting National Drama* (1837–50), which contained the first printing of many Adelphi dramas, including those by Buckstone and the early BOUCICAULT. This series was published by Chapman and Hall in association with the Dramatic Authors' Society as a defensive measure against Cumberland and other publishers who took advantage of the lamentable state of the copyright and stage-right laws to mulct authors. Other series were *Oxberry's Edition* (1820–1822) and *Dicks' Standard Plays* and Dicks' *The British Drama,* both launched in the 1880's. *Dicks' Standard Plays* contains more than three hundred items, among them much of the standard repertory as far back as Shakespeare as well as more recent "illegitimate," or minor, pieces. *The Cambridge Bibliography of English Literature* (Vol. III) lists series publishers, as does NICOLL (*Hand-List of Plays* in his *A History of Early Nineteenth Century Drama*), and RHODES is a useful guide for this period.

Thomas Hailes Lacy, who began publishing plays circa 1830, accumulated a very large list in his *Lacy's Acting Edition* (1851–

1860). His firm absorbed *Cumberland's British Theatre* and *Cumberland's Minor Theater*, which had previously swallowed up *Dolby's British Theatre* (1823–1825), and others; and Lacy in turn was absorbed by Samuel French, who began operations in London in 1872, after coming over from New York where he had been in the business since about 1845. Lacy's list—or what remained of it after drastic culling—was accommodated in the first five volumes of *French's Acting Edition.*

The Lacy list, at about the time French acquired it and as originally incorporated in French's list (before culling), consisted of one hundred volumes and French's of perhaps thirty-three, a volume averaging fifteen plays. The subsequent volumes beyond thirty-three comprise obscure plays not in much demand; this change in character of content (dating to about 1880) coincides with, and is probably explained by, the practice, spreading rapidly in three years, of withholding plays from print—which in turn may have some connection with the spread of local stock companies. To produce an uncopyrighted play which had not been published was a criminal offense under common law, and certainly the publication of plays of professional quality fell off sharply at this time. The Drury Lane melodramas of Pettitt, Meritt, and other writers, the Princess and Adelphi plays of the same period, and the great mass of the repertory of the Surrey Side and East End theatres (including the Brit), as well as the voluminous works of Frank Harvey and the Melville Brothers, never appeared in print. Even the dramas of W. G. Wills, on a higher literary level, remained in manuscript, including several produced by Irving.

There is extant a *Lacy List of Plays* (1865) and a *Samuel French International Descriptive Catalogue of Plays and Dramatic Works,* circa 1880. The latter contains listings of Dicks, Webster's *Acting Edition,* and Cumberland, under those separate headings.

For plot summaries and other information about the larger number of unprinted English melodramas in the final quarter of the century I have relied upon PASCOE (*Dramatic Notes*), reprinted reviews by KNIGHT, COOK, and others, chronicles and reminiscences by SHERSON, CLEMENT SCOTT, et al., and especially reviews in *The Theatre* (London). I have filled in the gaps in the Lyceum's records from the extensive Irving literature (BRERETON, LAURENCE IRVING, STOKER, etc.).

Terminology presents a problem with English as with French melodrama. During the nineteenth century a melodrama might have been designated on playbills and posters and in printed copies by any of a dozen terms, including burletta early in the century. Some of these terms are fairly unambiguous, such as sensational drama, historical drama, nautical drama, domestic drama, and even romantic drama and romantic opera. However, where the play was called simply a drama, some familiarity with the writer and the theatre involved, or even with the particular play, is usually necessary for more exact identification. As in France, "drama" was a prestigious label, whereas "melodrama" could be distinctly pejorative. *The Cambridge Bibliography* lumps melodrama and drama under the latter term.

Excellent collections of melodramas in the U.S.A. are at the Harvard College Library and the New York Public Library. Included are prompt copies used in the theatre.

Manuscripts

Plays submitted to the Lord Chamberlain's Examiner of Plays for approval are preserved in two places: the cellar of the Office of Works, London, and the Huntington Library, San Marino, California, which has possession of the Larpent Collection. This collection, consisting of 2,500 items covering the years 1778–1824, has been catalogued (MACMILLAN), and was used by NICOLL for his Hand-Lists of Plays. There are lacunae even in these, especially in the minor house repertory for early in the century, as noted by NICOLL in his volume for the early nineteenth century.

United States

There are several bibliographies of American plays: ATKINSON, WEGELIN, HILL, REED—each including melodramas. A Hand List of Plays in QUINN, *A History of American Drama from the Beginning to the Civil War* (2nd ed., N.Y., 1943), along the lines of NICOLL's lists, offers sketchy bibliographical, as well as production, data. A similar but shorter list in MOODY extends to the end of the century. In neither are melodramas designated as such, and serial publication is not indicated. In QUINN's *A History of the American Drama from the Civil War to the Present Day*, rev. ed. (N. Y., 1936) the listing is by authors with data given similar to that in the earlier volume.

The WEGELIN, HILL (based on Wegelin) and ATKINSON collections of early American plays deal with the period prior to 1830, Perley I. REED's work (chronological) stops with 1870 and ATKINSON's *Later American Plays*, which exists only in manuscript, carries the story to the end of the century. HILL is standard for its period; it includes references to the ten chief collections in which the plays are to be found. QUINN (the pre–Civil War volume) has a list of American libraries which have special collections of American plays. HASKELL (1916) lists American plays in the New York Public Library Collection.

An early American series was *Douglass Minor* (circa 1840). W. V. Spencer's *Boston Theatre* (1855——), in eight volumes, contains the first printing of important early native melodramas. Somewhat later are the "libraries" of Walter Baker, Boston; De Witt, New York; and Sergel's, Chicago. Samuel French started business about 1845 in New York. This publisher, thanks to his English connection, outdistanced his competitors after the Civil War. The Dramatic Publishing Company, Chicago, which absorbed Sergel's, put out several plays by BOUCICAULT, including *The Octoroon* and *Formosa*. Frederick Turner (*Turner's Dramatic Library*) was a Philadelphia publisher early in the century (circa 1820) and had a branch in New York. In the eighties houses such as De Witt, Sergel's and Ames (which operated from the unlikely location of Clyde, Ohio) appear to have specialized in their own versions of popular novels (*Lady Audley's Secret, East Lynne, Uncle Tom's Cabin*, etc.) and early plays then in the public domain; oddly enough, they managed also to get hold of several pieces by Tom TAYLOR and Wilkie Collins not published in England, probably by pirating.

Piracy was rampant in the U.S.A., and the passage in 1856 of a copyright law to protect dramatic authors did little to check it. This abuse gave rise to the practice of withholding plays from print, resorted to on a large scale after the Civil War. Forrest, who bought copyrights from authors, had not allowed any of his properties to be made public. Stars such as Mayo (*Davy Crockett*) and Chanfrau (*Kit, the Arkansas Traveller*) kept their famous vehicles out of print successfully. The plays of Bartley Campbell, Augustin Daly, the early BELASCO and Joseph Arthur (*Blue Jeans, The Still Alarm*), Bronson Howard's *Shenandoah*, and Lester Wallack's *Rosedale* were either not printed or printed privately. The result has been the perhaps permanent loss of many classical American melodramas. In the field of frontier drama alone such items as *Murrel Land Pirate, Si Slocum,* and the Buffalo Bill plays have disappeared.

A few long-lost melodramas have been recovered or resurrected from private printings and made generally available: *Horizon,* BELASCO dramas of the San Francisco period, *Shenandoah,* several Bartley Campbell thrillers, three Dunlap adaptations from the French, and BOUCICAULT items including *The Jilt.* Most of these recovered works are in the twenty-volume AMERICA'S LOST PLAYS, and a sprinkling of others were printed for the first time in recent collected editions for college study.

American melodramas of the period after the Civil War are poorly represented in the French editions as elsewhere.

The repertory of "ten, twent', thirt'," never saw print, but a few items have been incorporated in AMERICA'S LOST PLAYS, including Walter Woods' *Billy the Kid* and *The Great Diamond Robbery* by Alfriend and Wheeler.

Manuscripts

The United States never had a dramatic censorship, so no such treasures as the archives of the Lord Chamberlain and French Ministry of the Interior exist in this country. However, the deposit of manuscripts in connection with registration of copyright became a requirement in 1870, and the Library of Congress, as the principal repository, contains 400,000 pieces of drama in its book collection and 210,000 unpublished plays in manuscript and typescript, exclusive of 200,000 opera and operetta libretti.

The University of Chicago library houses the unique William Harlowe Briggs collection of 14,000 theatrical reviews. These cover performances in Chicago and New York in the late nineteenth and early twentieth century. Melodrama is represented among them, including many of the plays of Lincoln J. Carter.

Selected Bibliography

Albert, Maurice. *Les Théâtres de la foire*. Paris, 1900.

———. *Les Théâtres des Boulevards (1789–1848)*. Paris, 1902.

Albert, Paul. *La Littérature française au XIX siècle*. 2 vols. I, 5th ed., Paris, 1892; II, 3rd ed., Paris, 1893.

America's Lost Plays, ed. Barrett H. Clark. 20 vols. Princeton, 1940–1949. Contain valuable introductions.

L'Année littéraire et dramatique. See Vapereau.

Antoine, André. *Le Théâtre*. Paris, 1932.
A selective record of productions in the Paris theatre, from 1870 through 1905.

Archer, William. *English Dramatists of Today*. London, 1882.

———. *The Old Drama and the New*. Boston, 1923.

Armstrong, William. "The Art of the Minor Theatres in 1860," *Theatre Notebook*, X, 3 (Apr.–June 1956).

Arnold, Matthew. *Letters of an Old Playgoer*. New York, 1903; reissued in Columbia University Dramatic Museum Discussions of Drama Publications, Vol. IV, 1919.

Arundel, Dennis. *The Story of Sadler's Wells*. London, 1965.

Atkinson, F. W. Catalogue of the William August White collection of early American plays (1740–1830). University of Chicago library. Typescript.

———. "Later American Plays." MSS at the libraries of Harvard College, the University of Chicago, the University of Pennsylvania, and the Huntington Library.

Bachaumont, Louis le Petit de, et al. *Mémoirs secrets*. 36 vols. London, 1777–1789.

Baker, Blanch M. *Theatre and Allied Arts*. New York, 1952.
Bibliography.

Baker, H. Barton. *The London Stage; Its History and Traditions from 1576 to 1850*. London, 1889.

Baldick, Robert. *The Life and Times of Frederick Lemaître*. Fairlawn, N.J., 1959.

Barnes, Eric Wollencott. *The Lady of Fashion, the Life and Theatre of Ann Cora Mowatt*. New York, 1954.

Beaulieu, Henri. *Les Théâtres du Boulevard du Crime*. Paris, 1905.

Beaumarchais [P. A. Caron de]. *Théâtre complet, lettres relatives à son théâtre*. Paris, 1957.
Includes "Essai sur le genre dramatique sérieux."

Béclard, Leon. *Sébastien Mercier, sa vie, sa oeuvre, son temps*. Paris, 1905.

Belasco, David. *Plays Produced; a record*, ed. Louis Vincent Defoe. New York, privately printed, 1925.

———. *The Theatre through Its Stage Door*. New York, 1919.

Bernheim, Alfred L. *The Business of the Theatre; an economic history of the American theatre, 1750–1932*. 2nd ed. New York, 1960.

Bird, Robert Montgomery. *Nick of the Woods, or the Jibbenainosay.* London, 1837.

Boaden, James. *Memoirs of the Life of John Philip Kemble.* London, 1825.

Borgerhoff, Joseph L., ed. *Nineteenth Century French Plays.* New York & London, 1931.

Bory, Jean-Louis. *Eugene Süe; king of the popular novel.* Paris, 1962.

Boucicault, Dion [Dionysius Lardner]. "The Debut of a Dramatist," *North American Review,* CXLVIII (Apr. 1889).

———. "The Decline of the Drama," *ibid.,* CXXV (Sept. 1877).

———. "Early Days of a Dramatist," *ibid.,* CXLVIII (May 1889).

———. "Leaves from a Dramatist's Diary," *ibid.,* CXLIX (Aug. 1889).

———. "Theatres, Halls and Audiences," *ibid.,* CXLIX (Oct. 1889).

Brady, William A. *Showman.* New York, 1937; reprinted in *The Saturday Evening Post,* Jan. 11–Apr. 7, 1936.

Brayley, E. W. *Historical and Descriptive Account of the Theatres of London.* London, 1822.

Brazier, Nicolas. *Histoire des petits théâtres de Paris.* 2 vols. Paris, 1828; reprinted as *Chroniques des petits théâtres de Paris,* ed. George D'Heylli. Paris, 1883.

Brereton, Austin. *The Lyceum and Henry Irving.* London, 1903.

Broadbent, R. J. *Stage Whispers.* London, 1903.

Brougham, John. *John Brougham: An Autobiography,* ed. William Winters. New York, 1881.

Brown, T. Allston. *History of the New York Stage.* 3 vols. New York, 1903.

Bulwer-Lytton, Sir Edward. *Dramatic Works Now First Collected.* London, 1841.

———. *The Lady of Lyons,* Vol. CXV of French's Acting Edition of Plays.

———. *Richelieu; or, the Conspiracy,* Vol. CXVI of French's Acting Edition of Plays.

Bunn, Alfred R. *The Stage, both Before and Behind the Curtain.* 2 vols. Philadelphia, 1840.

Burgoyne, John. *The Lord of the Manor.* London, 1781.

Burnand, Sir Francis C. "An Autobiography," *The Theatre* (London) I, n.s., 107 (Feb. 1, 1883).

———. *Records and Reminiscences.* 2 vols. London, 1904.

Cain, Georges. *Anciens Théâtres de Paris.* Paris, 1920.

Campardon, Emile, ed. *Les Spectacles de la foire.* 2 vols. Paris & Nancy, 1877.

Carson, William G. *The Theatre on the Frontier.* Chicago, 1832.

Cerf, Bennett, and Van H. Cartmeell. *The Most Successful Plays of the American Stage.* New York, 1944.

Chapman, John, and Garrison P. Sherwood. *Best Plays: 1894–1899.* New York, 1955.

Charlemagne, Armand [Placide le Vieux]. *Le Mélodrame aux Boulevards.* Paris, 1809.

Chorley, Henry F. *Thirty Years' Musical Recollections.* 2 vols. London, 1862.

Clapp, John Bouvé and Edward Francis Edgett. *Plays of the Present*. New York, 1902.

Clapp, W. W. *Record of the Boston Stage*. Boston, 1853.

Clark, Barrett H. See *America's Lost Plays*.

Coates, Robert H. *The Outlaw Years*. New York, 1932.

Cody, Mrs. Louisa (Frederici), and Courtney Ryley Cooper. *Memories of Buffalo Bill*. New York, 1919.

Cole, J. W. *The Life and Theatrical Times of Charles Kean, F.S.A., including a summary of the English stage for the last fifty years*. 2 vols. London, 1859.

Coleman, John. *Charles Reade as I Knew Him*. London, 1904.

———. *Players and Playwrights I Have Known*. London, 1888.

Coleridge, Samuel Taylor. *Biographia Literaria*. New York, 1926.

Colman, George, the younger. *Random Records*. 2 vols. London, 1830.

Cook, Dutton. *A Book of the Play*. London, 1876.

———. *Hours with the Players*. London, 1880.

———. *Nights at the Play*. London, 1883.

———. *On the Stage*. London, 1883.

Cordell, Richard A. *Henry Arthur Jones and the Modern Drama*. New York, 1932.

Courtney, Marguerite. *Laurette*. New York, 1955.

Craig, Gordon. *Henry Irving*. New York & Toronto, 1930.

Creahan, John. *The Life of Laura Keene*. Philadelphia, 1897.

Cross, John C. *Circusiana*. 2 vols. London, 1809.

Cumberland, Richard. *The Mysterious Husband*. London, 1753.

Daly, Joseph. *The Life of Augustin Daly*. New York, 1917.

Daniel, George. See "D-G."

D'Arnaud, Baculard. *Comte de Comminge ou les amants malheureux*. Paris, 1764.
    Contains a famous preface explaining and defending *drame noir*.

Darton, F. J. *Vincent Crummles; his theatre and his times*. London, 1926.

Davis, Owen. *I'd Like to Do It Again*. New York, 1931.

———. "Why I Quit Writing Melodrama," *American Magazine*, Sept. 1914.

Desfontaines [P. F. Guyot]. *Observations sur les critiques modernes*, XXV, 25. Paris, 1737.

Des Granges, Charles Marc. *Geoffroy et la critique dramatique sous le Consulat et l'Empire (1800–1814)*. Paris, 1897.

Destouches [Philippe Néricault]. *Le Glorieux*. Paris, 1789.
    The preface is important.

"D-G." [Daniel, George]. Introductions to various items in *Cumberland's Minor Theatre*.

Dibdin, Charles, the younger. *Memoirs of . . .*, ed. George Speaight. London, 1956.

Dibdin, T. J. *The Reminiscences of a Literary Life*. 2 vols. London, 1827.

Dickens, Charles. "The Amusements of the People," 2 pts., *Household Words,* Apr. 30 & May 30, 1850.

———. "Cruikshank's The Drunkard's Children," *Examiner,* July 6, 1848.

———. *Miscellaneous Papers from "The Examiner," "Household Words," and "All the Year Round."* New York, n.d.

———. *The Uncommercial Traveller and Reprinted Pieces.* 2nd ed. London, 1964.

———. "Two Views of a Cheap Theatre," *The Uncommercial Traveler.* London, 1860.

———. "Virginie and Black Eyed Susan," *ibid.,* May 12, 1849.

Diderot, Denis. *Oeuvres completes,* eds. Assezat and Tourneux. 20 vols. Paris, 1875–1879.

———. *Writings on the Theatre,* ed. F. C. Green. Cambridge, 1936.
    Contains in chronological order all of this writer's discourses on the theatre, including "On *The Natural Son*" and "On Dramatic Poetry." In French.

Disher, M. Willson. *Blood and Thunder.* London, 1949.

———. *Melodrama: Plots That Thrilled.* London, 1954.

Doumic, Rene. "Le Mélodrame et le théâtre romantique," *Historie de la langue et de la littérature de France,* ed. Petit de Julleville. Vol. VII. Paris, 1889.

Draper, F. W. M. *The Rise and Fall of French Romantic Drama.* London, 1923.

Drew, Louisa (Lane) [Mrs. John Drew]. *Autobiographical Sketch of Mrs. Drew.* Introd. by her son, John Drew; with biographical notes by Douglas Taylor. New York, 1899.

Ducharte, Pierre Louis. *The Italian Comedy,* trans. Randolph R. Weaver. London, 1929.

Dumas, Alexandre, *pere. Souvenirs dramatiques.* 2 vols. Paris, 1881.

———. *Théâtre complet.* Paris. 1863–1874.

Eaton, Walter Pritchard. *The American Stage of Today.* Boston, 1908.

———. "Why Do You Fear Me, Nellie?" *Harper's,* July 1941.

Egan, Pierce. *Life in London.* London, 1821.

Elwin, Malcolm. *Charles Reade.* London, 1931.

Evans, Bertrand. *Gothic Drama from Walpole to Shelley.* Berkeley & Los Angeles, 1947.

Felheim, Marvin. *The Theatre of Augustin Daly.* Cambridge [U.S.A.], 1956.
    An account of the late nineteenth-century stage.

Field, Kate. *Charles Fechter.* Boston, 1882.

Fitzball, Edward. *Thirty-five Years of a Dramatic Author's Life.* London, 1859.

Fleetwood, Frances. *Conquest: The Story of a Theatre Family.* London, 1953.
    Includes complete list of plays produced by the Conquests at the Grecian and later at the Surrey.

Fleury, Abraham Joseph Bernard. *The French Stage and the French People as illustrated in the Memoires of M. Fleury,* ed. by Theodore Hook. 2 vols. London, 1841.

———. *Mémoires de la comédie française.* Paris, 1847.

Florian, J. P. C. *Nouvelles nouvelles.* Paris, 1792.
Contains the tale from which Pixerécourt's *Selico* (never printed) was adapted.

Forbes-Robertson, Gertrude Elliott. *My Aunt Maxine* [Elliott]. New York, 1964.

Foust, Clement. *Life and Dramatic Works of Robert Montgomery Bird.* Philadelphia, 1910.
Contains text of four of his plays.

Frohman, Daniel A. M. *Memories of a Manager.* New York, 1911.

Gaiffe, Félix. *Le Drame en France au XVIIIe siècle.* Paris, 1908.

Ganzel, Dewey. "Patent Wrongs and Patent Theatres, Drama and the Law in the Early Nineteenth Century," *PMLA*, Sept. 1961, 384–396.

Gautier, Théophile. *Histoire de l'art dramatique en France depuis vingt-cinq ans.* 6 vols. Paris, 1861.

———. *Histoire du romantisme.* Paris, 1874.

Genest, Rev. John. *Some Account of the English Stage from the Restoration to 1830.* 10 vols. Bath, 1832.

Geoffroy, Julien Louis. *Cours de littérature dramatique.* 2nd ed. Paris, 1825.

Gibbs, Lewis. *Sheridan.* London, 1947.

Gilder, Rosamond, and Vincent Freedley. *Theatre Collections in Libraries and Museums.* New York, 1936.

Gillette, William. An Address Delivered at the Fifth Joint Session of the American Academy of Arts and Letters and of the National Institute of Arts and Letters, held in Chicago on November 14, 1913; reprinted by The Dramatic Museum of Columbia University, New York, 1915.

———. *Held by the Enemy.* New York & London: French, n.d.

———. *Secret Service.* New York & London: French, n.d.

———. *Sherlock Holmes.* Garden City, 1936.

Ginisty, Paul. *Le Mélodrame.* Paris, 1910.

Harlow, Alvin. *Old Bowery Days.* New York & London, 1931.

Hartog, Willie G. *Guilbert de Pixerécourt.* Paris, 1913.

Haskell, D. C. *List of American Dramas in the New York Public Library.* New York, 1916.

Hazlitt, William. *The Complete Works of* . . . London & Toronto, 1930.

Herne, James A. *Sag Harbor and Other Plays.* New York, 1928.

Hervey, Charles. *Theatres of Paris.* Paris, 1846.

Hervey, James. *Meditations and Contemplations, containing his Meditations among the Tombs and Reflections on a Flower Garden . . . together with the life of the author.* Philadelphia, 1849.

Highfill, Philip H. "Edmund Simpson's Talent Raid on England in 1818," *Theatre Notebook*, XII, 3, 4, 5 (1958).

Hill, Frank P. *American Plays Printed, 1714–1830.* Palo Alto, 1934.
A bibliographical record compiled by Frank Pierce Hill. Dates of publication, when first produced, and where preserved. This compiler relied on Wegelin and Atkinson.

Holcroft, Thomas. *Memoirs of . . .* , ed. William Hazlitt. 3 vols. London, 1816.

———. *Travels from Hamburg through Westphalia, Holland and the Netherlands to Paris.* 2 vols. London, 1804.

Hollingshead, John. *My Lifetime.* 2 vols. London, 1895.

Hollingsworth, Keith. *The Newgate Novel.* Detroit, 1963.

Howard, J. Bannister. *Fifty Years a Showman.* London, 1938.

Hoyt, Harlowe R. *Town Hall Tonight.* Englewood Cliffs, N.J., 1955.

Hugo, Victor. Preface to *Cromwell.* Paris, 1827.

Hutton, Lawrence. *Curiosities of the American Stage.* New York, 1891.

Ireland, Joseph. *Records of the New York Stage from 1750 to 1860.* 2 vols. New York, 1866.

Irving, H. B. *Occasional Papers.* London, 1906.

Irving, Laurence. *Henry Irving, the Actor and His World by His Grandson.* New York, 1952.

James, Henry. *The Scenic Art,* ed. Allan Wade. New York, 1957.

———. *The Theatre and Friendship.* New York, 1932.
Some Henry James letters with a comment by Elizabeth Robins.

James, R. D. *Old Drury of Philadelphia, 1800–1835.* Philadelphia, 1932.

Janin, Jules. *Histoire de la littérature dramatique.* 2nd ed. 4 vols. Paris, 1855.

Jefferson, Joseph. *"Rip van Winkle": The Autobiography of Joseph Jefferson.* London, 1949.

Jerrold, Douglas, *Works of . . . .,* ed. W. Blanchard Jerrold, with memoir by the editor. 5 vols. London, 1851.

Jerrold, Walter. *Douglas Jerrold; dramatist and wit.* London, 1918.

Johnson, Edgar. *Charles Dickens, His Tragedy and Triumph.* 2 vols. New York, 1952.

Jones, Henry Arthur. *The Renascence of English Drama.* London, 1895.

———. *Representative Plays.* Boston, 1925. Includes *The Silver King.*

———. *The Shadow of Henry Irving.* New York, 1931.

Kelly, Michael. *Reminiscences of the King's Theatre and Theatre Royal, Drury Lane,* ed. Theodore Hook. London, 1826.

Knight, Joseph. *Theatrical Notes.* London, 1893.

Krows, Arthur Edwin. *Play Production in America.* New York, 1916.

Lacy, Alexander. *Pixerécourt and the French Romantic Drama.* Toronto, 1928.

Leigh, H. S. *Carols of Cockayne.* London, 1874.

Leonard, Elizabeth, and Julia Cody Goodman. *Buffalo Bill, King of the Old West.* Boston, 1955.

Leuchs, F. H. *The Early German Theatre in New York, 1840–1872.* New York, 1928.

Leverton, Garrett H., ed. *Plays for the College Theatre.* New York, 1932.

Lewes, George Henry. *On Actors and the Art of Acting.* London, 1939.

Lewis, Matthew Gregory. *Life and Correspondence of . . .* 2 vols. London, 1875.

Lough, John. *Paris Theatre Audiences in the Seventeenth and Eighteenth Centuries*. London, 1957.

Ludlow, Noah. *Dramatic Life as I Found It*. St. Louis, 1880.

Macgowan, Kenneth. *Behind the Screen; the history and technique of the motion picture*. New York, 1965.

Macmillan, Dougald. *Larpent Plays in the Huntington Library*. San Marino, Calif., 1939.

Macready, Charles. *Reminiscences*, ed. Sir Frederick Pollack. 2 vols. London, 1875.

Mander, Raymond, and Joe Mitcheson. *The Theatres of London*. New York, 1961.

Mantle, Robert Burns, ed. with Garrison P. Sherwood. *Best Plays: 1909-1919*. Annual *Best Plays* volumes from 1919 through 1947.

———. *Burns Mantle's Best Plays: 1899-1909*.

Marberry, M. M. *Splendid Poseur; Joaquin Miller, an American poet*. New York, 1953.

Marbury, Elisabeth. *My Crystal Ball*. New York, 1923.

March, Harold. *Frédéric Soulié, Novelist and Dramatist of the Romantic Period*. New Haven, 1951.

Marsan, Jules. "Le Mélodrame et Guilbert de Pixerécourt," *Revue d'histoire littéraire de la France*, July 1911.

Marshall, Thomas Frederic. *History of the Philadelphia Theatre, 1878-1890, and a check list of plays, 1878-1890*. Private printing, 1943.

Matthews, Brander. *A Book about the Theatre*. New York, 1916.

———. *Development of the Drama*. New York, 1930.

———. *These Many Years*. New York, 1917.

Mayhew, Henry. *Mayhew's London*, ed. Peter Quennell. London, n.d. Chapter on "The Vic Gallery."

Mayoraga, Margaret Gardner, ed. *A Short History of the American Drama*. New York, 1932. Contains bibliography.

Méjan, Maurice, ed. *Recueil des causes célèbres*. 21 vols. Paris, 1808-1814.

Mercier, Louis Sébastien. *De la Littérature et des Littérateurs, suivi d'un nouvel examen de la tragédie française*. Yverdon, 1778.

———. *Du Théâtre ou nouvel essai sur l'art dramatique*. Amsterdam, 1773.

———. *Théâtre complet*. 4 vols. Amsterdam, 1778-1784.

Monahan, James. *The Great Rascal: The Life and Adventures of Ned Buntline*. Boston, 1951.

Moncrieff, W. T. Various prefaces to plays published by Richardson's Minor (1829-1831).

Moody, Richard. *America Takes the Stage*. Indianapolis, 1955. Includes "selected" play list of approximately 630 entries, giving place and date of publication, first performance, theme and type of play.

Morehouse, Ward. *Matinee Tomorrow*. New York, 1949.

Morley, Henry. *The Journal of a London Playgoer*. London, 1866.

Morley, Malcolm. *The Old Marleybone Theatre London*. St. Marleybone Society Publication No. 2, London, 1960.

Morse, Frank P. *Backstage with Henry Miller*. New York, 1938.

Moses, Montrose J. *The American Dramatist*. Boston, 1917.

———. "Concerning a Certain Type of Melodrama: the 10, 20, 30," *The American Dramatist*, Boston, 1925.

———, ed. *Representative American Dramas, National and Local*. Boston, 1925.

———, ed. *Representative Plays by American Dramatists*. 3 vols. New York, 1917.

Moses, Montrose J., and John Mason Brown, eds. *The American Theatre as Seen by Its Critics, 1752-1934*. New York, 1934.

Mowatt, Anna Cora. *Autobiography of an Actress*. Boston, 1853.

———. *Mimic Life; or, Before and Behind the Curtain*. Boston, 1855.

Moynet, M. J. *L'Envers du théâtre*. Paris, 1874.

Newton, H. Chance ("Carados"). *Crime in the Drama*. London, 1927.

Nicholson, Watson. *The Struggle for a Free Stage in London*. Cambridge, Mass., 1906.

Nicoll, Allardyce. *A History of English Drama, 1660-1900*. 6 vols. III: *Late Eighteenth Century*. 2nd ed. Cambridge, 1952. IV: *Early Nineteenth Century*. rev. ed. Cambridge, 1955. V: *Late Nineteenth Century*. 2nd ed. Cambridge, 1959. Vol. VI: *A Short-Title Alphabetical Catalogue of Plays for the entire period covered by the History*. Cambridge, 1959. Volumes I–V each include a Hand-List of Plays giving place, theatre and date of first performance, type of piece, publication data, with an indication of where manuscripts are deposited (Lord Chamberlain and Larpent collections).

Nodier, Charles. "Du Movement intellectuel et littéraire sous le Directoire et le Consulat," *Revue de Paris*, XIX (July 1835).

———. Introduction to Pixerécourt, *Théâtre choisi*, I, i–xl.

Odell, George C. *Annals of the New York Stage*. 15 vols. New York, 1927–1949. Covers period from 1750 to 1894.

O'Keefe, John, *Recollections of the Life of John O'Keefe*. 2 vol. London, 1826.

Oliver, A. Richard. *Charles Nodier, Pilot of Romanticism*. Syracuse, 1964.

Ottenmiller, John Henry. *Index to Plays in Collections; an author and title index to plays appearing in collections published between 1900 and 1942*. 2nd ed. rev. New York, 1950.

Parigot, Hippolyte. *Le Drame d'Alexandre Dumas [père]*. Paris, 1899.

Parker, John, ed. *Who's Who in the Theatre*. Boston, 1922.

Pascoe, Charles Eyre, compiler. *The Dramatic List*. London, 1880. A theatrical who's who of the period.

———. *Dramatic Notes; a chronicle of the London stage*. London, 1883.

Pearson, Hesketh. *Labby; the life and character of Henry Labouchere*. New York & London, 1937.

Petit de Julleville. *Le Théâtre en France*. Paris; rev. ed., 1927.

Phelps, Henry Pitt. *Players of a Century; a record of the Albany stage*. Albany, 1880.

Pitou, Alexis. "Les Origines du mélodrame français à la fin du XVIII siècle," *Revue d'histoire littéraire*, June 1911.

Pixerécourt, René Charles Guilbert de. "Le Mélodrame," in *Paris ou le livres des Cent-et-un*, VI (1832), 319–352. (Reprinted as a pamphlet with the pagination unchanged.)

———. *Oeuvres completes*. Paris, 1796–1836.

———. *Théâtre choisi*. Introd. by Charles Nodier. 4 vols. Paris & Nancy, 1841–1843.
Includes text of twenty-two melodramas. Incorporated in the work are various autobiographical chapters, including "Souvenirs du jeune âge" and "Souvenirs de la Révolution," the prefaces respectively to Vols. I and II, and also "Dernières réflexions sur le Mélodrame."

Planché, J. R. *The Recollections and Reflections of* . . . 2 vols. London, 1843.

Purnell, Thomas ["Q"]. *Dramatists of the Present Day*. London, 1871.

Quinn, Arthur Hobson. *A History of the American Drama from the Beginning to the Civil War*. 2nd ed. New York, 1943.

———. *A History of the American Drama from the Civil War to the Present Day*. Rev. ed. New York, 1936.

———. *Representative American Plays, 1767 to the Present Day*. New York, 1917.

Rahill, Frank. "Dion Boucicault and the Royalty Payment for Playwrights," *Theatre Arts*, XXIII, 11 (Nov. 1939).

———. "The Murder Mystery Melodrama," *ibid.*, XXV, 3 (March 1952).

———. "When Heaven Protected the Working Girl," *ibid.*, XXXVIII, 10 (Oct. 1954).

———. "The World's Greatest Hit," *ibid.*, XXVI, 101 (Oct. 1952).

Reade, Charles, *The Eighth Commandment*. London, 1860.

Reed, Perley I. "Realistic Presentation of National Characters in Native American Plays Prior to 1870," *Ohio State University Bulletin XXII*, No. 26, May 1918.
A bibliography.

Rees, James. *The Dramatic Authors of America*. Philadelphia, 1845.

Reynolds, Frederick. *The Life and Times of* . . . 2 vols. London, 1827.

Rhodes, R. Compton. "The Early Nineteenth Century Drama," *Library XXI*, 91, 112 (1935–1936).

Rice, Charles. *The London Theatre in the Eighteen-Thirties*, ed. J. C. Sprague and Bertram Shuttleworth. London, 1950.

Richardson, Johanna. *Théophile Gautier*. London, 1959.

Roden, R. F. *Later American Plays, 1831–1900*. Dunlap Society. n.s. No. 12. New York, 1900.
Bibliography.

Rousseau, Jean Jacques. *Letter on French Music*. Paris, 1753.

———. *Letter on the Musical Drama in French and Italian*. Paris, 1751.

———. *Politics and the Arts*. Letter to M. D'Alembert on the Theatre. Trans. Allan Bloom. Glencoe, Ill., 1960.

———. *Pygmalion, scène lyrique*. Paris, 1775.

Rowell, George, ed. *Nineteenth Century Plays*. Oxford, 1953.

———. *The Victorian Theatre*. London, 1956.
    Contains a comprehensive bibliography.

Ruggles, Eleanor. *Prince of Players, Edwin Booth*. New York, 1953.

Saintsbury, George. *A History of the French Novel*. London, 1917.

Sala, George. *The Life and Adventures of . . .* 2 vols. London, 1895.

Sanger, Lord George. *Seventy Years a Showman*. London, 1926.

Schlegel, August William. *A Course of Lectures on Dramatic Art and Literature by . . .* Trans. John Black. London, 1846.

Scott, Clement. *The Drama of Yesterday and Today*. 2 vols. London, 1899.

———. *From The Bells to King Arthur*. London, 1896.

Scott, Sir Walter. *Essays on Chivalry, Romance and the Drama*. London, 1887.

Sedaine, Michel Jean. *Oeuvres choisies*. Paris, 1813.

Sedgwick, Ruth W. "Those Dear, Dead Days of Melodrama," *The Stage Magazine* (New York), XII, 11 (August, 1935).

Sell, Herbert Blackman, and Victor Weybright. *Buffalo Bill and the Wild West*. New York, 1955.

Shaw, George Bernard. *Dramatic Opinions and Essays*. New York, 1906.

Sherson, Errol. *London's Lost Theatres of the Nineteenth Century*. London, 1925.

Sims, George R. *My Life*. London, 1917.

Sitwell, Sacheverell. *The Dance of the Quick and the Dead*. Boston, 1922.

Skinner, Maude and Otis. *One Man in His Time*. Philadelphia, 1938.
    Deals with Harry Watkins, early American trouper.

Smith, Horace and James. *Rejected Addresses*. London, 1812.

Smith, Sol. *Theatrical Apprenticeship*. Philadelphia, 1846.

———. *Theatrical Management in the West and South for Thirty Years*. New York, 1868.

Stoker, Bram. *The Personal Reminiscences of Henry Irving*. London, 1906.

———. "Stage Lighting," *The Nineteenth Century*, May 1911.

Stout, Wesley Wynans. "Little Eva is Seventy Five," *The Saturday Evening Post*, Oct. 8, 1927.

Stuart, Donald Clive. *The Development of Dramatic Art*. New York, 1928.

Taine, Hippolyte. *History of English Literature*. Trans. Adolphe Laun. 4 vols. Philadelphia & Chicago [1908].

Talmey, Allene. "Sam Harris," *Stage* (New York) XII, 3 (Dec. 1934).

Taylor, Dwight. *Blood and Thunder*. New York, 1962.
    The reminiscences of Charles A. Taylor by his son.

Taylor, Tom. *Historical Dramas*. London, 1877.

———. *Three Dramas*. London, 1854.

Texte, J. *J. J. Rousseau and the Origins of Literary Cosmopolitanism*. Trans. J. W. Matthews, London, 1889.

Thackeray, William Makepeace. *The Paris Sketchbook*, Vol. XVI in *The Works of . . .* 26 vols. London, 1886.

Thomas, Augustus. *The Print of My Remembrance*. New York, 1922.

Thompson, Benjamin, ed. *German Theatre*. 6 vols. London, 1810–1811.

Tolles, Winston. *Tom Taylor and the Victorian Drama*. New York, 1940.

Tomlins, F. G. *A Brief View of the English Drama*. London, 1840.

Van Bellen, E. C. *Les Origines du mélodrame*. Utrecht, 1927.

Vapereau, G., ed. *L'Année littéraire et dramatique*. Paris, 1859–67.
  Nine annual volumes.

Vardac, A. Nicholas. *Stage to Screen*. Cambridge, Mass., 1926.

Veiller, Bayard. *Fun I've Had*. New York, 1941.

Vidocq, François Eugène. *Les vrais memoires de . . .* , ed. Jean Savant. Paris,
  1950.

Vidocq; the personal memoirs of the first great detective, ed. and trans. Edwin
  Gile Rich. Boston & Brighton, 1935.

Virely, André. *René Charles Guilbert de Pixerécourt*. Paris, 1909.

Wallack, Lester. *Memories of Fifty Years*. New York, 1889.

Walsh, Townsend. *The Career of Dion Boucicault*. New York, 1915.

Watson, Ernest Bradlee. *Sheridan to Robertson*. Cambridge, Mass., 1926.

Waugh, Evelyn. "The Jesuit Who Was Tuesday," *The Commonweal*, XLV,
  23 (March 27, 1947).

Wegelin, Oscar. *Early American Plays*. New York, 1900; revised 1905.
  A bibliography of American dramas published to 1830. Contains references to ten cheap printed collections; also a list of plays in manuscript.

Weiss, Jean Jacques. *Le Drame historique et le drame passionnel*. Paris, 1888.

Wicks, C. B. *The Parisian Stage*. University of Alabama Press: Part I (1800–
  1815), 1930; Part II (1815–1830), 1953.
  Contains alphabetical indices of plays and authors of the French stage for
  the first 30 years of the nineteenth century, based on notices in the
  newspapers.

Williams, Michael. *Some London Theatres*. London, 1883.

Wilson, A. E. *East End Entertainment*, London, 1954.

———. *The Edwardian Theatre*. London, 1951.

———. *Penny Plain, Two Pence Colored*. London, 1952.

Wilson, Arthur J. *A History of the Philadelphia Theatre, 1835–1855*. Philadelphia, 1933.

Winter, William. *Other Days*. New York, 1908.

Young, Edward. *The Complaint; or Night Thought*. 1742–45.

Zévaès, Alexandre. "Figures d'hier. Félix Pyat, homme de lettres et homme
  politique." *Nouvelle revue* (Paris). 1930. Ser. 4, tome 109, pp. 161–174,
  259–286; tome 10, pp. 60–68, 95–108.

Index